Local Transcendence

To Bill,

Thanks for your intellectual and collegial companionship over the years. — Alan

Local

Essays on Postmodern Historicism and the Database

Transcendence

Feb. 17, 2009

/ ALAN LIU

/ The University of Chicago Press
Chicago and London

Alan Liu is professor of English at the University of California at Santa Barbara. He is the author of several publications, including *The Laws of Cool: Knowledge Work and the Culture of Information*, also published by the University of Chicago Press.

The University of Chicago Press, Chicago 60637
The University of Chicago Press, Ltd., London
© 2008 by The University of Chicago
All rights reserved. Published 2008
Printed in the United States of America

17 16 15 14 13 12 11 10 09 08   1 2 3 4 5

ISBN-13: 978-0-226-48695-6 (cloth)
ISBN-13: 978-0-226-48696-3 (paper)
ISBN-10: 0-226-48695-8 (cloth)
ISBN-10: 0-226-48696-6 (paper)

Library of Congress Cataloging-in-Publication Data

Liu, Alan, 1953–
    Local transcendence : essays on postmodern historicism and the database / Alan Liu.
        p. cm.
    Includes bibliographical references and index.
    ISBN-13: 978-0-226-48695-6 (cloth : alk. paper)
    ISBN-13: 978-0-226-48696-3 (pbk. : alk. paper)
    ISBN-10: 0-226-48695-8 (cloth : alk. paper)
    ISBN-10: 0-226-48696-6 (pbk. : alk. paper)   1. Criticism—History—20th century.
2. Criticism—History—21st century. 3. Historicism. I. Title.
PN94 .L59 2008
801′.950904—dc22

2008006398

For Richard Helgerson

Contents /

Acknowledgments

In my previous books, I acknowledged many mentors, colleagues, friends, and family—a crowded, intricately woven society of influence that I was deeply happy to own up to, not just because the long solitude required to write any monograph is warmed by the thought of society, but because that society served as an image of the general reciprocity between individuals and larger history that was my theme, whether in the time of the French Revolution or of today's information revolution. The cover of my first book, on Wordsworth, was illustrated with a populous revolutionary crowd scene, while the cover of my second book, about information culture, imitated the Apple-like look of a computer whose uncrowded, minimalist, white design is punctuated by the mark of the individual: a cursor arrow. Somewhere between that lonely (romantic/cool) cursor and that crowd lay the trajectory of my argument.

The present book also owes much to many (named in individual chapters and notes). But I am clearing the field to let stand only a single acknowledgment. This book is dedicated to Richard Helgerson. Mentor, colleague, friend, and intimate of my family, Richard is himself a multitude—and unique. When I first met him at a conference on romanticism and the New Historicism at the University of California, Los Angeles, in 1986 (where, as I remember, I had the temerity as a young unknown to call on him in the audience to speak generally about the New Historicism from his vantage in the Renaissance field), I knew only that he was one of the leading intellects in a new movement with which I found my own work increasingly resonating. I did not know that in the next year he would bring me (and my spouse, the Renaissance scholar Patricia Fumerton) to the West Coast to join him at the University of California, Santa Barbara. Nor could I have known that, in the score of years since then, he would be such a champion and companion of my work, consult so generously when I made my risky, midcareer move into the field of information culture (suffering my cascades of e-mail when it was all new and I took the medium out for a ride), and maintain such a steady interest in my research even as it drifted further afield from his. I do not know of a more consummate citizen and leader of our profession: at once disciplined and open, rigorous and generous, pragmatic and idealistic, careful and caring, great and good.

Those who have followed Richard's work will by now be acquainted with the already legendary book he wrote in a single, sustained burst—both breaking new ground and summarizing his life's work—after he entered treatment for pancreatic cancer in 2005. That book, *A Sonnet from Carthage: Garcilaso de la Vega and the New Poetry of Sixteenth-Century Europe* (Philadelphia: University of Pennsylvania Press, 2007), is for me the model for what my own scholarship might one day hope to be. Emergent from a lifetime's rigorous and detailed knowledge, it strips away the inessential apparatus at last to lay bare the bones and the heart. The bones are the sociopolitical framework of early modernity—that coupling of expansive imperial desire and tight internal repression that set the mold for our own global modernity. The heart that pulses within is the poetic sensibility of Garcilaso, in whose sonnet we read the alternately diastolic and systolic, socially expansive and inwardly reflective rhythm of the individual caught in the great movements of history. The strategy of Richard's book on Garcilaso—reading multitudes in an individual, an epic within a sonnet—is the template for my present acknowledgment. As he is to Garcilaso, so I am to him.

I remember those heady days in the 1980s and 1990s when cultural criticism, the New Historicism, the New Cultural History, cultural anthropology, postmodern theory, and the other movements I address in the chapters that follow were new. This passage from Richard's book (which he calls an *essay*) about Garcilaso and the "new poetry" of the sixteenth-century seems to me to capture, mutatis mutandis, the spirit of the "new" movements—in, not out of, history—that are my theme:

> Though this essay concerns a very specific place and time, its implications reach well beyond those limits, reach to efforts at self-conscious literary renewal wherever and whenever they have occurred. The most obvious of those extensions, included within the essay itself, are back to Roman antiquity and to the fourteenth century of Petrarch's Italy. But they also extend forward. The five fundamental conditions I find working through Garcilaso's sonnet and through the new poetry of sixteenth-century Europe—(1) a political transformation needing a new literary expression, (2) a set of formal literary innovations responding to those changes, (3) a commitment to a particular place that sometimes challenges the grander designs of imperial politics, (4) a loss of self in desires that may arise from but often counter political ambition, and (5) the intimately immediate relations between the writers who collectively assume the task of radical literary change—have in different mixes and with different emphases recurred again and again. (xvi–xvii)

To be new in such a historically full sense, as Richard has been, is a high accomplishment and beyond the reach of most in today's season of start-ups.

Along with the introduction, two of the essays in this collection have not previously been published: chapter 6, which earlier appeared only in an abridged, German translation (by Jürgen Blasius) titled "Die interdisziplinäre Kriegsmaschine" (The interdisciplinary war machine) in *Texte zur Kunste*, no. 12 (November 1993): 127–37, and chapter 9, which has not before appeared at all. The other essays in this volume were previously published in earlier forms as follows: chapter 1, "The Power of Formalism: The New Historicism," in *ELH* 56 (1989): 721–71 (© 1989 The Johns Hopkins University Press); chapter 2, "Trying Cultural Criticism: Wordsworth and Subversion" (as "Wordsworth and Subversion, 1793–1804: Trying Cultural Criticism"), in *Yale Journal of Criticism* 2, no. 2 (Spring 1989): 55–100; chapter 3, "Local Transcendence: Cultural Criticism, Postmodernism, and the

Romanticism of Detail," in *Representations* 32 (Fall 1990): 75–113 (© 1990 by the Regents of the University of California); chapter 4, "Remembering the Spruce Goose: Historicism, Postmodernism, Romanticism," in *South Atlantic Quarterly* 102 (2003): 263–78; chapter 5, "The New Historicism and the Work of Mourning," in *Studies in Romanticism* 35 (1996): 553–62 (© 1996 by the Trustees of Boston University) (reprinted in slightly revised form in *The Wordsworthian Enlightenment: Romantic Poetry and the Ecology of Reading*, ed. Helen Regueiro Elam and Frances Ferguson [Baltimore: Johns Hopkins University Press, 2005]); chapter 7, "Sidney's Technology: A Critique by Technology of Literary History," in *Acts of Narrative*, ed. Carol Jacobs and Henry Sussman (Stanford, CA: Stanford University Press, 2003): 174–94 (© 2003 by the Board of Trustees of the Leland Stanford Junior University); and chapter 8, "Transcendental Data: Toward a Cultural History and Aesthetics of the New Encoded Discourse," in *Critical Inquiry* 31 (2004): 49–84 (© 2004 by The University of Chicago).

For the previously published essays, I have only occasionally made substantive additions or revisions. More commonly, I have added illustrations that earlier could not be included, expanded notes that were cut for journal publication, updated some references, consolidated citations, and made stylistic as well as other minor emendations. I have also altered the "time sense" of the essays wherever I felt that an especially noticeable mention of "recent" developments in the original might better be allowed to recede into a longer perspective—one from which, today, some of the trends I discuss appear in a sunset light announcing the coming of their own status as historical. But I have not altered the time sense too much, choosing to let the essays have their moment. Appropriate to my theme, *now* is a traversing, historical moment.

Introduction /

Contingent Methods

In the postindustrial West, the history of the new millennium has opened on a sense of loose beginnings and loose ends.

Chasing the new or innovative in business, technology, media, art, fashion, and so on, we seem to ourselves to slip the bonds of the past and become, again, aboriginals. We are post- rather than prehistorical aborigines (*ab* + *orīgine*: "from the origin") seeking a new beginning. Multibillion-dollar companies thus defend patents that legally eschew all "prior art."[1] Artistic and theoretical movements cut themselves off from the past with the prefix *post-* (the successor to twentieth-century movements signed *avant-*). And even our darkest collective visions—whether the postapocalyptic fantasies of the *Road Warrior* and *Matrix* films or the post–September 11 realities of terror—make us out to be survivors in a starkly new age. In short, we are the people of what Joseph Schumpeter—in a phrase of 1942 now widely applied to postindustrialism—called "creative destruction."[2] We make a sharp, jagged break with the past so that we can create. And all our creations, we decree, will be worlds—or at least patents, corporations, architectures, arts, intellectual movements, and now, above all, *information*—seeming ab ovo, sufficient unto themselves, knowing no historical other. Such is the beginning of a new millenarianism—a loosening of beginnings from all that gave beginnings their beginning.[3]

Never mind that the new beginnings expressed by "electronic frontier foundations," "declarations of the independence of cyberspace," doctrines of "spreading democracy," and so on also seem unaccountably needy of history (at least an Enlightenment, revolutionary history at the origin of the modern credo of the new).

But ours is a history of loose ends too. Symmetrical with the search for new beginnings is a search for a new concept of what it means to have an end. Once, the ends that truly mattered—the endings that made sense of beginnings—were eschatological or teleological: all things ended in a single design of God, spirit (*Geist*), classless society, and so on (and, in personal life, death, salvation, damnation). But now we crave an ending appropriate to a history of loose beginnings. If all our creations are imagined to be discrete worlds, then in the idiom of communications technology they are structurally "nodes"; and the end of a node—in the sense that a wire beginning at one node terminates in another—is connectivity. Expressed geopolitically as *globalism*, technologically as *networking*, and artistically as *intertextuality*, *appropriation*, *sampling*, and so on, connectivity is the presentist, "just-in-time" end—or loose end—of multiple, reconfigurable terminations. In the now-dominant information metaphor: it is all a web. We are all nodes sending "packets" (encoded with a brief TTL, or "time to live") to other nodes in a call for instantaneous, transient connectivity.[4]

Never mind that we seem simultaneously to crave the conviction of absolute endings, whether marked by a fallen Berlin Wall announcing the "end of history" or military pyrotechnics of "shock and awe" intended to end a war as soon as it begins.

Shall such a neoaboriginal, just-in-time, conflicted history—I will call it *postmodern historicism*—be our only sense of history? Or are there past experiences of history whose alternate balance between denying and needing history haunts us in ways that put in question the very notion of a uniquely postmodern historicism of pure beginnings and instantaneous endings? After all, it is history itself that incessantly loosens people from their land, ancestors, nation, and so on to make them look away from, yet hunger for, the haunted connectivity that is the sense of history in the first place. And a metaquestion: Might it be the task of the most advanced, recent expressions of postmodern historicism—the various new historicisms and cultural criticisms of the past few decades—not just to participate in postmodern historicism, but also to give utterance to such haunting by alter histories, thus saving a place within the age of creative destruction for premonitory or oppositional senses of history?

These are the questions that frame *Local Transcendence*. The essays collected here were written from 1986 to the present during a period when I, like others, was engaged in sustained projects of historicist cultural criticism yet felt the need to reflect on and—from the inside—criticize the methodology of such projects. The best way to characterize these essays, indeed, is to say that they are an internal critique of *the historicist way in contemporary cultural criticism*. The nature of such internal critique—or critical advocacy—will emerge from glossing the key concepts in this latter description of my topic: *historicism, cultural criticism, contemporary*, and *way*. I will do so in two movements, treating the first three terms as one related sequence, and then addressing the last as an expression of the inner logic of that relation.

Historicism

The underlying object of study in this book is historicism—specifically, postmodern historicism—as a pervasive sociocultural condition. Theorists of postmodernism or, on its socioeconomic and political side, postindustrialism have described this condition in large, systemic terms as, for example, "space-time compression" and the "end of history."[5] The late-capitalist and -democratic world system, essentially, has taken on the features of the global, just-in-time corporation that is its microcosm, and vice versa. But I prefer to personalize such a condition as the *ethos*—the generalizable character, posture, or attitude—of the individuals who live and work in the changed world system. In *The Laws of Cool: Knowledge Work and the Culture of Information*, I studied this ethos under the name *cool*, which, I asserted, is a fundamentally historical condition even if its presentist "now" seems to epitomize postmodern space-time compression. Who, I asked, are the people who "work here" but are "cool"?[6] They are the people whose folk, class, gender, racial, ethnic, religious, and other historical identities have been so thoroughly restructured by postindustrialism—for example, in organizations that "change their culture"—that they no longer have any effective means to assert an identity. Or, rather, they have no means to do so except through ad hoc instruments of style fashioned precisely from the antihistorical commodities, technologies, and media produced by postindustrialism. Internalizing just-in-time creative destruction, they—which is to say we—thus become the people of the cutting-edge new.

To ventriloquize: our company and our brave new world, they destroy all the history that makes us *us* in the name of innovation, which, because the cutting edge is sharp, we suffer as restructuring, downsizing, outsourcing, decreased benefits, scaled-back safety nets, and all the other weapons of mass destruction in the current corporate and government armament. But we're cool. Even as we bleed on that edge where the new world order comes down like a guillotine on historical identities, we internalize an edgy, avant-garde cool that both mimics postindustrialism and gestures toward a folk identity like that of old. We instant-message and blog at work, for example, using the coolest new tech to refresh old, communal habits. Or we retreat behind iPod earphones that save us from being cubicle-people shuffling documents by making us pod-people shuffling music in a phantom tribal dance.[7] The very practices, media, and tools we use to deny history, in sum, paradoxically declare our need for the experience of history.

The result of such a split sense of history—at once needy and in denial—is that history manifests in the distinctive style of the postmodern. We do not have history, but we have historicism. Historicism is a facade or screen history like a Hollywood history film or computer game in the style of *Civilization*.[8] It is a "pastiche" of special effects, virtual "worlds," or detachable "skins" (computer user interfaces) levitating just above historical foundations.[9] More destabilizing still, such screen (or, emphasizing its neediness) cling-wrap historicism subversively whispers that any sense of foundational history must itself have been only a misconstruction of the looser stuff of life, which may be history all the way down but—exactly for that reason—has no bottom. Foundation itself is just tectonic plates sliding free.

We remember, after all, that the analogism of the *as* in the "as it really was" (or "how it really was") of nineteenth-century historicism already implied such instability. The apparent robustness of Ranke's *wie es eigentlich gewesen*—the gusto of contact it enabled between the present and the immersive past—depended perilously on the slender thread of that simulational *wie*, which, as historicism developed from the nineteenth century to its so-called crisis of historicism circa World War I, proved to be a link that had to be looped around in complex, interpretive knots of hermeneutics to be made adequate to belief.[10] But now the link of experience between present and past is even more stretched, and we lack the patience to tie the complicated knots that would secure historicism—no matter how immersively simulated in detail and anecdote—to a history deeper than ourselves.

Cultural Criticism

In this book, the particular screen of historicism I study as a mediation of general postmodern historicism is the coolest of recent intellectual movements: cultural criticism. While my underlying topic is postmodern historicism in general, in other words, my proximate object of study consists of the interdisciplinary intellectual movements from the 1980s on that have shaped our most advanced understandings of such historicism. They have done so by situating any and all cultural phenomena within that great facsimile of historical experience: context. Intellectuals today worship few things they will admit to, whether beautiful or true. But they worship cultural context, which thus becomes the ark for whatever works, creeds, identities, ethics, and so on still retain the root sense of *cult* in *culture* that Walter Benjamin called "aura" and that cultural criticism renders through microauras of detailism, anecdotalism, subculturalism, and other nanohistoricisms that dedicate themselves to the universal by way of the holy local.[11]

In particular, the main witnesses I call are the subset of cultural criticisms that I have myself most engaged as participant and/or critic in the last two decades. These include the New Historicism (with whose variant in the romantics field my early work was associated), the New Cultural History, cultural anthropology, certain kinds of the New Pragmatism, the new Marxism, and various aspects of postmodern and postindustrial theory (French, German, and American).[12] There are omissions here, of course, since the boundaries of cultural criticism can also be drawn to include feminism and gender studies, race and ethnicity studies, postcolonial studies, popular culture studies, media studies, and so on. And there are new fields I would have liked to include too, such as "media archaeology," which resees the past as a history of disruptive new media technologies.[13] However, I have not tried to widen my horizon in all directions. Doing so would have not only taxed my own expertise beyond credibility but also blurred my main purpose, which is not to offer an equal, wide survey of recent cultural criticisms but to think specifically about the historicist program in such criticisms. In this regard, the movements I focus on form a kind of densely interconnected cluster on the side of the graph where there is plentiful work with historical materials combined with critical awareness of the problem of historicism itself.

In any case, the most important thing to say at the outset is that the cultural criticisms I address (in common with those I do not) *are* intellectual movements hosted by the contemporary academy and, thus, represent the general ethos of historicism only in a specific social sector. Such specificity has its cost, of course. I doubt that I will be invited onto radio talk shows to discuss cultural criticism, as I was to discuss cool. But it has its gains too. Part of what is at stake in the present volume, as I have suggested, is the hypothesis that, while expert formulations of historicism in the academy participate in broader contemporary movements, they also offer a distinctive critical vantage on those movements that my own standpoint of internal critique *within* academic cultural criticism models recursively.

Contemporary

Contemporary as the adjective of cultural criticism (together with *post-* as the prefix of modernism or industrialism) also requires explanation since in a book about historicism this term cannot be just indexical, like the minute hand on the clock. It is an argument. As might be expected, the sweet spot of contemporary cultural criticism in this book is from ca. 1980 to the present.[14] This is the moment of the post-1970s (post–May 1968, post–Vietnam War, post-counterculture) intellectual generation when cultural criticism came into dominance in tandem with the rise of the Internet, the relational database, and other key information technologies—the whole underscoring, but also criticizing or hacking, the mighty simultaneity of the postmodern *now*. (Cultural criticism and what Geert Lovink calls "net criticism" or "critical Internet culture" are isomorphic. One of the framing hypotheses of the essays in this book, especially the last three, is that there is a structural convergence between historicism and informationalism, with the consequence that critical approaches arose in both domains in parallel—the New Historicism inventing its microhistorical anecdote, for example, exactly when so-called computer lib in the 1970s and 1980s seized on the personal computer to challenge the mainframe and hypertext theorists emancipated the "lexia" or "link" from linear text.)[15]

But, in my usage, *contemporary* also flexes back from today's *now* to embrace a longer sense of modernity and its evolving critical sense of history. I argue that postmodern cultural criticism harbors within itself a succession of predecessor criticisms of culture traversing from early modern subversion (as formulated by the New Historicism), through romanticism, nineteenth-century historicism, and twentieth-century modernism (as witnessed in the New Criticism or Russian Formalism), ultimately to postmodernism (which in some fields is itself now historical).

Specifically, I concentrate in this book on the span of cultural criticism from romanticism through postmodernism—the terminus a quo and the terminus ad quem, respectively, of the post-Enlightenment critique of modernity. In Jay Clayton's words, "postmodernism has a hidden or repressed connection with nineteenth-century culture," and "romanticism and postmodernism share the distinction of being the two most significant counter-Enlightenment discourses produced in the West."[16] This book is thus in part a record of the trajectory I myself took from the topic of romantic historicism in *Wordsworth: The Sense of History* (1989) to that of postindustrial historicism (expressed as informationalism) in *The Laws of Cool* (2004). Both romanticism and postindustrialism appear in their own eyes to transcend history—the former in the name of the original self, the latter in that of just in time. (And the early modern period studied by New Historicists does much the same in the name of self-fashioning.)[17] But, however revolutionary or creatively destructive, romanticism and postindustrialism are also needy for history as their most profound condition of being and knowing, even if part of that condition is the willed *unknowing* and *unbeing* of history that I called *denial of history* in my book on Wordsworth and *the ethos of the unknown* in my book on cool.[18] This means that the swelling sense of contemporaneity in both periods was necessarily accompanied by an antithetical historicism *criticizing* the modern zeitgeist— a reaction epitomized, for example, in the young Wordsworth's near-treasonous identification with the ancient Celts against the English state during the French Revolution (the case study in chapter 2 below). While the early modern period may have had subversion, in other words, critique as we know it belongs to the epoch of modernization proper—from the era of Hegel on—as the specifically historicist engagement (dialectic) with modernization. Critique in the modern sense began in the transition between the Enlightenment and the counter-Enlightenment *as* historicism.[19]

I posit in this book, then, that a critical sense of history evolved in the period from ca. 1800 to 2000, with anticipations in the early modern period and the Enlightenment, and that it is the task of the new historicisms and cultural criticisms to inform today's contemporaneity of the history of that critique—history, indeed, being the inner form of such critique. The function of criticism at the present time is to show that, while innovation and just in time may be antihistorical, they are also inheritors of a modernity that comes along with an internal critique expressed as a particularly edgy kind of history: the history of modernization.

The Historicist Way

This leaves the term *way*, which will bring the critical logic I outlined in the preceding conceptual series—*historicism, cultural criticism, contemporary*—at last to bear on the expression of that logic I have termed *internal critique*.

When I speak of "the historicist way" in contemporary cultural criticism, I mean method (from *meta* + *hodos*, or meta-way). The essays in this book may take up specific historical or literary cases, but, in my recurrent effort to map the interrelations and antecedents of the various cultural criticisms, in my insistence that their habits of localism and detailism follow general principles, and in my sustained concern with their form, hermeneutics, discipline, technique, management, action, and practice as these interact with modern social processes, my intent is primarily methodological. Indeed, this book is ultimately *about* contemporary cultural criticism as the evolution of a method.

On the face of it, of course, this latter assertion may be surprising since many of the cultural criticisms I address are known to be antimethodological. We know this because they say so. A famous case, for instance, is the New Historicism, some of whose leading practitioners have avowed an aversion, or at best an agnosticism, toward theoretical systems. Catherine Gallagher and Stephen Greenblatt thus write retrospectively on the first page of *Practicing New Historicism*: "Surely, we of all people should know something of the history and the principles of new historicism, but what we knew above all was that it (or perhaps we) resisted systematization. We had never formulated a set of theoretical propositions or articulated a program."[20] Secondary or external reports of the New Historicism have taken such avowed aversion to be canonical. In her *New Literary Histories*, for instance (one of the best works published after the fact to explain the postmodern historicisms), Claire Colebrook comments: "New historicism has been reluctant to identify itself with any particular theorist or theory. Indeed, new historicism had, until recently, remained an ostensibly untheorised practice with its main exponent, Stephen Greenblatt, declaring that new historicism was actually 'no doctrine' at all."[21] Borrowing the distinctive voice of one branch of the New Pragmatism, Colebrook generalizes: "Perhaps the traditional problem of literary theory—the validity of interpretive method—is no longer possible. We just interpret, with a full recognition of the contingency and arbitrariness of our interpretive position. We no longer legitimate our practices through literary *theory*."[22]

But that's just one page in the book of the New Historicism. On the very next page, we note, Gallagher and Greenblatt argue the counterposition: "To be sure, we talked constantly about our methodological principles. We eagerly read works of 'theory' emanating principally from Paris, Konstanz, Berlin, Frankfurt, Budapest, Tartu, and Moscow. . . . One of the recurrent criticisms of new historicism is that it is insufficiently theorized. The criticism is certainly just, and yet it seems curiously out of touch with the simultaneous fascination with theory and resistance to it that has shaped from the start our whole attempt to rethink the practice of literary and cultural studies."[23] Aversion to method in the New Historicism, it turns out, is steeped in ambient method.

It's like walking a minefield. Spend enough time surveying the theory bombs, if only to avoid them (in mixed fascination and resistance), and one ends up following a path as tight, convoluted, and forced in its posture as any declared method—but with the difference that the path follows no line of doctrine but instead seems to strike off at crazy, unpredictable tangents. In the New Historicism, in the New Cultural History's micro- rather than macrohistory, in the locution of the "against-theory" New Pragmatists that things "just" are, in the matching preference of French neopragmatists for the "practice of everyday life" over "metanarratives," and so on, antimethod has the broken rhythm (in Gilles Deleuze and Félix Guattari's terms) of the rhizomatic. But a thousand plateaus of cultural criticism also generate what Deleuze and Guattari would call a "plane of consistency," a generic critical method.

Nor, it should be pointed out, are the zigzags of such method merely defensive. (In this regard, the minefield comparison is too limited.) More fully, my argument is that recent cultural criticism internalizes the entire critical scene of method *and* antimethod that was symptomatic of modernity, which, by definition, is a self-correcting, rather than God- or king-correcting, system. Such vows of "no doctrine" as those cited above— hauntingly reminiscent of previous "we have no method" doctrines (e.g., in late works of Russian Formalism such as Boris Eichenbaum's "The Theory of the 'Formal Method'")—are positions taken in the aftermath of a specifically modern system of dialectical argument, or self-quarrel. Modern method would not be method, in other words, if it did not correct itself antithetically from within in ways that, when they first appear, always seem to be antimethodologies from outside the system (intuitive, empirical, pragmatic, and so on)—such appearance from a putatively external frame of reference, inevitably appropriated to the label *new*, being part of the modern system that allows critique to emerge at all.

We thus need to desynonymize method from system in the singular if we are to recognize that cultural criticism is nothing if not methodological. Nineteenth-century dialectic started out destabilizing the idea of a single world system but at last reconstituted it in such neoimperial syntheses as Hegel's "absolute knowledge," Marx's "classless" state, American "scientific management" and corporatism, central European bureaucratism and gesellschaft, and so on—with Stalin, the great military-industrial war states, and other twentieth-century systems waiting in the wings. It has thus taken nearly another century of cultural criticism since then (roughly from the epoch of the early Frankfurt school, American Southern agrarianism and the New Criticism, and early structuralism) to discern that the inherently differential methods, approaches, and theories of modernization are not the same as totalitarian or even hegemonic system. Form, structure, deconstruction, and so on were some of the methods of difference making that made that recognition possible. There is no form without its irony or defamiliarization, the formalists said. There is no structure without its scandal, Claude Lévi-Strauss said (nor S without its Z, Roland Barthes elaborated). And there is no meaning without its *différance* or "resistance to theory," deconstruction added. Recent cultural criticism continues the trend, breaking system down, not into antithetical images, phrase regimes, words, and phonemes (the particles and antiparticles, as it were, that its predecessors had substituted for Newtonian, absolute meaning), but into their cultural equivalents: contestatory subcultures, microhistories, anecdotes, relative autonomies, practices of everyday life, and so on. All this is to say that, while the methods of cultural criticism may be approaches ("ways") to a system, they are by design *not* a closed system; and their very status as not-system—indeed, as systems that create their own not-system—is deployed critically within the modern world system as its internal critique.

The real question, therefore, is not whether contemporary cultural criticism is a modern method but how it is also specifically a *post*modern method. Dialectical, formal, structuralist, and deconstructive methods— the selective genealogy of thought I rapidly reviewed above—are demonstrably part of the heritage of a phrase like Gallagher and Greenblatt's "fascination with theory and resistance to it." But I think there is a remainder in excess of that heritage that is the specifically new contribution of the New Historicism and related cultural criticisms—a surplus style of dialectic, form, or (post)structure without which we would not be able to account for the sheer busyness, the kinetic restlessness, of their zigzags. Or, if "new" is too suspect in our present context, we might speak instead of a difference-making "overlay" of method—a critical intervention that, like a Photoshop layer, comes merely by way of *super*vention over the persistence of the old.

A passage I quoted earlier from Colebrook provides a convenient prompt. Recall her description of contemporary cultural criticism as a confession of the "contingency and arbitrariness of our interpretive position." This phrase, which redacts vocabulary common to many recent cultural criticisms, cues us to the distinctively postdialectical, posthermeneutical, postformalist, and poststructuralist quotient in the method of contemporary cultural criticism: contingency. Ours is an age "adrift in Late Contingency," Joshua Clover writes in his poem *Their Ambiguity* (which, in part, is a critique of the culture of the new).[24] From my early discussions in this book of ad hoc anecdotes, microhistories, and details to my final comparison of anecdotes to information in databases (which, in theory, free any datum from being locked into a context), I move toward understanding contingency as the distinctive method of late historicism. *Contingent method*, as I propose to call it, is the tangential method, or methodical tangency, of postmodern historicism. It is its zigzag mode (as I put it above) of striking off on crazy, unpredictable tangents. Or, again, as Marlon B. Ross has said about the New Historicism, a complex inner structure of contingency drives the "anti-methodical method (or methodical anti-method)" of the movement down accidental "cowpaths" (an image borrowed from Kenneth Burke).[25]

But how does contingency actually work as a critical method, rather than just as a symptom, of postmodern historicism? How does its detachable style of internal critique differ from—or, better, make a virtue of—loose beginnings and ends?

By the Way

I will begin by telling a fable, with the application—and, equally important, the method of that application—to be limned below. The fable consists of a postmodern reading of a section in the 1805 *Prelude* where William Wordsworth recounts a way he once walked through Salisbury Plain. In earlier poetry, Wordsworth had already narrated this walk (see chapter 2 below). But, late in *The Prelude*, he renarrates the walk in the form of a historical "reverie" that forecasts the whole romantic-to-postmodern lineage I have called the *historicist way*. The full verse paragraph is as follows (for convenience of analysis, I parse its structure as a preface followed by three discrete scenes):

> To such a mood,
> Once above all—a traveller at that time
> Upon the plain of Sarum—was I raised:
> There on the pastoral downs without a track

315

To guide me, or along the bare white roads
Lengthening in solitude their dreary line,
While through those vestiges of ancient times
I ranged, and by the solitude o'ercome,

[Scene 1]   I had reverie and saw the past,   320
Saw multitudes of men, and here and there
A single Briton in his wolf-skin vest,
With shield and stone-ax, stride across the wold;
The voice of spears was heard, the rattling spear
Shaken by arms of mighty bone, in strength   325
Long mouldered, of barbaric majesty.

[Scene 2]   I called upon the darkness, and it took—
A midnight darkness seemed to come and take—
All objects from my sight; and lo, again
The desart visible by dismal flames!   330
It is the sacrificial altar, fed
With living men—how deep the groans!—the voice
Of those in the gigantic wicker thrills
Throughout the region far and near, pervades
The monumental hillocks, and the pomp   335
Is for both worlds, the living and the dead.

[Scene 3]   At other moments, for through that wide waste
Three summer days I roamed, when 'twas my chance
To have before me on the downy plain
Lines, circles, mounts, a mystery of shapes   340
Such as in many quarters yet survive,
With intricate profusion figuring 'oer
The untilled ground (the work, as some divine,
Of infant science, imitative forms
By which the Druids covertly expressed   345
Their knowledge of the heavens, and imaged forth
The constellations), I was gently charmed,
Albeit with an antiquarian's dream,
And saw the bearded teachers, with white wands
Uplifted, pointing to the starry sky,   350
Alternately, and plain below, while breath
Of music seemed to guide them, and the waste
Was cheared with stillness and a pleasant sound.[26]

If in a first interpretive pass we set our optical resolution low to take in the reverie as a whole, we might conclude that Wordsworth's goal is total immersion in history, confirming that he stands near the beginning of nineteenth-century historicism in the manner of "as it really was." The poet "calls" on the past and, lo, "sees" the past ("I had reverie and saw the past"). Calling and seeing, encoding and rendering, are equated in a single, magical fiat of performative language. So powerful is the immersion effect—which, as Jennifer Jones has argued, is at least as important to the Wordsworthian sublime as transcendence[27]—that Wordsworth even drifts from past into present tense:

> again
> The desart visible by dismal flames!
> It is the sacrificial altar.

History is *now*, and, in the full-bandwidth immersion of that *now*, we are powerless to do more than watch the awful drama unfold with all the fatefulness that, at any moment, history always seems to endow the now of that moment. The tragic paradox of history, after all, is that our lived now appears perpetually alienated from the historical now. We seem powerless to act in the very moment in which we live, watching great events unfold instead. Most relevant to my argument, we seem powerless even to criticize effectively. We are paralyzed by synchrony with the zeitgeist.

But, if we set our resolution high, then a second interpretive pass will reveal that the immersion effect ends, and critique begins, in the decomposition of Wordsworth's reverie into a montage of discontinuous scenes. Indeed, a filmic vocabulary—or, more generally, a media analysis—is apt since our ultimate goal is to look ahead anachronistically to postromantic developments. From the later nineteenth century on, new linguistic, graphic, photographic, filmic, and other media not only updated "as it really was" into a distinctly modern form of reverie but also provided a new platform for critique. We might instance imagism, cubism, the New Typography, film montage in the style of Sergei Eisenstein, Russian Formalism, the New Criticism, and structural linguistics. All these movements set out in one way or another to make dialectical critique immanent in thick media effects— for example, by making defamiliarization, irony, paradox, and arbitrariness palpable in imagery, picture surface, collage, montage, or signifiers.

To see Wordsworth's reverie as a protomodernism, not just immersed in, but critical of history, in short, we need only inquire how we might shoot it as a film. In this light, it becomes immediately clear that the poet directs, not one, but a rapid sequence of scenes in a style akin to what Eisenstein later calls "montage" and—under the pressure of his own revolutionary moment—equates with dialectical critique.

Scene 1 (lines 320–26) celebrates the ancient Britons or Celts by condensing their multitudes in the image of a heroic "single Briton." The synecdoche, we note, is traditional to the trope by which the disconcertingly multiple British peoples fortify themselves as an individualist or stand-alone island unity in times of external threat. We think, for example, of Shakespeare's drama of

> this scept'red isle,
> This earth of majesty . . .
> This fortress built by Nature for herself

and Churchill's narrative of the Battle of Britain: "Never in the field of human conflict was so much owed by so many to so few."[28] According to the trope, the British multitudes (including the Celtic subalterns) rise as one in the person of the "single Briton."

But then there is a heavy-handed directorial intervention ("I called upon the darkness"), and we cut to *scene 2* (lines 327–36), which exposes the side of the ancient Britons devoted to superstition, Druidic sacrificial altars, and the Wicker Man, all swarming, at this juncture in the poem soon after the books about the French Revolution, with allusion to the very opposite of the "single Briton" just across the Channel: the French mobs.[29] Demonizing rather than heroicizing, this scene marks what must be taken to be the onset of critique in the episode. Yet it is a strangely detached, even amoral kind of critique. It is as if Wordsworth has absorbed only the scientific, observational personality of Enlightenment critique without the heavy-handed moralizing that typified philosophes of the period on both sides of the Channel. (One thinks, e.g., of Samuel Johnson's Juvenalian "observation" of mankind in "The Vanity of Human Wishes"; Edward Gibbon's reflection on the ages of superstition in *The Decline and Fall of the Roman Empire*; Edmund Burke's excoriation of the French in *Reflections on the Revolution in France*; and, of course, the pronouncements of the French philosophes and revolutionaries themselves against religion, aristocracy, and tyranny.) By contrast, the tone of Wordsworth's critique seems Hegelian in its soaring, metahistorical equanimity, its ability simply to pass from thesis to antithesis about the ancient Britons as if filling in the points on a graph of teleological civilizational development: "barbaric majesty" $\rightarrow$ "darkness" $\rightarrow$ synthesis ("the pomp / Is for both worlds, the living and the dead").

In hindsight, of course, critique in the Hegelian genealogy could itself appear heavy-handed as it evolved into modern apparatchik, avant-garde, and other forms of correctness. To see how Wordsworth's critique also anticipates postmodernity, therefore, we need to witness *scene 3* (lines 337–53), which begins with a curiously offhand salute to "chance" ("At other moments, . . . when 'twas my chance"). This last scene opens on a labyrinth of literal ways figured on Salisbury Plain—"Lines, circles, mounts, a mystery of shapes"—commanded again by the Druids. But now the Druids, who preside over the moment of enlightened synthesis in the passage, appear in a bright aspect that no historical method prior to romantic dialectic knew how to reconcile with their dark, barbarous, sacrificial alter ego—the total effect being an antithesis of bright and dark that only Hegelian logic and its aftermath (e.g., cold war logic) will "solve" (eventually allowing popular artists such as George Lucas, e.g., effortlessly to think the antithesis as a détente between Druid-like Jedi and the dark side of the Force).[30] Now the Druids are astronomers, natural philosophers, and teachers—in a word, *interpreters* of the mysterious ways of the world figured in all those henges and monoliths. And what they teach is a theory of worldly ways that is literally a meta-way or higher way: astronomy. Potentially, of course, that way also lies heavy-handed, didactic correct-ness (or Hegelian absolute knowledge): "with white wands / Uplifted," the Druids point "to the starry sky, / Alternately, and plain below." Yet, when prefaced by the poet's own offhandedness ("At other moments, . . . 'twas my chance"), and when excused as conducting a merely "gentle," "antiquarian," and so unmethodical charm, the felt effect is the opposite of heavy-handed. Though the Druids are the very theoreticians of the meta-way, or method, their whole magic in Wordsworth's passage seems to lie in conducting an offhand, ad hoc lightness of being. Fate may lie in the stars, in other words, but the proper conduct of fate on earth is as light and free as the fairy magic that always ensues when, after the day's labors or wars, we lift our eyes to the sky and imagine. Fate sublimes into what fairies make of chance: luck (or, as the angels would have it, grace).[31] There is at the last no overdetermined critique but, instead, an antithesis to the entire, previous antithesis of barbaric majesty and dark savagery imparted with immeasurable obliqueness through an arbitrariness—a zen—of chance. Not, "You must follow the method," in other words, but, "Oh, by the way, there's a method." The progress of civilization is as much a detour as a telos.

Such underdetermination of method in romanticism, I suggest, initi-ates a subplot of dialectical method that winds its way from the nineteenth century through modernism and postmodernism until at last it emerges as the main plot I name *contingency*. From dialectic to contingency: it's as if critical method becomes just an anecdote, a koan that rises free of immersion in history on a bubble of offhandedness. It's as if enlightenment becomes a peel-away *super-* rather than *inter*vention. Critical insight adheres to, as much as inheres in, history.

Contingent Method

We might have told other fables to reach the same goal, of course, but this strangely offhand episode in Wordsworth is as good a prelude as any to the contingent postmodern historicism I advocate for cultural criticism and that, in their various ways, these essays theorize or exemplify. Though no summary statement can be entirely true to the modus operandi of essays that have evolved over twenty years in response to particular needs rooted in their time, perhaps there may, nevertheless, be some value in distilling the principles of contingent postmodern historicism as I currently understand them. I do so through the following five recommendations, each untrue when taken alone, each adequate only when corrected by the others so as to ensure that the fallacies of general postmodern historicism—looseness of beginnings and ends, factitiousness of the new, screen-like detachment from history—criticize each other to sustain a compensatory, fragile bubble of historical understanding amid future worlds.

1. *Complicate history.* For my muse—but also for my countermuse—I summon up Walter Benjamin's familiar angel of history from "Theses on the Philosophy of History" (1940). The angel, we may say, acts out a modern version of the backward-looking *Prelude*. As such, he is an updated Druid with a specifically modern stance toward history:

> A Klee painting named "Angelus Novus" [figure 0.1] shows an angel looking as though he is about to move away from something he is fixedly contemplating. His eyes are staring, his mouth is open, his wings are spread. This is how one pictures the angel of history. His face is turned toward the past. Where we perceive a chain of events, he sees one single catastrophe which keeps piling wreckage upon wreckage and hurls it in front of his feet. The angel would like to stay, awaken the dead, and make whole what has been smashed. But a storm is blowing from Paradise; it has got caught in his wings with such a violence that the angel can no longer close them. The storm irresistibly propels him into the future to which his back is turned, while the pile of debris before him grows skyward. This storm is what we call progress. (Thesis 9)[32]

While Benjamin's stance toward history must be honored in its own time, for us, now, it must also be reoriented to unlock the legacy of *offhand*

Figure 0.1. Paul Klee, *Angelus Novus* (1920).

romanticism (as I earlier termed it) that it carries fragilely and secretly through straitened modernity to our postmodern times.

To begin with, the angel "sees one single catastrophe," a "pile of debris." But, for contemporary cultural criticism, history since even 1940 is at least several catastrophes, each with its own—and, recently, twin—piles of debris. My first recommendation is that cultural criticism today must differentiate between catastrophes in order to resist any too-easy piling up of today's enemies with yesterday's fascists, communists, imperialists, "axes of evil," and all other modern-style thousand-year-reich total histories (the catastrophic take-it-or-leave-it history symptomatic of modern "progress"). Or, to go micro, cultural criticism should look closely *into* individual catastrophes to detotalize them into internally differentiated fields of disaster. Sifted with the historiographic tools of *Annales* history, cultural materialism, Althusserian Marxism, Foucault's "epistemic" analysis, Geertz's "thick description," and so forth, the debris of history takes on an unaccountably rich interior structure. Indeed, in recent "catastrophe theory" or Ilya Prigogine's systems theory with its chaotic "bifurcation points," catastrophe itself has structure.[33] The historical "pile of debris," in other words, is complexly plied with essential, rather than accidental, plurality. Rather than gathering into either a single presence or the big bang explosion of such presence (Benjamin's "pile of debris," we recognize, precisely disintegrates the "aura" he theorized in "The Work of Art in the Age of Mechanical Reproduction"), history proliferates as a multi-layered, sedimented, turbulent, and self-organizing ecology of local determination. Lots of particulars in many kinds of structures, in other words, and even glimpses of metarelations between structures, but no one, grand structure vulnerable to equally totalizing collapses of structure.

Such, for example, is the vision of history that Manuel De Landa— blending Fernand Braudel's geologically inspired *Annales* historiography, Deleuze and Guattari's rhizomatics, and Prigogine's nonequilibrium systems theory—calls "a thousand years of nonlinear history."[34] Instead of conceptualizing the relation between past and present as linear, we might best think of it in De Landa's manner as a Braudelian multilayered sea, a Deleuze/Guattarian thousand plateaus, or a Prigogine dissipative system fractured with bifurcation points—that is, as a network or assemblage characterized by multiple rates of flow, redundant or interfering communication channels, and competing self-organizing and self-destructive behaviors. History is a complicated texture, which is what contemporary cultural criticism means by *context*.

2. Immerse ourselves in history. In the Second World War context of the full "Theses on the Philosophy of History," of course, Benjamin's angel is not just a horrified spectator but also an engaged cultural critic. He is one face of the "historical materialism" that Benjamin posed against the contemporary storm wind of "universal historicism," technocratic "progress," and—the storm trooper of all that—fascism. But the cost of the angel's dissent from the hyperprogressivism of his era is that—as captured in Thesis 9 (quoted above)—his mode of engagement appears the very opposite of engagement: a kind of retreat from or, at best, reluctant immersion in history ("looking as though he is about to move away from something he is fixedly contemplating"). In the context of 1940, we may say, the snapshot in which Thesis 9 captures him is like a passport photo. (Benjamin owned the Klee watercolor on which Thesis 9 is based, and, given his special admiration of Klee, it would not be far-fetched to see the watercolor as a kind of artistic personal identity document.)[35] Flash! It is as if the angel were presenting his papers to the SA or SS: "I have no meaningful history. I am just a bystander." A paradoxical blend of provocation and retreat to fight another day, Benjamin's essay is cultural criticism in survivor's mode.

My second recommendation for postmodern cultural criticism is to turn this Benjaminian mise-en-scène around to make it indeed about immersion in, rather than refuge from, history. In contemporary cultural criticism, the angel should appear as though he were about to move *into* something he is fixedly contemplating—specifically, a historical context complicated enough that, like a fractal sponge (Menger sponge), it exerts an absorptive rather than a repulsive power, sucking him *in*, rather than blowing him back.[36] Or, more fully, since the historical actors that cultural criticism contemplates are equally historical whether they pose as activists in or refugees from historical life, the task of cultural criticism today is to take some of the burden off the individual Benjaminian angel by revolving our observer's camera angle hemispherically around so that we view his stance from the back, framed against—in the act of confronting—history. Repositioning our viewpoint in this fashion will shift our regard from the individual participant-observer to the larger, contested historical patterns that emerge through, and around, individuals.

If postmodern society today is committed exorbitantly to the new, in short, then cultural criticism must compensate by dedicating itself with equal excess to confronting the old, where *old* is a relative term untethered to any particular lapse of years. (In some cases, even a short interval provides critical leverage.) Such immersion in history can be as ambient as what David Simpson calls "a good dose of antiquarian history: an excess of unassimilated information." Or it can be as ideologically shaped as Fredric Jameson's famous mission statement: "Always historicize." (Compare Benjamin: "Nothing that has ever happened should be regarded as lost for history" [Thesis 3]).[37] In either case, making it old (not new) is the prerequisite for any critical purpose whatsoever in the age of corporatized, total innovation.

3. Free ourselves from history. As Benjamin's angel is blown backward toward the future, he appears wholly passive in his wide-eyed witnessing of catastrophe. It is almost as if he were shot along a wire strung from past to future, never needing to worry that there might be a fork in the path to tomorrow, never considering that there might be alternative angles from which to view yesterday, and, therefore, never needing to look back and forth *between* past and future to ride the storm. In recent military parlance (the comparison is at first glance jarring, but no more so than keeping an ear cocked for V1 buzz bombs in Benjamin's own era), the angel is not just a wire-guided missile but a "fire-and-forget" smart missile. Only, in this case, the missile's nose camera is inexplicably reversed so that it looks away from its future target toward the history that launched it. A strange smart bomb, this, whose explosion is not its target but its origin and whose security is that not of homeland but of exile.

Complicating history and immersing ourselves in it, as I have recommended, are necessary first steps, but they are not by themselves adequate for critical engagement today. Also necessary is a step that will only at first seem contradictory: the strenuous (rather than facile) act of *freeing* ourselves from the complicated history we are immersed in or, phrased another way, of choosing ethically to be emancipated from historical context through the very act of allowing ourselves to be so fully and deeply absorbed in that context that we discern the alternative pathways between past and future emergent from its complexity.

The danger, of course, is enthrallment to the past in a manner that is conservative by default (in a way that avoids the hard ethical choices made by either political conservatives or progressives). I mean by this a version of what Nietzsche termed the "abuse of history," according to which immersion in history seems to lead to no more than a minimalist ethics of submission to the given, to that which simply, empirically, and inarguably (the greatest of all totalitarian arguments) "is."[38] One's ethical stance reduces to obeisance to reality. More strongly, one's stance reduces to what I term in chapter 9 *enslavement* to history (a reference to a specific context). Either *we* in the present become a facsimile of the historical *them* (as in modern political movements that have proceeded on the assumption of an unending American, French, Russian, or Chinese Revolution), or *they* in history become ghost projections of the modern *us* (as in business books that take historical leaders as types of the CEO).[39] Put in terms of causality rather than resemblance: either the present is determined by a history set in motion by the entirety of past context, or, inversely, the past is committed to a teleology of history whose outcome is the present. Of course, the tightest chains of such historical determinism conform to strictly linear relations between past and present. But complex, rhizomatic historical contexts of the sort I sketched above can create even more oppressive, hegemonic determinisms—like being tied down by a thousand fine chains. Context is enormously sticky.

Therefore, any contemporary use of history to critique culture needs not just to be immersive but also to imagine how culture can escape history by activating the potential for emancipation seeded within, but not without ethical choice able to emerge from, the complexity of the past. Among all the rich bifurcation points of history, where are the avenues that suggest alternative ways of thinking about the past and the future? Which is the way, or ways, to a future that can come into its own unchained from the forceful illusion, called *reality*, that there must always have been *one* past whose multifarious parts are locked together in a symphony of catastrophe? In one way or another, in short, contemporary historicism must imagine nonlinear history in a manner that exceeds the escapist fantasies of both popular historical entertainments and jingoistic freedom movements on all sides of the political spectrum.[40]

4. Make a method. The *Angelus Novus* watercolor that inspired Benjamin's Thesis 9 shows its angel frontally so that we do not see what he flinches away from, only that his eyes are turned askance, to his left, as if he were not just shying, but looking, away—a Laocöon of the shifty glance rather than uprolled eyes (see figure 0.1 above). But there is also another kind of looking away in the painting: the distinctively postimpressionist, postcubist, and postexpressionist style through which Klee, in the now-classic method of modern painting, shifts our gaze away from the representational subject to the play of the medium itself on the plane of the picture surface. Such is one of the methods by which modernity—as also attested, for example, by Picasso's *Guernica* (1937) or the anti-"Northern" irony of the New Critical formalists—at once immersed itself in history and freed itself from history.[41]

The moderns, I think, pointed the way. How can contemporary historicism at once acknowledge the condition of being bound to history and claim another sense of "conditionality" (as when we say that something is conditional) able to open a space of freedom from/in history—the necessary paradox of any critical historicism? After the original, nineteenth-century moment of historicism, the answer was to play up the antithetical, ironic, or otherwise difference-making component of Hegelian method. As Joel Fineman remarks: "We can say . . . that it has been the project of post-Hegelian philosophy, insofar as it remains Hegelian, and concerned therefore with history, to find some way to introduce into the ahistorical historicality of Hegelian philosophy of history some break or interruption of the fullness and repletion of the Spirit's self-reflection, so as thereby to introduce to history the temporality of time."[42] This post-

Hegelian project later descended into twentieth-century method specifically as a breakaway concept of method itself. The central modern critical concept, we may say, was a *method* (any method) able to insist both that the modern *us* rigorously acknowledge its relation to the historical *them* and that it break away on its own. Like some cubist, expressionist, or abstract expressionist style, method itself served as the emancipatory cutout between us and them.

In the first chapter of this book (chronologically the first essay I wrote on cultural criticism), I sketch the underlying rationale of such breakaway method as follows:

> Code the identification between *us* and *them* into our interviewing procedure (by making method harbor an interior otherness, a will to estrange its own most comfortable assumptions), and the identification between *them* and *us* will no longer be quite so naked. When *they* are in our method, then—as in the moment of tragic recognition—the realization that man is finally man and we only who we are (the tautological statement of historicism) will be redeemed by a detachment akin to that once signed by the deus ex machina. This is why my choice of exempla ("I am that I am") and, perhaps, very tone intimate that historical understanding is bound to forms of interpretation seeming as inevitable as the gods or fate. There is a Hermes in hermeneutics: it is precisely the sense that we are being led by a method of understanding as puzzling, inconsistent, and alien as any historical other (from the viewpoint of single explanatory models) that saves our knowledge of the past from too immediate an act of identification. (49)

I can now expand on this summary statement in the following way. On the one hand, clearly, method is good for creating a sense that we are not free to interpret history just any old way. Method implies subjection to the real of the past according to some system of discovery, validation, and interpretation that answers to the real both empirically and normatively (constructively) by incorporating within itself some of the a priori givenness of the real. Yet, on the other hand, such latter construction, when fully developed, acquires an autonomy, not only registering, but also offsetting or displacing the found truth of history. From a fundamentalist perspective, that displacement is toward some apparently more transcendental reality. Method has thus been used to elevate the real of history to the fuller reality of theology, idealism, materialism, or any other big picture that shows us we need to conform to a metahistory beyond the known scope and mandate of history. But, from a more latitudinarian perspective, method displaces us not so much toward some other reality as—the logical kernel here—toward the sense of otherness itself. At this core level, prior to any proposition about ultimate origins or goals, the only thing that registers is a break in the tight, clenched little history of our selves; and the most accurate statement of that break is a method (like a grammar or a syntax we would ourselves not naturally speak) that enacts a certain alienation or remove from ourselves. After all, from Descartes's *Discourse on Method* (1637) at the onset of the Enlightenment on, method (and, even more so, theory) has had the reputation of being disembodied, inorganic, abstract, technical, or alien—the opposite of organically rooted, organic, or intuitive. But *good* method, we may say, applies conceptual alienation for a critical, rather than merely technical, purpose. It dedicates modernity to seeking a history that can be other than it is.

5. *Mediate our method.* But it is not on modern method itself that I would conclude. The postmodern supplement to the modern critical concept is a method that might free the contemporary *us* from the historical *them* in a manner buffered from the severity of modern method itself. Again I take my cue from formal innovation in the Benjamin passage quoted above. The experimentalism of the Klee painting on which Benjamin meditates, of course, is matched by the formal innovation of Benjamin's writing itself in the overall "Theses on the Philosophy of History," which mixes and matches the aphoristic style of the German romantic philosophers, the manifesto style of the early modernists (e.g., Victor Shklovsky's "Art as Technique"), and the hypothesis style of the scientists that modernist poets ironized (as in the paradoxical formula in Archibald MacLeish's "Ars Poetica": "A poem should be equal to: / Not true").[43] Or, to recur to my earlier mention of modernist media innovations, perhaps *formal innovation* in my present vocabulary is too stilted a concept. *Media innovation* instead may be the key to seeing how modernism has passed on its experimental method to postmodernism in a manner allowing us now both to bind ourselves to historical context and—in a manner more complete than modernism itself—to free ourselves from it.

I can best articulate this position by offering a fresh defense of the New Historicist anecdote as it has emerged into prominence in controversies about postmodern historicism (especially, but not exclusively, in regard to the New Historicism). Or, better, since both the reductive charge of being "just anecdotal" and rebuttals against such charges have now been well rehearsed, I will defend the broader paradigm that links the postmodern-historicist anecdote to such past innovations in the romantic-modern-postmodern genealogy I sketch as the Wordsworthian spot of time or the formalist close reading. For convenience, we can call this broader paradigm the method of *bubble universes*. We can start by taking a page from Fineman's well-known essay reflecting on the anecdote: "In formal terms, my thesis is the following: that the anecdote is the literary form that uniquely *lets history happen* by virtue of the way it introduces an opening into the teleological, and therefore timeless, narration of beginning, middle, and end. The anecdote produces the effect of the real, the occurrence of contingency, by establishing an event as an event within and yet without the framing context of historical successivity, i.e., it does so only in so far as its narrative both comprises and refracts the narration it reports."[44] Continuing in psychoanalytic terms, Fineman speaks of the anecdote as a paradoxical "orifice" set inside, but also issuing outside, history (an "opening of history . . . the hole and rim—using psychoanalytic language, the orifice—traced out . . . within the totalizing whole of history").[45] In short, the anecdotes or other microhistories that populate the work of the New Historicists, the New Cultural Historians, and so on are bubble universes at once contained *in* historical reality and admitting of freedom *from* that reality.[46]

My own approach to the problem is to complement Fineman's psychoanalytic framework with that of media analysis, which would start by noticing the unacknowledged elephant in the little room of the anecdote: before it is a method, the anecdote (derived from oral culture, the post-Montaigne essay, the vignette, journalistic print culture, the electronic sound bite, and, more recently, the Internet blog post, etc.) is a media form. Or, more strongly, the anecdote can be a method precisely *because* it is now an advanced, historically layered media form. Consider that the various postmodern historicisms have been acutely attuned to history as a medium of representations, symbols, interpretations, and so on. My hypothesis is that there is a link between such an understanding of history as a set of semiautonomous, "subversive," or never fully governable representational forms hosted in artifacts, arts, language, and other cultural substrates—*media* in my usage here—and the media form of the anecdote itself as it has become one of postmodern historicism's own signature acts of representation. Such recursion of past media in present media is a method for at once receiving the force of historical determination as causality and mediating such causality as a *communication* between past and present that is undecidably both performative and symbolic, both determined by history and free enough from strict conditioning (via unpredictable, two-way feedback modulations between past and present media) to allow us to imagine other avenues of possibility leading from the complexity of the past to that of the future.

In short, postmodern historicism introduces the thought of *mediation* in the relation of past to future. My culminating recommendation, therefore, is that postmodern historicism can best do so by visibly signaling the act of such mediation through actual media innovation or allusions to such innovation in its own form, thereby methodically bringing to view a sense of simultaneous sameness and otherness in our relation to history. Or, more carefully, lest we fall into the trap of innovation *über alles* on which I commented at the start of this introduction, let us say instead that media innovation of the sort I indicate is really any mediation that produces a sense of anachronism (residual or emergent, in Raymond Williams's vocabulary) able to make us see history as a compound relation of proximity and distance between past and present. Readable either as regression to oral storytelling or progression to electronic age sound bites or blog posts, the anecdote is barely the beginning of such possible self-aware media innovation.

It's like holding a microphone up to the far past: a way of committing ourselves to hearing the past but, through the conscious election of a media paradigm from a different era, also of holding open the possibility of freedom from the past. Bubble universes of history, that is, are necessarily shaped through the "orifices" of lenses, microphones, screens, and sundry other instruments of mediation that, via the act of mediation itself, register the paradox of immersive freedom from history constitutive of contingency. Only through such mediation, it may be posited, can cultural criticism today engage critically with, rather than merely mirror, the general phenomenon of contemporary postmodern historicism. Moreover, it may be suggested that, in the near future, cultural criticism will indeed need to experiment with its actual media to address meaningfully a postmodern historicism that, as in the case of so-called Web 2.0, is both highly socially aware and—as attested by blog archives that vainly try to give an afterlife to dynamic, contingent postings ceaselessly rolling out of sight—in need of historical awareness.

For the present, however, this book of essays still hews to the media forms of *book* and *essay*, but with a strong tendency to thematize and/or allude to media anachronisms of the sort theorized above. Thus, in chapter 1 ("The Power of Formalism: The New Historicism"), I adopt a variety of media metaphors—Fellini's cinema, Wölfflin's slide projectors, photography—to sketch the dialectic I term the *governing line* and the *disturbed array*. Chapter 2 ("Trying Cultural Criticism: Wordsworth and Subversion") adopts the framing paradigm of the legal trial with its exhibits of evidence. Chapter 3 ("Local Transcendence: Cultural Criticism, Postmodernism, and the Romanticism of Detail") begins by imagining Wordsworth at a personal computer, goes on to present a matrix with multiple "channels" from postmodern cultural criticism, and at last meditates on the "cybernetic, televisionary, rhapsodic" way in which such criticism projects its "version of romantic nature: a screen" (137). Chapter 4 ("Remembering the Spruce Goose: Historicism, Postmodernism, Romanticism") extends the media paradigm, enacting in its own form the media exhibits, simulations, and screens that constitute its object of study (the Spruce Goose exhibit then in Long Beach, California). And so the tactic of self-aware media paradigms continues through most of the succeeding chapters—for example, chapter 5 ("The New Historicism and the Work of Mourning"), with its introductory, explicitly postmodern depiction of Wordsworth's dead brother as a kind of found-object collage or "body/plank/sand assemblage," or chapter 6 ("The Interdisciplinary War Machine"), which concludes with a conjecture on the incommensurable, unpresentable relation between the "interdisciplinary" and the "intermediated" (not to mention new media).

The culmination of this method then comes in the final three chapters, where I reflect specifically on the link—at once bound and free, determinative and contingent—that runs between older methods of understanding history and contemporary information media. Chapter 7 ("Sidney's Technology: A Critique by Technology of Literary History") adopts the paradigms of modern and postmodern communication systems (from the telephone to the Internet) to critique historical method in a manner whose anachronism I explicitly justify. Chapter 8 ("Transcendental Data: Toward a Cultural History and Aesthetics of the New Encoded Discourse") borrows the form of XML encoding to title the sections of its argument about the relation between recent text-encoding and database practices and early-twentieth-century work regimes and office media. And chapter 9 ("Escaping History: The New Historicism, Databases, and Contingency") explores the strange, cross-historical link between abolition as Charles Babbage thought about it at the time of his Analytical Engine and our own "information wants to be free" era of random access and relational databases.

January 2007, Goleta, California

Though it will doubtless be required some day to change its character, semiology must first of all, if not exactly take definite shape, at least *try* itself out, explore its possibilities and impossibilities. . . . It must be acknowledged in advance that such an investigation is both diffident and rash.

ROLAND BARTHES, *ELEMENTS OF SEMIOLOGY*

I compare . . . a certain number of structures which I seek where they may be found, and not elsewhere: in other words, in the kinship system, political ideology, mythology, ritual, art, code of etiquette, and—why not?—cooking.

CLAUDE LÉVI-STRAUSS, *STRUCTURAL ANTHROPOLOGY*

The Power of Formalism
The New Historicism

Why Not?

To understand the New Historicism, it will be useful to start by considering the version of rhetorical *exordium* the method uses to place its argument in play. Just as Sidney solicits his audience in the *Apology for Poetry* by beginning on the anecdote of Pugliano's horsemanship, so Stephen Greenblatt and others—to quote Jean E. Howard's early criticism of the technique—broach their argument through "painstaking description of a particular historical event, place, or experience" whose "supposedly paradigmatic moment" sketches "a cultural law."[1] So thoroughgoing is such paradigmatism that *exordium* is convertible with *digressio*: even when a New Historicist study internalizes a paradigm as its centerpiece rather than its opening, the paradigm retains a throwaway quality. Serendipitous and adventitious—always

merely found, always merely picked up—these models compose a bri-
colage substituting for what was once the more methodical *narratio* or
presentation of facts in the history of ideas: the recording of such master
paradigms, for example, as the chain of being, the mirror, and the lamp.
Where the history of ideas straightened world pictures, Elizabethan or
otherwise, New Historicism hangs them anew—seemingly by accident,
off any hook, at any angle.[2] It not only cherishes paradigms thematizing
obliqueness, as in Greenblatt's anamorphic reading of Holbein's *Ambassadors* in *Renaissance Self-Fashioning*,[3] but also speaks those paradigms in
a vocabulary of anecdotal virtuosity so oblique—itself tending at times
to anamorphosis, paradox, oxymoron, and chiasmus—that the result is a
kind of intellectual *sprezzatura*.[4] To allude to the structuralist strain in the
ancestry of the method, the paradigms of the New Historicism bare a shy
rashness, a supremely cavalier *why not?* assertive of their marginality.

It is my thesis that the *why not?* of the New Historicism serves primarily
to repress the urgency of its real questions about literature and history
and that the reason the repression is necessary is that the urgency of these
questions is motivated not by curiosity about literature and history in the
past so much as by deep embarrassment about the marginality of literary history now. For what most distinguishes the *New* Historicism may
be read in the brash nervousness with which it wears its title in an intellectual climate commonly prefixed *post-*. As I will suggest, the spurious,
avant-garde novelty of the method (in which my own early work has been
as implicated as any) is really a rearguard action spurred by the postmodern fear that, in the face of history, *literary* history or any such mere show
of intellect is passé.

I want to trace a trajectory, then, from the *why not?* of the New Historicism to a *why* that will allow us to set an agenda for understanding
the method's anxiety of marginality. And to begin with (assuming here a
barker's voice in advance of future argument): *view* the carnival of New
Historicist paradigms; *see* the sideshows of the overparadigm I will call—
why not?—the contest of the *governing line* and the *disturbed array*.[5]

Imagine Charles I seated at a court play—at the masque-like *Florimène* in
1635, for example, as Stephen Orgel has reconstructed the scene. Centered
in conspicuous visibility amid the audience, who occupy seats along three
walls facing him, he sees along the exact medial axis of the hall directly
into Inigo Jones's stage with its strongly illusionistic perspective effects—
into the recessional avenue between trees and cottages, for instance, hung
in the opening scene (figures 1.1–1.3). King and vanishing point: the apexes
of royal presence and representation rule the universe between them.[6]

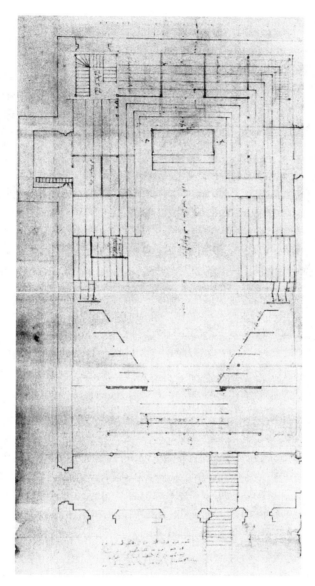

Figure 1.1. *Florimène*: plan of the stage and hall, ca. 1635. Discussed by Stephen Orgel in *The Illusion of Power*, 27–29.

Figure 1.2. Unknown artist, *Cardinal Richelieu Entertains the King and Queen in the Theatre of the Palais Cardinal*. Used comparatively by Orgel to illustrate the centrality of the monarch's viewing position at the time of *Florimène* ("The Royal Theatre and the Role of the King," 265–66).

This scene visualizes one of the two leading paradigms of New Historicist poetics: a "cultural poetics," as Greenblatt names it, whose donnée of interpretation is neither the historical nor the literary fact but the feigned, illusional, or otherwise *made* structure of the cultural artifact encompassing both realms.[7] The paradigm is that of theatricality, which in Renaissance studies and its romantics counterpart (the latter increasingly influenced by French Revolution studies) starts in the actual theater but then aggressively spills out of doors to make *mise-en-scène, social drama, playfulness, improvisation, rehearsal, tragedy,* and *illusion* the master tropes of culture.[8] With the possible exception of Greenblatt's study of self-made Renaissance men, theatricality has been used primarily to model the *mentalité* of monarch-centered aristocracy or its overthrow—the experience of the Elizabethan and Stuart court theater as recounted by Orgel, for example, or that of the court spectacle (in another sense) registered by Marie-Hélène Huet at the trial of Louis XVI.[9]

As in the case of New Historicist paradigms generally, theatricality models *power*.[10] Power, especially in Renaissance studies, designates the

Figure 1.3. Inigo Jones, stage, proscenium, and standing scene for opening scene of *Florimène* (1635). Discussed in Orgel, *The Illusion of Power*, 30–34.

negotiation of social, personal, and literary authority that yields a single regulation of culture. But the regulated state, we should immediately note, is so far from being monolithic that at every level its distinguishing feature is inner dynamism—a self-tensed, *internecine* action of power. The New Historicism imagines an existentially precarious power secured on the incipient civil war between, on the one hand, cultural plurality and, on the other (to borrow an apt term from Russian Formalism), the cultural dominant able to bind plurality within structure.[11] Theatricality in particular is the paradigm that stresses the slender control of dominance *over* plurality.

Thus it is that Orgel observes the plural jostle for court rank and ambassadorial privilege in the seating arrangements at *Florimène* and that Huet reconstructs the multitudinous vivacity, inebriation, and sometimes plain boredom that sounded from the spectators at Louis's trial in 1793.[12] But thus it is also that both authors stress the ability of the dominant, in the person of Charles or Louis, to structure plurality into the *show* of a single state. Throned at the only point in the room perfect for viewing the perspective effects, Charles literally ruled: his being-seen-to-watch-the-show, as Orgel conceives it,[13] organized aristocracy around a single line of perfect vision, a single symbolic rule allowing each participant in the masque universe to calibrate his place near or far, to the right or the left of the royal lineage.[14] Just so Louis XVI, even as he was *de*throned, commanded all eyes in his spectacle-court as powerfully as some Richard II asking for a mirror. The theatricality that once maintained the illusion of a king was now the perfect mirror of magistrates to *di*sillusion another king—but in such a way as still to maintain around the king's lineage the symmetry of right and left (those who voted no and yes to Louis's death) that was constitutive of ruled state. Only when the king had played his last performance, as Huet shows, did the Revolution then propagate plays about Marat and other heroes showing anew the *people's* rule.

Charles and Louis, illusion and disillusion: these two states and their actors, we realize, are finally as indistinguishable in the analytic of theatricality as the two halves of the anamorphic answer Richard II returns to Bolingbroke in Shakespeare's deposition scene: "Ay, no; no, ay."[15] Once we premise the theatricality of all culture and enter the bottomless spectatorship of New Historicist consciousness, we know that any cultural backdrop, at any time, can turn into its inversion as easily as some Inigo Jones *machina versatilis* (turning machine) opening up a new scene. Every facade is merely the reversal or repetition of a previous facade. A double paradigm conflating the Stuart and Bourbon, English and French revolutionary scenes comes to mind. As reported with special emphasis in the London press, Louis in his last days took care to read the "account of the death of Charles the First."[16] What Louis-as-actor read, we can imagine, was the script for a prior drama foreshadowing his own—a script, as Patricia Fumerton's researches suggest, that Charles himself performed in an uncanny reenactment of an even earlier theater of act. With high sense of drama, Charles went to his death almost exactly as he would have gone to a masque—through the same sequence of rooms in the Banqueting House at Whitehall, through a window in the hall where masques were performed, and at last out onto the stage of the blade where he enacted a scene of death so self-controlled and riveting that it can truly be said to have been a command performance.[17] Just so, as I have recounted in *Wordsworth: The Sense of History*, Louis rose to the occasion on his own platform of the guillotine, giving a command performance so self-possessed, devout, and potentially subversive of the new state that the managers of the carefully staged event ordered a drumroll silencing his soliloquy.[18] Play-within-a-play: in the endlessly receding playhouse that is New Historicist

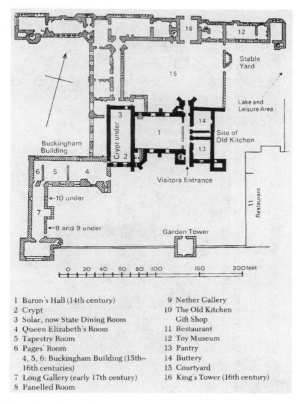

Figure 1.4. "Plan of Penshurst Place showing various stages of construction and the present disposition of rooms open to visitors. The darker areas demark the walls of the original fourteenth-century manor house." Discussed (with above caption) by Don E. Wayne in *Penshurst*, 47, 50.

history, there is no death. Finality is only the possibility of theatrical revival, cultural determination a casting call for future improvisation.

Again, imagine visiting Penshurst Place. As explored in Don E. Wayne's *Penshurst*, the core of the building consists of a fourteenth-century manor house with its Baron's or Great Hall, while the later additions of the Sidney family sprawl outward—but in such a way as to feign seamlessness (figure 1.4). Looking through the newer main entrance at the north, we sight down the perspective recession created by a vista of arches: first the entrance span, then the arch of the service passage through the manor house, and, finally, the arched aperture of the newer Garden Tower toward

Figure 1.5. "Penshurst Place. Perspective of arches (King's Tower—Great Hall—Garden Tower) viewed through the open doors of the main entrance at the North Front." Discussed (with above caption) in Wayne, *Penshurst*, 85, 91.

the south (figure 1.5).[19] Fore-, middle-, and background planes frame visual space within a box of time measured with the typological certainty of a Fra Angelico *Annunciation* (in which recessed planes showing the Garden situate Mary's *humiliatio* within the longest vista of human history).[20] The eye's walk into Penshurst's manorial past has all the stateliness of procession: we are humbled before a history seen in ceremonial review.

Such is a visualization of the architectural and what might be called *inventorial* paradigm characterizing not just Wayne's intriguing book but also such other inquiries as Jonathan Goldberg's study of the triumphal arches ushering James I into London, Catherine Belsey's sketch of split representation in Felbrigg Hall, Fumerton's work on Whitehall Palace and Renaissance miniature cabinets, and Steven Mullaney's look into Renaissance wonder cabinets.[21] Again, the project is to reconstruct the mentality of monarch-centered power—here concretized in the organization of a house or monument, the successive experience of rooms within a house, or, within rooms themselves, such interior galleries as the wonder or miniature cabinet. And, once more, such space projects a ruling line able to dominate plurality.

Even as other courtiers talked business in Elizabeth I's innermost bedchamber, Fumerton shows, Elizabeth was able to maintain the illusion that she was taking the ambassador from Mary Queen of Scots ever inward into her confidence: down the labyrinthine line of her apartments at Whitehall, into her bedchamber, into her miniature cabinet, through the wrappings of her miniature portraits (in this case of the Earl of Leicester and of Mary), through the layered aesthetics of these images of putative dear ones, and at last into the aura of feminine intimacy that was one with her politics of virginal rule.[22] Division of state became a communion of confidantes over the heart's secrets. Just so, Wayne argues, cultural plurality at Penshurst was aligned through a strategem analogous to the ruling line of vision at a masque or the subtler Ariadnean threading of Elizabeth's architecture. How to imagine continuity where there was discontinuity (between the baronial legitimacy of the manor house and the additions of the Sidney clan representing the new court-oriented aristocracy)? One lineage where there were two? The answer, as Wayne compellingly demonstrates, lay in creating the special perspective on history that we have reviewed: the recession that laminated the baronial Great Hall between fore- and far planes of aristocratic veneer. Thus was an image created that, reinforced by the effect of other architectural and heraldic devices, authored the vision of a single descent of greatness. Like the ambassador entering Elizabeth's bedchamber, a visitor proceeding to the central hall stepped into an aura of familiarity, into the very hearth warmth of a mythic family of long possession.

Once more, imagine viewing the cells in the rotunda of Jeremy Bentham's Panopticon prison from the central inspection tower—perhaps from the visitor's gallery that Bentham left room for in his plans. Specifically, envisage this panorama of reform in the manner of John Bender's *Imagining the Penitentiary*: as the demonstration of the eye's *omniscience* while it inspects with narratological power the scene of character development (figure 1.6).[23] Or, again, to create a strange sympathy of sights, imagine touring the then-celebrated Lower Rydal Falls in the English Lake District—as described, for example, by Wordsworth in his *An Evening Walk*, where the falls provide the leading exemplum of landscape. As I have argued in discussing

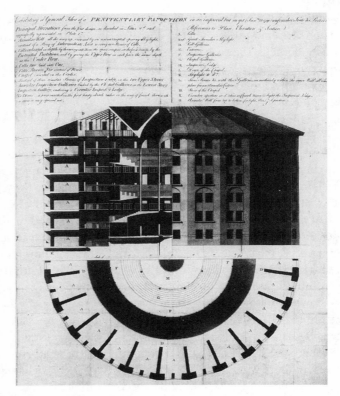

Figure 1.6. Jeremy Bentham, Samuel Bentham, and Willey Reveley, *Penitentiary Panopticon* (1791). Discussed by John Bender in *Imagining the Penitentiary*, 23–24.

the picturesque in my *Wordsworth: The Sense of History*, Lower Rydal Falls naturalizes in its central perspective recession and perfectly reposed bridge in the middle distance a certain kind of supervision, regulation, and *rule* of landscape (figure 1.7). Not a glimpse of proportion or poise but declares the surveillance of picturesque irregularity by an enclosing, correcting, and governing eye.[24]

There are two paradigms represented here, of course, but we can hang them together to highlight what might be called, very broadly, the *middle-classing* of the New Historicism—the imperative, especially in studies of the eighteenth century and its aftermath, to mold the shaping models of the method to the bourgeois and its ascendant forms: the novel, preeminently, but also the poetry (and prose) of description that foreshadowed romantic lyric. The two paradigms are the prison and the recreational tour (the latter modernizes a supplementary paradigm of Renaissance studies, the monarch's progress and entry pageant).[25] Seen in overview, the common project of these paradigms is to conceive a shift in power from aristocracy and monarchical rule to the middle classes and the rule of the individualistic self. Once more, the picture of power forms around a line dominating plurality. Meditating such penitentiary projects as Bentham's Panopticon, Bender arrives at the thesis that it was, in part, the novel (often explicitly concerned with penal themes) that shaped the assumptions about human character necessary to imagine the new prison. Novelistic narrative and the mentality it expressed, that is, helped inculcate the notions of individual consciousness, character development, and the reformatory power of the spectator that gave later-eighteenth-century prisons their object of reform. *We*—you and I—novel reader, are the inspector at the center of Bentham's prison able to see along the pitiless, radial axis of the Panopticon into each cell of murderous, larcenous, or otherwise plural human character. Misrule is submitted to the rule of omniscience.

Or, again, to escape from prison to my own paradigm, *we*—the eighteenth- and nineteenth-century tourist—rule a British landscape of plural "variety." But perhaps we have not truly escaped prison after all. As signaled by Bentham's own description of his scene of reform as "pictur-

Figure 1.7. Joseph Wright of Derby (1734–97), *Rydal Waterfall* (Lower Rydal Falls; 1795). © 2007 Derby Museums and Art Gallery. Discussed in Liu, *Wordsworth: The Sense of History*, 81–82.

Figure 1.8. Lower Rydal Falls with summerhouse in foreground. A shuttered window in the summerhouse was designed to provide the perfect view of the falls. (Photograph: Alan Liu.) Discussed in Liu, *Wordsworth: The Sense of History*, 88–90.

esque" or by Wordsworth's politicized view of landscape from the tower of Lancaster Castle (then a prison) in an essay associated with his *Guide to the Lakes*, the novelistic assumptions that Bender recounts communicate strangely with the "nature"—this lime-tree bower my prison—of romantic poetry.[26] Nature was a *cultural* artifact to be ruled by the recreational eye. Sighting down the "visto of the brook" at Lower Rydal Falls, for example (which we may also see displayed graphically in innumerable contemporary pictures), our eye rules irregularity according to a perspective that was also political. The picturesque was liberalism. It was the nation of freedom that Richard Payne Knight and Uvedale Price propagated with such Foxite Whiggishness that the public linked their theories outright to the Jacobinism of the French Revolution. Like the French Revolution in the early liberal view, that is, nature was "free" and "bold," but hopefully never *too* free or bold. It was captured in especially arresting views that framed any too-licentious or -"violent" irregularities in a sort of checks and balances or constitution of nature: *repose* (one of the most common of picturesque epithets). So too the picturesque was social structure. As attested by Knight's and Price's persistent concern with ownership, nature in repose wedded liberality to security by imagining a nation of exchangeable *property*. Or, where the tourist was not himself a large property owner like Knight and Price, he had to be able (in William Gilpin's phrase) to "appropriate" the imaginary property of such splendidly waste—that is, largely unowned—scenes as the Lake District. The picturesque was the enclosure act of the eye.

Perhaps now we can see why Wordsworth would soon become so unhappy with the picturesque eye that, in *The Prelude* (11.170–79), he likens it to "despotic" "tyranny." Consider that Lower Rydal Falls was situated on the estate of Sir Michael Le Fleming—a property owner who, as Wordsworth and Coleridge found out the hard way, took strict measures with trespassers. The picture-perfect scene could be seen only by *permission*—from a viewing enclosure (a small summerhouse at Rydal Hall) specifically designed to frame it through a window, along the perspective recession, as if in a picture (figure 1.8).[27] The famously sharawaggian plurality and liberty of picturesque experience thus came under the rule of a central eye not unlike Bentham's inspector.

Finally, imagine the interior of the Rotunda at Ranelagh as glimpsed (through Canaletto's picture of 1754) in Terry Castle's *Masquerade and Civilization* (figure 1.9). In a scene not unlike Bentham's Panopticon, a central

Figure 1.9. Giovanni Antonio Canal (Canaletto), *Interior of the Rotunda at Ranelagh* (1754). Used by Terry Castle to illustrate the English adaptation of Continental masquerades in *Masquerade and Civilization*, 14–21.

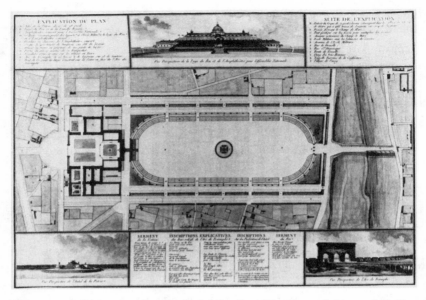

Figure 1.10. Tinted engraving by Meunier and Gaucher of the Champ-de-Mars and the Nouveau Cirque. Used by Mona Ozouf to illustrate her discussion of the construction of the site for the Fête of Federation in 1790 (*Festivals and the French Revolution*, 45–47).

hub of columns commands the round of revelry. Or, to cross the Channel to further festivity, imagine the Paris Champ-de-Mars amphitheater during the Fête of Federation in 1790, as recorded in the plan reproduced in Mona Ozouf's *Festivals and the French Revolution* (figure 1.10). A central altar focuses the oath of the nation while, as contemporary prints record, the massed representatives of the people bear witness all around from an earthwork perimeter specially raised for the event. Space itself during *l'année heureuse* was a centered revolution.[28]

Welcome, at last, to the carnival I earlier barked. If theatricality is New Historicism's paradigm of high culture and monarchy, the carnivalesque—the other most pervasive paradigm of the method—is the matching paradigm of the Bakhtinian low, of the universe in which, as the work of Peter Stallybrass, Allon White, and Michael D. Bristol has shown, the pig and the fish are as nice an object for study as any king or author.[29] The carnivalesque has been imagined with Rabelaisian fullness not only by the Renaissance critics just cited but also by such others in the field as Jonathan Haynes, Richard Helgerson, Leonard Tennenhouse, and Leah S. Marcus (the last of whom, in her book *The Politics of Mirth*, fits high and low together by studying the relation between theater and James I's politicization of British pastimes and sports).[30] Moreover, as shown by Marjorie Levinson's notice of the French revolutionary fête screened by Wordsworth's "Intimations" ode, festivity is one of our most suggestive approaches to romanticism.[31] The child in the ode, after all, *plays* not only theatrically, conning his parts like a "little Actor," but literally, festively: he shapes "a wedding or a festival."[32]

What the carnivalesque conceives is a universe of authority exactly congruent with that of theatricality—but with the opposite emphasis. Rather than stress the dominance of a ruling or central perspective, it watches as perspective itself dips and wavers, gets drunk, gets lost in a plural recession of fun-house mirrors. Part of Castle's argument about the masquerade Rotunda at Ranelagh and other such structures, for example, is that carnival—at least in its English manifestation—was lorded over by a king of impresarios, John James ("Count") Heidegger, and bounded within containing structures that might remind us of the Panopticon. Yet, even in such contained, regulated forms (not to mention the street-filling carnivals of the Continent), misrule tumbled rule. Where the court masque once submitted the antimasque universe to the harmonizing rule of the concluding revels, that is, masquerade reversed the rule to make revel itself an antic discord of plurality.[33] In the fun house, under the great tent, inside the arena of the Champ-de-Mars as it was constructed in a holiday mood by 200,000 Parisian volunteers of every description,[34] all the pent-up kinesis of plurality broke forth in dangerous glee.

So ends our show of the paradigms of the New Historicism, appropriately, with the circus animals' desertion of our survey: theatrical play becomes house, prison, tour, and rounds back to play in an altered state. Each of the models I have sketched, of course, would require fuller elucidation to demonstrate the characteristically obsessive detail with which New Historicism thinks through its props. Furthermore, there are many other paradigms that I could not pack into my already strained categorizations—for example, the circuit of Renaissance gifts studied by Montrose and Fumerton, the destructive exploration of primitive cultures studied by Greenblatt, the first detailed mapping of England scrutinized with provocative results by Helgerson, or the poetics of romantic money (economics and property) seizing the imagination of such romanticists as Levinson, Kurt Heinzelman, David Simpson, and Susan Eilenberg.[35] But perhaps I have gathered sufficient material at this point to hazard a generalization and an incipient criticism.

Why: The Motive behind New Historicism

If we review the paradigms thus far surveyed, we see a common *dialectic*—one of the most pervasive of the terms the New Historicism (especially in Renaissance studies) has used to describe the interrelated patterns of history and literature.[36] The dialectic opposes what I term the *disturbed array* and the *governing line*. I invoke two elder spirits of the New Historicism, Foucault and Bakhtin. Recall the celebrated laugh that breaks from Foucault when, in the preface to *The Order of Things*, he reads the lunatic "Chinese encyclopaedia" with its disturbed catalog of dogs.[37] Or, again, recall the Rabelaisian license that inspires Bakhtin to imagine a universe of carnival not unlike some market square in his own language-rich country: heteroglossic, polysemous, dialogic rather than monologic, Babel-like in its insistent toppling of high authority.[38] Putting the case cinematically: what Foucault and Bakhtin have taught the New Historicism to film is something like that disturbed array of characters that the hero of Fellini's 8½ at last sees revolving in the dream circuses of his fantasy.[39] The disturbed array is the grid that dissolves into moiré pattern, the asylum that erupts in Bedlam, the Mardi Gras parade that jazzes up the pedestrian rhythm of everyday life. The governing line, on the other hand, is the self-centered, axial gaze of Foucault's Benthamite inspector; or, again, it is what Bakhtin calls the "centripetal" impulse always striving to rein in the "centrifugal" dizzyness of heteroglossia within "centralizing," "unitary languages."[40] The governing line, in short, is the whip Marcello Mastroianni cracks: it is the perspective that would see all the disturbed array of culture as *pénétré* with rule, structure, authority.

Why such paradigmatism? To paradigmatize, or, in the root sense, to show side by side (as in the art-historical pedagogy of dual slide projection invented by Heinrich Wölfflin), is to project the question, most simply: What is the connection?[41] Given the New Historicism's dialecticism, this question of connection might be rendered Hegelian (What is the common *Geist*?) or Marxist (What is the material determinant?). But it will be useful to suspend the operation of dialectic for the moment to pose the question precisely in Wölfflin's terms as it influenced Russian Formalism and, eventually, structural study and its aftermath.[42] In the formalist tradition, to ask, What is the connection? is to ask, What is the motif? (Wölfflin) or, again, What is the motive? (Eichenbaum, Shklovsky, Tomashevsky), linking the disturbed array and the governing line.[43] What, that is, is the formal principle of connection holding plurality in unity? Furthermore, what is the motive linking historical and literary fact—kings and plays, for example, or pigs and authors—within the unified, cultural artifact? We

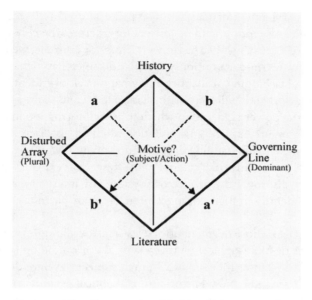

Figure 1.11. Coordinate system of the New Historicist paradigm.

might schematize the overall coordinate system of the New Historicist paradigm according to the quadrate in figure 1.11.

What I most want to suggest with this oblique world picture is that the question of connection or motive posed by the New Historicism—which I have broached in a purely formal idiom—resolves in sharper focus into two complementary issues: What is the subject of literary history, and what is the action of literary history?

What is the subject of literary history? As witness, I call here on such works obsessively preoccupied with the "subject" as Greenblatt's *Renaissance Self-Fashioning* and "Psychoanalysis and Renaissance Culture," Montrose's "The Elizabethan Subject and the Spenserian Text," Dollimore's *Radical Tragedy*, Helgerson's *Self-Crowned Laureates*, Catherine Belsey's *The Subject of Tragedy*, and many other studies not just in the Renaissance field but in the very heartland of subjectivity, romantic studies.[44] The common enterprise of all these works, it seems to me, is not only the Foucauldian one of critiquing the subject, "humanity,"[45] but also more basically that of *searching* for the subject, *any* subject able to tell us what *it* is (authority, author, identity, ideology, consciousness, humanity) that connects the plural to the dominant, historical context to literary text, and so creates a single movement of culture, a single motivated artifact. Though the New Historicism has renamed formalist motive *power* and complicated any faith in homogeneous culture with its instinct for fracture, the core question it asks is still recognizably, *Who* has power? Thus, for example, we may reject as our given the modern notions of self and subjectivity when we study the historical fashioning of identity. But what unit of overidentity—court, household, work unit, village, parish, class, nation, and so on—do we then assume as the power field within which to *see* self-formation in its process of empowerment? As such interpretation-oriented historicists as Dilthey knew, historical understanding depends fundamentally on *some* "category of identity," even if any such category able to serve as explanatory ground is inevitably also only the arbiter of "systems of interactions," of other spheres of identity in their complex interchange of harmony and dissension.[46]

In a criticism whose hermeneutics serve a history far removed from any divine spirit or philosophical truth, in sum, there can be no secure oversubject able to center the study of human subjects. Where divinity said, "I am that I am," the New Historicism is skeptical even of such watered down humanist tautologies as, "Man is man." The tautology of universal explanation must instead be made to branch laterally into an endless quest for definition by alterity ("man is class, state, gender, or ideological struggle against other men"). Yet such a quest only defers the realization that, in order to be satisfying, historical explanation must at some point round back to tautology. The hidden telos of any analysis of ideological struggle, after all, is that at the end of struggle lies new, free, or true man (in a relativistic idiom: the salient class or type of man at the time). And so, if the critical task of searching for the definitive subject of historical study were only to integrate into one equation all its differentia of alterity (class, state, gender, and so on), man would inevitably reduce once more to being understood as man. Such, it may be said, is at once the failing and promise of the New Historicist search for the subject: though it desires to define *man* nontautologically by differentiation from other men (or kinds of identity), the very condition of its desire is made possible by the postdivine faith that there can never really *be* "other men." Only demons and gods unknown to history could be so other.

The New Historicist search for other subjective experience or *mentalité* is, thus, doomed to a tragic recognition. Though *we* would understand the historical *them* in all their strangeness, the forms of our understanding are fated at last to reveal that *they* are a remembrance or prophecy of *us*. Historical understanding is validated by the assumption that man is man, and, of the two terms *past men* and *present men*, only the latter is concrete evidence. As I discuss below, the New Historicist interpreter is thus a subject looking into the past for some other subject able to define what he himself, or she herself, is; but all the search shows in its uncanny historical mirror is the same subject he or she already knows: a simulacrum of the postmodern self insecure in its identity. This is why New Historicist books and essays, despite their splendid diversity of material, feel so much the same: the search for the history of the subject is big with the *same* personality of search, the same detached/committed, ironic/awed, playful/solemn intensity betraying in its nervous force the identity of an intellect itself our base paradigm of class, state, gender, ideological (and so on) uncertainty.

It is not to be marveled at, then, that the New Historicism has such talent for theater: the past is a costume drama in which the interpreter's subject plays. Historical understanding, or what Collingwood called the "re-enactment of past experience," is an act.[47]

What is the action of literary history? Except in a structuralism that originated in the linguistics of the phoneme and morpheme, subject predicates a *sentence* of action. "It" is as it does; motive *moves*. But, in the Wölfflinesque slide show of the New Historicism, what moves other than the scholar's pointer? Here I call as witness not only the long file of Renaissance New Historicists who have made the question of transgression or subversion/containment paramount but also what is probably the even longer file of romanticists who have wondered whether to think their poets incipient revolutionaries or Tory conservatives.[48] The common plight of all these inquiries, as demonstrated with penetrating clarity in Greenblatt's "Invisible Bullets" (originally subtitled "Renaissance Authority and Its Subversion"), is what now seems a genuinely undecidable crux: Do literary or even historical subjects *do* anything?[49] Does the plural movement of a carnival or a satire, for example, truly *subvert* dominant authority? Or, to cite the so-called escape-valve theory, does the dominant merely release a little gas through the Bakhtinian "material bodily lower stratum," thus acknowledging movement within itself but also containing that movement?[50] Indeed, what kind of movement *is* subversion anyway—the single action still allowed in a New Historicist universe become like a gigantic, too-quiet house within which, somewhere, in one of the walls, perhaps, insects chew? Given New Historicism's prejudice for synchronic structure—for the paradigmatic moment in time in which the whole pattern of historical context may be gazed at in rapt stasis—is any *action* conceivable at all? Or is the subject of cultural and literary history capable only of a static, reversible, self-contained rictus of action not unlike myth in Lévi-Strauss's formulation?[51]

Not only, Who has power? then, but also, What is it that power (a concept wholly mythic unless placed in action) *does?* As Nigel Smith has said in an essay touching on the journal *Representations*: "'Non-literary' texts have been seized by literary and cultural critics and deconstructed in order to understand their location in history, and, to a more limited degree, their role in social or political processes. All well and good, if we simply wish to read the map of the world in its tropological complexity. . . . But what happens after representation? What about circulation, dissemination, affect?"[52] Or, as I phrase the problem below in chapter 2, what is the nature of that moment of propagation when identity and its cultural formations are constituted not as the subject formed in history-as-representation and -interpretation, virtually the exclusive realm of the New Historicism so far, but as an action formed in politics-as-*active*-representation (publicity or propaganda, e.g.) and -as-*active*-interpretation (evaluation, justification, and so on)? The issue, of course, is not that action is a more real ground of explanation than subjective representation but, rather, that action—freed of its old chains of causal explanation—is a hermeneutics necessary to complement interpretations of representation descended, ultimately, from the Hegelian phenomenology of the subject (in which *Geist* is represented or displayed in various historical epiphenomena).

History, in sum, must be studied not just as an expressive action of self-, monarch, or hegemonic-state display (the purely theatrical "action" of New Historicist unrealpolitik) but also as action qua action—as action, that is, seen as an alternate ground of explanation definitive of what we mean by identities and their coercive representations. From the perspective of representation, subject may be the central phenomenon, with the consequence that any causal action allowing subjects to exert power over other subjects is incommensurable with the explanatory logic of identity: causation and influence diminish to, and become mystified as, a sympathetic magic or voodoo of resemblance (the mystery of "reproduction" or ideological action, e.g., that Althusser seeks to rationalize in his work on "relative autonomy").[53] But, from the perspective of action, the phenomenal basis lies in transitions within material, demographic, and social masses with their attendant remarshaling of practices, methods, and habits; and *subject* (the ephemeral identity that allows us to narrativize transitional moments in systems of action) is the great illusion. Without both these concepts of subject *and* action, of identities on display and practices creative of such modes of self-fashioning as display itself, there could be no fully satisfying historical explanation.

Neither, I suggest, could there be an explanation that meliorates satisfaction with method. We can put the case intuitively in this way: we want to know what *they did;* but between such terms as *they* and *did,* subject and action, historical being and historical becoming, opens a slight misfit. This misfit is the mystery of predication, the core puzzle of any historicism. If subject and action are explanatory frameworks each separately understandable, each is also made strange in its interplay with the other: was what Charles I *did* supportive or subversive of his *identity* as king, for example? And is not any predication more complex than the copula ("Charles *is* king" or, in a romantic context, Coleridge's "I AM" the imagination) a moment of perilous vulnerability in syntax, genealogy, law, and all the other institutions created to shelter the exercise of predicative power in a convention of regularity? When subject impinges on predicate nominative or object, after all, there is necessarily a contact—and thus a confusion or undermining—of identity. Witness the confusion in the language of subjectivity itself that the New Historicism, under the sway of Althusser, plays on—phrased schematically, the kingly subject (noun) subjects (verb) its subjects (object).[54]

The result of the misfit in historical explanation between the frameworks of subject and action, I suggest, is an instability that reproduces in our own understanding the sense of transition and incommensurability characterizing historical *mentalité* itself. Only through such mimetic instability can we know the sense of history—and *also* know it with the only kind of objectivity possible. If historicism begins as the desire to interview the other across a temporal divide, then we require a seminal otherness or alterity within the very mode of our explanation to ensure that the interview is conducted not just in a single discourse—wholly according to the narratives of self-fashioning or the annals of action, for example—but in a complex dialogue of the two.[55] Only so can the ultimate recognition that *they* are really *us*, as I set forth above, be mediated by method. Code the identification between *us* and *them* into our interviewing procedure (by making method harbor an interior otherness, a will to estrange its own most comfortable assumptions), and the identification between *them* and *us* will no longer be quite so naked. When *they* are in our method, then—as in the moment of tragic recognition—the realization that man is finally man and we only who we are (the tautological statement of historicism) will be redeemed by a detachment akin to that once signed by the deus ex machina. This is why my choice of exempla ("I am that I am") and, perhaps, very tone intimate that historical understanding is bound to forms of interpretation seeming as inevitable as the gods or fate. There is a Hermes in hermeneutics: it is precisely the sense that we are being led by a method of understanding as puzzling, inconsistent, and alien as any historical other (from the viewpoint of single explanatory models) that saves our knowledge of the past from too immediate an act of identification.

What begins to become clear, I suggest, is that these two intervolved questions—what is the subject, and what is the action such a subject predicates?—bring the New Historicism into the fold of the general structuralist and poststructuralist enterprise of rethinking mimesis. It was Aristotelian mimesis, after all, that first dictated to literary history, not only the relation between unified structure and plural episode, but also the canonical relation of history to literature. To recover the ghost form of mimesis embedded within the New Historicism, we need only operate on the schematic quadrate I posed earlier as follows (see figure 1.11 above). Make history as Aristotle saw it—specific, discrete, bound to accidental reality—stand for cultural plurality (establishing the representational linkage a in my figure). Correspondingly, make literature—the more general and probable truth—represent (along a') the dominant unity, the ruling line of beginning-middle-end. Once the quadrate is thus resolved into a binary, then a fully motivated *imitation* becomes possible. Posit in the middle a subject (the hero) whose entire action consists of "discovering" or "recognizing" in the plural episodes of lived history a fearsome unity that is chorused as sacral, otherworldly, *literary*. Thus does plurality become unity and history from the first implicitly literary, implicitly a mimeable action. This is the meaning of Aristotelian mimesis: a total integration of the realms of the many and the one, the real and the fictive into that original monism, the universe of tragedy.

But now premise that nineteenth-century subversion of mimesis at the wellspring of Russian Formalism and, ultimately, of structuralism (and, on Anglo-American shores, of the New Criticism): symbolism. Caught in the wake of the modern flagship of mimesis, the realistic novel, the drunken boat of symbolism saw history not so much as discrete and plural as massive and monolithic—as a line of determination as normative as the "same middle-class magic" Rimbaud imagines wherever the "mail train puts us down!" in his "Historic Evening" (thus establishing the linkage b in my schema).[56] Correspondingly, the literary was that which dissolved history into whirling orbits of plural indeterminacy, into the "imagery" of Potebnyaism that Russian Formalism struck with its hammer to forge its first thinking tools (b' in my schema).[57] Once the quadrate was thus resolved into a new binary, then a wholly different concept of motivation became possible. Whereas, before, the action of the hero discovered historical plurality to be literary unity, the expressive action of the new hero, modern subjectivity, discovered just the reverse. *History* was now the dominating unity that had to be expressed as literary plurality. The light of everyday existence now had to be transmitted through a subjectivity more dispersive and diffractive than any Shelleyan many-colored glass to become the estranged imagery that Russian Formalism knew as its peripety: defamiliarization.[58]

Formalism and its sequelae (up to and including the New Historicism) can be understood at least provisionally, I hazard, as a reflection on the transition between mimetic and symbolist credos. Here, I supply the missing piece in my broad account of the history of the New Historicism. The transition may be located most conveniently in the romantic period between the classic and the symbolist: the period in which history originally became a *historicism* transitional between the universes of the governing line and the disturbed array, with the corollary that literature simultaneously became undecided.[59] Very schematically, was the French Revolution, for example, a movement of tyranny or of plurality? And was history in general a line dominated by political event or, instead, by a blurred contest of diverse political, economic, social, and cultural movements whose composite weltanschauung was as much decentered as centered? What the Germans called *Historismus*—as deployed from Thierry and Michelet through Ranke and Burckhardt—effected a transition in the answers to such questions. Simultaneously, romantic poets and novelists altered the notion of literary structure. Schematically once more, was *The Prelude* or Goethe's *Faust* unified? Or episodic? Or, again, was Scott's *Waverley* about one world or two? Caught in the flux of such historicist and literary transition, the very notion of the subject had to be rethought in the shape of that strangely unmotivated or unconsciously motivated being haunting both literary and historiographic romanticism: the folk, with its post-Hegelian spirit (*Geist*). So too—as demonstrated in England's self-consciously defensive posture during the invasion scares of the Napoleonic wars or in such excruciatingly inactive characters as Mortimer in Wordsworth's *Borderers*—action had to be rethought. Action, as Michelet, Burckhardt, and other historicists demonstrated, occurred on many quieter, social fronts flanking the point of obvious political or military event.

We might apply anew William Empson's celebrated criticism of the "something far more deeply interfused" passage in "Tintern Abbey": "Whether man or some form of God is subject here, [Wordsworth] distinguishes between *things* which are objects or subjects of *thought*, these he *impels*; and *things* which are neither objects nor subjects of *thought*, through these he merely *rolls*. . . . The only advantage I can see in this distinction is that it makes the *spirit* at once intelligent and without intelligence; at once God and nature. . . . There is something rather shuffling about this attempt to be uplifting yet non-denominational."[60] What is the subject of this shuffling poem, Empson asks, and what variously impelled or rolled action is that subject taking? Thus does a modern reflect on romanticism, the period in which (in my initiatory history of the New Historicism) the mimetic turned symbolist.

We are not very far here, it may be seen, from modern formalism full-blown and the long sequence of criticisms that brings us at last to the New Historicism: a further reflection, as I called it, on the transition between mimesis and symbolism initiated in romanticism. To move from Empson's denunciation of "shuffling" to Russian Formalism's atomization of "motive," to Saussure's hugely demotivated langue (a structure of the arbitrary, contentless, unconscious), to Lévi-Strauss's savage mind, to Foucault's agentless archive, to mindless (i.e., Logos-less) *différance*, and to the New Historicism's paradigms uncertain in their subject and action is only to change our valorization. Empson's "shuffling," we may speculate, was a demobilized, post–world war nightmare of the action the nineteenth century accounted to its problematized subject: the mob, crowd, folk, race, nation, and, ultimately, "spirit of the times." Mob-like "*spirit* at once intelligent and without intelligence" is what formalism in its successive states from Russian Formalism and American Southern agrarianism on has attempted to find a safe, a literate, way to enact.

Form, after all, is that which contains the mobility of subversive plurality within a myth of organic wholeness, "ambiguity" within "unity." Or, where organic wholes have been demystified, form contains *différance* within paper tiger wholes (in many ways just as compulsive and necessary to the system) on the order of Derrida's "entire history of metaphysics" or poststructuralism's boundless, all-containing textuality. Whether offered as myth or demystification, the unity of the New Critical poem and the omnium-gatherum of deconstructive metaphysics-into-textuality are, finally, only very delimited wholes—like schoolyards—designed to allow formal thought to play safely. They shelter a place where subject and action may be mobilized (ambiguously or differentially) by claiming preemptively that such place is all there is; it is total, global (in the deconstructive reversal, abyssal). Thus is denied cultural history, the truly global abyss in which are risked the deepest plays of social mobility.[61]

The Embarrassment of the New Historicism

I now venture on my primary thesis. The New Historicism is our most embarrassed "safe" enactment of the forces once mobilizing the old historicist spirit.[62] In its very motive (not to mention critical vocabulary and often style), it is our newest version of the movement that first taught criticism how to be embarrassed by history: formalism.

Early formalism, we know, was embarrassed enough of the historical subject or *Geist* (whether in the avatar of the author's biography or the story of his or her times) to transform poems into artifacts as seemingly emptied of historical subject as a Grecian urn.[63] Yet, still, a recalcitrant concern for general culture survived in the preoccupation of the Russian Formalists with the *skaz*, or folk narrative (not to mention the movement's late, desperate accommodation to state ideology), and of the New Critics with general society and religion—even if such concern was marked as outside the bounds of specifically literary study. Indeed, while Russian Formalism was eventually curtailed by ideology, the New Criticism was free to elaborate within its chosen bounds its apparently abstract, but originally political (anti-Northern), subjects and actions—ironic unity and resistance, respectively[64]—precisely because it took its politics underground, ceding explicit responsibility for historical context to a different method of the time—the history of ideas—with the appearance of neutral, scientistic historicism free of ideology.

Of course, the neutrality of the history of ideas was itself a style of ideology. With its unit-ideas analysis of historical spirit and quasi-causal laws for the transmission and combination of such ideas ("influence"), the history of ideas was a science of subject and action.[65] But in the era after the Scopes "monkey trial" of 1925, which so deeply affected John Crowe Ransom as well as others in the early Nashville milieu of the New Criticism, science was an issue as fully political as the divide between the New and Old Souths.[66] In essence, we may say, the physics-model atomism of Arthur O. Lovejoy and other historians of ideas helped write the political constitution of an individualist and pluralist Platonic republic of intellect eminently adapted to the spirit of the modern, progressive new. Scientific rationalism was a kind of enlightened liberalism. We may adduce, for example, Lovejoy's celebration of the diverse "life histories" of his intellectualized individual, the unit idea, or his implicit panegyric on pluralism in "On the Discrimination of Romanticisms."[67] Or, again, there is George Boas's credo of pluralistic tolerance:

> Hence it is clear that before one can write the history of an idea one must disentangle it from all the ambiguities that it has acquired in the course of time. One must expect to find it appearing in contexts that vary from age to age. One must not be puzzled to find it used as a basis for praise and blame. To do all this requires very wide, indeed indiscriminate, reading, tolerance of inconsistency in a given man or book, and a willingness to accept wobbling from fact to value and from value to fact. In doing this, one is always tempted to quarrel with the men whose ideas one is discussing. This temptation is hard to avoid but nevertheless argument is not historical

narration. . . . Let me say for myself that this book is written from the point of view of one who believes—or assumes, if you prefer—that ideas may be held regardless of their relevance to economics or politics or religion.[68]

It was under the constitution of such a universal pluralism disentangled from all the fractious "ambiguities . . . acquired in the course of time" and integrated within a single diverse republic of ideas that the New Criticism in the academy became ever freer of historically conditioned ideas—that is, disencumbered of the direct responsibility for thinking such ideas by the very atmosphere of intellect encouraging the divestiture of study areas into other specialties in the university.[69] Or, rather, we can say that the New Criticism seceded to pursue in an *interiorized* realm its characteristic early political agenda—a stance at once celebratory and denunciatory of the spirit of the new and similarly at once praising and condemnatory of the old. It became free, that is, to create its "Fugitive," agrarian, and, at last, academic state (a fifty-first state, we might say) of embarrassed, recidivist, and contestatory pluralism: first in the circle of intellects gathered around Sidney Mttron Hirsch in Nashville (as well as the subsequent versions of the circle),[70] later the quintessential New Critical seminar in the university, and, finally, the sublimated state of the poem. In this interior world, the spirit and actions of modern pluralism could be accepted in such a way as to retain all the old antebellum charm of internal dissension: ambiguity, paradox, irony, tension, resistance, and so forth. Dissension in the intellectual circle, classroom, or text was sanctioned because it was a "discussion" always implicitly presided over by a philosopher-king (whether Hirsch, the seminar teacher, or textual unity).

In short, it is certain (though often today forgotten) that early formalism cared deeply about historical spirit and action; but it did so in a complex antithetical manner that surrendered the direct regulation of historical understanding to the history of ideas with its adjuncts in other disciplines on the campus so that the literary critic (now aggressively differentiated from the literary scholar or historian) could regulate the same province of concerns in internalized, marginalized, and sublimated form—as art to be talked about, argued over, *battled* over in an enduring civil war of polemical dissension.[71] To refuse to paraphrase ideas (in Brooks's formulation) was to be ironic; and to be ironic—ambiguous, paradoxical, tense, resistant, and so forth—was to be recusant. Or, again, it was to be subversive in the manner of gadfly Socrates in relation to the dominant understanding of the plural republic and of the way such a republic influences ideas. It is thus perhaps appropriate that one of the most comprehensive testaments of the views of the New Critics—at once explicitly ideological and strangely innocent in feel—is the long Socratic dialogue that Warren constructed from talks between himself and Brooks on literature, culture, and religion titled "A Conversation with Cleanth Brooks." This, we feel, is the home form of the method.

Now we can understand the acute embarrassment that is the New Historicism, a resumption by other means of the New Criticism's own subsumption of the Civil War, its covert (ironic, ambiguous) marshaling of literature as a kind of irregular action against modern industrial society. The New Historicism would pour the spirit of the *skaz*—of the combined tragedy and joke work of the folk—directly into the literary text once more and so reunite the primary republic of society and the marginal republic of literature in a single poetics of culture where literature might conceivably make a rebel difference. But the entire interdisciplinary realm of the history of ideas that once *thought* the border between historical society and literature—that organized the mediating zone of ideas and influence according to a science, respectively, of subject and action—has fallen away. Though still often applied in practical form, the apparatus of unit ideas and influence has become unviable at the theoretical level under the assault of a host of competing notions: *mentalité, episteme, longue durée*, Althusserian "ideology," and (more generally) structural or quasi-structural rebuttals to positivist explanation.[72] Historical context and literary text thus now confront each other and interpenetrate directly—the desideratum of the New Historicism—but with the disturbing corollary that they do so in what seems an unthought, even unthinkable, manner.

More precisely: the diverse body of structural or quasi-structural thought I indicate above *could* substitute for the history of ideas in the modern understanding of the relation between context and text; but in most works that follow a New Historicist approach it is surprisingly underthought at the theoretical level and, it would appear, poorly grasped. At best, the New Historicism either is pseudo-Foucauldian in feel or, when it alludes to its methodological base at all, merely points without reflection or overall perspective to select extrapolations of the structural development of formalism—for example, to anthropology or Althusser. It then too often overleaps the whole domain of the structural intervention to borrow from a deconstruction that, decapitated from the structural body integral with its foundation, appears merely Orphic, merely a lyrical invocation of *mise-en-abyme* or some other neosymbolist whirl of "vertiginous" possibility.[73] In the end, the title conferred on this wonder cabinet of ill-sorted methods is then *interdisciplinary study*, the most seriously underthought critical, pedagogical, and institutional concept in the modern academy.[74]

Such, I suggest, is the deep origin of the "paradigm." A New Historicist paradigm holds up to view a historical context on one side, a literary text on the other, and, in between, a connection of pure nothing. Or, rather, what now substitutes for the history of ideas between context and text is the fantastic interdisciplinary nothingness of metaphor (more fully, the whole province of "resemblances" that Foucault charts in his "Prose of the World" applied *without* its historicized and theorized basis).[75] As I can attest from experience, "metaphor" is the most frequent and pointed charge against New Historicist approaches that pose a context, text, and, in between, a relation of pure suggestiveness. Physical concepts originating in positivist explanations of reality—power, for example—drift over the gap to figure the work of texts; and, inversely, the *exact* forms of a formalism the New Historicism claims to have left behind (ambiguity, paradox, contradiction, irony, and so forth) drift from their origination in literary study to figure the operations of history. (Greenblatt writes, e.g.: "Within this theatrical setting [of royal power], there is a notable insistence upon the paradoxes, ambiguities, and tensions of authority. . . . The form itself [of theatricality], as a primary expression of Renaissance power, helps to contain the radical doubts it continually provokes." Montrose observes: "In *A Midsummer Night's Dream*, as in *The Faerie Queene*, the ostensible project of elaborating Queen Elizabeth's personal mythology subverts itself—generates ironies, contradictions, resistances which undo the royal magic.")[76] What is merely "convenient" in a resemblance between context and text (in Foucault's sense of contiguity) soon seems an emulation; emulation is compounded in analogy; and, before we know it, analogy seems magical "sympathy": a quasi-magical *action* of resemblance between text and context (akin to the action that once seemed to make the warm and light fire strive sympathetically upward into the air).[77] Instead of the influence that had organized the cross-flow between context and text, in short, now there is only a metaphoric transference pointed out (again, we may see the back-and-forth shuttling of the scholar's pointer) through a deft manipulation that might well seem to older historians of ideas a wave of the wizard's wand.

The overall result is that the New Historicism is at once more frank than the New Criticism—because it makes no bones about wishing to establish a subversive intersubjectivity and interaction between texts and their contexts—*and* excruciatingly more embarrassed (etymologically, "barred, obstructed"). While driven to refer literature to history (most literally in its notes referring to historical documents), it is self-barred from any method able to ground, or even to *think*, reference more secure than trope. Indeed, the very concept of reference becomes taboo. Ignoring the fact that historical evidence by and large *is* referred to in its notes (which has the effect of lending documentary material an a priori status denied the literary works and anecdotes it reads and rereads), the New Historicism proceeds tropologically *as if* literary texts and historical contexts had equal priority. Literary "authors" thus claim an equivalence with political "authority," and "subjected" intellects with their monarchical "subject," through an argument of paradox, ambiguity, irony, or (to recur to dialectic) lordship/bondage not far removed at base from the etymological wordplay of deconstruction. As deconstructive catachresis is to reference, then, so subversion is to power—but *without* the considered defense of tropology allowing deconstruction to found alogical figuration in the very substrate of its version of historical context: the intertext. New Historicist contextuality is an intertextuality of culture without a functional philosophy or antiphilosophy. No Derrida of the field has made of the subversive relation between authors and authority what deconstruction makes of its subversion of reference: deferral or supplementarity. After all, it would be too embarrassing to admit that subversion of historical power (and of all the ontological and referential hierarchies still retained by Althusser in the gestural phrase "in the last instance") is just another *différance*.[78] Such would be to confess the formalism of the New Historicism.

Put reductively: when I compare Wordsworth's picturesque eye to Bentham's panoptic inspector or the New Critics to the Civil War, I am embarrassed. All New Historicists embarrass themselves in this manner; all create a metaphysical conceit of text-*like*-context as cryptoformalist as a Donne poem interpreted by the New Criticism. But I know how to change my embarrassment into a special bravura: a thrown-glove *why not?* unsecured upon any considered defense of figure, trope, or conceit (i.e., "language") comparable to that of deconstruction and, we might remember, of the New Criticism itself with its theorems of "icon" and "image."

Finally, however, I do not mean to be reductive. If the New Historicism continues in a higher register the embarrassment that formalism first experienced in the face of history, we must also grant it its own place and occasion. The New Historicism is a uniquely postmodern personality of intellect transuming all the earlier personae by which formalism had outbraved the embarrassment of history (the aggressive voice of the polemical critic in the New Criticism, e.g., or the Mosaic persona of the critic-in-the-wilderness or the critic-as-artist in deconstruction). Specifically: if the method braves out its embarrassment with its characteristic *why not?* such bravura is at last also self-effacing—but only in a manner carrying effrontery to a second degree. The New Historicism *declares* its self-effacement in the face of history; it authoritatively arrogates to itself the lack of authority that is the perceived role of the intellectual in latter-day society. The New Historicism, I will thus at last define, is the supremely *self-conscious* embarrassment of the postmodern intellect as expressed in the medium of historical consciousness. It is the sense of history become one with what we might call the interpreter's *intentionality of embarrassment.*

By *intentionality*, I mean that there is understood to be no influence (no subject acting causally) in the void between literary text and historical context because there is finally only the marginalized and consciously figural intention underlying all New Historicist conceits of culture: the interpreter's own self-conflicted subject or intellect in its acknowledged failure of influence. Or, to psychologize slightly, what emerges from the endlessly impeded effort of the New Historicism to know the *Geist* of past culture without the history-of-ideas apparatus once mediating such knowledge is the chagrin of the postmodern interpreter in his or her too-naked, futile *desire* for the old spirit. "Like all authors, critics, and other intellects," we might hear the interpreter saying, "I wish to be engaged with general culture and history. But I also want to study literature. Therefore, I am without influence." Nostalgia for history thus embarrasses literary appreciation; literary appreciation embarrasses historicism; and at the intersection of this chiastic flux of chagrin forms the only subject and action still possible: the critic (and the historical author serving as the critic's surrogate) thinking about subversion.

This is what I mean at last by defining the New Historicism as a "reflection" on romanticism (keeping in mind that I use romanticism synecdochically as the key intervention from the early nineteenth century on). To return to my earlier suggestion that the New Historicist *we* finally sees only itself in *them*: the New Historicism is, in effect, a profoundly narcissistic method. It romanticizes the Renaissance or early modern, to take the most prominent example, but wakes up to the realization that what it sees in the other of the past through lenses of subjectivity, dialecticism, or the very notion of literature inherited from the nineteenth century and after is the image of its own *post*modern anxiety of intellect. Disbelieving in any regulated method of reaching the historical other from the domain of the text, it at last studies itself in the anxious pose of reaching for the other. *Power* is the interpreter's figure for powerlessness.

The evidence, I believe, is overwhelming. Most signally, there is the consistently heightened self-reflexivity of the New Historicism. Whether in its aspect as British cultural materialism, which aggressively deploys self-consciousness as a political stance in the present, or as the American *Representations* school, whose self-consciousness has no ready outlet, reflexiveness is more than a matter of chiastic, oxymoronic, or otherwise self-conflicted style. We could look at any number of American studies, for example, to notice that, if the method tends to open on a paradigm of historical otherness, it also frequently closes on an acutely self-aware passage—at times, indeed, no less than a meditation on the postmodern condition. Thus, there is the striking epilogue to Greenblatt's *Renaissance Self-Fashioning*, the last paragraphs of Montrose's "The Elizabethan Subject and the Spenserian Text" (together with that of its brief precursor, "Renaissance Literary Studies and the Subject of History"), or the last paragraph of Tennenhouse's "Strategies of State and Political Plays." More broadly, New Historicist studies, however they begin or end, can at any moment open out into a meditation on postmodernity. The two components of this overall meditation can be articulated as follows (where I ventriloquize a composite voice of the New Historicist interpreter modeled primarily on the work of Greenblatt and Montrose):

1. *I am embarrassed of my marginality as interpreter—specifically, of the whole enterprise of literary history, the academy, and the intellect in which I am implicated.* The extent to which the origin of such chagrin may be traced to a particular period and locale of failed politics (e.g., the carnival/tragedy of the academy in the aftermath of May 1968 or 1970) is contested.[79] But, certainly, the recognition in the New Historicism that postmodern intellect is a failed political power cannot be mistaken. In a moment of piercing self-reflexiveness, Montrose writes:

> Many of those who profess "the Humanities" see themselves and their calling as threatened by marginalization within a system of higher education increasingly geared to the provision of highly specialized technological and preprofessional training. In its anti-reflectionism, its shift of emphasis from the formal analysis of verbal *artifacts* to the ideological analysis of discursive *practices*, . . . the emergent historical orientation in literary studies is pervasively concerned with writing as a mode of *action*. I do not believe that it compromises the intellectual seriousness of this concern to see it as impelled by a questioning of our very capacity for action—by a nagging sense of professional, institutional, and political impotence.[80]

Or, again, in the original lead-in to this passage in its earlier published form: "One way to view the recent revival of interest in questions of history in literary studies may be as a compensation for that acceleration in the forgetting of history which seems to characterize an increasingly technocratic and future-oriented academy and society. To the painfully dismissive expression, 'Oh, that's academic,' we must add another, more pernicious: 'Oh, that's history.'"[81] A remembrance of Sidney would not be out of place. "Oh, that's poetic," we might hear Sidney say in mimicry of the *mysomousoi* or "poet-haters" featured in his strong compensation: the *Apology for Poetry*.[82] "Oh, that's academic history," the New Historicism mouths instead in a genuflection before general culture before launching on its own compensation: a defense of literature, historiography, the academy, and the intellect that, while it respects general culture, would make a space of subversion/containment in it for the monastic "impotence" of scholarship to continue.

2. I would compensate for my embarrassment at the postmodern intellect by making a Renaissance. Here, the root of *fact* is useful. The cultural artifact within which the New Historicism places the text in proximity to factual context is very definitely a made or done thing. Made-up or done-up in New Historicist fashion as the age of subversion, oppositionality, contestation, or transgression, the "Renaissance" is the romanticization of the postmodern scholar. Relevant are the explanations that have been offered for the precedence of the Renaissance or early modern field in New Historicist study. After the passage on academic impotence quoted above, for example, Montrose concludes "The Elizabethan Subject and the Spenserian Text":

> That Renaissance literary studies should now be alive to such concerns is not to be explained in terms of any single cause. But one of the determinations here may be that during the sixteenth and seventeenth centuries, the separation of "Literature" and "Art" from explicitly didactic and political discourses or from such disciplines as history or moral and natural philosophy was as yet incipient. Both the pervasiveness of rhetorical models in Renaissance poetics and the predominance of patronage as a mode of literary production may have worked to foreground rather than to efface the status of texts as social and not merely literary productions. Such texts may more actively invite sociohistorical analysis than do those later works of our literary canon that have been produced within an ideology of aesthetic disinterestedness. Because we now seem to be moving beyond this modern, essentialist orientation to "Literature," we can begin to grasp it as an historical formation that was only beginning to emerge at the end of the sixteenth century. Interpreters of Tudor-Stuart literature thus find themselves now particularly well placed to rearticulate literature as a social practice—and, by so doing, to rearticulate criticism as a social practice. In reflecting upon my own practice in the foregoing essay, I am aware of a strong stake, not in any illusion of individual autonomy but in the possibilities for limited and localized agency within the regime of power and knowledge that at once sustains and constrains us.[83]

We are now most interested in the Renaissance, Montrose says, because the discourse of that epoch shares our standards of interestedness—of the implication of literature in politics—and so is most "inviting" to current sensibility. Yet, as sounded most loudly in the first-person self-reflexiveness of the last sentence here ("In reflecting upon my own practice"), the hospitality of the Renaissance is, perhaps, a little too generous, too unresisting before the intrusion of the postmodern. By the time of Montrose's last sentence, the Renaissance is all about the anxiety of the postmodern intellect in its academic confines. Or, to look up the page to the penultimate sentence, "interpreters of Tudor-Stuart literature" are indeed "particularly well placed to rearticulate literature as a social practice—and, by so doing, to rearticulate criticism as a social practice." They are well placed because the Renaissance they articulate is really a simulation, a dream academy. Like the Spenserian text and other Tudor-Stuart tomes literally locked away in the academy and its adjuncts (e.g., the Newberry, Huntington, and Beinecke libraries; the Elizabethan Club at Yale), the New Historicist Renaissance is coincident with the corridors and vaults of the postmodern intellect. It is the quiet room, muffled by that great silencer of politics, history, where the postmodern intellect fantasizes safely about subversion and transgression against "the regime of power and knowledge that at once sustains and constrains us."

To support this interpretation of the self-reflexiveness of the New Historicism, I turn to its even more suggestive formulation in Greenblatt's work. To begin with, we can observe that the membrane of history between the Renaissance and postmodernity in Greenblatt's studies sometimes stretches so thin that there is virtually no separation at all. Speaking of More, for example, Greenblatt speculates: "There are periods in which the relation between intellectuals and power is redefined, in which the old forms have decayed and new forms have yet to be developed."[84] What we read in the plural *periods* here is that the Renaissance is the primal scene of any number of other intellectual dis- or reempowerings extending up through the revolutions, cultural or otherwise, of the twentieth century. It is a repression or sublimation of our own scenes of intellectual trauma. Addressing directly the modern perception of the past in "Invisible Bullets," Greenblatt argues in a provocative passage that the subversion recent interpreters see in the past is a function of their own condition:

> Indeed we may feel at this point that subversion scarcely exists and may legitimately ask ourselves how our perception of the subversive and orthodox is generated. The answer, I think, is that the term *subversive* for us designates those elements in Renaissance culture that contemporary

audiences tried to contain or, when containment seemed impossible, to destroy and that now conform to our own sense of truth and reality. That is, we find "subversive" in the past precisely those things that are *not* subversive to ourselves, that pose no threat to the order by which we live and allocate resources: in Harriot's *Brief and True Report*, the function of illusion in the establishment of religion, the displacement of a providential conception of disease by one focused on "invisible bullets," the exposure of the psychological and material interests served by a certain conception of divine power. Conversely, we identify as principles of order and authority in Renaissance texts what we would, if we took them seriously, find subversive for ourselves: religious and political absolutism, aristocracy of birth, demonology, humoral psychology, and the like. That we do not find such notions subversive, that we complacently identify them as principles of aesthetic or political order, replicates the process of containment that licensed the elements we call subversive in Renaissance texts: that is, our own values are sufficiently strong for us to contain alien forces almost effortlessly.[85]

That which the postmodern interpreter champions as subversive in the past is an enlightened attitude that recognizes "illusion in the establishment of religion" and so forth and, thus, sympathizes with *ourselves*—the only substantive meaning of which in Greenblatt's usage is the postmodern, academic community. (After all, whole segments of current society, no matter their actual secularism, *would* be threatened by deliberate "exposure of the psychological and material interests served by a certain conception of divine power.") Conversely, that which the postmodern interpreter in the academy sees as "order and authority" in the past ("religious and political absolutism" etc.) sympathizes with such current trends as Montrose's "preprofessionalism" to endanger the disciplines of intellect. Or, rather, past absolutism *would* be dangerous to intellect if the latter did not have a mechanism by which to avoid taking "seriously" any connection between past and present absolutisms. Suspended belief is provided by intellectual "values . . . sufficiently strong for us to contain alien forces almost effortlessly"—that is, to make past dominance appear precisely *alien* and, thus, removed from present possibility.

The overall relation between present and past in the New Historicism can thus be schematized as follows. The postmodern intellect identifies its own desire to subvert dominance with the subversiveness of an earlier era (where identification is experienced as fascination with, and comfortable acceptance of, past resistance). Yet what the strange mirror between postmodernity and the Renaissance obscures is the total process of contestation—a differential process in which subversive values play only one part.

The subversion of the present, after all, can truly be mapped over that of the past only if the *relation* between subversive and dominant elements in the present is like that of the past. Yet the too-easy identification of the present will-to-subversion with that of the Renaissance blocks any hard look at the relation constitutive of contestation because it merely assumes a correlation between Renaissance and postmodern dominants each of which is left in assumption. Essays or books on subversion thus often spotlight the subversive and leave in unexamined cliché or convention the detail of dominant norms.[86] (Some open questions for research, e.g.: was the "providential conception of disease" that checked belief in viral "invisible bullets" wholly effective in everyday folk life in England, let alone the New World? or, again, how effective or exclusive in practice is the current preprofessionalism that aims students straight as bullets toward medical or other professional schools?)

The consequence of such selective identification with the past is that, in the mirror of desire named the *Renaissance*, the interpreter can fantasize about subverting dominance while dreaming away the total commitments of contestation. While interpreters assume their values to be minority opinions transgressive of society, they also deflect any serious consideration *of* that society or of the political and institutional costs exacted of those committed to the practical application of subversion. Such costs are merely presumed to be *like* those of past contestation between subversion and dominance, and the effect of such assumption is, paradoxically, to make the costs of subversion more comfortable in imagination (since hanging, drawing, and quartering, e.g., is now less palpable a punishment than loss of tenure). In short, the real resistance of the New Historicist interpreter is to any conscious appraisal of what it means to resist powers inimical to intellect. No weighing of risk or gain, no cost-benefit analysis (to speak in bureaucratese) disturbs the academese of historicist study. And the dream work that makes such repression possible is a scholarly page overwrought with subversions of passé kings, queens, creeds, or—at best—Tillyards.

Howard observes about the New Historicism: "At *this* historical moment, an analysis of Renaissance culture can be made to speak to the concerns of late twentieth-century culture." And later: "In short, I would argue that the Renaissance, seen as the last refuge of preindustrial man, is of such interest to scholars of the postindustrial era because these scholars construe the period in terms reflecting their own sense of the exhilaration and fearfulness of living inside a gap in history, when the paradigms that structured the past seem facile and new paradigms uncertain."[87] The truly operative word here, I suggest, is *refuge*, which would have no place

in historicism if *post*modern man did not reshape the past with teleological foreknowledge of postindustrial preprofessionalism so as to open for
himself a refuge of pure mind named the *Renaissance,* an early modern
arche-academy hidden from the exigencies of the present within history
itself.

"I think, therefore I am powerless," is the credo of the postmodern
Cartesian, with the corollary: "I am powerless, therefore I would make a
Renaissance."

The New Historicism, I conclude, is our latest post–May 1970, post–
May 1968, post-1917, . . . , post-1789 (and so forth) imagination of an active role for intellect in the renascence of society—an imagination that
elides the fact that truly subversive renascences on the scale of revolution
have had an uncanny habit of immediately disempowering, containing,
or recuperating subversive practitioners of intellect. To apply my period
synecdoche for this process of imagination once more: it is our latest romanticization of the Renaissance, our latest use of the assumptions that
achieved their most intense form in the epoch of the original historicism
to restore a past that images (and we at last know it) our best selves. I
do not mean to exempt romantic studies from this thesis, of course. But,
besides being a fainter echo of Renaissance New Historicism, romantic
studies has had its great chastener in Jerome McGann, whose *The Romantic
Ideology* sets out precisely to embarrass romanticizers of romanticism—
critics, in other words, who open a channel of indiscriminate cross-flow
between past and present concerns by using romantic assumptions to read
romanticism. The New Historicism is our latest romantic ideology unable
to differentiate meaningfully between then and now, unable—at least at
its present level of thought—to do more than be driven toward a refuge
of intellect lost in history.

Toward a fuller consideration of the New Historicism—which I criticize but to which I continue to be committed—I set forth as my *peroratio*
an agenda of three future areas of improvement. The main thrust of this
agenda is that the narcissism of the New Historicism is not at last weakness
so much as the possibility of a strengthened method to come. I suggest:

1. A New Historicist study of New Historicism. Recognizing the necessary
intervention of the postmodern interpreter in the past, Howard concludes
her evaluation of the New Historicism in Renaissance studies:

> Finally, it seems to me that the historically-minded critic must increasingly
> be willing to acknowledge the non-objectivity of his or her own stance and
> the inevitably political nature of interpretive and even descriptive acts. . . .
> I am not suggesting that it is desirable to look at the past with the willful

intention of seeing one's own prejudices and concerns. Nonetheless, since objectivity is not in any pure form a possibility, let us acknowledge that fact and acknowledge as well that any move into history is an *intervention*, an attempt to reach from the present moment into the past to rescue both from meaningless banality.[88]

I would go further. I *do* suggest that "it is desirable to look at the past with the willful intention of seeing one's own prejudices and concerns" as a first step to filling in what "acknowledgment" of nonobjectivity must become to be a serviceable critical tool. A concept with eminently academic overtones, acknowledgment of the present's intervention in the past should blossom into disciplined study. We *should* see our own prejudices and concerns in such constructs as the Renaissance, in other words, and that which will redeem such vision from mere partiality is research into the contexts and texts of the prejudices intervening between past and present.

A fully capable New Historicism should be able to overcome the embarrassment of its own implication in history to take a hard look first at the assumptions it carries over from the nineteenth century. As I have already intimated, truly to understand the method (and its close analogue in current historiography proper, the New Cultural History) requires that we place it in a long view reaching back to the original historicism.[89] In this sense, the term *New Historicism* is wholly deceptive. Whether it was invented by Greenblatt or should be traced back to Wesley Morris's 1972 *Toward a New Historicism* is immaterial: wherever we look in the New Historicism we see resemblances to the original historicism so striking and deep—even down to the epithet *new*—that it might provoke speculation that the category of the new is the oldest instinct of historiography.[90] Thus it is, for example, that the very excitement over a "new history" first peaked in France in the early nineteenth century; that it followed a period of revolutionary fervor not unlike our own 1960s; that it expressed itself in a few key journals analogous to our own *Representations*; that it became interdisciplinary in the combined efforts of its historical, literary, legal, economic, and philological researchers; and that it problematized the notions of subject (individual, nation, or spirit) and action (event).[91] And thus it is as well that the original historicism turned from the *wie es eigentlich gewesen* of Ranke to the skeptical relativism of Ernst Troeltsch during the "crisis of historicism" of the early twentieth century and so predicted the embarrassment at the heart of New Historicist concern. If each culture of the past "as it really was" consisted of a self-contained complex with its own unique spirit, how could it ever be known since the modern historian lives in his or her own cultural complex? Thus was the basic hermeneutical question activated leading to the so-called crisis in historicism and the tentative solutions offered in the early and mid-twentieth century: R. G. Collingwood's *The Idea of History* (1946), for example, which postulated that the modern historian can know history only by reenacting it in consciousness through an act of "historical imagination."[92]

But, by itself, research into the nineteenth-century precedent of the New Historicism is too restrictive. We need also to study other culturally rooted senses of history both prior and posterior to *Historismus*. In the posterior realm especially, the documentation is all around us. To take one example, why are we too embarrassed to study the relation, whether of subversion or containment, between New Historicist discourse and the language of the protest movements of the 1960s? Or between the discourse of modern protest and that of current academic interdisciplinarity with its recuperated instinct of transgression (across boundaries, periods, canons, paradigms, etc.)? Or, perhaps most constructively, how can we turn the sources of postmodern intellectual embarrassment into resources of historical understanding? How, that is, build the awareness of postmodernity into our criticism as *method*.

2. *A full-scale theory of the New Historicism.* Only on the basis of an adequate history of the New Historicism, I suggest, can an adequate theory of the method be articulated. This is because only an awareness of shared cultural contexts will provide the missing medium in which to see the commonality of the New Historicism with those criticisms that it has so far sought to distinguish itself from and that actually furnish the genealogy of what I have called its *contingent method*. As I have throughout implied, it is simply not the case that the New Historicism is essentially different from formalism. It is more true to say that it is an ultimate formalism so powerful that it colonizes the very world as its text. The New Historicism opens the door between text and context in a spirit of seeming equivalence such that the metaphoricity I earlier signaled ultimately confuses tenor and vehicle: the context *is* the text, and vice versa (e.g., Montrose: "The new orientation to history . . . may be succinctly characterized, on the one hand, by its acknowledgement of the *historicity of texts* . . . [and] on the other hand . . . by its acknowledgement of the *textuality of history*").[93] But from the perspective of literary studies, we recognize, the result is an imperialism of textual and specifically formal analysis: a sudden expansion of methods of thought previously segregated to paradoxical, ambiguous, or ironic literature. To *read* the world, after all, is not an ideologically neutral act. It is to appropriate the world from the masses of the less articulate and literate. It is a statement of privilege.[94]

A theory of the New Historicism, then, should not eschew its formalist origins but embrace those origins together with the historical conditions that prompted them. It should seek to explain both contextually and textually its borrowings from formalisms early and late, New Critical or deconstructive. Particularly illuminating in regard to contingency, for example, is the resemblance between the interpretation of history as understood by Greenblatt and Montrose and the hermeneutics of allegory or figure as understood by de Man.[95] To argue as Montrose does repeatedly that texts are historical and history textual, I suggest, is to draw yet another version of the hermeneutical circle. But to argue also that literary historians are implicated in, yet historically distanced from, their object of study is to emphasize a particular vision of that circle. As in the case of de Man, such vision places textual interpretation or reading always at a temporal remove from the historical inscription it desires to approach—a temporal remove identical with figural remove. Put simply, and in a way that explains why it is sometimes so guiltily easy for sophisticated readers of literature to change into readers of history: the New Historicism is an allegory for history. It erects an intricately wrought veil of allegory that figures not so much any holy of holies behind the veil (history) as the shadow cast by the interpreter in his or her complex posture of adoration/skepticism before the temple of "as it really was." The New Historicism, in other words, has only a contingent knowledge of history. The inner form of New Historicist allegory—its theory—is contingency. Or, to cite the title of de Man's essay on allegory, its inner form is "the rhetoric of temporality."

3. *A renewed rhetoric.* Here I place in play the incipient argument I have sustained in invocations of *exordium, digressio, narratio,* and *peroratio.*[96] The New Historicism, I earlier suggested, is a method of metaphor void of any rigorously considered philosophy of cultural figure, trope, conceit, or "language" of its own. While joining text and context figuratively to create its Geertzian symbolic of culture, it lacks the means to *think* the interdisciplinary medium of contingent conjunction except by rote allusion to a miscellany of "discursive systems" and other borrowed methodology. Of course, "philosophy" or "thought" may be too Aristotelian a goal. In its implicit rewriting of the *Poetics,* the New Historicism should ask, not which is the more philosophical, poetry or history, but instead how both poetry and philosophy engage history. The New Historicism thus requires a method of contextualization founded on a historically realized philosophy of discourse—that is, some notion of rhetoric (or, more broadly, of language) that can exceed the de Manian notion by casting discourse as historically active event. Indeed, the ultimate rationale for the proliferat-

ing paradigms of the New Historicism that I began by inventorying may well be that they imagine a way to return historicism not just from postmodern to romantic or Renaissance cultural poetics but, at last, to classical rhetoric. Masques, guillotine stages, architecture, miniature cabinets, prisons, picturesque tours, carnivals, fêtes, and so on: these are staging grounds of symbols in action, not just of symbols in representation. The promise of the New Historicism, I submit (and argue more fully in chapter 2 below), is thus to develop the philosophy of allegory into a true—which is to say *not* philosophically true but instead sophistically contingent— speaking in the agora: a rhetorical notion of literature as text-cum-action performed by historical subjects on other subjects. That which needs to be unthought, in other words, is the idea of the "text" as such.

The beginnings of such a development are clear, for example, in Orgel's insistence that theater in the Renaissance was primarily a rhetorical discourse or again, more broadly, in a recent wave of books experimenting in what John Frow has called a "general rhetoric" at once social and literary.[97] New Historicism can proceed to a further stage of inquiry if a colloquy can be created between its Renaissance and its romantic participants, as well as between its practitioners and its theorists, and thus a sufficient parallax established to calibrate our most recent rediscovery of that old concept of literature to one side of Aristotelian mimesis: rhetorical action.

In short (reading through my proposed program of study in reverse): no understanding of text as action is possible without a theory; and no theory of the New Historicism is possible without a fully historical, if also entirely contingent (both allegorical and rhetorical), sense of itself as method. Renaissance New Historicism in itself would be a dead end. So too would a New Historicism centered on any succeeding period be truncated. What is needed is a New Historicism that, like the process of history, finds itself crossing the periods so that it sees the Renaissance opening out in calibrated stops into the Enlightenment, romanticism, symbolism, modernism, postmodernism, or whatever other stops of the camera lens we denominate in our effort to see at once the object of our study and the shadow of the photographer.

/ / / / / / / / / / /

Trying Cultural Criticism
Wordsworth and Subversion

Subvert, oppose, contest, transgress; but also *contain, assimilate,* and—to draw on the language of post–May 1968 Paris—*recuperate*. These are the words that in the New Historicism and affiliated cultural criticisms now serve much the same function as did in the New Criticism *ambiguity, tension, paradox,* and *irony*, on the one hand, and *unity, harmony,* and *pattern,* on the other. Literature or intellect, we increasingly say, is subversive of dominant culture; yet dominance, we also recognize, is uncannily subversive of subversion. Releasing disruptive tensions in its marginal spaces—a page in a book, a carnival in the streets, or, in Steven Mullaney's paradigm, the "place of the stage" in the Liberties zone of old London—dominance at last contains the radical tension, gives it a place among the commonplaces.[1] In Pierre Gaudibert's view of the post–May 1968 milieu: "La récupération, c'est ce mouvement social pour lequel une agressivité qui se veut subversive se trouve apprivoisée, édulcorée, émasculée, assimilée, digérée par l'idéologie et la culture dominantes. L'oeuvre d'art voit ses griffes émoussées, ses dents élimées: elle devient spectacle, marchandise, décor, gadget culturel, icône inoffensive, foyer éteint; elle cesse d'être active, de dégager sa charge de déflagration."[2]

Or, in any case, such is the analytic of subversion/containment that "we" recognize (to repeat my pronoun above)—where *we* are the intellectual generation(s) whose primal scene is the intersection between the breakout on the streets in the late 1960s and early 1970s and the simultaneous breakout "beyond formalism" in literary criticism.[3] In that turbulent intersection, we remember, all the old verbal icons of the New Criticism became a swirl of slogans, protest signs, and poststructuralist anti-icons (deconstruction's hymen, pharmakon, gram, *mise-en-abyme*, etc.). But, from the 1980s on, the slogans themselves came to seem icons as *inoffensive* as some deconstructive paradigm drawn from the commercial image on a cocoa box.[4] Subvert, oppose, contest, transgress—the purposely slogan-like chant on which I began—is a protest banner hung within cultural criticism as if in some museum of popular culture. It is contained, even as it appreciates in critical value.

What I offer are two concurrent investigations. The first is a reexplanation, by means of the subversion/containment analytic, of Wordsworth's turn from radicalism in the aftermath of the Revolution of 1789. The second is an examination of the revolution manqué expressed in the subversion/containment analytic itself, specifically as spoken by cultural criticism in its American New Historicist or *Representations* inflection.[5] The collation of these inquiries will be a way to try out—and, as I will imagine it, to bring to trial—the basic assumptions of cultural criticism as a method of reading. What kind of contextual and textual event does the method explain that could not be explained before? And what drops out of the picture to make the explanation possible? A working hypothesis: there is something suspiciously *easy* about the equipollent symmetry of subversion and containment that suggests that the stasis of their contest—of subversive intellects always already contained and of dominant cultures always already big with subversion—is a much-reduced, tamed antithesis. In an age when absolute knowledge and/or dialectical materialism has become the "interpretation of cultures" with its exclusive attention to symbol, display, and representation, the dynamics of lordship/bondage is itself bound.[6] It is "décor, gadget culturel" contained within a room of larger interpretive possibilities.

The thesis I will shape from this hypothesis: if there is a cultural fallacy, pace the New Critical biographical fallacy, it lies in the constrictive interpretation of social representations empowered by the notion of the subject. The hermeneutics of representation applauds the primarily theatrical power plays of subversion (a subject's *display* of resistance to subjection) while merely hanging a backdrop to indicate the detail of the zone beyond the theater.[7] That zone is containment, the place *before* the stage where actions are not just dramatic or representational but also physical, logistic, rhetorical, and political—that is, involved in a hermeneutics of movement and suasion not wholly coincident with the hermeneutics of representation. Subversion/containment can be unbound from its present stasis only when we see that subversion need not be just a stage act. It is an activity bound up with and within equally active *processes* of containment that do not so much recuperate subversion as enable the possibility of any action, subversive or otherwise.

Silent Subversion: An Indictment

I begin with a series of evidences, as in a trial, bearing on the start of what may be called Wordsworth's *long decade of subversion*, 1793–1804. In the *Biographia Literaria*, Coleridge remarks about an incident in the Alfoxden area during the 1797 invasion scares: "One of these sycophantic law mongrels, discoursing on the *politics* of the neighbourhood, uttered the following *deep* remark: 'As to *Coleridge*, there is not so much harm in him, for he is a whirl brain that talks whatever comes uppermost; but that [Wordsworth]! he is the *dark* traitor. *You never hear* HIM *say a syllable on the subject.*'"[8] Indeed, to read the decade I refer to requires opening not with the quietist Wordsworth of *The Ruined Cottage* or *Lyrical Ballads* but with a strangely silent, if also politically radical, persona that would seem as out-of-the-way as it is unexpected if the poetry and life records for the period after the return from France in late 1792 were not so full on this subject. The persona is the "Welsh" or, more broadly, "Celtic" Wordsworth, and its inclusion among our accepted types alters the sequence of the poet's familiar personalities such that we will need to see at the end of the long decade, not just the champion of imagination in the 1805 *Prelude*, but also another champion still unassimilated in mainstream romantic studies: the jingoistic, bloody-minded, and supremely *British* patriot.

Exhibit A is from the 1805 *Prelude*. Reading from the account of war between Britain and France in book 10:

> And now the strength of Britain was put forth
> In league with the confederated host;
> Not in my single self alone I found,

But in the minds of all ingenuous youth,
Change and subversion from this hour. No shock
Given to my moral nature had I known
Down to that very moment—neither lapse
Nor turn of sentiment—that might be named
A revolution, save at this one time. . . .
                                        I rejoiced,
Yes, afterwards, truth painful to record,
Exulted in the triumph of my soul
When Englishmen by thousands were o'erthrown,
Left without glory on the field, or driven,
Brave hearts, to shameful flight. It was a grief—
Grief call it not, 'twas anything but that—
A conflict of sensations without name,
Of which he only who may love the sight
Of a village steeple as I do can judge,
When in the congregation, bending all
To their great Father, prayers were offered up,
Or praises for our country's victories,
And, 'mid the simple worshippers perchance
I only, like an uninvited guest
Whom no one owned, sate silent—shall I add,
Fed on the day of vengeance yet to come![9]

The time of prayer here is late summer 1793, possibly mid-September if
the overthrow of Englishmen is the defeat at Hondeschoote. The place, as
Mary Moorman suggests, is North Wales, where Wordsworth was visiting
his recently ordained college friend Robert Jones, and where patriotic sermons were symptomatic of the gathering Welsh counterrevolution led by
Anglican churchmen.[10] Donald Hayden's reenactment of the poet's Welsh
trip indicates how oppressive the church would have been even if Wordsworth had not been forced to sit through a patriotic sermon. Jones's village (about five miles from Denbigh) consisted of only a few farmhouses
and, up the hill, the church together with the Jones house: Plas-yn-Llan,
literally "hall-at-the-church."[11]

Exhibit B is from *Salisbury Plain*, which Wordsworth wrote precisely on
his 1793 trip to visit Jones (he left London to sojourn on the Isle of Wight,
walked up through Salisbury Plain, and entered Wales by way of the Wye
Valley). Again, we witness an imagination of war fixated on overthrown
soldiers; again, a "hush" of silence amid religious rites (this time Druidic);

and, again, fresh stirrings of violence akin to the "day of vengeance" invoked at the end of the *Prelude* passage. Reading from the Stonehenge hallucination in the middle of the poem:

And oft a night-fire mounting to the clouds
Reveals the desert and with dismal red
Clothes the black bodies of encircling crowds.
It is the sacrificial altar fed
With living men. How deep it groans—the dead
Thrilled in their yawning tombs their helms uprear;
The sword that slept beneath the warriour's head
Thunders in fiery air: red arms appear
Uplifted thro' the gloom and shake the rattling spear.

Not thus where clear moons spread their pleasing light.
—Long bearded forms with wands uplifted shew
To vast assemblies, while each breath of night
Is hushed, the living fires that bright and slow
Rounding th'aetherial field in order go.

And from the reprise of the theme in the poem's closing movement:

Though from huge wickers paled with circling fire
No longer horrid shrieks and dying cries
To ears of Daemon-Gods in peals aspire,
To Daemon-Gods a human sacrifice;
Though Treachery her sword no longer dyes
In the cold blood of Truce, still, reason's ray,
What does it more than while the tempests rise,
With starless glooms and sounds of loud dismay,
Reveal with still-born glimpse the terrors of our way?[12]

Exhibit C, finally, speaks forte to the whispered silences of violence in 1793 but adds a note of racial humor.[13] The exhibit is Wordsworth's 1829 letter relating his visit to Montgomeryshire, Wales (whether on his 1793 or his 1791 Welsh trip is unclear).[14] After interpolating associatively a long mention of his call on Thomas Pennant (one of the great forces behind the contemporary Welsh cultural revival or renascence), the poet concentrates on a visit with the squire Thomas Thomas that proved memorable because it exposed him to the closest recorded threat of personal violence in his life.[15] The vehemence of the threat, we may note, was powered by a long history of Welsh resentment against Englishmen and the English language then coming to a head (again) in the 1790s. Even the form of the threat—the alcoholic boast/curse—was established in local Anglophobic tradition.[16] I abbreviate the mention of Pennant for clarity, though in the logic of the letter his "library" of Welsh cultural revivalism is strangely coincident with the fine points of philology discussed at Thomas's table:

> Five and thirty days ago I passed a few days in one of [Montgomeryshire's] most retired vallies at the house of a Mr Thomas some time since dead. His ordinary residence was upon an estate of his in Flintshire close to Mr Pennant's of Downing with whom, I mean [Pennant], . . . I passed several agreeable hours in his library. . . . All this has led me from his neighbour Mr Thomas' seat in Montgom: where an event took place so characteristic of the Cambro Britons that I will venture upon a recital of it. . . . One day we sat down une partie quarrée at the Squire's Table, himself at the head; the Parson of the Parish, a bulky broad-faced man between 50 and 60 at the foot and Jones and I opposite each other. I must observe that "the Man of God" had not unprofessionally been employed most part of the morning in bottling the Squire's "Cwrrw" anglisé strong Ale, this had redden'd his visage (we will suppose by the fumes) but I sat at table not apprehending mischief. The conversation proceeded with the cheerfulness good appetite, and good cheer, naturally inspire—the Topic—the powers of the Welsh Language. "They are marvellous," said the revd Taffy. "Your English is not to be compared especially in conciseness, we can often express in one word what you can scarcely do in a long sentence." "That," said I, "is indeed wonderful be so kind as to favor me with an instance?" "That I will" he answered. "You know perhaps the word Tad?" "Yes." "What does it mean?" "Father" I replied. "Well," stammer'd the Priest in triumph, "Tad and Father there you have it"—on hearing this odd illustration of his confused notions I could not help smiling on my friend opposite; whereupon, the incensed Welshman rose from his chair and brandished over me a huge sharp pointed carving knife. I held up my arm in a defensive attitude; judge of the consternation of the Squire, the dismay of my friend, and my own astonishment not unmixed with fear whilst he stood threat[e]ning me in this manner and heaping on my poor English head every reproachful epithet which his scanty knowledge of our language could supply to lungs almost stifled with rage. "You vile Saxon!" I recollect was one of his terms, "To come here and insult me an ancient Briton on my own territory!"[17]

And an extra note, in strangely precise counterpoint. "Treachery" once dyed her sword at Stonehenge "in the cold blood of Truce," we remember Wordsworth saying in *Salisbury Plain*. This is an unmistakable allusion to the "treason of the long knives"—a legend that exerted so strong an influence on the Welsh cause that it later inspired the naming of a nineteenth-century Welsh agitation the *treason of the Blue Books*.[18] The original legend about the massacre of Celts by Hengist (leading to the Saxon domination of Britain) appeared in Geoffrey of Monmouth's *Historia Regum Britanniae* (in a translation taken from the excerpt that appeared in the discussion of "Druid" monuments near Penrith in Hutchinson's *History of the County of Cumberland* [1793–96]):

> Hengist (a subtle and malicious man) . . . under colour of peace, devised the subversion of all the nobility of Britain, and chose out, to come to this assembly, his faithfullest and hardiest men, commanding every one of them to hide, under his garment, a long knif . . . as long as their thies; with which, when he should give the watch-word *nymyá ywr Sexys* [take your knives], he commanded that every one should kill the Briton next him. . . . And the Saxons with their long knives, violently murdered the innocent and unarmed Britons, none of them having on him so much as a knif.[19]

The Welsh priest who pulled a knife on Wordsworth, we realize, was taking revenge for an old subversion. Out of control he may have been, but the very form of his outburst was shaped, not only by local drinking conventions and the standing dispute over language, but also by one of the most commonplace and politically charged myths in the Welsh revivalist canon. (Even drunkenness, we may note, had its precedent in the "tipsiness" of the gullible British leader in the Monmouth legend).[20]

Three exhibits and a coda, then, of barely contained violence: the silent poet in a Welsh church thinking bloody thoughts; hushed Druids at Stonehenge subliming sacrificial into celestial "living fires"; a loud Welsh priest at table taking sharp pride in race and language; and the treason of the long knives. All these were embedded within Wordsworth's generally violent imagination of Celtism at the time, realized in the giant warrior skeleton and tumulus in the 1794 revisions to *An Evening Walk*, his extensive background readings in Druidism recorded in a bibliography jotted down in the *Borderers* Rough Notebook, and even perhaps his near-regicidal *Letter to the Bishop of Llandaff* of 1793, whose rebuke of the ex-liberal bishop for political apostasy gains extra force when we realize that Llandaff (like the Denbigh area near Jones's house) had of old set a standard for Welsh resistance to English supremacy and uniformity.[21] Moreover, all these moments big with violence and treason "talk" to each other through a structured set of shared motifs: of warrior versus priest, assassination versus sacrifice, loudness versus silence, fire versus dark, knives versus language, Celt versus English. Indeed (and I am being leading here), they talk to each other almost as if they were a corresponding society of the time, a *conspiracy* of shared intent whose overall design—depending on how one viewed it— was either spontaneous or secretly meditated.

The prima facie evidence, in sum, is very strong: returning from France in late 1792, and touring the next year to Wales, Wordsworth *was* subversive, especially when in mind he took up the long knives of Celtic contest. Indeed, given his Revolution Society–like "triumph" in the death of English soldiers in the *Prelude* passage—alluding here to the 1789 "triumphal" sermon by the prorevolutionary Welsh revivalist Richard Price that triggered Burke's *Reflections on the Revolution in France*—the prima facie evidence is so strong as to be possibly actionable.[22] Or at least it might seem so to someone like the Home Office agent sent to the west coast in 1797 to spy on Wordsworth and Coleridge in the aftermath of the French landing in Wales; to the French revolutionary look-alike of such an agent (a watch committee member); or, perhaps, to the uncanny postmodern analogue of all such home-front spies, the cultural critic watching for subversiveness.[23]

Let me be extreme for a moment. Acting government agent and cultural critic without distinction, let me actually indict Wordsworth for subversion as if drawing up one of the sedition or treason cases of the Pittite repression in the mid-1790s. The poet's own declaration of "subversion" in the *Prelude* passage, of course, means in context that *he* was subverted: in myself, he says, "I found . . . / Change and subversion from this hour." But, as shown by the long French, English, and American traditions of conspiracy fear (with its lore of aristocrats, Jacobins, Illuminati, Mormons, "Huns within," Jews, Yellow Perils, Communists, and so forth), the intentional structure of subversion *has* no "inside"—except, to invoke Theodore Roosevelt's polemics, as a "Hun within our gates" or a Trojan horse inside.[24] Even for the most radical reformers, the true subverters are always some *other* cabal: ministers or Pittites, for example. Therefore, in the words of one of the standard indictments for sedition in 1793 and 1794: let it be found that William Wordsworth, "being a malicious, seditious, and ill-disposed person, and wickedly and seditiously devising and intending to move and incite the liege subjects of our said lord the king to hatred and dislike of the constitution of the government of this realm, and to cause the said subjects to wish for, and to endeavour to procure a subversion of the said constitution," in late 1793 at the church of . . . (borrowing from the 1793 English indictment of Thomas Briellat for seditious words).[25] We can leave the sentence hanging for the moment.

But an objection, which will winnow out the cultural critic from the government agent to open a parallel trial of the postmodern will-to-subversion. My objection is to the tendency—with such exceptions as Stephen Greenblatt's "Invisible Bullets," Paul Brown's "'This thing of darkness I acknowledge mine': *The Tempest* and the Discourse of Colonialism," Walter Cohen's "Political Criticism of Shakespeare," or Jonathan Dollimore's "Introduction: Shakespeare, Cultural Materialism and the New Historicism"—to inflate even the barest hint of subversiveness into an afflatus of literature-*as*-subversion. To vary a question that Dollimore has raised: What is the difference, after all, between subversiveness and subversion (as the latter appears in my historically accurate indictment, e.g.).[26] What, in other words, is the difference definitive of the *active* element in literature that Brown has called the moment in "excess" of simple containment?[27]

We left our indictment of Wordsworth, of course, crucially hanging. To be historically accurate, we would need to add to wicked or subversive intent—*malus animus*, as it was known—some such charge as follows (to borrow again from the Briellat trial for seditious spoken words): that Wordsworth did "unlawfully and seditiously . . . utter, publish, and declare with a loud voice, . . . malicious, seditious, and inflammatory words."[28] Here is where the historical venue of subversion and recent cultural criticism part company. As in the Scottish sedition trials of 1793–94, a defense attorney would at this point be expected to object on the grounds of irrelevancy.[29] Wordsworth was sitting in church, after all, *silent*—in a silence that is not *necessarily* irrelevant, to take issue with M. H. Abrams's blunt criticism of New Historicist method, but that would appear to be so in this particular context.[30] Our newer cultural criticisms, however, tend to overlook the bar of relevancy. All tendencies possible to be interpreted as subversive—through the back-corridor logic that hermeneutics shares with House Committees on Un-American Activities—become nascent subversions. *Argumentum e silentio* amplifies; less, as it were, is More, every poet a man for all seasons. Transmuted by the analytic of subversiveness, the negative, refused, or interiorized politics that the New Historicism addresses through its other primary analytic of "displaced" or occluded topicality suddenly breaks forth (as if from a Trojan horse), the ultimate politics.[31]

Yet, if we prosecute the newer cultural criticisms in the midst of prosecuting Wordsworth, we must also at last defend. Whatever its drawbacks,
the discourse of subversion/containment is at least an initiatory approach
toward what to date has been the blind side of cultural criticism. Put
abstractly for the moment: what is the nature of that broad interface of
"publishing" or propagation where *malus animus* is constituted, not as the
literary subject contained within history-as-representation and -interpre-
tation (virtually the exclusive realm of the New Historicism so far), but as
a dynamic *action* contained within politics-as-*active*-representation (publicity) and -*active*-interpretation (evaluation)? The containment that cultural
criticism senses, in other words, is partly its own containment within a relatively small room of thought, called *history*, occupied by representations
of self-fashioning and subjectivity (of the identities of More and Tyndale,
e.g., to allude to Greenblatt's influential *Renaissance Self-Fashioning*).[32] But,
beyond that room, there is a whole other set of containment structures
within which, as in a courtroom, literary action may be explored *as* action
rather than as representational displays contingent on a historicized phenomenology of the subject.[33] If subversion is to containment as bondage
was to lordship, in sum, the excess subversiveness that cultural criticism
seeks must stem from some *activity* resident in Hegelian sublation that it
has not even begun to think in more than subject-oriented dialectic.

Indeed, it may be said that, in its too-comfortable reliance on the synchronic paradigm of "discursive systems," cultural criticism has ceded the
real thinking of literary action to deconstruction. I refer specifically to
the later move that deconstruction made to appropriate the task of reading culture.[34] Particularly intriguing in our context is the strong salient
of deconstruction: the study of rhetorical trope. Though figurative, the
notion of dissemination by catachresis, for example, is in some ways the
reenactment of a classical rhetoric propagating words sophistically and
dynamically outward to others. "Catachresis," as J. Hillis Miller places it
in play in *The Linguistic Moment*, "is the violent, forced, or abusive use of a
word to name something that has no literal name . . . something that has
not, cannot have, a proper name." "That something," Miller continues,
"is the abyss."[35] What would be recognized by a cultural criticism of the
active moment (as opposed to Miller's *linguistic* moment) is that the true
abyss is social. Put simply, the abusive naming of something that "has not,
cannot have, a proper name" because it has no being is a version of prejudice. Catachresis is culture at large considered as a design of lived nega-
tivities or social differentiations (hates, slurs, condescensions, discriminations, distinctions, privileges, and so forth). Over such ungrounded social
differences, prejudice erects culture's great covers of repression (to play

here on Miller's notion of "curing" or caring for/covering the abyss); and, from deep romantic chasms under the containing covers, subversive forces work momently to turn the ground from under.[36]

The Derridean "solicitation" or violent shaking of the earth enacted by deconstruction, we may say, is really an opium allegory for the contest of repression and subversion involved in any propagation of suasive language intended to create from the social abyss a single state, a single Leviathan. In short, that greatest of Burkean "prejudices," "Culture" with a capital *C* (or *K*, as Pound would have it), consists of the glossary of catachrestic misnamings telling us what the ever-groundless, mobile, or mob-like *we* (civilization, humanity, man, Englishman, subject) *are*. Or, to enlist the other cachets of deconstruction, catachresis is like deferral, decentered-ness, contradiction, undecidability, and figuration of all sorts in imagining the *normally* fractured and alogical processes of social dialogism: gossip, for example, or opinion, rumor, propaganda. The linguistic moment is not just linguistic: it is also the moment of publishing or active dissemination that cultural criticism, if it is to read politics adequately, needs to think with a rigor matching the best of deconstruction. The Millerian ethics of *différance* is really a regulation of cultural difference; and dissemination is not just the "joy" of reading/writing/teaching but also the conduct of such joy amid the whole carnival of raucous glee, catcalls, irreverence, ob-scenity, anger, and plain hate laying siege to literacy during, for example, any university protest or (drawing on the most divisive aspect of Yale his-tory in the past few decades) university strike action.[37]

The essence of my critique of the newer cultural criticisms, then, comes to this: an ideological subject "contained" in history-as-representa-tional-structure is slightly different from a principle of action contained in politics-as-regulated-activity. And it is this slight difference between con-tainment by purely "ideological state apparatuses," on the one hand, and containment by the "repressive state apparatuses" directly governing ac-tions, on the other (to use Althusser's conceptualization), that is definitive of any possible excess of subversiveness—whether or not we then actually want to read that exorbitancy of subversiveness in the rarified terms of deconstruction.[38] Such excess, it is to be feared, is not finally thinkable as freedom; it is thinkable only as the escape of literature from one contain-ment to *another*—specifically, from engagement with ideological to en-gagement with repressive apparatuses (the actual police, law, or military). As enacted in the ease with which Althusser himself passes over repressive state apparatuses in the subject- and representation-oriented postulates of his celebrated essay, the domain of repression has become the blindness of our insight into ideology.[39] Caught up in the seductively easy project of ideology-speak, cultural criticism no longer knows how, as it were, to come up to and touch the police barrier effectively rather than simply intelligently. It has lost the touch for a considered notion of action (including nonviolent action) because it cannot think the principle of containment—the *content*, we might call it, of barriers of repression.

The recommendation I thus offer extends Foucault's in his *Power/Knowledge* collection: repressive containment—the limit of intellect—is not just a homogeneously negative or no-saying power that cultural criticism should rush to think *through* (as through a barrier) but, rather, an intricately articulated, plenitudinous, pleasure-giving, and "productive" realm.[40] It is not a two-dimensional limit, that is, but a *thick* Circean zone of complicity whose overlapping and intramurally contestatory containment structures intellectuals of the post–May 1968 generations must learn to reinhabit before *we* can even begin thinking what a genuinely active or excessive literature might be. Or, rather, the notion of containment structures does not do justice to the dynamism of containment, which is not a static system but a plenum of hyperactive detecting, policing, coercing, prosecuting, defending, judging, and other activities. The limits imposed by this plenum (often at cross-purposes with each other) are ipso facto vectors of motion/force to be pushed, pulled, or otherwise engaged with *in action*.

Or as John Frow has argued: "The possibility of unsettling limits is always both given and limited by an actual condition of power. There is no outside of power. But to write, within discursive limits, with a recognition of what these limits are and of the forms of discursive objects and relations delimited by a discursive formation is to push at these limits, to lay them open to the inspection of a counterpower whose force is not completely contained or foreseen. Without this possibility no system could ever change, it could only collapse from its own inertia."[41] I would add that to effect change by pushing at the limits is not so much to lay open for inspection "the forms of discursive objects and relations delimited by a discursive formation" as to resee the very notion of discursive formations. Such formations are made up of the myriad physical, logistic, rhetorical, political, and other actions constitutive of the "laws," respectively, of natural movement, mob mobilization, crowd persuasion, party formation, and so forth—heuristics of action necessary both to governments and to factions committed to subverting government. Ultimately, the New Historicism has believed subversion to be inevitably bound by containment because it confuses containment *within* such laws of action (some as fixed as military ballistics, some as contingent as mob logistics in a particular city) with containment *by* the regime that uses such laws for its own purposes. What is truly oppressive to cultural criticism is the thought of action. Compared to the quick set changes of the representational stage, the mechanics of real-time action are too slow, too bound by details of place and circumstance, too eroded by merely entropic rather than contestatory frictions. They are bad theater.

Does cultural criticism indeed want to read deconstructively the plenum of disseminatory or publishing actions that are the true arena of literary subversion/containment? Probably not. Though deconstruction offers one of the most sophisticated means to sift the ceaselessly figurative or rhetorical actions of deferral versus logos, subversion versus containment, cultural criticism has responded not so much by accepting deconstruction as by reappropriating its vision of rhetoric. Prompted by inner entelechy as well as by such factors as British cultural materialism, the new Marxisms, and a wave of applied research into the politics of language and dialect, the method would reconstruct deconstruction from the ground up in its own idiom and with a distinctively anti- or nonaesthetic feel. I refer to relatively recent explorations by politically conscious linguists and rhetoricians as well as intellectual historians, anthropologists, and literary critics in a mode that might be called a *new rhetorical historicism*—that is, a method that views cultural discourse less as symbolic representation or figure than as performative act.

Indicative of the politicization of rhetorical and linguistic approaches, for example, are such works as David Aers et al.'s *Literature, Language and Society in England*, George L. Dillon's *Rhetoric as Social Imagination*, James W. Fernandez's *Persuasions and Performances*, Roger Fowler et al.'s *Language and Control*, Roger Fowler's *Literature as Social Discourse*, Gunther Kress and Robert Hodge's *Language as Ideology*, and Frederick J. Newmeyer's *The Politics of Linguistics*.[42] These may, at first glance, seem to differ from cultural criticism originating in a more recognizably *literary* criticism and history. But, as exemplified by historicizing literary-critical works such as Jon Klancher's *The Making of English Reading Audiences, 1790–1832* (which reads in noncanonical periodical literature an active shaping or "making" of audiences) or David Simpson's *The Politics of American English, 1776–1850* (which considers the acculturation of language in both literature and non-literature), historicist rhetoric and rhetorical literary history are rapidly allying. Together, they sketch what Frow has called a "general rhetoric" focused, not just on the high literature and philosophy of deconstruction, but on the whole range of social texts from the cry of the street vendor up through the most rarified lyrical ballad.[43]

In the perspective of a general rhetoric, our question becomes: What are the features of subversion as an action published or performed in the forum of particular containments? How, that is, do we test for active subversion in literary and other discourses of the past? After all, however blocked subversion may be in its subject, a rhetorical rather than a merely representational performance of blockage *can* be registered as social action. In some forums of containment, indeed, silence *may* be subversion.

Rehearing Silence: Subversion and the Pittite Containment

I return to Wordsworth's long decade to retry his silence in the context of the productive potential, specifically, of the Pittite repression of the 1790s. By producing one subversive radical after another in court and elsewhere, the repression articulated for its period the basic conditions of possibility for active subversion. Reading this articulation will allow us to attempt a general formulation of subversion able to differentiate between the excessive in discourse and the purely representational.

A first brief holds documents relating to the two supreme institutional contexts available at the time for thinking publishing or the activation of literature—institutions, however, that Wordsworth was not ready to engage with until the later 1790s when he shaped what I have elsewhere called his *vocational imagination* (i.e., his self-placement as a poet relative to the economies and legitimating structures of other vocations).[44] I refer to economics and the law—sites eminently suited to the brutal negotiation between authors, intervening agents, censors, and audiences creative of *contestatory* rather than interpretive communities. Economy and law, that is, are fragmented and antagonistic venues regulating literature as action rather than as that privileged object of interpretation: meaning. Simply to follow up on my primary thought vehicle in this essay, for example, there is the venue of the law. The main point may be sketched by comparing the precedent-setting treason law enacted under Edward III and such later revisions as the Treasonable and Seditious Practices Act of 1795. Reading with elision: in 25 Edw. 3 a person is treasonous "if [he] compasses or imagines the death of our lord the king" by "overt act."[45] In the 1795 Gagging Law, by contrast, a person is treasonous if he shall "compass, imagine, invent, devise, or intend death or destruction, or any bodily harm tending to death or destruction, maim or wounding, imprisonment or restraint of the person of the . . . king . . . or to deprive or depose him . . . or to levy war against his majesty . . . and such . . . intentions . . . shall express, utter, or declare by publishing any printing or writing or by any overt act or deed."[46]

What is clear—and would be even more so with the inclusion of the intervening laws—is that the repressive state apparatus of the courts was an immensely "constructive" generator of thought about what publishing actually was. In parallel to the multiplication of inferred injuries to the king, the treason and sedition laws generated out of "compass[ing] or imagin[ing]" by "overt act" in 25 Edw. 3 an increasingly fulsome articulation of both literary *imagination* and *action*. Indeed, what opens to view in the statutes, the indictments, and the voluminous proceedings of the sedition and treason trials of the 1790s is one of the most sustained—and also fractious—inquiries on record into authorship, intertextuality or (as it was known) conspiracy, the dynamics of the performative act, the relation between author and witnessing audience needed for an interpretable (or, rather, actionable) literary action to take place, the distribution of reading power (between witnesses, advocates, jury, and judges), and, finally, the second-order publishing of that ultimate active reading, the verdict and sentence.[47] All these contestatory inquiries into the literary act, it may be added, are susceptible, not just of historicist, but of structural and deconstructive understandings. What was articulated by the law was an entire systematics—and countersystematics—of the verbal act in its catachrestic and often-meaningless transmission from party to party. When Thomas Muir, for example, was transported by the Scottish court in 1793 partly because someone, against his recommendation, took a copy of Paine's works with uncut pages from the pocket of his greatcoat lying on a chair, the literally prejudicial or prejudged precedent of "publishing" thus set was certainly a catachresis, an *abusio*, in every sense.[48]

A fuller examination of the sedition and treason trials (together, e.g., with cases of political patronage and copyright law) would tell us much about the legal/economic constraints shaping literary acts at the time.[49] In particular, one finding will be crucial in formulating a testing principle for determining the presence of active subversion in discourse. What we witness in the controversy over the sedition and treason trials is that there was no rhetorical action, subversive or otherwise, that was not accompanied by a parallel action situated at the limit between the primary action and the society that contained it. This limit was where the legitimacy or illegitimacy of the original action was decided, and its resident action was characteristically a legal system *itself* big with contests of subversion/containment. Thus, in the 1790s, subversive speech or writing was delimited or defined as action by celebrated contests between Thomas Erskine (for the defense) and the government. Moreover, such limary contests of legitimation were then themselves paralleled by second-degree legitimating contests situated at a further limit of containment big with its own subversions. Erskine versus the government was itself defined *as* action by newspapers and books that immediately published the trial proceedings for political motive.[50] In short, action opened out into the official chambers of legitimation (or, depending on the verdict, delegitimation), and the latter opened out into the court of public opinion in such a way that the journalism of this latter court could then see the journalists themselves under indictment (or summoned to Privy Council) for too-zealous reporting.[51]

The puzzle about cultural containment or limitation, we begin to perceive, is that it is an open system: there is no limit that is not (to co-opt a word we applied previously only to subversion) excessive of its limitations. Limits ceaselessly spill outward into other limits, and it is this principle of disseminatory limitation that we will need to build into our notion of what is contained in limitation's open-ended box: subversion.

It will be most useful, however, to concentrate on a second brief documenting the vision of the Pittite containment that Wordsworth *did* use to conceive subversion in the early and mid-1790s. This vision was of English imperialism. Empire, of course, incorporated in its broad regime of social control the legal and economic institutions cited above, but it did so in a manner that charged not so much individuals as whole peoples or, as we will see, "races." For the legally and economically naive poet, the legitimacy of subversive discourse was to be tried as much as possible outside the courtroom (or the purview of political or bookseller patronage) in a limitary zone where the subversion of entire peoples ran up against what he perceived to be the hardest and most vivid repressive agency of the time: the military that maintained empires. As witnessed by the fascinated repulsion with which he daydreamed the death of English soldiers in church, brooded about the British fleet off the Isle of Wight at the start of his 1793 tour (recorded in a fragmentary poem of the time as well as the later Advertisement to *Guilt and Sorrow*), or imagined the horrors of veterans and their families in *An Evening Walk* and *Salisbury Plain*, the real contest for Wordsworth was that of peoples versus armies.[52]

Some geography will help us identify the specific limitary zone where this vision of imperialism came home to the poet. If we map Wordsworth's mobility during his long decade, we find a pedestrian-cum-poetic description of Britain analogous to the localizing English cartography that Richard Helgerson has suggested first helped subvert the image of a monarch-centered land.[53] Wordsworth's progress described what was virtually a complete orbit of literal and intellectual marginality around the island—simplifying somewhat, first London, then the Isle of Wight, Salisbury Plain, the Wye Valley, Wales, various locations in the northwest, Newcastle, London again, the Bristol-Racedown-Alfoxden triangle, Wales briefly once more, and at last (after the trip to Germany) Grasmere (interrupted in 1802 by the antihoneymoon to say good-bye to Annette in France).[54] It was this outline of marginality around England—punctuated periodically by trips to London and the Godwin circle that were journeys not so much to the center as to the political fringe—that situated the specifically Celtic segment of subversiveness with which I began.

Here, we can make our most direct contact with the previously cited essays by Greenblatt ("Invisible Bullets") and Brown ("'This thing of darkness I acknowledge mine'"), both of which address subversion in Renaissance *colonial* discourse.[55] What Wordsworth's literal and poetic geography of the British fringe describes, I believe, and what our opening exhibits of the poet in a Welsh church, Druidic priests at Stonehenge, the Welsh priest at table, and the treason of the long knives finally evidence, is that, in the early 1790s, the poet honed his long knife of subversion specifically on Welsh colonial discourse—a subversive language, as we will see, that protested what it took to be English imperialism exerted on a subordinate people in Britain itself. That is, Wordsworth inhabited a marginal frame of mind and a discourse coincident with *internal colonialism* (to cite the title of Michael Hechter's book, which has had a marked impact on Welsh studies). Or, to vary on Immanuel Wallerstein's general taxonomy of empire, the poet's subversive silence approximated the language of a semiperipheral state that saw itself positioned between the core of England and the far periphery of England's actual (and former) colonies, where the specter of her armies loomed large.[56]

In this regard, the comparison of the Solitary's story in book 3 of Wordsworth's later *Excursion* (1814) is revealing. After a personal tragedy, the Solitary remembers, he awoke once more to social life in sympathy with the French Revolution—even to the point of singing thanksgiving "in still groves, / Where mild enthusiasts tuned a pensive lay" and resuming an "office in the House / Of public worship" where he conducted "prayer" and "prophecy." But despondency came with the war on France and repression at home, and he felt claustrophobically contained:

> The tranquil shores
> Of Britain circumscribed me; else, perhaps
> I might have been entangled among deeds,
> Which, now, as infamous, I should abhor.

Choosing not to express his radicalism in any "infamous" resistance or criminality, he fled Britain, where "all was quieted by iron bonds / Of military sway," for the American republic—where in a further rejection of containment he immediately grew disgusted with postcolonial civilization and retreated farther into the Indian wilderness. Ensconced in his private Arden, however, he must still be Jacques. The noble savagery, he says with fastidious Hobbesianism, was "squalid, vengeful, and impure."[57]

In 1793 and following, of course, Wordsworth himself did not take either his radical enthusiasm or his malcontent solitude quite so far as to sing in groves, preach revolution, emigrate to America, or search for Indians. Yet *The Excursion*'s imagination of a postrevolutionary and colony-ho trajectory away from repressive "iron bonds / Of military sway" is essentially accurate. Indeed, the Solitary's story offers us a uniquely helpful way to look back on our opening exhibits of the "Welsh" Wordsworth with insight into their total embeddedness within Welsh colonial discourse. The Solitary is Scottish rather than Welsh, of course, but his singing, preaching, emigrating, and searching retrace *exactly* (though with a northerly displacement we will need to address later) the archetypal myth of Welsh resistance to England in the 1790s. In every detail, the Solitary's life told the single great story, the long march, of Welsh colonial discourse.

What was Welsh colonial discourse? I have entered my argument by citing the most relevant application of the internal colonialism thesis that became prominent in late-twentieth-century historical, economic, and sociological studies (the thesis took its precedent from Marxist-based work on Latin America).[58] But, for our purposes, the specifically postmodern premises and vocabulary of the thesis are dispensable. The colonial frame of thought was so strongly rooted in the lived and ideological state of 1790s Wales itself that its relevance to our discussion stands firm—if anything, more firm—without obvious postmodern intervention. Drawing on the historical and sociological material in Hechter as well as works on Wales by Rees Davies, E. D. Evans, Geraint H. Jenkins, Bud B. Khleif, Prys Morgan, D. Huw Owen, and especially Gwyn A. Williams (whose detailed and incisively conceived discussion of Welsh radicalism in the 1790s is the most germane), I put forward the following model of Wales at the end of the eighteenth century organized around a variant of *Annales* and *histoire de mentalités* methodology.[59]

We can initiate the model with an overview: Wales in the 1790s was structured as a *divide* or differentiation in *longue durée* patterns of geography, property, economy, and population that together fostered a corresponding *mentalité* of alienated "Welshness." This latter mentality had many facets in popular pastimes, education, religion, and so forth, but, for our purposes, its most expressive form in the years from the American

Revolution through the French Revolution was the conjunction between renewed agitation over the Welsh language and the imagination of Wales as a colony. It was this conjunction that was constitutive of a subversive discourse or way of speaking Wales-as-colony that went deeper than any mere idiom or figuration and that, while it was spoken most vociferously by the Welsh intelligentsia, moved masses and even affected in some fashion the silencing majority who suppressed Welsh subversion after the French invasion scares (at least until its resurgence as the famous Welsh radicalism of the nineteenth century).

Moreover, since no wholly structural model can accommodate a sense of historicity, we need to be aware that the contemporary way of speaking Wales, as I put it, was mapped over deep structural divisions through the mediation of a historical imagination so dominant that it may remind us of such other history-full peoples as the Hebrews (with whom some Welsh thought the Druids were kin).[60] Alienation in present experience, that is, was imagined almost exclusively on the basis of deeply felt past alienations. To be Welsh was to be aware in every moment of the relation between *then* and *now*—specifically, of a continuity of calamity so embedded in prehistorical and irrecoverable tradition that calamitous change (with its three eighteenth-century inversions of reformism, millenarianism, and prophetic or apocalyptic revolutionism) seemed as fixed in the Welsh character as the *longue durée* lay of the land itself. In sum, Welsh historical imagination brought deep structure and *mentalité* together in a single vision that Eric Hobsbawm and Terence Ranger have called "the invention of tradition."[61] For our purposes, it is especially suggestive that the invented traditions of the Welsh characteristically took the form of what Lévi-Strauss might have considered savage-minded "myths" converting structure into historical narrative. The divide imposed by the central Welsh mountains or by such ancient boundaries as Offa's Dyke (with their correlative rifts between competing economies, properties, and cultures) emerged in story form as a legendary history—or, rather, tragedy—of agon.[62]

Specifically, Wales agonistes may be modeled as follows.

Wales in the 1790s was a land divided in mind between what historians for lack of better terminology describe as two "races," the "Celtic" and the "English" (or often "Saxon")—an exaggerated racial differentiation whose contemporary function was to deploy outmoded notions of tribal distinction to make (polemical) sense of the deepest and most confusing structural divisions of actual Welsh existence.[63] *Race* was how *tribe* could be modernized to give meaningful shape to the social contradictions of current Wales.

The reason I place *races* in quotation marks, of course, is that, in Wales, the population base could not be discriminated by color or any other physical mark.[64] It was the very invisibility of race, indeed, that gave the concept heightened power. In essence, race was a notion locating in invisible distinctions of tribal origin or blood a whole range of other invisibilities. These included ancient distinctions in geography, property, law, economy, and political administration whose increasing disappearance within more recent organizations and institutions was the very definition of Welsh history—that is, the history of a disappeared or "nonhistorical" people assimilated to a conquering culture. To begin with, we know that Wales was formed by accumulated divisions between the postconquest Celtic tribes and the Saxon/Norman English (and, of course, the Romans earlier). These divisions were originally defined by precise geographic, proprietary, legal, political, and, ultimately, social discriminations (e.g., between western Wales and the Marches, between Welsh communities and "Englishries," and between the Welsh Law of Hywel and English property law).[65] However, by the 1790s, many of these divisions had become blurred within more contemporary manifestations of geographic, economic, social, and other divisions in which the purely Celt versus English divide had grown either amorphous or wholly contradictory (e.g., Welshmen claiming English ancestry and names and Englishmen claiming Welsh law for financial reasons).[66]

Thus, while it could be said that current rifts between sections of Wales stemmed originally from a divide between English and Celtic patterns of land use, the contemporary connection between those rifts and actual Englishmen or Welshmen was hard to pin down.[67] The result was that the Celt versus English divide increasingly reappeared in an internalized and figurative prejudice of race. The Welsh were divided racially *within* themselves. As in the case of the "London Welsh" we will come upon who went by two names (one a colorfully Welsh "bardic" title, the other a common English-Welsh patronym such as Jones or Williams), to be Welsh was to be as English as the Prince of Wales.

This, perhaps, is the deep motive for such myths as the treason of the long knives, which reaffirmed the disappeared, hard-and-fast distinctions between Welsh and English tribes and made ideological sense of the actual social divisions of the time. Without foundation in recoverable fact, and possibly even borrowed from one of the Saxons's own myths, the treason of the long knives pitted the ancient Britons against the English in a manner that recovered apparently clear patterns of "racial" discrimination.[68]

Such stories romanticized discrimination as a defense against a contemporary reality in which poverty, ignorance, and lack of social status could no longer be attributed automatically to differences of blood.

What at once prompted the explanation of race and constantly undermined its adequacy were deep structural divisions whose original link to competition between the Welsh and English had changed into an internal contest situating something like a Welsh Mason-Dixon Line. Most important, Wales was a land divided between highland and lowland as well as country and urban populations and, thus, correspondingly, between agrarian and increasingly industrial economies. Gwyn A. Williams is particularly perceptive on these issues. As he notes, the original English settlers in postconquest Wales were soldiers, craftsmen, and adventurers whose urban Englishries excluded the native Welsh so strictly that the ultimate result was the definition of the Welsh as a "peculiarly non-urban people."[69] Moreover, the pattern of conquest and subsequent cultural assimilation by England had articulated Wales into a land split not just between country and city but also between the backward "mountain core of Wale's hollow heart" (together with the traditional culture of the west and southwest beyond the mountains) and the changeful regions of the south and northeast facing England.[70] The most salient eighteenth-century manifestation of this division was what Williams has called the reemergence of the "old frontier" between the conquered and unconquered Wales of times past: a rapidly widening rift between the industrializing shires (especially Monmouth and Glanmorgan in the south and Denbigh and Flint in the northeast) and the conservative counties of central and southwestern Wales where the old agrarian and great landlord economy was deeply entrenched.[71]

Faced with the reemergence of an old frontier no longer easily described as Celt versus English, race discourse—the most primitive of the available idioms at the time—increasingly spilled over into other ways of describing Wales agonistes. All these competing discourses were in some way primitive. Indeed, Williams has drawn on Hobsbawm's thesis of the "primitive rebel" to declare Wales in the 1790s "overpoweringly over-populated by primitive rebels": "social bandits, millenarians by the score, labour sects, ritualistic revolts."[72] But it was only the most organized and theorized primitivities among these (if the oxymoron be allowed) that succeeded in redeploying the energy behind ancient ethnic strife to shape the divided Welsh scene into a new, directed sense of Welshness.

The first such movement was Nonconformity, which, in its overall vector from the south and east into the rest of Wales, retraced the great geographic and economic divides.[73] Established in the three sects of Independents (Congregationalists), Baptists, and Presbyterians, Old Dissent was joined after the 1730s and particularly in the 1790s by an explosive Methodism that theorized primitivism as fundamentalism.[74] Growing by such means as mass mission drives in the 1790s, Methodism with its populist base polarized, energized, and, ultimately, extremized the whole Nonconformist movement such that an unprecedented shift in the religious population from primarily Anglican to primarily Nonconformist occurred after 1790 in the space of about a generation.[75] The significance of the shift was that an entirely new sense of Welshness, with its own discourse for describing inner division, arose to supplement racial or ethnic discourse. As Morgan has pointed out, Methodism was particularly efficient in extirpating older Welsh customs in order to devise "a new Welsh way of life which cut the people away from the past."[76] When, as Williams reports, young men still nominally within the Anglican fold "started to stand up in the open air and to bear witness, to ram home awareness of sin and, employing every device known to reach the senses as well as the intellect, to achieve the cataclysmic 'conversion' which had men and women 'born again,'" a new way of defining the Welsh became possible, one based on a mythic revivalism.[77] To be Welsh was not to be Celt versus Saxon but to be Nonconformist versus Anglican and, within the individual himself, to be the born-again versus the old self. Thus were deep divisions in Wales refashioned by spiritual conflict into a new sense of the Welsh people complete with a new name, the *gwerin* or "common people."[78]

The other most relevant theoretical primitivity followed in the footsteps of Nonconformity: the radicalism that, after the 1760s and especially in the period spanning the American and French revolutions, foreshadowed the Welsh radicalism of the succeeding century. It was no accident that some of the leading prorevolutionary spokesmen in Britain at the end of the eighteenth century were Welsh churchmen such as Richard Price and Bishop Watson of Llandaff. As Evans notes, after 1760 the tradition of Nonconformity (to which even Watson was assimilated in this instance) had become increasingly politicized and liberal in its campaigns for religious and constitutional reform.[79] Taking advantage of this politicization (and despite the fact that Methodism itself was politically conservative), radicalism launched itself from what until the end of the eighteenth century was the only widespread platform of specifically Welsh mentality: oral discourse broadcast from the pulpit.[80] Even the route of radicalism's proselytizings in Wales was set in advance by the path of the pulpit. Much like Nonconformity, radicalism moved most strongly into the industrializing south (Glanmorgan) and northeast (Denbighshire and Flintshire). Indeed, in the period of the highly politicized food riots in Denbighshire in the 1790s, it was possible for alarmists in north Wales to point simultaneously to "hordes of Methodists" and champions of "the Rights of Man."[81]

But we must leave the church for Druidic groves and grottoes if we are to grasp the full vision of the "friends of liberty": Welsh radicalism theorized a primitivity not so much of the *gwerin* as of an ancient Welsh Cymmrodorion ("Aborigine") nation. And the rediscovery of this nation, paradoxically, occurred in London. The first signs of Welsh radicalism, as Evans notes, were fomented by the Association movement of 1779–83 (for economic and constitutional reform) in areas including Denbighshire and Flintshire. Enlisting such revivalists as Thomas Pennant, Association-ism in Wales peaked in a sedition trial in which Erskine (defending the chairman of the Flintshire Association) delivered a celebrated speech on seditious libel prophetic of his later exertions in the 1790s.[82] But such home movements could not fully blossom (into Druidic groves and grottoes) until the Welsh intelligentsia had created an intense expatriate circle in London in the 1790s. It was the ghettoization of the Welsh away from home that focused Welsh radicalism into a revolutionism that could then be reimported back home via corresponding societies.

I refer to the seething, left-bank, and, in some instances, slightly mad underworld of the London Welsh that Williams, Evans, Morgan, Jenkins, and others have documented.[83] Even before the years of the Associations, antiquarianism had created the mold for Welsh radicalism in London by organizing the Cymmrodorion Society and later the more populist Gwyn-eddigion or "Men of North Wales" (which drew members particularly from Denbighshire exiles). Meeting festively and turbulently in London taverns, the latter society was particularly rife with radicalism. In its mul-tifarious capacity as a literary-debating-singing-harping-drinking forum, it drifted increasingly away from antiquarianism in the direction of French *sociétés de pensée* and, ultimately, Jacobin clubs, even to the point of taking for its motto "Liberty in Church and State."[84] Together with such other radical London Welsh clubs as the Caradogion and Cymreigyddion as well as the corresponding societies in Wales attached to their London *mère* societies (to borrow from the Jacobin model), the Gwyneddigion inter-sected with a circulating pool of often gorgeously named "bardic" Welsh radicals both in London and Wales.[85] These included Tomos Glyn Cothi (Thomas Evans), a poet of freedom imprisoned for sedition in 1801; David Davis, a poet and revolutionary; Jac Glan y Gors (John Jones), the renderer of Thomas Paine in Welsh; William Jones, "the rural Voltaire" and author of *Liberty and Oppression*; Iolo Morganwg (Edward Williams), the stonemason "Bard of Liberty" and laudanum addict; Owain Myfyr (Owen Jones), a Denbighshire radical who remained extremist throughout the Pittite repression; David Williams, a declared Girondin republican whose ideas influenced Robespierre's "Cult of the Supreme Being" and who was made a French citizen in 1792 (soon to be imprisoned in the Terror); and Morgan John Rhys, the apostle radical who created a Bible Society to spread the Word in France in the service of ameliorating the Revolution.[86]

What emerged from this underworld of Welsh radicalism was not the perfectibility of man—the future-oriented vision of the Godwin circle in London—but a thoroughly past-oriented and primitivist credo of the Welsh nation. Wales agonistes was reimagined in terms of legends of days of yore when the English supposedly massacred the bards. With sponsorship from the Gwyneddigion, a group of north Welshmen in 1789 thus revived the tradition of the Eisteddfod, or bardic and singing contest, which overlapped with the hallucinatory reestablishment of the ritual of the Gorsedd (or Bards of Britain) by Iolo Morganwg and others. Eisteddfod and Gorsedd together propagated a wholesale reinvention of "ancient" bardic and Druidic arcana with a distinctly democratic bias. In 1791, the singing competition of the Eisteddfod was commemorated by medals designed by the official sculptor of the French Republic. And, on the equinox of 23 September 1792, Iolo instituted on London's Primrose Hill a ceremony in which the democratic Bards of Wales performed a ritual with a sword in a circle of stones. From such revisionist liturgy—the extreme, we might say, of Nonconformity—arose the continuing tradition of neo-Bards pacing reconstructed Druidic henges or grottoes in gardens.[87] Internal division or contest in Wales thus became a singing contest amid groves and henges; ceremonies with naked swords refashioned the treason of the long knives into a Welsh fête cognate with those staged by David in Paris.

Here we arrive at the culmination of our model of Wales. All the above racial, religious, and political visions of a new Welsh people intersected in the 1790s in the climactic resurgence of two of the most widely shared and intensely lived expressions of Welsh protest: *language* and *emigration*. Revived linguistic contest and renewed emigration were the distinctive forms of mass resistance in the 1790s. They were overlapping discourses—or, rather, a single conjoined discourse—spoken by the tongue and ratified by the feet. What we discover here is not so much the postmodern notion of a discursive system as what might be better called a discursive *movement* at once textual and contextual, discursive and active, akin to what we now know as demonstration, rally, or protest march (eighteenth-century analogues include enclosure, food, or militia riots).[88] Language and emigration together rallied an *active* rhetoric and gesture (up to the point of translating the entire body in a gesture toward liberty across the ocean) that signed a Welsh declaration of independence.

Language, first of all, was the common focus of all the Welsh controversies of the time. We can look back to the discourse of race, for example. If race in Wales was not diacriticized by physical mark, it *was* accented by an invisibility that had all the felt presence of color: language. To speak monoglot Welsh (as in the case of the vast majority of the Welsh population), to speak broken English, or even to speak bilingually in good English was, in one way or another, to betray—to reveal or commit treason against—one's race.[89] But there was one further linguistic stance that increasingly allowed the Welsh at home and in London to escape the dialectic of betrayal: the language of *contest* that issued in the loud and proud use of Welsh even when the speaker was bilingual and the milieu English. Thus it was that *Sais yw ef syn* (He is a Saxon, beware) became a common watchword to be spoken within earshot of English travelers. As one such traveler put it, he was shocked to find that the Welsh "language has kept up" the notion that England was a foreign country.[90] Language—not inner disseminations of meaning but the basic *fact* of the language—was the cherished burden of the Welsh race.

So too we can reprise in the hearing of language the other controversies we modeled above as if singing a ballad or hymnal burden whose deepest meaning lies in the fact *of* burden, of a piece of language signifying by lilt more than content and whose deepest significance is the bonding of those who carry the same tune. The Welsh language in the 1790s was the burden not just of race but also of Nonconformity and radicalism. Nonconformity marshaled the legacy of Babel for its own purposes by depending for its oral ministry on the Welsh Word (the Welsh-language Bible) as propagated by preachers and the instructors of the flourishing circulating schools. Moreover, the effort to communicate the Word in oral discourse increasingly led to a supplementary drive to spread the printed word. Using not only the Welsh Bible but also other religious books in Welsh, Nonconformity had by the end of the eighteenth century succeeded in making most of the adult Welsh population to some degree literate.[91]

Similarly, radicalism took up the cause of language and took it further in both the oral mode (in singing and poetry contests) and written form. Most important, it developed an extensive array of apparatuses by which to publish the Welsh language as a demonstration of the most fundamental freedom of speech and press possible: the freedom to express oneself in one's language of choice and to imagine a time when the official language (of government, law, finance, higher education, etc.) would be one's own.

Political liberty and freedom of speech/press became inseparable in the invention of a performative rhetoric whose point-and-pica attention to the minutia of publishing in all its forms helped define language as ipso facto active. Specifically, a large proportion of the Denbighshire young men who came to London became ghettoized as printers while other London Welsh radicals located themselves in the Grub Street underworld as journalists and pseudo-Johnsonian hacks-of-all-trades.[92] What these printers, journalists, and radicals invented within Grub Street was the obverse of Johnsonian English: a literature of enthusiasm in Welsh. With accelerating pace in the latter decades of the century, Welsh dictionaries (in one case *larger* than Johnson's), orthographies, grammar books, philological studies, literary histories, poetry anthologies, biographies, registers, translations (e.g., of Paine and *Paradise Lost*), songs, and even national anthems spilled forth to carry the Welsh burden.[93] All these works were at once scholarly and thoroughly polemical. Indeed, this is one of the clearest instances of scholarship conceived as a direct political agenda. The very *fact* of Welsh scholarship was a manifesto of nationalism.

Not surprisingly, therefore, the growing bibliography of Welsh studies fostered at last a full-scale Welsh political press whose publications in the 1790s accounted for one-fifth of total Welsh publications. Indeed, if we count explicitly politicized works in related fields of literature, theology, and so forth, the fraction swells to nearly half.[94] Welsh political periodicals, including the *Cylchgrawn Cynmraeg* (Welsh journal), *Trysorfa Gymmysgedig* (Miscellaneous treasury), and *Geirgrawn* or *Trysorfa Gwybodaeth* (Treasury of knowledge), rallied radicalism through political discussion, coverage of the Pittite treason trials, and popularizations of Priestleyan and other ideas.[95] Such publications, we may note, incurred a reaction from the government and loyalist associations that documents the extent to which they were perceived as active subversions: authorities were alerted, books burned by government spies, periodicals suppressed, counterrevolutionary demonstrations and propaganda sponsored, and journalists sent into hiding.[96]

Second, overlapping with the Welsh linguistic contest in the 1790s was a revived emigration movement spurred on by sermonizing and journalistic propaganda. It is at this point that we come to the burden of our own discussion: Welsh colonial discourse. The drive to declare the independence of the Welsh language at the end of the eighteenth century was cognate with an emigration movement declaring literal independence from British colonialism. Wales set out to become "American," and the literature of emigration heralded a New Wales complete with "native" Welsh-speaking aborigines already in place. To find a true home for the Welsh language, that is, seemed to require a transference—a sort of actualized metaphor—of the tribe across the Atlantic.

Again, all the previous race, Nonconformist, and radical discourses we surveyed find their common focus in the emigration movement. The origin of the movement earlier in the century was thus centrally tied to Dissent and political protest. The primary fact here is the vast number of Welshmen, primarily Nonconformist, who crossed to America in the first half of the eighteenth century in denominational groups (sometimes shipping as entire congregations) and who by the time of the American Revolution were so ubiquitously and visibly established in American political, religious, and educational institutions (sixteen Welsh Americans, e.g., signed the Declaration of Independence) that such areas as Pennsylvania and Delaware seemed not a "new England" but a "second Wales."[97] Importantly, the American Welsh saw themselves as part of "an intense transatlantic world" maintained by frequent communication with their brethren in the Old World.[98] At the onset of the American Revolution, the result was an extensive pro-American sympathy in Wales that peaked in such registrations of protest against the government as Richard Price's celebrated Americanist publications, the appearance of other prorevolutionary tracts, and published protests against militia taxation. As some loyalists in Wales charged, Welsh Nonconformism, especially among "seditious writers," was the real origin of the American Revolution.[99]

The first wave of Welsh emigration and Americanism then succeeded to the second wave in the 1790s—and in such a way as to bolster dissent and protest with the old "racial" imperative. As Williams has commented: "These were the years of 'the rage to go to America,' when the emigrants' handbooks came pouring from the presses."[100] Again, we may note, Welsh mythic imagination played a crucial role. The American rage was popularized, not just by emigrant literature and a swell of sermonizing and journalistic propaganda, but by a particularly strong myth allowing Nonconformist and radical discourses, as it were, to return to their roots. We come here on the Welsh Columbus: Madoc of the Indians. In 1792, a tribe of Indians was found on the upper Missouri who were "white like Europeans." Immediately, the Welsh both in America and at home remembered old stories propagated by Dr. John Dee in the sixteenth century (and recently retold in a publication of 1790) about the Welshman Madoc who discovered and colonized America three centuries before Columbus—a story originally used to press Tudor claims against Spain.[101] The result in both Nonconformist and radical circles was the so-called Madogian

movement that prompted Iolo Morganwg to forge materials showing the
Indians to be Welsh-speaking descendants of Madoc, William Owen to
found an expeditionary society, John Evans to ship for America and search
for Welsh Indians (his maps were later used by the Lewis and Clarke ex-
pedition), Southey to write *Madoc* (first complete draft 1797–99), and—at
last—hundreds of Welsh families to emigrate en masse to the New World
(led in the mid-1790s and at the turn of the century by such radicals as
Morgan John Rhys). As many of the emigrants declared on arriving in
America, they had come to found "the Kingdom of Wales"; or, as Rhys an-
nounced on Bastille Day 1795, on the prairie west of Ohio, the American
West was to be the *gwladfa*, the new home of the Welsh race.[102] The nation
of the Cymmrodorion or Aborigines came "home" to the Indian nations.

Such was the Wales (as opposed to Wales-part-of-Britain) imagined
and enacted in the 1790s under the shadow of the Pittite repression. This
Wales emerged from the mentality of a people (especially in some areas,
among some groups) who just before the invasion scares and the triumph
of conservatism at home increasingly saw themselves as American rebels
and who simultaneously reinvented Welsh as a performative language
each of whose words was a declaration of independence. As Khleif has
commented: "Welshmen like to say, Wales was England's *first* colony."[103]

We can close our model with a final observation: a legacy in part of
Welsh sympathy for the Americans was that during both the American
and the French revolutions resentment of established government hard-
ened into actual Welsh resistance to the military and to recruitment. In the
mid- to late 1790s, indeed, the map of popular protest shows that militia
riots were especially prevalent in the whole Celtic fringe running from
Wales (through the Lakes) to Scotland.[104] As Williams reports:

> A strong and often very radical popular movement developed around Wrex-
> ham and Denbigh [both in Denbighshire]. At the height of the troubles of
> 1795, as magistrates met at Denbigh to raise men for the militia and the
> navy, some 500 men in a military formation of fourteen squads marched
> in, took over the town, jailed the magistrates and forced them to renounce
> their project, before marching on circuit through the north-east to stop the
> export of grain. . . . In the north-east there was a popular movement which
> was not only violent but highly ideological; they were making pikes there
> in 1800 and government feared insurrection.

Meanwhile in nearby Bangor, Williams adds, "papers went up on doors . . .
calling for people to pray for a British defeat in the war against France."[105]
Faced with such opposition aimed against the very muscle of British con-

tainment, the government at last exploited the invasion scares to establish a home militia or Volunteer Movement in Wales with the special purpose of enlisting loyalists in a rearguard action against radicals. As Evans observes about Welsh Volunteerism: "In 1794, the Government launched the Volunteer Movement as a national conservative coalition with a view to discrediting the opposition and to initiating judicial persecution against radicals. Men of property were prominent in it which made it a useful police force and it kept a watchful eye on radicals, protestors against high prices and malcontents. The Volunteers were armed."[106]

Toward a Theory of Subversion

Now we can return from Wales to Wordsworth. Or, rather, our discovery should be that, in modeling Wales, we have really throughout been modeling the poet. Singing in groves, preaching revolution, emigrating to America, searching for Indians: all these actions of the Solitary in his effort to break out of the containment of "iron bonds / Of military sway" reenact the Welsh saga with uncanny precision. So too, we realize, our opening exhibits of Wordsworth wishing the death of English soldiers in a Welsh church, imagining Druids at Stonehenge, confronting the Welsh priest at table, and invoking the treason of the long knives are so intricately and multiply interwoven with the major Welsh discourses of race, Nonconformity, radicalism, language, and, ultimately, internal colonialism that the circumstantial evidence becomes overwhelming. For a radical just back from France, to sojourn at length in Wales—and particularly in Denbighshire with trips to Flintshire—was to be immersed in a fulsome language of subversion produced in counteraction to the Pittite repression. The Celts, we may say, were Wordsworth's vision of British sansculottes.

A fuller study of the poet's early radicalism would also need to consider his involvement with English radicalism. Particularly suggestive is his occasional contact in 1795–97 with the political journalists of the Godwin circle in London, some of whom, Kenneth R. Johnston speculates, he may have joined in publishing the *Philanthropist* (which appeared in 1795 a year after Wordsworth planned, and apparently shelved, a somewhat more radical magazine of the same name).[107] There is also the nexus of Wordsworth, Coleridge, and John Thelwall in the Alfoxden area in 1797 that resulted in the arrival of the government spy. Acquitted of treason in 1794, we may note, Thelwall eventually sought to retire from political agitation to Wales, where, however, he found his neighborhood so politicized that he could not escape hostility (to the point of assault by pickax).[108] But the scene of Wales I have sketched impinged on the poet earlier in the 1790s while he was most desperately radical (and did so, we may note, with no more uncertain influence than the shadowy, difficult-to-pin-down incitement of the English radicals in London). Welsh colonial discourse and Celtism provide a first, a minimum explanation of the subversion the poet sought to model himself on when he came home from France and cast about for a political stance.

Specifically, and here I approach my home chord, the scene of Wales, or what I have called *Welsh colonial discourse*, may well have provided the stance for Wordsworth's subversive silence. In this instance, silence has as much evidentiary status as any mute but still-smoking gun. Or, rather, the analogy of physical evidence is misleading. To refute Abrams's categorical rejection of the New Historicist use of negative evidence or silence, we need to recognize that silence is a metaphor drawn from physical experience. But, in culture, there is no such thing as a silence of pure absence (as in the lack of sound waves); there is only that which is unheard, insignificant, or silenced.[109] Silence, that is, is an undervoice. And, insofar as every culture consists in a differentiation between those who possess their voice and those who do not have a significant voice or are dispossessed of it, *silence is part of the very organization of culture.* If the history of ideas disbelieves in all evidence of silence, then that is because the idea is not an idea of culture. After all, the question may be put: Where within the comparatist and philosophical symphony of circuitous journeys or apocalyptic marriages is there any scoring of the anticomparatist (i.e., chauvinist) and antiphilosophical prejudices, discriminations, spites, revenges, and hates sequestering major voices from undervoices and so orchestrating the bars of actual culture? Or, to use Mary Douglas's terms, if high philosophical culture is purity, then where is the dirt marking the bounds and shape of purity?[110] The dirt, of course, is swept aside into certain areas decreed invisible; the undervoices are silenced.

How did Welsh colonial discourse set the pattern for Wordsworth's subversive silence? A flashback to Tudor times is telling. As Mullaney observes: "Henry VIII had addressed the problem of linguistic variety with characteristic bluntness when he outlawed Welsh, finding that 'great Discord Variance Debate Division Murmur and Sedition' had arisen, due to the fact that the Welsh 'have and do daily use a Speech nothing like, nor consonant to the natural Mother Tongue within this Realm.'"[111] Like the Welsh language in Tudor times, Welsh colonial discourse in the 1790s was by statutory definition that which was *silenced* in the name of Great Britain. Thus the pattern established for the early Wordsworth, a pattern that may well have extended even to the mature poet in his quest for an aboriginal language "really used by men": the subversion that Wordsworth sought to imitate through silence in the early 1790s was one that extended from the intelligentsia down through the Cymmrodorion or *gwerin* rural folk, that centered in a religion (sometimes of groves and grottoes) outside the established church, that spoke itself as a proud affirmation of the language really used by men, that was located at the limit or periphery of Britain, and that relied on memorialization of the traditional past. It was subversion, in other words, that helped prepare the ground for the Preface to *Lyrical Ballads* and for the personal traditionalism (as James Chandler has conceived it) of the years following the long decade.[112] Such subversion spoke itself as a silenced Welsh and Celtic undervoice from which issued loud seditious tracts, songs, and poems performed in groves. In the early 1790s, Wordsworth's silence was the mimesis of an active, *published* discourse of subversion.

Yet there was a difference, of course. It would be going too far to say that the poet's characteristic early political stance of silence—silent in church during patriotic prayers, silent in *not* publishing the dangerous *Letter to the Bishop of Llandaff*, silent in refusing to come to London to bring out the *Philanthropist* as he originally conceived it—was exactly the same as the silenced voice of loud Welsh protest.[113] Like his Scottish Solitary, Wordsworth was not Welsh, could not speak Welsh, and so could not participate in Welsh discourse directly even if he had wished. No more so was he truly Gallic in Paris, Orléans, and Blois in 1791–92 (where his spoken French was far from fluent).[114] Rather, Wordsworth was native to another region just slightly *removed* from the Celtic heartlands. Indeed, we may say that removed or distantiated subversiveness is the quintessential Wordsworthian politics. Even from the first, the poet's silence was distanced from the loud silences of actual subversion in a way predictive of his later total removal from radical politics.

How at last to judge his silence? In unreconstructed form, the subversion/containment analytic would require that we judge it a submission to the forces of recuperation. The poet, after all, was not willing to take a fully published stand. And he would soon become so recuperated that he enthusiastically embraced the epitome of Pittite repression. He enlisted in the Grasmere Volunteers in 1803.[115] Yet I would put it that what really comes clear in this instance is the total inadequacy of an unreconstructed subversion/containment dialectic in reading either history or literature. Viewing containment as an active, thick, and productive zone of limitation, we can also judge Wordsworth's distantiated silence in a different fashion that will allow us to complete our reformulation of subversion/containment and establish a test for subversion in discourse.

Crucial here is the specific route of the poet's distantiation from radicalism and of his recuperation within mainstream British politics. I bring us back to Wordsworth in church, silent, and to that odd blend in his postrevolutionary experience of political and sacerdotal contestation—a blend that need not be understood *exclusively* on the basis of contemporary Celtic politics and Nonconformist dissent. After all, keeping silence in church is not exactly the same as standing up "to bear witness, to ram home awareness of sin," and to dissent in the full voice of Protestant Nonconformity. There is at least one alternative reading of the poet's contestatory silence in church: as a borrowing from a much older discourse of resistance native to the whole Celtic fringe from Wales up through the Lakes into Scotland. Additional references at this point might include the reputation of north Wales (and especially the Denbigh area) as a center of Catholic resistance in the Renaissance, the use of Wales as a staging site for Jesuit and Continentally trained Welsh priests infiltrating back into Tudor England, Wordsworth's imaginative sympathy for the old northern Catholic uprising in his later *White Doe of Rylstone*, the fact that book 10 of *The Prelude* moves on to a ruined "Romish chapel" where the poet, in essence, says mass after the death of Robespierre (see 10.515–66), and the fact that book 10 generally speaks a religiosity centered on paradigms of apostasy.[116] Soon after the silent-in-church episode, for example, the poet expatiates:

> When I began at first, in early youth,
> To yield myself to Nature—when that strong
> And holy passion overcame me first—
> Neither day nor night, evening or morn,
> Were free from that oppression, but, great God, . . .
>   what a change is here!
> How different ritual for this after-worship.[117]

As a first mediation of the contemporary discourse of subversion, I suggest, Wordsworth borrowed the older discourse of recusancy, which in Wales and the north in the era of the Supremacy and Uniformity acts was the primary focus of contest between English domination and local resistance. *Now* we have a context in which less is, indeed, More (alluding here to More's celebrated answer of silence in 1534). Or, rather, as was true of historical resistance to the Acts of Uniformity, Wordsworth's was a recusancy of crypto-Catholic *and* Dissenting persuasion. Silent in church during prayers for the country, but inspired by prophecy elsewhere in book 10 of *The Prelude*, he enacted a recusancy of Catholicism conflated with Miltonic inner heroism. A recusancy miming politics in silence, in sum, was a fitting close to an era of radicalism opened so loudly from the pulpit of Price, Watson (the bishop of Llandaff), and others. Indeed, to look forward to the conspiracy (as it may be called) of the One Life in Wordsworth's revised imagination of Wales in 1798, we might improvise on William Empson's churchly criticism of "Tintern Abbey." What, after all, is that disturbance rolling through all things but a subversively recusant way of *not* naming God in the authorized manner? To be a "worshipper of Nature," as the poem confesses and as Empson detects with unerring precision in his idiom of "ambiguity," was to be exactly like a recusant "shuffling" his way out of any firm commitment to the Act of Uniformity and setting up alternative services. As Empson puts it (in a passage I previously discussed in a different context in chapter 1 above): "Whether man or some form of God is subject here, [Wordsworth] distinguishes between *things* which are objects or subjects of *thought*, these he *impels*; and *things* which are neither objects nor subjects of *thought*, through these he merely *rolls*. . . . The only advantage I can see in this distinction is that it makes the *spirit* at once intelligent and without intelligence; at once God and nature. . . . There is something rather shuffling about this attempt to be uplifting yet non-denominational."

I argue, then, that, in his search for ways of subversion during wartime repression, Wordsworth fell into local conventions in part acclimated to Welsh colonial discourse of the 1790s but also in part descended from the older, broader strife of recusancy and Jacobitism. It is not to the contemporary scene of radical journalism, perhaps, but instead to the "publishing" procedures of recusancy with its antecedents—most canonically, Christ, who, when "accused of the chief priests and elders, . . . answered nothing" (Matt. 27:12)—that we might turn to discover how Wordsworth first started thinking the publication of his autobiographical gospel. In particular, it is intriguing to look to the tradition of recusant martyr publications celebrating the Welsh and northern martyrs for the old faith. What such moments of hallowed transgression as the poet in church or the Druidic priests at Stonehenge will ultimately reveal themselves to be in Wordsworth's work, of course, are "spots of time"; and the spots of time draw on, among other conventions, hagiography with its tremendously literal obsession for instruments of torture capable of publishing in the medium of the body, even in its enforced silence, the good Word.[118] "I would enshrine the spirit of the past / For future restoration," Wordsworth says after the Gibbet-Mast spot of time, his holy day marking the origin not just of imaginative subjectivity but of what seems almost a pure "publication" independent of subject: that monumental writing carved by an "unknown hand" and blessed finally by the Mariology of the girl with the pitcher.[119]

The overall significance of the recusant strain in the crypto-Catholic or old-religion Wordsworth, as he has been studied by Katherine Mary Peek and others,[120] is that it allowed him to retrace in mind the supremacy and uniformity of the *British* nation—a nation in which Wales was one with the Lakes and (the implicit argument of the Preface to *Lyrical Ballads* and other works) the Lakes one with the (ideal) nation. Mediated by the older contestation of recusancy and Jacobitism especially suited to the northern imagination, that is, the subversiveness of radical discourse in the 1790s could be redeployed as the alter ego of colonial rebellion: *nationalist* discourse. Thus, I conclude, Wordsworth in his wish to support Britain at the end of his long decade could simply press subversion back into service: subversion *became* patriotism. For, and this is also the conclusion I come to by parallel means in my *Wordsworth: The Sense of History*, the poet in 1802–4 finally propagandized—that is, publicized and evaluated rather than simply represented and interpreted—the British nation as itself the quintessentially subversive state. The two great instances here are, first, the political sonnets of 1802–3, which exploit the octet-sestet of the Italianate form to think nationalism as innately split between the fallen ethos of a nation of shopkeepers (characteristically in the octet) and the high old Miltonic faith (in the sestet), and, second, that grand Welsh mountain that Wordsworth posted at the close of *The Prelude* in 1804 roughly at the time Napoleon crowned himself emperor and, as recorded in both the French and the English papers, proceeded on coronation day through the streets under a miraculous sunburst through clouds much like that instant light "like a flash" on Snowdon.[121] Wordsworth's imperialism of vision on Snowdon—of a "mighty mind" whose "domination" "moulds . . . , endues, abstracts, combines"[122]—finally opposed not just his own dialectical mind but the internally rifted English nation-state against French empire: as subversion against containment. The Welsh mountain was not the resistance of the colonized Celts to English empire—as might have been the case in the 1790s—but Britain's resistance to Napoleon, or, more broadly, to the *wrong* kind of domination molding, enduing, abstracting, combining. It was *Britain* in the years of the greatest invasion scares that was threatened with colonization. And out of *this* stance of nationalism, of speaking subversively against the worst aspects of England in the service of speaking *for* England's subversion of French empire, the poet now began the long process of publishing his political poems "collected"—as he put it—alongside his personal and quietist ones.

What is subversion? As may be evident by this point, my answer is that subversion has no possibility as an active rhetorical stance unless it is contained. *And this is because containment is the very form of subversion.* I invoke once more the notion of disseminatory limitation we discovered while watching Erskine for the defense and the journalism that then defended Erskine's defense. The final realization we should come to in observing Wordsworth's long decade is that, in displacing Celtic subversion first into the distanced scene of recusancy (more generally, of the north) and then into its more legitimate avatar as British nationalism, the poet played a role structurally cognate with Erskine for the defense. In both cases, subversion was advocated or *represented* (in a legalistic, active sense co-opting symbolic representation). It was represented in a limitary zone at the outer bounds of subversion. And the judgment whether such advocacy is merely safe (recuperated within legitimacy) or itself actively subversive *depends on the further advocatory representation of some other spokesman situated at an even more distant limit between subversion and legitimacy.* Here is a definition of *subversion* and, implicitly, of what we mean by *action* in a critical universe teethed on intertextuality: there is no subversion without its advocate; and the measure of a subversion's effectivity—of its excessiveness—is whether that advocate is willing to proceed in such a way as himself or herself to require advocacy. Only when subversion is laterally displaced in this fashion is it received as social act.

Such, then, is the testing principle I offer for determining the presence of subversion in discourse. To read subversion, we need to sift the contexts of its containment in search of an advocate willing to be put at risk. In intuitive terms: there are personal, familial, social, economic, legal, political, linguistic (and so forth) battles to be fought in all provinces of cultural experience; and whether the particular battle one chooses or "must" engage in is subversive in an incipiently revolutionary way is never the business of the battler. It is always the judgment of an advocate at a remove or in the future. Thus, it is possible to fail to "make a difference" one way or the other even when setting out to battle within what is conventionally recognized as a crucial limitary zone (e.g., university administration buildings in the 1968–70 milieu); and, inversely, it is possible to make a difference in a zone no one ever thought of spotlighting as the central scene of contest (e.g., the Watergate-era press that grew up covering administration building *journées*). A thought experiment: what if Napoleon *had* successfully invaded Britain in the first years of the nineteenth century and altered the world in such a way that this essay would now be written in French? Would not Wordsworth, through his published attacks on Napoleon, have been at risk and, thus, possibly have inspired some advocate equally willing to be put at risk?

Of course, such a what-if historical imagination is productive only of bad novels, and I am not seriously suggesting that the reading of subversion in literary discourse invent such historical experiments in its effort to test for socially registered subversions. As even positivism now knows, there is no test without its uncertainty principle. Thus it is that we need to add one further codicil to our definition of *subversion* that will bring it back from any specious scientism to the dilemma of hermeneutics attending any truly historical or critical understanding. Where do we go to look for the advocate of subversion who can register subversion as a socially received act? The answer, of course, is to the most likely or available places. And such likelihood or accessibility is determined by our own cultural circumstances—by a scene that we may know in our bones but that we cannot know with critical definition until some distant or future observer writes it. For all practical purposes, therefore, Wordsworth in his jingoistic patriot voice at the end of the long decade was not truly subversive. In our own recent political climate (i.e., as experienced in the academy), we do not expect—and cannot really understand—the possibility of a subversion expressed as total conservatism. Or, more accurately, we cannot do so unless we look outside the academy.

Rewriting Kafka on hope, Greenblatt in "Invisible Bullets" writes: "There is subversion, no end of subversion, only not for us."[123] Phrased another way: there is subversion, no end of subversion, only for us it is called *containment*. Subversion contributes to historical changes that condition us, when we look back from the changed world, to see subversion as part of the way things were established.

/ / / / / / / / / / /

Local Transcendence

Cultural Criticism, Postmodernism, and the Romanticism of Detail

Release 1.0

> I struck, and struck again,
> And, growing still in stature, the huge cliff
> Rose up between me and the stars, and still
> With measured motion, like a living thing
> Strode after me. With trembling hands I turned
> And through the silent water stole my way
> Back to the cavern of the willow-tree.
>
> . . . .
>   after I had seen
> That spectacle, for many days my brain
> Worked with a dim and undetermined sense
> Of unknown modes of being. In my thoughts
> There was a darkness—call it solitude

Or blank desertion—no familiar shapes
Of hourly objects, images of trees,
Of sea or sky, no colours of green fields,
But huge and mighty forms that do not live
Like living men moved slowly through my mind
By day, and were the trouble of my dreams.

William Wordsworth, *The Prelude* (1805)

A year here and he still dreamed of cyberspace, hope fading nightly. All the speed
he took, all the turns he'd taken and the corners he'd cut in Night City, and still he'd
see the matrix in his sleep, bright lattices of logic unfolding across that colorless
void. . . . The dreams came on in the Japanese night like livewire voodoo, and he'd
cry for it, cry in his sleep, and wake alone in the dark, curled in his capsule in some
coffin hotel, his hands clawed into the bedslab, temperfoam bunched between his
fingers, trying to reach the console that wasn't there.

"Cyberspace. A consensual hallucination experienced daily by billions of legitimate
operators, in every nation. . . . A graphic representation of data abstracted from the
banks of every computer in the human system. Unthinkable complexity. Lines of light
ranged in the nonspace of the mind, clusters and constellations of data. Like city
lights, receding. . . ."

William Gibson, *Neuromancer* (1984)

*To imagine Wordsworth with his hands on a personal computer is to glimpse a
descent, as if of software, from the romantic release of imagination to its various postmodern releases. Cyberpunk, for example. Romantic imagination is the
source code (by way of Edgar Allan Poe, the Beats, Thomas Pynchon, and others)
of* Neuromancer, *the novel that marked the emergence of the cyberpunk or mirrorshades movement in postmodern science fiction.[1] The comparison is vulgar, but
precisely so. Perhaps only our vulgate bards match the original banality, the transcendental everydayness, of the poet of* Lyrical Ballads.

*Transcendence is the issue. Romantic imagination was a mediation between
the worldly and the otherworldly whose definitive act was the simulation of transcendental release. In such spots of time in* The Prelude *as the Boat Stealing or
Snowdon episodes, the mind was the visionary medium that coded the world as
otherworldly. But the dark ricorso of such simulation was what Geoffrey Hartman (in his book on Wordsworth) called the "return to nature."[2] The thief in the
boat turns back from transgressive transcendence to a Platonic cave of legitimacy.
The poet on Snowdon views a cloud-video "perfect image of a mighty mind" but
then corrects the simulation, turns it at last into an ode to duty: "hence religion,
faith," "Hence truth in moral judgements; and delight / That fails not, in the*

external universe."[3] Transcendence is recuperated within the banal—the denotative banal of commonplace experience and perhaps also the connotative and ideological banal, the trite, hackneyed, contained, bourgeois.[4]

Just so, neuromantic imagination simulates release. The visionary medium is now mind in direct interface with silicon (and, secondarily, with a kaleidoscope of synthetic drugs updating romantic opium), and the function of the synthetic imagination is once more to allow the world—now corporate, multinational, informatic—to feign the otherworldly. Fashioned in much the same mold of existential theft as Wordsworth's boat stealer, the hero of Gibson's novel, Case, is an outlaw, a "cowboy" hacker riding "viruses" into bright corporate databases. Gliding in cool stealth along the data-path traceries of the corporate network, Case is Kerouac on the road, Slothrop in the Zone, the street that jinks between corporation headquarters. But, at last, this thief also ends in the double bind of transgression become legitimation. In the great legitimation crisis of the novel, he raids an evil corporate colossus that is the postindustrial imagination of Milton's Pandemonium. The resulting subversion is transcendental, apocalyptically so, but also, we recognize, indistinguishable in outcome from what economic journalism calls a minor adjustment of the market triggered by a corporate raid, a takeover, a taking care of what Case—in his street talk—has all along called "biz." In Neuromancer too, transcendence is, ultimately, banal, which in postmodern science fiction often means that it is parasitic on a mock-Japanese ideology of ordinariness: corporation consensus, performativity, zaibatsu rectitude. In Gibson's drug-sharp image of his hero bunching his fingers in cold withdrawal from his keyboard (in the electric "Japanese night"), we recognize a consummate need for the corporate grid.

On one great screen, then: romantic "unknown modes of being." On the other: "cyberspace" or, in other cyberpunk idiom, the "matrix," "network," "grid," "Plateau."[5] The medium of dependency in both instances is the same: an ecstatic mind caught in an endless loop between transgressive transcendence and corrective legitimation. Transcendence is a go-to routine of the imagination that goes nowhere.

But a detail: What about that insistent "willow-tree" in Wordsworth (thrice mentioned in the Boat Stealing episode)? Or the "temperfoam" in the passage from Gibson? What do these ultrabanal details embedded in the routine of transcendence—together with a whole manifold of arbitrary particulars elsewhere in these works—offer the romantic or neuromantic imagination? Haiku, after all, shows how little is needed to simulate a world. Why does the vision of One Life or One Matrix need such a level of detail in its simulation of release from the world? Why not be content with a more select repertory of motifs or images adequate for simulation: Wordsworth's imagery of "darkness," for example, or Gibson's of "bright lattices of logic . . . like city lights, receding"?[6] Or is it the case that gray

background—neutrality, static, the noise between channels—is the very possibil-
ity of romantic/postmodern simulation? The meanest flower that blows as well
as such routine products of materials science as temperfoam: is this the stuff of
underallegory, undersymbol, or, perhaps, the most hallucinatory of all simula-
tions, context?

Overview: The Rhetoric of Detail

I wish in this essay to criticize cultural criticism in what can be called its
high postmodernist forms: cultural anthropology, the New Cultural History, the New Historicism, the New Pragmatism, the new and/or post-
Marxism, and, finally, that side of French theory—overlapping with
post-Marxism—that may be labeled *French pragmatism* (i.e., the "practice"
philosophy and/or semiotic "pragmatics" of the later Michel Foucault,
Pierre Bourdieu, Michel de Certeau, and Jean-François Lyotard). These
aggressively new forms of contextualism do not exhaust the field of postmodern cultural criticism, and a fuller study would need to include the
different emphases of ethnic, gender, and area studies as well as of British
cultural materialism.[7] But for now we can stay high. *High* distinguishes
neither the theoretical from the practical, the high cultural from the populist, nor the neoconservative from the leftist. Rather, it indicates a shared
mode of cultural engagement that undercuts all such polemics dividing
the field to project an increasingly generic discourse of contextualism.[8]
This mode of engagement can be called *detached immanence.* Detached immanence amid worlds of context is the distinctively postmodern, the new,
in cultural criticism.

But we must descend to particulars. I refer to a tenet so elementary,
pervasive, and insistent in all the high cultural criticisms that it appears
foundational (despite the method's avowed philosophical antifoundation-
alism). The basis of high cultural criticism is its belief that criticism can,
and must, engage with context in a manner so close, bitmapped, or mi-
crobial (to use some of the method's paradigms) that the critic appears no
farther from the cultural object than a cybernetic or biological virus from
its host at the moment of code exchange. We live in an age of "detailism"
characterized by the "pervasive valorization of the minute, the partial,
and the marginal," Naomi Schor says in her intriguing *Reading in Detail,*
a study of the genealogy of detailism leading up to modernist and poststructuralist aesthetics.[9] High cultural criticism is an aesthetics—and much
more—of specifically postmodern detailism.[10] Or, to name the method's
related leading concepts, it is particularism, localism, regionalism, relative autonomism, incommensurabilism, accidentalism (or contingency),

anecdotalism, historicism, and—to draw attention to a set of curiously prominent Greek prefixes in the method—*micro-*, *hetero-*, and *poly*-ism. "All these," we may say in words borrowed from Clifford Geertz's *Local Knowledge*, "are products of a certain cast of thought, one rather entranced with the diversity of things."[11] Or as Richard Rorty sums it up: "All that can be done to explicate 'truth,' 'knowledge,' 'morality,' 'virtue' is to refer us back to the concrete details of the culture in which these terms grew up."[12] And, most succinctly, that unofficial motto repeated several times in Jerome J. McGann's *Social Values and Poetic Acts*: "I make for myself a picture of great detail."[13]

I will later return to Schor's and McGann's books in particular because their emphases are eminently relevant for us here, but at present I borrow only McGann's recommendation of a nonnarrative form suited to displaying detailism: the array or matrix.[14] Here is a matrix of cultural-critical phrases rendered in all their (self-thematized) disconnection as if they were so many piles of Lyotardian phrases, snatches of Rortyian conversation, pastiches of New Historicist paradigms, or sound bites of Baudrillardian media. Media-oriented readers, indeed, may wish to view this matrix as if with remote control in hand—flitting from channel to channel and sentence fragment to sentence fragment in a hallucinatory blur of strangely continuous discontinuity:[15]

The Matrix of Detail

Channel 1. Cultural Anthropology

Clifford Geertz: "local knowledge" "the massive fact of cultural and historical particularity" "the most local of local detail" "the road to the grand abstractions of science winds through a thicket of singular facts."

Channel 2. The New Cultural History

Roger Chartier: "multiple intellectual configurations by which reality is constructed in contradictory ways" "a specific way of being in the world" "history is turning to practices that give meaning to the world in plural and even contradictory ways." *Robert Darnton*: "a patchwork of regions" "a specific field for the exercise of cat power" "he wanted to capture his entire city, every bit of it, and so he wrote on and on—for 426 manuscript pages, covering every chapel, every wig maker, every stray dog." *Natalie Zemon Davis*: "consider the disorderly woman in more detail" "rather than thinking diffusely about 'the people,' I am trying wherever possible to ask how printing affected more carefully defined milieus" "local context" "a salty, particularistic, resourceful layer of culture." *Carlo Ginzburg*: "reconstruct a fragment" "a narrow investigation on a solitary miller" "the anecdote" "a microcosm." *Emmanuel Le Roy Ladurie*: "analysis that is not only general . . . but also *detailed*" "particular detail" "*regional* evidence" "in its smallest detail."

Channel 3. The New Historicism

Renaissance studies. Stephen Greenblatt: "some fragment of a lost life" "my vision is necessarily more fragmentary" "particular and local pressures" "partial, fragmentary, conflictual." *Richard Helgerson*: "the experience of particular communities" "individual autonomy . . . communal autonomy . . . national autonomy" "the land in all its most particular divisions." *Leah S. Marcus*: "particular cultural situations" "'local' reading" "localization" "radical varieties of regionalism" "a patchwork of local differences." *Louis Adrian Montrose*: "the cultural specificity, the social embedment, of all modes of writing" "the pressure and particularity of material interests" "*relative* autonomy of specific discourses." *Steven Mullaney*: "a detailed mise-en-scène of Brazilian culture" "richly detailed," "preternatural detail."

    Romantic studies. Jon P. Klancher: "a reader situated in a particular social space" "crowding of cultural fragments" "a rich array of socially individuated types." *Marjorie Levinson*: "disturbing particular" "very concretely situated" "the particular and particularly constrained" "deeply specific" "epochal specificity" "*we are the effects* of particular pasts." *Alan Liu*: "concrete, highly charged phenomena . . . phenomenal spots of history" "uncountable local variations" "the scandal of the particular and partisan." *Jerome J. McGann*: "the concrete, the material, and the particular" "the local, the topical, the circumstantial" "the polymorphous and the heteroglot" "daily life in a particular community" "incommensurate detail" "elementary particulars" "heuristic isolates" "minute particulars" "grains of sand in which the world may be seen" "minute particulars of time, place, and circumstance." *David Simpson*: "particular details—the details of disposition and empirical contingency" "small details of everyday life" "we are inevitably committed to a careful and detailed examination of particulars" "minute particulars."

Channel 4. The New Pragmatism

Stanley Fish: "all aesthetics, then, are local and conventional" "context specific" "parochial perspective of some local or partisan point of view" "contingent practices of particular communities." *Frank Lentricchia*: "specific, detailed, everyday functioning" "real local effects" "beliefs . . . are born locally in crisis and have local consequences only" "a heterogeneous space of dispersed histories" "the 'eaches'" "the particular, the local, the secret self" "pragmatism is an epistemology for *isolatos* who experiment at the frontier." *Richard Rorty*: "criticism of one's culture can only be piecemeal and partial" "micro-processes" "ordinary, retail, detailed, concrete" "alternative, concrete, detailed cosmologies" "thousands of small mutations finding niches" "atoms in a DNA molecule" "local final vocabulary."

Channel 5. The New Marxism

Louis Althusser: "specific object of a specific discourse" "this particular unity" "a peculiar real system . . . a *specific* system" "no practice in general, but only *distinct practices*" "I shall call Ideological State Apparatuses a certain number of realities which present themselves . . . in the form of distinct and specialized institutions." *Fredric Jameson*: "the specificity and radical difference of the social and cultural past" "the specificity of the political content of everyday life" "a purely local validity in cultural analysis" "the fragments, the incommensurable levels, the heterogeneous impulses" "isolated, disconnected, discontinuous material signifiers." *Pierre Macherey*: "the specificity of the literary work" "product of a specific labour" "a specific but undisguised . . . relation with history."

Channel 6. French Post-Marxism/Pragmatism

Jean Baudrillard: "bits" "little black boxes" "bodily cells, electronic cells, party cells, microbiological cells . . . the tiniest, indivisible element" "the play of molecules . . . the play of infinitesimal signifiers" "tiniest disjunctive unities" "the operationalism of the smallest detail." *Pierre Bourdieu*: "an acquired system of generative schemes objectively adjusted to the particular conditions in which it is constituted, the habitus" "the discontinuous, patchy space of practical paths" "polythesis." *Michel de Certeau*: "a *science of singularity*" "microbe-like operations" "a 'polytheism' of scattered practices" "encysted in particularity" "microbe-like, singular and plural practices" "micro-stories." *Jean-François Lyotard*: "a pragmatics of language particles . . . a heterogeneity of elements . . . institutions in patches—local determinism" "'nodal points' of specific communication circuits, however tiny" "*petit récit*" "*petite histoires*." *Michel Foucault*: "a 'new micro-physics' of power" "a political economy of detail" "a multiple network of diverse forces" "particular, local, regional knowledge" "the 'specific' intellectual" "dispersed, heteromorphous, localised procedures of power" "a plurality of resistances, each of them a special case" "a specific type of discourse on sex . . . appearing historically and in specific places."[16]

This, we recognize, is the rhetoric of a method, a sheer virtuosity of detail. Of course, this is not the whole picture of great detail. Indeed, it may be appropriate to interject a rhetorical gesture of our own imitating a topos we will see throughout the discourses of particularity: inexpressibility or incompletion. A fuller study of detail would need to bolster its canon, not only with more authors than I have been able to array here, but also with other disciplines (historicist film studies, e.g., where Philip Rosen's work on cinematic detail and film studio production is provocative).[17] It would also need to consider at length the applied side of cultural criticism: the grounding of its rhetoric on variously thorough or haphazard projects of recovering specific contexts of detail. Methodological vocabulary alone tells us relatively little, for example, about the assumptions embedded in the genre, style, tense, quotation strategy, and even type size of the New Historicism's paradigms, Geertz's cockfights, or Bourdieu's slices of anthropology. Finally, a fuller study would advert to the sometimes massive discourse of detailism in such modern or structuralist forebears of the postmodern scene as traditional American pragmatism, Fernand Braudel's historiography, Georg Lukács on the "special," Theodor Adorno's "micrological" aesthetics, Mikhail Bakhtin's "heteroglossia," formalist close reading, or Roland Barthes on the "reality effect."[18]

But all such gestures of incompletion, we know, end by crossing their fingers: let us say, then, that the matrix I have presented is sufficient to simulate the whole. What we observe in the matrix is a revisionary idea of culture whose full sweep could be conveniently analyzed as a cultural *empirics*, *pragmatics*, and *dialogics*—in short, a whole methodology for thinking the cultural world. Or, rather, "thinking" should not put us too much in mind of an orderly discourse of knowledge based on a set of operations for transforming discrete perceptions into cognition. Detail is the very instrument of the antifoundational and antiepistemological imperative in high cultural criticism: its contention that there is no reason (other than fidelity to quaint notions of philosophy) why contexts of discretely perceived particulars should resolve into culture as a single, grounded, and knowable order. The empirics, pragmatics, and dialogics of high cultural criticism are finally methodologies as much *against* as of knowledge—a methodical antimethod.

But there is a danger in antimethod, of course. It is possible to discern in the sometimes all too trenchant formulations of cultural criticism precisely an incipient method or meta-way (*meta* + *hodos*) of alternative knowledge harder in mold than the ground state of contingent method I discussed in the introduction to this book. This is the accusation of foundationalism that has long haunted Marxist criticism, for example, and pertains in lesser degree to late or neo-Marxist theories premised (as in the case of Althusser) on materialist axioms only "in the last instance." Or, again, we can think of the polemical hard edges of other cultural criticisms: Geertz's antifunctionalism, the New Historicism's antiformalism, or the anti-*Annales* movement in the New Cultural History—all of which wear their dissent, perhaps, with too heightened a sense of the sanctity of their meta-way.[19] As when we read through the sequence of Rorty's works, which have essentially one thing to say but are adept at repeating the gospel again and again with wider relevance, the method of antimethod can, at times, seem too dogmatic, too much of a piece—precisely not contingent. It overdoes Rorty's prescription for pragmatist philosophy: to improvise on one of his favorite phrases, the picture of detail not only shows "how things, in the broadest possible sense of the term, hang together" but also, perhaps, hangs together all too much, like a history painting on a wall. The picture of great detail, as it were, threatens to become a *great picture* of detail.[20]

How to discern in our matrix a "thought" or "idea" of culture, then, without being too knowing even in the way of antiknowing? The answer, I suggest, lies precisely under the sign of a very old antifoundationalism or sophistry: rhetoric. In reading our matrix and the methods it indexes, we should be aware that we are, indeed, *reading*—that we are dealing with rhetoric as the facsimile knowledge or pseudoanalytic whose distinctive method is its tendency to lose its way at decisive moments, to pose a logic of detail, only then to thwart itself (in the essential de Manian reading) by interposing incommensurable logics.[21] In particular, our matrix of phrases declares that the methodology of high cultural criticism is really an incoherence of three rhetorical "moments." For ease of reference, these can be called *immanence, commitment,* and *detachment.* It is immanence that speaks within cultural criticism's empirics of the real, commitment within its pragmatics of variously oppositional or neoconservative practice, and detachment within its cool dialogics of improvised conversation or *petits récits* (the "culture rap," in other words, thematized by authors as diverse as Rorty, Darnton, de Certeau, and Lyotard). Each such rhetorical moment at the core of the method, I suggest, is, not an integral discourse, but the site of an instability or turning in rhetoric. After all, only inner troping allows method to be perceived *as* rhetoricity in the first place—as a way of knowing prevented from hardening into dogma (*especially* when it is being most polemical or rhetorical) by the arbitrary intervention of its media.

Of course, our most recent avatar of rhetoricity certainly holds to its own meta-way. But deconstructive method will serve as a salutary corrective to cultural-critical method so long as we persist in seeing rhetoric as mediational to the end—that is, as perpetually a medium or means rather than an end. Rhetoric will be our means of referring cultural-critical method to the ultimate antifoundationalism or endless end: history. History, or *elsewhereness*, as I have called it elsewhere, is alienated foundation.[22] It is what orders the thought and, within thought, the rhetoric of cultural criticism into a characteristic sequence whose logical necessity is subordinated to the phantom necessity of contingency.

What I mean here may be educed from the detectable tug of diachrony in high cultural-critical argument, the tendency in the method to marshal reasons and discourses in a certain order unpredictable from within the system. As thought, to begin with, cultural criticism follows a logical order that is pseudosyllogistic. Consider as evidence, for instance, the strong drift in Geertz's cockfight essay *from* counting bets *to* meditating on aesthetics; or, again, witness the glide in Rorty's *Contingency, Irony, and Solidarity* toward a culminating discussion of literature.[23] Paralleling such linear movements of exposition are cultural-critical works that establish an axiology according to which art is the highest, most privileged, or otherwise most special form. (Thus, one of the distinctive features of McGann's *Social Values and Poetic Acts* is its strong advocacy of poetry as a unique discourse that "performs a critical function which is not found in other forms of discourse.")[24] What such directional arguments indicate is that high cultural critics more often than not argue *from* the major premise of empirical reality, *through* minor premises of pragmatism (the idea of "specific" practice, indeed, is analogous in function to a minor premise in classical syllogism), *to* a conclusion in aesthetics, dialogics, or media studies. "In conclusion," we hear them say, "it is as if reality enacted in a rich texture of specific practices were art."

The arbitrariness of such syllogism comes clear when we remember that cultural criticism (at least in theory) eschews any foundational major premise or conclusion and makes *reality*, *practice*, and *discourse* all equivalent minor premises. What is it that drives the system of thought in a particular direction? The answer is already whispered in the deflected logic of the figurative/aesthetic "as if" at the conclusion of the cultural-critical syllogism (as I ventriloquized it above: "it is as if reality enacted in a rich texture of specific practices . . ."). Such deflection is the very signature of the fact that the arbitrary direction of the syllogism is controlled internally by an equally arbitrary sequence of rhetorical moments *from* immanence *through* commitment *to* aesthetic detachment. And driving this discursive sequence, in turn, is the bottomless foundation that generates any arbitrary sequence: a series of purely contingent, historical moments each of which premises its reality on the "as it really was" of another. Putting the case in overview: high cultural criticism is a system in which thought is subjected through the mediation of rhetoric to that ultimate disruption of thought, the *history* of thought, such that the force of the disruption is at once revealed and concealed as aesthetic response.[25]

We will need to grow more specific in identifying the historical moments that regulate the system of mediations constitutive of high cultural criticism. In terms of a general history of thought, however (no doubt too neat to serve as more than a scaffolding for research into the history of cultural criticism), it may be suggested that the interior trajectory of high cultural criticism is along a succession of intellectual-historical moments from the premodern through the modern to the postmodern— from immanental empirics through an originally Deweyan, Marxist, or New Critical praxis to distantiated dialogics.[26] The historically given logics of the real, the practical, and the simulated—with their underlying rhetorics of immanence, commitment, and detachment—blur in fast-forward or filmic dissolve, and the overall result is the Baudrillardian sense of simulated reality, of mediated tele-engagement, that I have called *detached immanence.*

The Romanticism of Detail

The present essay focuses on immanence, the first or opening rhetoric of high cultural criticism, though my argument will require that I also look, at times, to the matching moments of commitment and detachment that complete the overall rhetorical experience I have dubbed *detached immanence.* With immanence we are closest to the appearance of foundationalism. Like pitons driven by the climber into a mountain face, details in the rhetoric of immanence are points of attachment where we experience such hands-on knowledge of the gritty cultural mass that we seem to feel the very quiddity of culture, the real.

We will have reason to climb mountains later, but perhaps first we should be empirical and look at atoms. The sense of immanental reality I indicate lies screened behind the scientist logic of high cultural criticism: the Whole Sick Crew (to allude to Pynchon's technovisionary fiction) of "highly charged phenomena," "atoms," "molecules," "microphysics," "microprocesses," "DNA molecules," "microbiological cells," "microbe-like operations," "small mutations," "little black boxes," and so forth (all phrases from our matrix). More generally, immanence is screened by a broadly empirical view of culture; and, if scientific idiom will not serve, then equally technical-sounding terminology must be invented—"micro-stories," for instance, or "multiple intellectual configurations," "a specific field for the exercise of cat power," "heuristic isolates." And this is not even to mention the massive traces of scientism in the more anthropological, sociological, statistical, or structuralist cultural criticisms.

What such an empirics projects is a view of cultural matter (economic, social, political, or ideological) so objective that materialism seems to obey the dynamics of literal matter. We can take as our explanatory paradigm the sometimes explicit conceit in cultural criticism that details are "atoms." Observe that our matrix of phrases repeatedly isolates "atoms," "tiniest, indivisible elements," "elementary particulars," "highly charged phenomena," and, ultimately, "molecules" akin to what Arthur O. Lovejoy's history of ideas called "unit ideas." Details, that is, are elementary particles engaged in an overall systemics of combination much like the molecularism for which Louis O. Mink once criticized Lovejoy.[27] But a discrimination is in order. As calibrated by such pervasive cultural-critical modifiers as *determinate* and *specific* ("deeply specific," Levinson says), elementary particularism is innocent of the fuzzy probabilities of current particle science. The Greek prefixes I earlier touched on are emblematic: cultural criticism remembers in the detail something like Democritan atomism as well as the geopolitical insularity of Greek city-states. The atom of detail is a classically hard, discrete unit. Or, put *neo*classically, the unit-detail analytic indicates the residual hold of Newtonian physics and of the emergent philosophy of Newton's age: Locke's program of elementary "ideas" and/ or social-contract individuals associating in compound aggregates. With associational mechanics in mind, indeed, we might reinforce that great pillar of materialism throughout cultural criticism: the "concrete." Phrases in our matrix such as "concretely situated," "the concrete, the material, and the particular," and "ordinary, retail, detailed, concrete" build a world that is exactly concrete: a cement aggregate of specific and determinate particularity.

Such unit-detail atomism is ubiquitous, affecting even the most sophisticated interpreter whenever argument turns in the direction of empirical investigation. To come directly to the heart of the "matter," we need only foreground what our matrix of phrases has already enacted: the strangely overdetermined role of matrix forms throughout cultural criticism.[28] Matrices are the method's great aggregates of atomistic detail. To read at any length in cultural criticism, after all, is often precisely to read *at length*— an effect consisting not so much in the actual number of pages as in the wet-cement quality of the reading experience. Cultural criticism dilates discourse through interpolated arrays of particulars, a sort of *blason* of the mundane or what Rorty (inspired by a Philip Larkin poem) calls "lading lists" of the world.[29] Indeed, it is precisely the list form (or the simple matrix of one axis) that is most pervasive. Here is a short list of lists:

> *Darnton*: "The Italian motifs remained recognizable enough for one to be able to classify the tale in the Aarne-Thompson scheme (it is tale type 2032). But everything else about the story—its frame, figures of speech, allusions, style, and general feel—had become intensely Zuni."[30]

> *Geertz*: "Actually, the typing of cocks, which is extremely elaborate (I have collected more than twenty classes, certainly not a complete list), is not based on color alone, but on a series of independent, interacting, dimensions, which include—besides color—size, bone thickness, plumage, and temperament."[31]

> *Althusser*: "I shall call Ideological State Apparatuses [ISAs] a certain number of realities which present themselves to the immediate observer in the form of distinct and specialized institutions. I propose an empirical list of these which will obviously have to be examined in detail . . . the religious ISA . . . the educational ISA . . . the family ISA, the legal ISA, the political ISA."[32]

> *Lyotard*: "To paragraph is to write *And, And moreover, And nevertheless* . . . The differend is reintroduced [the elision is Lyotard's]."[33]

The science of the list may be stated: wholes are knowable only as aggregates in which the detail *has no interior detail*. Cultural-critical detail, that is, is as much a resistance to as an enactment of the more radical detailism of fractal and chaos theory in postmodern science proper. It is clear that the particulars gathered by Darnton and Geertz, for example, have no visible interior detail—no more so than the *"And, And moreover, And nevertheless"* in Lyotard's great work of/about lists (what he terms phrases "linked" in disconnection by their "differends"). "Frame, figures of speech," "size, bone thickness," and, and, . . . , exist at that lower event horizon known to all empirical investigators of culture where evidentiary authority must at last rest on sketchy, borrowed, or otherwise uncooked "facts" collected without linkage in a notebook.[34] At that event horizon, there is no substantive difference between traditional empiricists and such outré "scientists" of culture as structural anthropologists or structural Marxists. Structure itself reduces to lists. However much Althusser's overall theory is structural, for example, it is evident that his "empirical list" in "Ideology and Ideological State Apparatuses" cements rough-hewn institutions en bloc in an essentially aggregate social whole. Similarly, the few details he does offer about the internal practices of religious and educational institutions accrue in an essentially mechanistic manner. "Apparatus," we may say, is the bureaucratization of the Lockean aggregate. "Thus Schools and Churches use suitable methods of punishment, expulsion, selection, etc.," Althusser says at one point, checking off the particulars of superstructure on a lading list of undetailed details punctuated by an *etc.*[35]

And with this *etc.* we come to the heart of the matter: the strange interface where the science of the list reveals its rhetoricity and, indexed by rhetoricity, its historicity. Seen one way, after all, the science of lists depends on a convention of figuration rather than of induction: a syntagmatics or metonymics whose illusion is that wholes are polymers of parts. What makes such figuration visible is an interior instability where saying one thing—in this case, listing atoms—suddenly seems equivalent to saying something else. What else does high cultural criticism have to say in the very act of reciting lists as if syntagm were its only discourse?

It has a lot to say, namely *etc.* One of Althusser's most characteristic devices, we recognize, is the *etc.* in alliance with such cognates as the elision (". . ."). The very subtitle of the "Ideological State Apparatuses" essay is an implicit elision: "Notes towards an Investigation." So too review in our list of lists Geertz's "certainly not a complete list" or Lyotard's ". . . ." In every cultural critic, I hazard, there is an essential *et cetera* or similar stigma of incompletion far in excess of the margin-of-error requirements of normal science. What is the thought behind the *et* or troubled Lyotardian *and* haunting cultural criticism? The antifoundational answer, of course, is that there is no thought: thought, logic, grounded Newtonian science ends. Once we walk off the plank of serial evidence into seas of *etc.*, there can be heard only cultural-critical topoi of inexpressibility, vain apologies, elegiac or whimsical plays on incompletion, and other such recognitions that the science of the atomistic list was all along rhetorical.[36]

Etc., I suggest, is a *trope* of inexpressibility that introduces within atomism a rhetoric-within-rhetoric. Besides metonymy, after all, there is also that variant, more expansive play on particulars: synecdoche. It is synecdoche that redeems the *etc.* from the wasteland of endless syntagm (which some cultural criticisms also call *consumerism*) by transforming incompletion into the figure of fulfillment: a symbolics or iconic metaphorics putting the part *for* the cultural whole.[37] I refer to the implicit rhetorical turn heard in such phrases from our matrix as "some fragment of a lost life," "my vision is necessarily more fragmentary," or "the fragments, the incommensurable levels, the heterogeneous impulses." Such rhetoric clearly confesses incompletion, but, at last, also the unmistakable sign of synecdoche. Fragments, after all, are by definition not particles (which exist whether or not they join in a larger unit); they can only be parts of a whole. A phrase such as "some fragment of a lost life" thus implies by its genitive construction that "lost life" is not really lost, that despite its discontinuity with the lost life-world "some fragment" can be discovered to be part "of" the lost world and, thus, to be big with wholeness. Not a scientific method in which limits of error bracket literal incompletenesses, then (or, more recently, in which incompletely known "butterfly effects" wander a local-chaos universe of patterned error), but the kind of *etc.* by which Everyman in his very partialness once figured the whole body politic or cosmos. The fragmentary atomism of cultural-critical detail harbors a huge error or trope: *microcosm* in the old sense.[38]

Or, rather, the detail is big with a slightly more recent rhetoric of microcosm—with the rhetoric of parts become wholes, indeed, that originally arose to combat Lockean systemics. Here, I advance the historical complement to rhetorical analysis. The moment of immanence is "first" in cultural criticism, as I have said, not because it is a priori, but because it initiates an embedded historical sequence of rhetorics. It would be possible, for example, to refer postmodern cultural criticism at this point to modernist aesthetics. The "ontological particularity" or "iconics" that John Crowe Ransom argued in notably scientistic style is apropos, as are the discrete literary "devices" that the Russian Formalists observed with even more quasi-engineered precision.[39] Or, to vary on the other prescriptives of close reading, it is now culture that is ambiguous and paradoxical in its tense complexity of particularity, its texture of "local irrelevance." It is culture that should, not mean, but—with all the ontological zing of the real—be. Thus arises our new concrete universal: the *cultural* rather than the verbal icon. But, instead of bringing us back to the regime of T. S. Eliot's fragments shored against ruin, I will here drink deeply from the source. Let me refer postmodern cultural criticism to the movement that modernist aesthetics itself—together with such coevals as Deweyan philosophy—so aggressively sublated: romanticism. Cultural criticism is "first" of all an allusion to the moment when the rhetoric of empiricism confronted the early regime of the fragment: an emerging romantic rhetoric.

Witness, therefore, the broad, deep, and explicit remembrance of high romanticism—both literary and philosophical—in high postmodern cultural criticism. Without exaggeration, it can be said that romanticism is the most common ancestor of the various cultural criticisms: more basic, more shared than such polemically charged and relatively recent parent figures as Marx, Nietzsche, Dewey, Braudel, or Malinowski. Romanticism, as it were, is the grandparent or grand-muse: a grand-matrix of thought that, precisely because it is more distanced from current struggles for and against Marx, Nietzsche, Dewey, etc., indulges the most uncritical statements. A first evidence consists in such unabashed allusions in our matrix as "minute particulars," "grains of sand in which the world may be seen," "minute particulars of time, place, and circumstance," and (in imitation of Wordsworth's spots of time) "phenomenal spots of history." But the evidence runs deeper than spot allusions. There is a whole subgenre in cultural criticism of sustained and egregiously adventitious uses of romanticism, gorgeous insets of romantic consciousness so well wrought, so self-sustaining, that we wonder whether cultural criticism is at last something like Keats's Grecian urn: a mere fretwork of culture (some "little town by river or sea shore . . . emptied of [its] folk") silhouetted against an ideal ground.[40]

A prime example is the New Historicism, whose frequent dependence on assumptions of romanticism and nineteenth-century historicism I discussed earlier in this book. In its many invocations of Hegelian "dialectic" together with its master/servant or "containment/subversion" analytic of power, for instance, Renaissance New Historicism is big with *Geist*.[41] Greenblatt's massively antithetical notion of Renaissance self-fashioning could thus be mapped directly over a previous, celebrated work about self-fashioning: Hartman's *Wordsworth's Poetry*.[42] But it is in romantics New Historicism that romanticism redux is most brazen. McGann's *Social Values and Poetic Acts*, for example, is an exhilaratingly polymorphous, hetero-cosmic, or—Americanizing the prefix—coon-curious work that chases the argument of cultural detailism through many fields of inquiry. Two fields, however, stand out: romantic literature and postmodernism. Whether these two are polymorphs or isomorphs is open to question: there is a strong presumption throughout the book that Blakean, Byronic, and other aspects of romanticism simply *are* postmodern. "Insofar as works like [Blake's] *Songs* and *Marriage* are nonnarratives which do not involve themselves in forms of atonement," McGann can thus say, "they resemble various kinds of poststructural discourse, in particular the work now commonly known as L=A=N=G=U=A=G=E Writing."[43] My own book on Wordsworth, I am compelled to add, is a sustained project of detailism that jumps implicitly (and, at times, explicitly) between the particulars of the French Revolution period and our postmodern sense of a differential, fractured, refugee culture. Or, again, there is David Simpson's *Wordsworth's Historical Imagination*, whose attack on totalizing theory in favor of minute particularity parallels Wordsworth's own cultural-linguistic attack on "gaudiness and inane phraseology" in defense of the "language really used by men."[44]

Similarly, romanticism exerts an inordinate influence on the against-theory variant of the New Pragmatism that arose in tandem with the other postmodern cultural criticisms. It is intriguing, for instance, to consider the infamous set piece at the center of Steven Knapp and Walter Benn Michaels's "Against Theory."[45] When that Lucy poem by Words-worth ("A Slumber Did My Spirit Seal") washes up on the beach as if by natural process without "intention," we are certainly being instructed in the manner of the philosophical traditions succeeding original prag-matism: analytic philosophy and its strong revision, "ordinary-language" philosophy. Compensating for a bluntly denotative style with loony, pure thought-experiment examples ("The universe has expanded to twice its original size this night," "Suppose that in a distant galaxy there is the twin of our earth," "1227 is a rhombus," "Caesar is a prime number," "Should unusual, brilliant patterns suddenly appear in the sky—even if they took the form of letters which seemed to compose a sentence . . ."), analytic and ordinary-language philosophy formed the New Pragmatism in its image.[46] Plain, blunt, and trenchant to the point of exaggeration, New Pragmatist discourse in its against-theory personality also favors pure examples—par-adigms so denotatively complex but connotatively insensitive that they re-semble Rube Goldberg contraptions. "Suppose that you're walking along a beach and you come upon a curious sequence of squiggles in the sand," Knapp and Michaels begin. They then set up their contraption: "You step back a few paces and notice that they spell out the following words: 'A slumber did my spirit seal. . . .'"[47]

But, if we attend to the undertow of allusion, we will recognize that the contraption washes up on a berm of romanticism. Surely, after all, we are in the wake of Wordsworth's *Lyrical Ballads* with its original "ordinary language."[48] Surely (to allude to *The Prelude*) we stand by some glimmering lake where a boy halts his owl songs to feel with shock the "voice" and "im-agery" of the landscape sinking "unawares into his mind."[49] Or, again, to invoke "The Sensitive-Plant," we pause by some Shelleyan ocean "whose waves never mark, though they ever impress / The light sand which paves it—Consciousness."[50] What hidden romantic current, after all, washes a Lucy poem onto Knapp and Michaels's shifting sands of antifoundation-alism?[51] Further considerations: Knapp and Michaels's full thesis is that the notion of an unauthored and intentionless Lucy poem is absurd. In-tentionality is innately part of what we mean by texts because we would not otherwise perceive textuality in the first place (only "squiggles" in the sand). Is innately intentional textuality therefore the same as romantic nature, every part of which—whether a Lucy-poem landscape or squiggles of "little lines / Of sportive wood run wild"[52]—is an inscription signing some fulfillment (or tragedy) of romantic intention (i.e., "mind," "imagination")? Or, again, when Knapp and Michaels state that "the meaning of a text is simply identical to the author's intended meaning" such that "the project of *grounding* meaning in intention becomes incoherent," what does *simple* mean?[53] Does the standard New Pragmatist argument by dismissal (of the sort: "It simply *is* this way," "Nothing interesting can be said; they just *are* that way") mean that the premise of authorial intention is so natural that it could be an appendix to that romantic theory of simplicity: the Preface to *Lyrical Ballads*? (Wordsworth on intention: rustic existence is paradigmatic because "in that condition of life our elementary feelings co-exist in a state of greater simplicity" and because rustics "convey their feelings and notions in simple and unelaborated expressions.")[54] Is intention, in sum, as "simple" as Lucy, whatever Wordsworth intended by that name?[55]

But perhaps I make too much of Wordsworth, the original against-theorist (or, as James K. Chandler conceives it, Burkean ideologue-against-ideology), in Knapp and Michaels's essay.[56] The full significance of such romantic vignettes set within New Pragmatist discourse comes to view only when we peruse the broad wash effects of romanticism in an extended corpus of cultural criticism such as Richard Rorty's (and, in the background, John Dewey's and William James's).[57] There are Rorty's direct quotations and allusions, for example: "something far more deeply interfused," "murder to dissect," "negative capability," "clerisy of the nation," "create the taste by which he will be judged," "I must Create a System, or be enslav'd by another Man's," and so forth.[58] (Dewey: "The 'magic' of poetry—and pregnant experience has poetical quality—is precisely the revelation of meaning in the old effected by its presentation through the new. It radiates the light that never was on land and sea." James: "As Wordsworth says, 'thought is not; in enjoyment it expires.'")[59] And there is Rorty's consistent use of *romantic* as a period concept designed at once to instruct philosophy in the imaginative groundlessness of romantic world making and to criticize the too-idealist goal of the original romantic world makers. Particularly dependent on the romantic period concept are essays such as "Professionalized Philosophy," "Idealism and Textualism," and the "Contingency" series. To make a collage:

> Let me call "romanticism" the thesis that what is most important for
> human life is not what propositions we believe but what vocabulary we

use. . . . Not until the Romantics did books become so various as to create readers who see what has been written as having no containing frame-work. . . . Since the Romantics, we have been helped most of all by the poets, the novelists, and the ideologues. . . . The *Phenomenology of Spirit* taught us to see not only the history of philosophy, but that of Europe, as portions of a *Bildungsroman*. . . . What survived from the disappearance of metaphysical idealism as a scientific, arguable thesis was, simply, romanti-cism. . . . Romanticism was *aufgehoben* in pragmatism. . . . The important philosophers of our own century are those who have tried to follow through on the Romantic poets.[60]

It is not coincidental that one of Rorty's heroes of "postphilosophical" culture is Harold Bloom.[61] Romanticism is Rorty's archetype for a uni-verse in which the ground is stable only between world-expunging and world-making swerves.

Finally, I invoke just one other side of high postmodern cultural criti-cism: French postmodern/pragmatist theory as represented, for example, by Lyotard's *The Differend*.[62] *The Differend* is emphatically a work of cultural criticism not only because it draws its semiotics from the "pragmatics" tra-dition launched by C. S. Peirce, G. H. Mead, and Charles Morris, but also because it sets its finally *post*semiotic world of splintered phrase universes on a primal scene of (post)culture: Auschwitz.[63] Auschwitz—and, since this remains an ineluctably French work, secondarily the terror of the French Revolution—is where old philosophers come to dispute their final truth solutions: epistemological, metaphysical, even syntactic "realities." Is there a speakable and verifiable truth communicable between phrase universes? How can there be such linkage if some final solutions silence an entire class of speakers, an entire testament of phrases? In truth, did the Final Solution, did Auschwitz really happen?[64] Philosophers come to offer their judgments. And two of the philosophers who walk most largely are Kant and Hegel. Tutelary geniuses of some of Lyotard's most sustained "Notices," Kant and Hegel are the bookends of Enlightenment and ro-manticism between which the differend is the book burning. The differ-end is a "feeling" for the unspeakability of any truth about final solutions, a noncognitive reaching after unspeakable words, a silent grasping for . . . As Lyotard says immediately after his third Kant Notice: "Is this the sense in which we are not modern? Incommensurability, heterogeneity, the dif-ferend, the persistence of proper names, the absence of a supreme tribu-nal? Or, on the other hand, is this the continuation of romanticism, the nostalgia that accompanies the retreat of . . . , etc.?" (Lyotard's elision).[65]

More such fragments of romanticism could be gathered. Cultural criticism's pragmatics of "everyday" or ordinary experience, for example, is, in part, certifiably romantic. So too there is romanticism in the dialogics of cultural criticism: the view that culture is no more than a series of conversational improvisations, stories, or *petits récits*. The ordinary and the storied, after all, are the heartland of *Lyrical Ballads*. But perhaps our fragments already limn the whole. To view cultural-critical atomism in historical perspective is to discover precisely what I earlier called an *iconic metaphorics*, or, to use the romantic rather than modernist concept, the symbol. As Coleridge might phrase it, cultural-critical detail is the part through which the whole shines translucently.[66] Thus, listen again to the unmistakable allusions in our matrix: "minute particulars," "grains of sand in which the world may be seen," "minute particulars of time, place, and circumstance," and "phenomenal spots of history."

Or we might look from the grain of sand to the parallel Blakean symbolics of inverted space—of "vortexes," "ordered spaces," or visionary "Globules of Man's blood" each of which expands into a whole cosmos when viewed from inside. Cultural criticism remembers the process of microworld making by which children sporting on the shore, the boy in the boat, the gibbet mast, and so on once created phenomenally entire universes *within* the local or regional. I underscore here an aspect of high cultural criticism so sustained and colorful that, in all likelihood, it will be the method's most anthologized element, its "best" work. Cultural criticism's best is its passion for constructing microworlds each as intricately detailed, yet also as expansive in mythic possibility (*bubble universes*, I called them in the introduction to this book), as a Wordsworthian Lakeland, a Blakean ordered space, a Keatsian Grecian urn, or—to cite a modern but deeply romantic analogue—Faulkner's Yoknapatawpha County. When we sift the richly worked anecdotes of the New Historicism (e.g., any of Greenblatt's or Mullaney's inaugural paradigms); when we caress the even more lovingly reconstructed microworlds of the New Cultural History (the universes of heretic millers, false Martin Guerres, cat-killing apprentices, or Le Roy Ladurie's Pays d'Oc); when we regard the intricately meditated Cashinahua "Notice" and other vignettes of philosophy-as-life in Lyotard's *Differend*; and when we enjoy the New Pragmatism's comically inventive alternate universes done up in analytic-philosophy fashion (worlds in which poems wash up on beaches complete with submarines in the distance, Rorty's neo-Swiftian society of Antipodeans)[67]—in sum, when we read any of these miraculously sustained bubbles of re-created or created context, we are for a moment again a child shaking one of those globed, water-filled landscapes filled with miniature snowflakes. The flakes of detail fall into place, and we are charmed by both their slow suspense and the crystal clarity of the scene when all has settled into mock reality. Or, to magnify the miniature, this is what Jean Baudrillard calls "our only architecture today: great screens on which are reflected atoms, particles, molecules in motion. Not a public scene or true public space but gigantic spaces of circulation, ventilation and ephemeral connections."[68]

In the picture of great detail, in sum, the local threatens to go transcendental: detailism becomes what Baudrillard calls "molecular transcendence," the "idealism of the molecule."[69] Cultural critics, we note, recognize this witching moment of local transcendence in their works. In some of their most meditative passages, they pause on the threshold of transcendence aware that Keatsian magic casements of detail are about to open on a foam of perilous seas, in faery lands forlorn. In this moment ("Forlorn! the very word is like a bell / To toll [them] back . . ."),[70] they become critics of cultural criticism. Only so does their *critical* sense survive, in a self-reflexive rather than a social gaze. Marcus thus observes reflexively in the epilogue to her fine book on topical or local reading, *Puzzling Shakespeare*: "The project for localization sets itself resolutely against the general and the universal, but has its own ways of creating generalities, leaping over difference in order to construct an alternative order of 'essences' out of the materials of history." And again: "Generating a plenitude of particulars is not the same as appealing to a realm of ultimate truths, yet there may be important ways in which the two activities are functionally similar."[71] Greenblatt inquires: "But what if we refuse the lure of a totalizing vision? The alternative frequently proposed is a relativism that refuses to privilege one narrative over another, that celebrates the uniqueness of each cultural moment. But this stance—akin to congratulating both the real and the pretended Martin Guerre for their superb performances—is not, I think, either promising or realistic. For thorough-going relativism has a curious resemblance to the universalizing that it proposes to displace."[72] Foucault adds: "Is it not perhaps the case that these fragments of genealogies are no sooner brought to light . . . than they run the risk of re-codification, re-colonisation [within unitary discourses]? . . . And if we want to protect these only lately liberated fragments are we not in danger of ourselves constructing, with our own hands, that unitary discourse. . . ?"[73] And I have accused myself: "There is the faintest unmistakable taint of transcendence about your whole project."[74]

Now we can take a page from Schor's *Reading in Detail*. The "threshold" of transcendence on which high cultural criticism pauses is the sublime. In a series of chapters tracing the tradition of detailism from Sir Joshua Reynolds through Hegel, Freud, Barthes (and others), Schor comes to the crucial insight that detailism overthrew neoclassical generalization to dominate in the age of romanticism and the realistic novel only because it was made subservient to the aesthetics of sublimity.[75] The spot-of-time detail was a help (and, in Schor's gender argument, a helpmeet) to transcendence. It is our own modernist and poststructuralist age, she argues, that at last "desublimates" the "detail ideal."[76] Addressed specifically to the postmodern, my own argument diverges in a direction suggested by Lyotard's essay "Answering the Question: What Is Postmodernism?" Lyotard argues: "Modern aesthetics is an aesthetic of the sublime, though a nostalgic one. . . . The postmodern would be that which, in the modern . . . searches for new presentations . . . in order to impart a stronger sense of the [sublimely] unpresentable."[77] Postmodernism, that is, re-presents modernism but is continuous with it and its romantic predecessor: the moment of sublimity is there at the root.

If Thomas Weiskel were writing now, perhaps, he would enroll cultural criticism alongside structuralism and psychoanalysis in *The Romantic Sublime* (1976). The *etc.* of cultural-critical detail is, at base, emphatically sublime. Cultural criticism looks out on perilous seas of detail but—blocked from any overview by its casement view or local perspectivism—experiences a crisis of incompletion, of significance drowned in insignificance. The details are so many details. Only the reactive phase of the romantic sublime (specifically, Kant's "mathematical sublime") can intervene: insignificance becomes the trope of transcendental meaning.[78] By this trope, the least detail points to total understanding; as we say, history is in the details. Culture, that is, can be understood in its totality only if we believe that our inability to understand totality *is* the total truth.

And, with this copular *is*, we at last come to the real. The real in cultural criticism is indistinguishable from figure. How else could we understand what *is* by what *is not* except by synecdoche, metaphor, or symbol so extreme that it is catachresis? To change our own figure from perilous seas to high sierras: when we face the massif of detail piled up by high cultural criticism, we at last truly climb mountains. We end on some cloud-wrapped Snowdon or nimbus-noumenon where any visible detail—say the way a rift in the clouds sublimes all the underlying voices of the world—marks the threshold of the visionary.[79] The visionary *is* the real.

Or perhaps *visionary* and *transcendental* are too otherworldly to map cultural criticism, which, while it eschews foundational ground, makes its home, not in the abyss of seas or the inverted abyss of mountains (the two sublime bounds of Braudel's precedent-setting work of detailism, *The Mediterranean and the Mediterranean World*), but on the firm terra cognita of the great coastal plains of civilization. Let us say instead, therefore, that the objectivist and scientistic discourse of cultural criticism at last sublimes into immanence. Immanence is transcendence sunk in the mundane. It is what Dewey, in his modern anticipation, meant when he said: "Modern life involves the deification of the here and the now; of the specific, the particular, the unique, that which happens once and has no measure of value save such as it brings with itself. Such deification is monstrous fetishism, unless the deity be there; unless the universal lives, moves, and has its being in experience as individualized."[80]

To complete this picture of great detail, we need now only rename the atom so as to restore the discourse of scientism and immanence to the sphere of culture proper. Other names in high cultural criticism for the atom are *individual* and *community*—the progressively enlarged horizons of local detail.

What is the subject, that vexed unit of identity in cultural criticism? In one view, it is the immanental individual: the individual who fends off totalism in de Certeau's *The Practice of Everyday Life* and that Lentricchia in his "The Return of William James" calls "the particular, the local, the secret self," the "*isolatos* . . . at the frontier."[81] In its reverence for detail, I suggest, cultural criticism reveals a hidden agenda of Western individualism not clearly distinguished from what Lentricchia recalls to us in his essay on James: an original-pragmatist nostalgia for the colonial or nineteenth-century frontiersman of can-do sufficiency. Such is true also of all the more or less Marxist authors in our matrix. It may be said about the materialist side of the New Historicism, for example, that detailism is, in part, a sustained allegory for individualism: when we subscribe to "the concrete, the material, and the particular" or "the particular and particularly constrained," we are really rewriting the biography of what old-line Marxism made taboo: individualities behaving with all the relative autonomy of "real" people in the ideal Western democracy. People, as it were, are personified details.

The highest stakes involved in mapping the atomistic detail over the individual then appear if we enlarge our horizons to "community." Here I refer to what may be the single most promising, if also problematic, front of cultural criticism: its exploration of the communally *parochial, local,* and *regional.* These latter terms, which crisscross our matrix, herald worlds of research.[82] Marcus's and Helgerson's works about localism, for instance, Bourdieu's project of the habitus, or Geertz's essays on local knowledge focus localism as the underexplored zone between the discretely individual and the massively collective. But localism is assuredly also problematic. We can witness such phrases from our matrix as "the experience of particular communities," "individual autonomy . . . communal autonomy," "a reader situated in a particular social space," or "daily life in a particular community." By defining hyperdiscrete communities that behave as if they were particular individuals, these phrases indicate what sometimes seems a too-resistless mapping of the person concept *over* localism.[83] The regional community functions as if it were a solidarity of one, as if, in other words, it were immanent with identity.

Perhaps the boldest in this regard is the branch of high postmodern cultural criticism that has made the most of the local-community concept for theoretical (or, rather, *anti*theoretical) purposes: the New Pragmatism. Whether we consider Rorty's idolization of local context—especially his aggrandizement of the "liberal community"—or Fish's "interpretive communities," *we* (using the pronoun enactively here) sense what is, perhaps, an entirely too-comfortable sense of solidarity signed by the heavy-handed pronouns of the method: characteristically, *we* and *us* versus *they* and *them* (sometimes *I* and *me* vs. *you*). Witness the following statement by Rorty: "The point of these examples is that *our* sense of solidarity is strongest when those with whom solidarity is expressed are thought of as 'one of us,' where 'us' means something smaller and more local than the human race. That is why 'because she is a human being' is a weak, unconvincing explanation of a generous action" (emphasis added).[84] What seemingly universal solidarity authorizes the *our* (outside quotation marks) that, in a secondary operation, then thinks about the smaller and more local "us" or "she" (inside quotation marks)?[85] Or, again, from Fish: "The only 'proof' of membership is fellowship, the nod of recognition from someone in the same community, someone who says to you what neither of us could ever prove to a third party: 'we know.' I say it to you now, knowing full well that you will agree with me (that is, understand) only if you already agree with me."[86] My question to you: Who is the generalizable *I* or *me* here in this solidaristic *we*-community of *I*'s? Is Fish (or anyone), after all, always the same?

The problem of change aside, even the most instantiated context for a community of fellowship—e.g., a lecture hall in 1989–90 in which a professor delivers this essay as a paper before an audience of other professors and graduate students—poses a problem of infinite regress in the determination of the *I*. For what is the protocol that confers membership on the speaker-in-this-community such that the various competing aspects of his relevant identity (e.g., teacher, student, specialist, generalist, administrator in charge of telling some graduate students they do not belong in the professional community) agree to speak as a proper "member," a suitably consistent *I*? And this is not even to mention the outposts of relevant identity (e.g., not just professional but also son, parent, spouse, voter, taxpayer, American, man, etc.) that always, for better or worse, inform one's focal roles with deeper, broader, but also conflicting knowledge? The heart of the problem, of course, is that there are very few contexts of interest in which the local community provides enough external signals ("nods" from the audience) to govern the relationship of a self's "selves" without uncertainty or anxiety. Indeed, the most urgent contexts motivating the invocation of such adjudicating principles as *interpretive community* in the first place are precisely those that do *not* offer pure, strong, or harmonic signals—as in the case of contradictions between the roles of teacher and administrator, teacher and taxpayer, teacher and consumer, or teacher and American. It would thus seem that the *I* that gestures its membership in Fish's interpretive community requires for its constitution the supplement of an internal interpretive community—a mental scene in which its selves nod to *each other* in a fellowship governed by an internally imagined or memorial context. Of course, to take the regress much further (what, after all, defines each of the self's interior selves?) would stretch this kind of analysis—and perhaps any kind of analysis—beyond what it is designed to do. The main point is that a local-community concept that takes us back only *one* step of the regress to an elemental *I* void of internal distinction has the felt effect of being immanental, foundational. Tied notionally to an undifferentiated *I*, the interpretive community appears to act as if it were itself a person concept.[87]

In the New Pragmatism, in sum, and to varying degrees in all the cultural criticisms, there resides a deeply troubled us-versus-them problem that is not resolved by the bare recognition that the interpretive community of us *does* confront them. The very denomination or pronomination of an *us* (and an *I*) by which to make statements about us and them is the blindness of cultural criticism's insight. It leaves in darkness all that is truly of moment about the us-versus-them, self-versus-other, problem: the procedures of emigration/immigration, border inspection/recognition, confrontation/negotiation, and, ultimately, terror/desire creating an us *from* them. What assures us, after all, that the local, regional, or parochial community we study *is* a community—or collective unity—in the first place?[88] Nothing but a direct mapping of the *isolatos* concept over community (in a spirit directly contrary to Lentricchia's intention in "The Return of William James" to challenge imperialist appropriations of world identity). And the possibilities for then multiplying such implicitly imperialist mappings by creating even larger communities such as *nation* or *world* are fearsome.

The detail, we might say, is as small as Napoleon.[89]

Release 2.0

> The mistress gave the order, enjoining the boys above all to avoid frightening her
> *grise*. Gleefully Jerome and Léveillé set to work, aided by the journeymen. Armed with
> broom handles, bars of the press, and other tools of their trade, they went after every
> cat they could find, beginning with *la grise*. Léveillé smashed its spine with an iron
> bar and Jerome finished it off. Then they stashed it in a gutter while the journeymen
> drove the other cats across the rooftops, bludgeoning every one within reach and
> trapping those who tried to escape in strategically placed sacks. . . . Roused by gales
> of laughter, the mistress arrived. She let out a shriek as soon as she saw a bloody cat
> dangling from a noose. Then she realized it might be *la grise*. Certainly not, the men
> assured her: they had too much respect for the house to do such a thing.
>
> **Robert Darnton, *The Great Cat Massacre* (1984)**

> Pain is nonlinguistic: It is what we human beings have that ties us to the
> nonlanguage-using beasts. So victims of cruelty, people who are suffering, do not
> have much in the way of a language. That is why there is no such thing as the "voice
> of the oppressed" or the "language of the victims." The language the victims once
> used is not working anymore, and they are suffering too much to put new words to-
> gether. So the job of putting their situation into language is going to have to be done
> for them by somebody else. The liberal novelist, poet, or journalist is good at that.
>
> **Richard Rorty, *Contingency, Irony, and Solidarity* (1989)**

> You are informed that human beings endowed with language were placed in a
> situation such that none of them is now able to tell about it. Most of them disap-
> peared then, and the survivors rarely speak about it. When they do speak about it,
> their testimony bears only upon a minute part of this situation. How can you know
> that the situation itself existed? . . . "I have analyzed thousands of documents. I have
> tirelessly pursued specialists and historians with my questions. I have tried in vain to
> find a single former deportee capable of proving to me that he had really seen, with
> his own eyes, a gas chamber."
>
> **Jean-François Lyotard, *The Differend* (1983)**

*In Robert Darnton's essay "The Great Cat Massacre," the most disturbing de-
tail is the killing of the* grise, *the favorite cat of the master printer's wife. We
hear in our inner ear the brittle, wet breaking of the grey's spine as the iron bar,
wielded by a subversive apprentice, descends. We see in our inner eye the con-
vulsions of the beast as an accomplice finishes the deed. But that is not what is
finally disturbing—what stays with us in mind as well as in the viscera. What
lingers is the facility with which a victim of violence becomes a symbol. Darnton
comments: "Cats as symbols conjured up sex as well as violence, a combination*

perfectly suited for an attack on the mistress. The narrative identified her with la grise, *her* chatte *favorite. In killing it, the boys struck at her.*"[90]

Raised to the meta-level, such ease of symbolization is the hallmark of the New Cultural History itself. Darnton—among the best of the New Cultural Historians specializing in "symbolic" analysis—deploys his bloody story to construct our most potent postmodern symbolism: cultural representation. Cultural representation or social drama is figuration interpreted according to the preferred metanarrative of high cultural criticism: neither the tale of liberation, nor that of philosophical integration (the two metanarratives addressed in Lyotard's Postmodern Condition*), but, instead, the great, arrested story—its climax suspended in perpetual agon—of subversion/containment. From his opening historical anecdote on, in other words, Darnton on cats is akin to Greenblatt, Mullaney, Montrose, and other New Historicists whose paradigms dramatize the world as all a representation of struggle between subversives and dominants.*[91]

But what happened to the body of the grey? To the irreducible facticity and uniqueness of the beast? For the purposes of representing subversion versus containment, the grise *must be disappeared. A particular cat's agony, after all, is insignificant compared to what we can make it stand for. Let such agony represent an entire agon of class strife, partisan battle, the differential struggle of local context versus local context. Never mind that a cat's back must be broken to create the fulcrum point of the* versus *itself. The cat has no language. It is not a survivor. Let the liberal intellectual, writing past scenes of strife as a simulacrum of praxis, speak for it.*

Toward a Practiced Detachment: A Prospective Conclusion

When high postmodern cultural critics sing the detail, I have argued, they rehearse a rhetoric of immanental reality descended most famously from romanticism. But that is not all there is to the romance of contextualism.

There is also the *rhetoric of commitment* to detail. Commitment is not neutral attachment to reality but partisan attachment to one side or the other in the existential combat, the essential *binarism*, of culture—of culture, that is, conceived as local us versus them and, within any us, as less versus more powerful subcultures.[92] Or, more fully (since not all cultural critics express political sympathy with one side or the other), high postmodern cultural criticism is committed to the antitotalistic vision of culture as the *or* or *versus* of struggle itself. For high cultural critics, that is, culture is a tragedy, an eternal agon. Details are the supporting cast. The bodies of detail—Darnton's cats among them—pile up in the theater of catfights, cockfights, treason trials, executions, razings, plagues, rebellions, revolutions, Terrors, and so on. Yet, however high the pile, such details evidencing the agony of the dominated versus the dominating remain strangely faceless, anonymous. They are never more than throwaway markers, representations, symbols of a contest enacted in the *name* of detail but greater than any particular detail. While high cultural critics may commit themselves to an agonist in the contest, in sum, the very facility with which they process interchangeable details argues their greater commitment to *struggle, resistance, opposition, subversion*, and *transgression* as abstract, perfect forms of contest.

The logic that issues from such commitment to the idea of contest is *practice*. Increasingly heard in high cultural criticism across all its denominations, practice is the analytic of culture as digital rather than atomic— as a field of zero versus one, dominated versus dominating. According to this logic, cultural contestants are essentially bits, and the function of bit people is to enact through myriad "microtactics" and "-techniques" of resistance what de Certeau calls "the practice of everyday life" and what Foucault, gazing reciprocally on repression, calls the practice of "power."

A question for high cultural criticism: What is the common denominator of *practice* as spoken on both sides of the Atlantic and across the political spectrum that makes the details of practice at once so fulsome and so faceless? Why does the very word *practice* at times seem so overdetermined—so overstrong, repetitive, and, at last, ritualistic that it threatens to become compulsory? And, in our post- or against-theory ambience, is there such a thing as a "resistance to practice" akin to the resistance to theory?

A further question that an extended version of this essay would need to ask: What *about* that moment of remove when the critic views the perfect form of cultural agony as if from across the proscenium? How is it that the detailed and practical battles of culture can finally seem as distantiated as little, regional wars glimpsed on the television screen or in a computer war game? If postmodern culture is agonic, in short, it is also ironic and aesthetic: commitment to a staged scene of resistance lasts until the show is over and the critic touches the control to bring up the next riveting *petit récit* on the cable. The rhetoric of commitment ends in the *rhetoric of detachment*. And the logic that this latter, ironic rhetoric makes possible is postmodern dialogism: the view that every set of cultural practices is, finally, just the outcome of a local vocabulary, perspective, or simulation whose conversational improvisations, little stories, "spatial stories," styles, and so on make culture—from the view of the ironist rather than those trapped in the simulation—all a detachable facade.[93] High cultural criticism, we may say vulgarly, is a culture-*spiel* as determinedly depthless in its play with representational surfaces, facades, screens, and media of all sorts as a vinyl LP handspun by a rap artist, that master of culture-*spiel* able to fragment long-play metanarrative into *petits récits*.

Cybernetic, televisionary, rhapsodic: such models of mediated and detached cultural experience could be multiplied. The array of surfaces that is the cultural matrix grows thick all about us, and it comforts more than it disturbs. Once we insulated ourselves from reality in universals and totalisms. Now we wrap ourselves in detailed layers of context as thick and multiform as cotton or Gibson's temperfoam. If I had to put my criticism of high postmodern cultural criticism in brief, it would come to this: context is not the same as culture. Context throws over the surface of culture an articulated grid, a way of speaking and thinking culture, that allows us to model the scenes of human experience with more felt significance— more reality, more practicality, more aesthetic impact—than appears anywhere but on the postmodern version of romantic nature: a screen.

Remembering the Spruce Goose

Historicism, Postmodernism, Romanticism

We enter the great, white dome and gather in the reception theater. Computer-coordinated slide projectors whir to life to tell us in a rapid montage of images and voices the Story. "A success story, a driving power, a dynamic tycoon, the envy of Wall Street, a world-record-breaking pilot, the toast of the nation: a man who could make things happen," the voices recite. "Who was this man? Howard Hughes. His mission: to build the world's largest airplane. . . ."

The story draws to a close; the screen rises slowly; we walk through the space of the screen to see—alone in its black, reflecting pool—the Plane. (figures 4.1–4.2)

Commonplaces

Whether we read Jean Baudrillard on Disneyland, Fredric Jameson on the Hotel Bonaventure, Jean-François Lyotard on the

Figure 4.1. Photograph of the Spruce Goose projected onscreen during the introductory slide show at the Long Beach Spruce Goose exhibit, 1992. (The screen rises into the ceiling at the end of the show to allow visitors to walk into the exhibition dome.) Photograph of screen: Alan Liu.

"Pacific Wall," or Paul Virilio on Howard Hughes, we know that southern California—more broadly, the North American Pacific Rim—has become the commonplace of the postmodern world.[1] Installed all along the arc that runs up from La Jolla through Anaheim, Hollywood, Silicon Valley, Bill Gates's or David Lynch's Washington State, to William Gibson's Vancouver are the topoi—small as a microchip or large as the LA sprawl—of the postmodern dystopia. This dystopia appears variously on phenomenal, psychosexual, socioeconomic, and other planes as the society of "simulation," "hyperreality," "hyperspace," "depthless surface," "cyborg couplings," "flexible accumulation," "schizophrenia," "speed," and so on. Perhaps most fabulously, it appears on the historical plane as "the end of history"—as the fabled new world order, that is, where the completion of history's work rewards us with a leisure of pure *representations* of history modeling the past (in Jameson's words) "as fashion-plate images that entertain no determinable ideological relationship to other moments of time."[2] Postmodern buildings thus wear facades of history, postmodern cities fill with gentrified "Old Townes" or retro malls, postmodern television goes Nick-at-Nite, and everywhere on the LA dial we hear oldies rock. As Baudrillard says in his 1985 essay "The Year 2000 Has Already Happened": "History itself is or was only an immense model of simulation."[3]

I wish here to install in the postmodern canon yet another Pacific Rim commonplace. But I do so to challenge the very theory of the commonplace that underlies postmodern thought. The theory is that at the center of popular culture there is a commonplace that once functioned as an agora (place of public assembly or marketplace) but that is now dysfunctional—that no longer grounds the truth difference between agora and allegory (from *allos* + *agoreuein*, "other than speaking openly as if in the agora") or between reality and hyperreality, that fractures the universality of ethical standards, that similarly scandalizes the generality of aesthetic criteria, and that at last revokes the very language pragmatics designed to negotiate agreement on (and between) truth, morality, and art claims. The village square of the global village, in short, has been emptied of the kind of founded, integral cognition—total cognition, we may say—that once made the *sensus communis* a closed circuit of the true, good, and beautiful. And so in the agora, where people once spoke the mutuality of their cognition and, hence, *recognized* each other, there remains only something other than total cognition.

Or, more precisely (and this is the particular trauma of postmodern theory), there remains an agonic contest between two forms of other-than-total-cognition. One, the antagonist, is the Weberian regime that

Figure 4.2. The Spruce Goose installed in the exhibition dome, Long Beach, California, July 1992. Photograph: Alan Liu.

Lyotard names "performativity" and Habermas the "colonization of the lifeworld": the modernizing regime, in other words, that, in the abeyance of total cognition, reifies just one faculty of cognition, the truth function, into an "instrumental rationality" capable of absorbing all other faculties into a bureaucratized, "expert" culture of specialized subsystems.[4] To vary on Max Weber's "iron cage" image: society becomes something like a computer motherboard on which dedicated ethics and aesthetics chips now serve the truth processor at the top of the instrumental hierarchy. The second form of other-than-total-cognition is then the tragic or sublime agonist of postmodern theory. This hero, as often mourned as celebrated, is the stubbornly noncognitive *and* noninstrumental aesthetics—a sort of survivor or guerrilla aesthetics—that Benjamin in his "Work of Art in the Age of Mechanical Reproduction" early on dubbed "reception in a state of distraction" and that postmodern theory has updated into a whole aesthetics of everyday distraction.[5] I refer to the microstylistics of sensation or feeling that so fascinates postmodern theory: Lyotard's "feeling" for the "unpresentable"; Deleuze and Guattari's "pure intensities"; Baudrillard's "ecstasy"; Haraway's "pleasure in the confusion of boundaries"; de Certeau's "almost invisible pleasures, little extras"; Jameson's "*boredom* as an aesthetic response," "'hysterical' sublime," video "panic"; and so on.[6]

The best we have to hope for, it seems, is to live in a gigantic, mindless commonplace—named *America* or *California*—that distracts us eternally from total cognition and its head administrator, performativity, through an aesthetics so mind-numbing (borrowing here from Susan Buck-Morss's "Aesthetics and Anesthetics") that it is precisely "*an*esthetic." "Eternally," I add, because the ultimate postmodern anesthetics is the rigorously mindless assertion—a sort of parody of Hegel's teleology of absolute knowledge—that history has ended and the feeling of distraction is for all time. Distraction, the simulation of historical contingency, is how we pass the time.

My suggestion in this essay is that we have been too quick to believe that total cognition has vanished totally and thus also too quick to make a triage choice between the two, consequent postures of postmodern theory: the one that looks to aesthetic distraction for resistance to the reification of instrumental rationality (the Lyotardian heresy) and the one that looks past aesthetics to a revenant *return* of total cognition (the Jamesonian and Habermasian piety). We have been too quick because the preoccupation of postmodern theory with the family quarrel between postmodernity and modernity has made it easy to forget a crucial fact about the "totality" in such concepts as "total cognition." The only totality there has ever been is history, where history (in the view I have espoused elsewhere) is understood as that which teaches by contingency that there has never been any such thing as *a* totality—universal, unified, stable—with enough bounded presence to be judged either totally here or not here.[7]

Imagine, then, that the postmodern commonplace is cannier, just plain smarter than we give it credit for because total cognition has never totally vanished but is still resident in a retrievable *history* of cognition. Imagine that within the state of distraction—that is, the state of an "everyday" consciousness suspended between the horizons of the collective and the individual, the necessary and the contingent, the mind and the body—there exists a whole archive of negotiations between rational, ethical, and aesthetic thought. Imagine in particular that the aesthetics of distraction is, thus, always also cognitive *traction*: an engagement of aesthetics *with* cognition capable on various occasions of drawing on all the permutations in the dialectical relation between sensation and thought that Terry Eagleton reminds us is the *history* of aesthetics.[8]

Imagine, if you will, the visit of a Wordsworth critic to the Disney-managed Spruce Goose installation in Long Beach, California, as it stood in the spring and summer of 1992 soon before it became history.

On our way to the plane, we are distracted by the exhibits scattered across the dome floor. Here is the original mock-up of the Spruce Goose cockpit, in which, the sign tells us, Hughes "spent more time . . . than in the actual . . . cockpit." Next is an "authentic Sherman tank" rolling out of a dummy version of the plane's front bay doors.

Let's sit and rest for a moment at the Hughes the Filmmaker exhibit, where the video shows clips from Hell's Angels *featuring Hughes's fleet of original World War I airplanes. And there's Jane Russell in a clip from* The Outlaw *showing off the breasts for which Hughes designed extra lift. (A woman near us laughs and walks away.)*

Finally, we are climbing the staircase that takes us over the reflecting pool to the Spruce Goose. They've cut a hole in the fuselage to let us in. Only, what we see when we enter is, not the full length of the interior, which extends back from where we stand a hundred feet or so to the tail, but, instead, a false-perspective mock-up of the interior going back only some fifty feet. There's even a miniature dummy of a crew member.

On our way to the exit through the gift shop, we notice that the plane is not alone in the pool. Exhibited on its own island is a 1939 Fleetwood Cadillac. The sign reads: "You are looking at a one-of-a-kind. This motoring legend was one of 27 produced . . . and is speculated to be the only one left in existence."

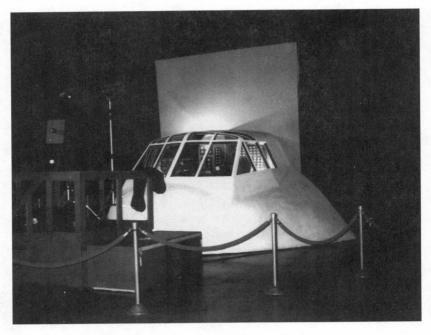

Figure 4.3. Mock-up of the Spruce Goose cockpit. Photograph: Alan Liu.

Also, we see the trees—real, natural trees—growing in pots. How do trees live in this dark dome shut away from the sun? (figures 4.3–4.6)

Exit Nature

We can best describe the postmodern agora installed at the Spruce Goose by adopting a socioeconomic analytic—one that, up to a point, will be predictable. Where Benjamin had his Arcades, we can say, LA had its Spruce Goose. The Spruce Goose, that is, structured the contemporary agora as an exemplary spectacle market of commodity logic. Or, rather, it structured a distracting transition between two such commodity logics, one the heartland of Benjaminian modernity and the other that of postmodern simulation.

Modernity, first of all. In Benjamin's terms, the Spruce Goose installation was a paradigm of the fetishism with which the age of mechanical reproduction transfigures auratic "originals" and "uniques" into equipment-assisted facsimiles. From the moment we walked *through* the space of the slide screen to see the original plane—the one and only Spruce Goose

Figure 4.4. Sherman tank emerging from mock-up of the Spruce Goose front bay doors. Photograph: Alan Liu.

Figure 4.5. Interior view of the Spruce Goose fuselage, looking toward the tail with false-perspective mock-up of the tail section (illuminated by lights) and half-scale dummy of crewman (near center of photograph). Photograph: Alan Liu.

Figure 4.6. 1939 Fleetwood Cadillac on display beside the Spruce Goose, mounted on pedestal in reflecting pool. Photograph: Alan Liu.

flown one time by the one and only Howard Hughes—all the dome's phantasmagoria of reproduction was foreseen: all its transference of aura from originals into images, mock-ups, models, and dummies, all its origami-ontology folding "authentic" Sherman tanks into trompe l'oeil bay doors, even the inexplicable insertion of a stage set–like replication within the body of the original. And, just in case we missed the modern in all this, the entirety of the phantasmagoria, of course, was mounted in a Disney-perfect ambience of modernity finished in excruciating detail with music, photographs, mementos, planes, cars, and other bric-a-brac from the period of that great, Fordist entrepreneur of speed and mass entertainment: Howard Hughes. In this context, indeed, Hughes's twin manias for airspeed and film production are equivalent registers of the need for reproduction. World-record speed was what allowed Hughes to reproduce himself as if instantly before cameras in New York and Paris, and film was what allowed him to change one instrument of reproduction, the airplane, for an even faster one, the camera itself.

Modernism (as opposed to modernity) was then the critical or utopian myth that arose to represent reproduction: "dreamwork" Benjamin calls the myth in his Arcades Project; a "dream" of progress, the Spruce Goose exhibits said instead. We note, however, that modernist myths of reproduction rest on a prior, foundational myth secreted within the notion of the original itself. The myth is "nature." Consider these two statements together:

> From Benjamin's artwork essay: "The concept of aura . . . may usefully be illustrated with reference to the aura of natural [objects]. . . . If, while resting on a summer afternoon, you follow with your eyes a mountain range on the horizon or a branch which casts its shadow over you, you experience the aura of those mountains, of that branch."[9]

> Voice-over in the video at the Hughes as Filmmaker exhibit: "Howard Hughes was a man of great natural talent, ability, and intelligence. . . . It was only natural that . . . Hughes would make a name for himself [in Hollywood]."

Whether reproduction is seen as the Fall or, instead, the *felix culpa* of originality, in other words, there *was* a primordial originality as real as nature. Or, at least, such originality could be fabricated.[10] For what is curious about such eminently modern artifacts as the Spruce Goose, we recognize, is that their authenticity depends on conflating the categories of the *natural original* (as it may be called) and the *manufactured original*. The result is that highly interesting, synthetic category (mock-heroicized by Duchamp's "Readymades") of the *found original*. Hughes, after all, had meant to build three prototypes of the Spruce Goose and, eventually, a working fleet. If the plane turned out to be uniquely original, therefore, such singularity has at best a found status akin to that of a hapax: authenticity derives only from the extinction or suppression of reproductions *contemporary* with originality.

But now we come to postmodern commodity logic. The crucial fact here, of course, is that the Spruce Goose installation was unable to let the modernist conflation of natural and manufactured originals alone. Rather, it worried at that seam of foundation so obsessively that it at last disclosed the fissure of postmodern hyperreality. Item: we notice that curious, *other* found original sharing the pool with the Spruce Goose, the one-of-a-kind 1939 Cadillac. Item: Hughes's originality was dogged throughout the exhibits by the specter of another, prior original, Charles Lindbergh. "In 1927," the sign at the Hughes and Aircraft exhibit proclaimed, "Charles Lindbergh completed a historic flight . . . launching the golden age of aviation. Hughes became caught up in the excitement of the age." Again, in the exhibit's video: "President Roosevelt himself presented the Harmon Trophy to Hughes, whose fame was now equal to Charles Lindbergh's."

And item: the entirety of the Spruce Goose installation competed with an even more massive singularity tied up at the same Long Beach dock, the Disney-run *Queen Mary* ocean liner with its homage to the identical era of modernity (complete with historical photographs, mementos, restored staterooms, etc.). At the Spruce Goose, in sum, the modern market of exchange between auratic originals and mechanical reproductions was overlaid by a gigantic double image: the ghost image of a whole, other market of exchange between *competing* originals each of which hollows out the authenticity of other originals and so exposes the unstable natural/manufactured basis of the whole system.[11]

Thus it is that we discover ourselves in the postmodern agora. This agora is not the scene of modernist alienation or (put spatially) "spacing" between originals and reproductions. Nor is it in any fully stable way the postmodern spacing *within* originality that alienates us from modernist myths of alienation themselves. Rather, the postmodern agora is what Jameson calls a cognitive "hyperspace" yawning open in strange, disorienting torsion *between* those two, primary spaces of alienation—a meta- or hyperspace in which, as Margaret Morse says in her study of the "ontology of everyday distraction" on freeways, malls, and television, we are profoundly "spaced out."[12] If modernity had witnessed the alienation of reproductions from their originals, after all, at least it had a compass bearing on those mythic originals by which to measure its own exile (i.e., if Hughes wasn't original, then Lindbergh or someone else must have been). Thus, modernism cut athwart all the old symmetries at a critical slant but—as emblematized in the bold diagonals of modernist graphic design (e.g., El Lissitzky or Jan Tschichold)—implied in that very slant its own grid of certitudes (e.g., the "grid" principle of layout design within which diagonals worked their precise transgressions).[13] The critical slant that made a manifesto out of alienation became the mark of avant-garde originality. But now we have neither the old symmetries nor any clear diagonals designed to snap everything back into an alternative, critical focus. As in Jameson's paradigm of the Hotel Bonaventure, the Benjaminian flaneur gives way to the postmodern consumer-tourist wandering in malls and Spruce Goose installations through a cognitively unmappable zone of hyperalienation where the only foundation to be grasped is somatic: the purely local universe of the body in which we feel our estrangement from total cognition.

We visit the Spruce Goose once more in late summer soon before it is to be disassembled. Jazz Age music plays to no one at the snack bar; just a few people sit at the video exhibits, faces lit by flickering screens; one child stands before the Cut-

Figure 4.7. Discarded tree from the Spruce Goose exhibition dome. "Art," presumably, is the name of the local garbage company. Photograph: Alan Liu.

away Engine display, watching a mock-up of the plane's gigantic engines cease-lessly propelling itself nowhere.

Looking around, we notice that the trees in pots are gone—all except one left out in the refuse for Art to pick up. (figure 4.7)

Toward a History of Distraction

My sketch of the postmodern agora, as indicated, is so far predictable. What is *un*predictable because unthought by postmodern theory?

It is time to remember the laugh of that woman at Jane Russell's breasts (exhibited without irony as yet another Hughes engineering project along-side the world's largest airplane).[14] The laugh itself, perhaps, is theoretically accountable. The woman utters a great, Foucauldian laugh, we deduce, because she sees in the Russell icon the exposure, not just of the modern gap between the natural or original woman and her inflated screen image, but of the postmodern scission we previously remarked within the status of the natural/original itself.[15] According to the exhibit, after all, Russell was in effect man-made: it was the man Hughes who originated the image of the natural woman. (And, extending the analysis further, we notice that not even the man Hughes is fundamental; instead, it is a construction constantly effeminized in the exhibit by allusions to Hughes's shy and retreating boyhood spent under the wings of his mother.)

What is theoretically unpredictable, however, is simply that the woman walked away—an act that may stand here for the larger fact that so many people walked away from the Spruce Goose that Disney at last had to shut it down. To my knowledge, nothing in postmodern theory adequately explains such a discrimination *within* the realm of the commonplace. While theory deploys sophisticated analytics to describe the distractions of hyperreality, it has assumed that such a postmodern condition is essentially homogeneous (homogeneous in its heterogeneity, it might be said) and so too that our distracted navigation through this condition is indiscriminate. But what we learn from such commonplaces as the Spruce Goose is that some distractions are more attractive than others—Disneyland itself, for example, as opposed to Hughes-land. And, while the discrimination involved in choosing distractions is, in part, aesthetic (one could, I suppose, build a case for Disneyland as an extra-hyperreality furnishing *more* feeling, more pleasure, more boredom, more panic, etc.), surely in everyday practice aesthetic and rational discriminations mix. Rationally considered, for instance, the Spruce Goose was simply harder to get to and offered relatively little bang for the buck compared with other acmes of hyperreality. So too it is at least conceivable that ethical discriminations may have come into play: shadowed by the eccentricities of his late life, Howard simply could not be Walt on the family circuit.

Of course, my particular speculations here are disputable. But more interesting than any such dispute is what the very possibility of making speculations of this sort points to: the great, blind zone of cognition *in* the commonplace that theory elides because it characteristically stops just at the point of discovering the sublime, panicked, ecstatic, bored, and other aesthetics of distraction prior to looking closely *into* those aesthetics to descry their internal dynamics and external affiliations. This blind zone where aesthetics links up with other cognitive domains has been the absolute limit of inquiry that Baudrillard personifies as the "silent majorities." "What are they; what do they do; what do they become?" he asks about the silent masses, and then answers immediately in his usual spirit of burlesque sublimity: "They turn themselves into an impenetrable and meaningless surface."[16] So too for Lyotard the blind zone where aesthetics links up with other cognitive "phrase regimes" marks the absolute limit of knowledge he calls—with a much more serious invocation of the sublime—the "differend." But pause to look closely *into* the meaninglessness of distracted feeling, I am saying, and discover that the horizon of postmodern aesthetics merely opens up rather than closes off a whole, further horizon of questions—questions about the commonplace interrelations of reason, ethics, *and* aesthetics that allow some people on some occasions to be critical in their distraction.

I come now to the core suggestion of this essay. How to look into the blind zone of commonplace intelligence? What is required, I believe, is a hermeneutic of the commonplace designed to be sensitive to the peculiar combination of meaninglessness *and* cognition constitutive of the blur of everyday consciousness—the blur of *collective* practical thought, in other words, that other hermeneutics still busy affirming or negating the notion of the individual cogito pass over. And the best hermeneutic in this regard is historical understanding.[17] While the sometimes bizarre linkages of reason, ethics, and aesthetics created in commonplace thought have no transcendental foundation (they are, in this sense, meaningless), they *are* founded in the contingency of the *history* of thought. There are historically different kinds of meaningless engagements or differends between reason, ethics, and aesthetics, in other words, and at least some past kinds (historiography has a wealth of collectivist names for these kinds: *custom, habitus, episteme, mentality, ideology,* and so on) enter into conjunction with postmodernity as a repertory of habitual ways of thinking *about* and *through* feeling. To understand how it is possible to think in the postmodern agora, therefore, we need to look into the archive of prepared forms of cognition to see just what past commonplaces (and in what configurations) are available to the present commonplace.

I cannot here provide the history of distraction I am calling for except to suggest the usefulness of exploring a particular episode in such a history: what might be called the *romanticism of postmodernism*.[18] After all, consider that tree, of many one, left standing outside the Spruce Goose dome (figure 4.7 above).[19] Whatever one thinks of the ultimate conclusions of Habermas's work, I believe, the historicizing impulse he demonstrates in such writings as the chapter on Nietzsche and romantic aesthetics in his *Philosophical Discourse of Modernity* is worthy of emulation.[20] Romanticism—which originally worried the relation between cognition and the commonplace, which inflected that cognition in the direction of feeling, which named the resulting distraction *memory* or *imagination,* and which finally subjectified the whole problem in a tense relation between nature and originality—such romanticism is not the same as postmodernism. But, without the historical lens provided by such topics as romanticism *and* postmodernism, neither term in the comparison can now be illuminated.

Methodological Afterword

A defining feature of the debate on postmodernism has been what may be termed the *historicism paradox*. On the one hand, postmodern experience has been described as the aestheticization of historical reality. Where once things mattered, historical matter (economic, social, political, cultural) now appears indistinguishable from the phantasmatic. Nothing matters except the imagery, spectacle, or simulacra of reality, and the essence of such simulation is that—as when we surf effortlessly across channels on the cable or sites on the Web—it seems to have none of the stubborn, gritty determinacy or resistance of historical matter. Even late- rather than post-Marxists such as Fredric Jameson, David Harvey, and Edward W. Soja have effectively abandoned the materialist premise to cleave to a hollower notion of geosocial space.[21] Postmodern space is all configurations, relations, distances, and timings: it is a circuit etched on a world-size silicon chip whose material substrate (the equivalent of silicon) is functionally neutral, totally clean of history, in other words, except for the dope (as in the impurities purposely added to silicon to make it a semiconductor) that postmodern cultural criticism retains as accidental, contingent, or anecdotal reminders of history. As we have already seen Baudrillard sum it up: "History itself is or was only an immense model of simulation." History becomes an image-generating circuit that models, rather than constitutes, reality.

But, on the other hand, formulations of postmodernism have been simultaneously haunted by the need to account *historically* for postmodernism as the end of history. Characteristically, therefore, postmodernism is inflected as a "postmodernity" or "postmodern condition" whose origin is sought above all in its relation to modernity. And the fierce debate over whether this period relation is discontinuous or continuous proceeds precisely on the grounds of economic, social, political, and cultural matter—that is, on the presumption of a substrate able to determine the rise of the new world order of indeterminacy. Jameson puts the paradox nicely when he says about his late-capitalism thesis: "What follows is not to be read as stylistic description. . . . I have rather meant to offer a periodizing hypothesis, and that at a moment in which the very conception of historical periodization has come to seem most problematical indeed."[22] In a manner similarly problematic, postmodernism has been determined as post-Fordism, postindustrialism, postnationalism, the postpolitical, post-print, posthumanism, and so on.

Interpreters crave a history of postmodernism, in sum, but have no ground to stand on. For, if postmodernity is the period that conditions us to experience sim-history rather than history, then to what period or condition do interpreters themselves belong when they seek to explain the end of history historically?

The methodological premise of this essay is that the hermeneutical groundlessness fostered by the historicism paradox is, in great part, a function of the narrowness of the modern versus postmodern debate. When attempts to explain the historical emergence of postmodernism restrict their baseline to twentieth-century modernity, then the conceptual ground of any resulting historicism is undercut from the start. As Habermas notes, after all, modern modernity was itself "that radicalized consciousness . . . which freed itself from all specific historical ties."[23] In a debate where modern modernity and postmodernity are the only options, history tellers or seekers such as Jameson (as is sometimes averred) necessarily appear atavistic: critical dinosaurs. Yet, of course, Jameson is not the only atavism to stalk the Jurassic Park of the postmodern. One has only to review, for instance, such major, historicizing gambits as Lyotard's comparison of postmodernity to romantic sublimity or Habermas's contrast of the Enlightenment to the Nietzschean "entry into postmodernity."[24] The general argument offered above in the conclusion of my essay is that, since history is demonstrably required by our ablest interpreters of postmodernism yet does not fit on the modern versus postmodern gameboard, then it is the gameboard itself that must be expanded to accommodate the moves of historical understanding. The only solution to the historicism paradox, in other words, is to place postmodernism in a longer view, one that significantly deepens modernity beyond modern modernity, embraces centuries rather than just one century, and differentiates discrete moments in the process of modernization: premodern, early modern, Enlightenment, romantic, and so on. Historicism may still be a simulation (descended, we recall, from the *as* in *as it really was*), but the expansion of the historical continuum allows for recognitions of nuance and delay that make a difference—the difference that allows each age and its citizens to make a life of their own through slight demurrals of, or distractions from, the big bang singularity of the original.[25]

My more specific argument is that while much can be gained by referring postmodernism to any past period of history, it is especially pertinent to initiate an interview between the postmodern and the romantic. Contact between postmodernity and such older epochs as the classical, pre-

Christian, or medieval is, in essence, exotic. When Deleuze and Guattari investigate paradigms of nomadic life or medieval cathedral building in *A Thousand Plateaus*, for example, they produce within our contemporary sensibility an effect akin to what Foucault, at the beginning of *The Order of Things*, calls "the exotic charm of another system of thought[,] . . . the stark impossibility of thinking *that*."[26] The emphasis is on a delicious frisson of momentary contact between modernity and the (pre)historical other: other than Western modernity, subjectivity, *mentalité*, and so on. But, when Lyotard and Habermas link postmodernism to romanticism in the latter's complex emergence from the Enlightenment, then a different theater of hermeneutics opens in which it is, not the charm of the exotic, but the uncanny compulsion of the familiar that dominates interpretation. The difficult relation of similarity and otherness characterizing the birth of romanticism from the Enlightenment is itself—to the second power— the progenitor of the equally complex relation of similarity and otherness characterizing the breach of postmodernism from modernism. The track that romanticism made as it broke out of the furrow of reason was the antecedent of the unfurrowing, the delirium, of postmodernism.[27]

After all, it was romanticism (or "romantic modernity," as Habermas calls it) that first confronted the historicism paradox ("I am 'new' or 'original,'" it said, but also: "Let us remember origins").[28] It was romanticism that thus constructed what might be called an oxymoronic *history of the new* (Wordsworth: "I would enshrine the spirit of the past / For future restoration").[29] And it was thus romanticism that precipitated nineteenth-century historicism and so helped establish the very primacy of historical understanding whose paradox has now returned to haunt us. If at the "end of history" we are once more perplexed by the historicism paradox, then it is not surprising that such interpreters as Habermas and Lyotard implicitly recommend measuring the history of the new that is postmodernism against the history of the new that was romanticism.

The list of themes that romanticism and postmodernism share is surprisingly replete: the sublime, subjectivity, simulation (imagination), reproduction (the status of copies relative to auratic naturals), mass culture, political revolution (July 1789/May 1968), industrial and technological revolution, the aestheticization of cognition (as feelings or intensities), organicism and antiorganicism, neoconservatism, aesthetic improvisation, fragmentary artistic forms, and many more. So many and so important are these shared problems, and so often do interpreters of postmodernism allude to romanticism, that there is every reason to think that the two epochs intersect in more than an accidental way. More than other periods, perhaps, romanticism and postmodernism are, not just part of the centuries-long process of modernization, but the stages in that process wherein modernity reflects self-consciously on the historical bounds of its freedom to be new. The two periods may differ in the answers they offer, but their question is the same: What does it mean to be historically determined to be indeterminate, to be conditioned to be free?

5 /

The New Historicism and the Work of Mourning

Imagine that a creature—let us leave it nameless, ageless, even speciesless—drowns. The rope it had been clinging to slips away as the creature begins its slow descent to the tidal shelf twelve fathoms down. Here, on the pale bottom sands, the rough sea is only a massive but gentle surge. The body rocks back and forth on the sands, one arm half raised and adrift. Planking rains down nearby, one iron-bound section pinning the arm to the sand. Time passes, and the soft parts of the body lose their definition, swell, and break open bloodlessly against the planking and sand. The body becomes no longer quite a body; it is a body/plank/sand assemblage. Fish pick at the flesh and graze the algae on the plank. They become fish/body/algae assemblages. Shell-fish, small crabs, and other bottom-feeders join the ensemble. Microorganisms are at work, too, churning the mass's internal structure and chemistry, fusing certain tissues more tightly, disassembling others, and offering their elements up to the seawater as a subtle scent.

At the end of six weeks, the body lies cradled in an encrusted, rooted, intricate matrix linked by thin trails of molecules (borne along tidal currents and fish migration paths) to a host of static and motile assemblages elsewhere—the total aggregate gradually propagating outward like a network of veins across the larger body of the ocean.

Nothing of the original creature has been lost: not an atom.

Such is a fable of the death of John Wordsworth—last seen clinging to a rope, not washed ashore until after six weeks—imagined from a point of view incapable of the perception of loss. However much this point of view resembles the vision in "Tintern Abbey" of

> something far more deeply interfused,
> Whose dwelling is the light of setting suns,
> And the round ocean,[1]

we know that it would have been unfathomable to William Wordsworth. For in this fable there never was loss requiring abundant recompense. ("Our loss is one which never can be made up," "we know what we have lost," "my loss is great, and irreparable," Wordsworth's letters of early 1805 chant.)[2] In the vision of the universe-as-assemblage, no organisms die to be redeemed in a transcendentally organic One Life. There are only assemblages passing into other assemblages.

But *we* know how to fathom this point of view because we recognize in it the makings of our modernity—or, more accurately, postmodernity. Freud and Weber (who may stand here for the modern) saw the dawning of that point of view. For them, the relevant universe—mind and society, respectively—was not so much organism as an "economy" or a "system." The system was normally a closed one (to generalize Weber's image: an "iron cage") and so homeostatic, retentive, lossless. Energies flowed from one mental faculty or social institution to another, at times cathecting in pathologies and reifications, but the systemic economy as a whole neither gained nor lost. Psychically or socially significant charges thus did not come unmediated from pure exteriority. ("Freud was definitely and remarkably immune to the sublime moment," Thomas Weiskel comments in remarking our modern skepticism of infinitude.)[3] Rather, such energies came from other zones of the system. And, reciprocally, charges never disappeared; they just went from *here* to *there*. However repressed, reified, or otherwise dysfunctional the system became, in short, all its essential being remained, waiting to be unpacked by the analyst.

Or perhaps we would do better in interpreting our fable to follow the French *post*modernists in saying that such "being" in the system—constantly shuttled to and fro from assemblage to assemblage—is not being at all but "happening." Lyotard and Deleuze/Guattari are apropos here (my fable of the body/plank/sand assemblage is thus recognizably "rhizomatic," and its very form alludes to Lyotard's "A Postmodern Fable"). But, for present purposes, I will cite only Jean-Luc Nancy's "Finite History." Characterizing postmodernity as the end to history he calls "finite history," Nancy writes:

> *Finitude* does not mean that we are noninfinite—like small, insignificant beings within a grand, universal, and continuous being—but it means that we are *infinitely* finite, infinitely exposed to our existence as a nonessence, infinitely exposed to the otherness of our own "being." . . . We begin and we end without beginning and ending: without having a beginning and an end that is *ours*, but having (or being) them only as others', and through others. . . .
>
>   What results is that *we happen*. . . . We are not a "being" but a "happening."[4]

The *we happen* that Nancy celebrates here, we recognize, is the very declaration by which postmodernism frees itself from both the older *I am* of divine and Cartesian identity and the newer *we are* of modernity. While modernity had previously dispersed the *I* of that *I am* into a plural *we* of mental and social faculties governed by parental or bureaucratic apparatuses, it nevertheless insisted on saying in place of *I am* "the *system* is." The systemic *we*, in other words, retained a residually organic being identified with the very systematicity of system—with the premise that there *is* such a thing as bounded, self-conserving system. *We* are the system of mental and social regimes that create the hegemony of *a* mind or society. Postmodernism, on the other hand, completes the dismantling of the *I am* by then subtracting even the *are* from modernity's *we are* to leave only the finitely historical statement: *we happen*. Sometimes our faculties and regimes happen to fall in with each other so as to seem *a* mind or society, that is, but sometimes they also happen to fall out so that mind or society deterritorializes. We are no longer a system whose ghost in the machine is organic being; as the Borg might say, we are assemblage.[5]

And so, from this infinitely finite perspective, John Wordsworth never *was*, so how could he be lost? John Wordsworth was always a *we* or an assemblage whose boundaries overlapped constitutionally with that of other people, creatures, the sea itself. In becoming the sea and the creatures of that sea (becoming animal, becoming woman, becoming intense . . . , Deleuze and Guattari say in their mantra),[6] he was still the happening or becoming he always was. He could have no end because he also had no beginning.

"Organic and subjective our reading of Wordsworth once would have been,—'tis so no more; / We have submitted to a new controul: / With the New Historicism a power is gone, which nothing can restore; / A deep distress hath humanized our Soul. // Not for a moment could we now behold / A smiling sea and be what we have been: / The feeling of our loss will ne'er be old. . . ."[7]

This, I take it, is the fundamentally elegiac posture—not just about but *of* elegy—adopted by one of the most interesting critiques of the New Historicism in the romanticism field. In 1993, Kevis Goodman, R. Clifton Spargo, and Leon Waldoff collaboratively addressed the topic "Wordsworth's 'Invisible Workmanship' and the Work of New Historicism" in a set of essays that took the New Historicism to task on grounds different from the now-standard criticisms that it is neither positivist enough as history nor textualist enough as reading.[8] Conditioned by the apparent opposition between historical contexts and literary texts that has typified advanced literary criticism from the New Criticism through deconstruction, the standard criticisms have conformed to a fearful symmetry: either there is too much interpretive reading in New Historicist history (making it seem metaphoric), or there is too much history in New Historicist reading (making it seem a vitiated deconstruction craving reference). In both cases, the debate has tended not to be very illuminating because it is at the level of first principles: the ships, as it were, pass in the night. By contrast, Goodman, Spargo, Waldoff, and other *post–New Historicists* (as they might be called) are willing to test the New Historicist premise that historicism is a compound act of "reading history" rather than the explication of either the context or the text separately and, therefore, that advanced techniques of deconstructive interpretation can, in principle, be brought to bear on absences that are historically *there* (e.g., modern debt financing as determinedly *not* thematized in Wordsworth's *The Ruined Cottage*; the usurpative Napoleon *not* there in the Simplon Pass episode of *The Prelude*).[9] In the vocabulary of the New Historicism itself, what is there in a poem is precisely what is not there: all the history that has been "displaced," "erased," "suppressed," "elided," "overlooked," "overwritten," "omitted," "obscured," "expunged," "repudiated," "excluded," "annihilated," and "denied."[10]

But, having tested the principle, the post–New Historicists find that the New Historicism comes up short even in its own terms. "Look at all we *lose* when we read in this manner," they object, voicing a plaint that a common thematization of drowned men allows me to pose as elegiac. (Goodman's essay centers on the Drowned Man episode in bk. 5 of *The Prelude*, while Spargo's and Waldoff's essays focus on Wordsworth's "Elegiac Stanzas Suggested by a Picture of Peele Castle.") Look at all the historical matter, in particular, that the New Historicism itself displaces to concentrate on just the most dramatic displacements of history in literature—displacements on the scale of Napoleon or above.

What is lost? Each of the post–New Historicist essays I refer to has its own trajectory, so any generalization I can offer will be a compromise. But I believe that we can understand the shared work of mourning that is the project of those essays by saying that all grieve for the loss of *personal* history. *Personal* here is not at all synonymous with *subjective*. Indeed, far from trying to reclaim the *I am*, Goodman, Spargo, and Waldoff hold a seat at the table for a concept as much the deconstruction as the construction of the subject. We can call this concept, broadly, the *pragmatics of subjectivity*. It may well be that the subject has become for the New Historicism a deconstructed Platonic sun or Derridean "white mythology": at once a flare of solar intensity (like the New Historicist focus on "Renaissance self-fashioning") and an epistemological and ontological nullity, a white zero on the retina that can be rescued from the heart of whiteness only by populating it with visions of social collectivity, like shades of ancestors crowding back in.[11] But, rejecting such all-or-nothing logic (either all subject or all collectivity), Goodman, Spargo, and Waldoff cannily look just *to one side* of the subject (as if just to the left or the right of the blinding sun) to show that there exists a corona of subjectivity effects not the same as public, collective history but also not exactly nothing. The New Historicism, in other words, perhaps commits the fallacy of the excluded middle: the universe is not completely distributed between the nothingness of an illusory subject (to be discounted) and the somethingness of Napoleonic history (to be recovered). Also happening is the history of intra- and interpersonal communication, relation, negotiation, and responsibility—a work of communicative action (as Habermas might put it) that not only cannot occur in solitude (in this sense, the personal is the antonym of subjectivity) but also is the very means for converting the subject from "being" into a "being *in*" the historical world. Thus, Goodman looks to one side of the subject to appreciate the personal "responsiveness" to history fostered by words that euphemistically—that is, pragmatically—allow us to cope, make, do, live in history. So too Spargo sights to one side of the subject to underscore subjectivity's necessarily self-undermining, ethical openness to alterity. "The personal is no longer an extension of the poet's self-interest in the world—his harmonizing or totalizing self," he says, "but signifies the other and requires response and justice." And, similarly, Waldoff looks past the subject to glimpse the work of the subjectivity effect that he calls (with some analogy to Spargo on alterity) the "transitional self."

Much is valid in such a post–New Historicist critique of the New Historicism. One can, at this point, only await the completion of these lines of thought to see what new expanses of history—perhaps a history of romantic privacy, everyday life, and ethics—will, in fact, be brought to the table to broaden the taste of the New Historicism for Napoleons. And much there is to question too. Most urgent, I believe, is the way in which such critique—centered in this case specifically on "Wordsworth's 'invisible workmanship'"—participates indirectly in one of the major intellectual adventures of our time: the sudden rescoring of issues of labor in the post-Marxist key of practice. Somehow, it might be suggested, the romance of pragmatism that makes de Certeau's tricky individual walking around the city in a personal way one with the personalized subjects in the essays by Goodman, Spargo, and Waldoff has seemed to justify literature as practical without thinking at all about that other evolution of labor in postindustrial economies: service (as in the Orwellian euphemism we so often hear today, *the service sector*). To prove that the practice of language is labor, perhaps, is now a hollow victory without also proving that the labor of words provides a service.

But I will here truncate my notice of the revisionary difference in such critique to observe, more fundamentally, that the post–New Historicists are also profoundly in common with the New Historicism they criticize. What is common, I believe, and what positions them finally *with* the New Historicism as critics of the end of history, is an anxiety that may be called the *fear of the loss of loss*. After all, if the thematization of elegy in the essays by Goodman, Spargo, and Waldoff has allowed me to figure their project as a keening over the loss of the personal, that thematization should also prompt us to recognize that the New Historicism itself is all about—and of—loss. Both schools, in other words, rehearse keen loss. Let me rehearse again the dark brood of the method Levinson calls "negative allegory": displacement, erasure, suppression, elision, overlooking, overwriting, omission, obscuration, expunging, repudiation, exclusion, annihilation, denial. Certainly, there is a note of denunciation—even anger—in such criticism that views poetry as nothing but the loss of historical truth.

But always also, I hazard, there comes a moment in the New Historicist denunciation when the critic's perception of lost history acknowledges that it has been strangely preempted by the perception of historical loss *in* the poetry itself—a moment, in other words, when the loss of history can no longer be spoken of as itself lost on the poet. In her "Elegiac Stanzas" chapter, therefore, Levinson writes, the poem not only "consummates . . . displacement logic" but "turns around and *registers* what . . . has thereby [been] lost." "Far more profoundly and inclusively elegiac than we have guessed," she continues, "'Elegiac Stanzas' is *about* the loss of an order of referentiality . . . of a concept of external and independent otherness" (second emphasis added).[12]

This moment, when the critic of the loss of history suddenly sympathizes with the poet of the loss of history,[13] may be called the *elegiac moment* in the New Historicism—or, rather, the moment that opens the scene of elegy. In this moment of secret romantic ideology, all the critic's anger of denunciation turns into something else. It is incorporated within a critical work of mourning able to acknowledge that the poetry itself is a work of mourning and, as such, entitled to normative stages of displacement and repudiation on its way toward registering, not just the loss of particular history, but (and this is the deepest grief of the New Historicism) the fact that history considered universally *is* loss. History, as it were, is the perpetuation or retention of the process of loss. Thus, listen to the distinctively elegiac note that sounds the largest theses of history in romantics New Historicism. "All discourse may well be about loss," Levinson says in opening the final section of her "Elegiac Stanzas" chapter, continuing: "Peele Castle is a reminder, indeed, the reification, of a *lost* Real."[14] And I have myself thrown ashes on the grave by saying: "History is the absence that is the very possibility of the 'here and now.' The reason poetic denial is ipso facto a realization of history . . . is that history is the very category of denial. It is history that says, 'This "is" but neither was nor will be.' Or in terms of social space: 'This is your place but was/is/shall be another's.'"[15]

In sum, what the post–New Historicist essays I have referred to might teach us to see is that, even more so than Renaissance New Historicism (which mourns the "power" of "Elegiac Stanzas" that "is gone" as the subversive marginality of literature), romantics New Historicism is primarily a form of elegy.[16]

What is the significance of such elegiasm? Let me close by recurring to the lossless assemblage universe I began on in order to map out—with the aid of Freud's "Mourning and Melancholia"—two antithetical, contemporary understandings of that universe. In Freud's terms, the French understanding of the postorganic/postsystemic world I previously sketched can be called "manic." At its best, French postmodern theory is about the joyous reinvention of the ethics, politics, and art of the closed world so that our iron cage will no longer *feel* so closed but instead radically open-ended, free. "Freedom," Jean-Luc Nancy says, "shall be understood precisely as the proper character of the happening and exposure of existence. Not simply a way of being 'free' of causality or destiny, but a way of being *destined* to deal with them. . . . Freedom would mean: to have history, in its happening, as one's destiny."[17] Freedom in this acceptation, in other words, means learning how to be just, effective, and playful within the very interstices of contingency that constitute the assemblage universe as an arbitrary system.

By contrast, the New Historicism participates in what appears to be the major Anglo-American and Germanic understanding of postmodernity. It too dedicates itself to addressing the assemblage universe. But its habit (matched by that of Jameson mourning the loss of "cognitive mapping" or Habermas the loss of "lifeworld") is the flip side of mania in Freud's schema: a mourning so existential as to be comparable to melancholia. "In what, now, does the work which mourning performs consist?" Freud asks, and then embarks on the general theory of mourning (of which melancholia is the special case) in the following sentence: "Reality-testing has shown that the loved object no longer exists, and it proceeds to demand that all libido shall be withdrawn from its attachments to that object."[18] When the object is known to exist no longer, that is, *then* the proper work of mourning ensues. But the New Historicism cannot take it for granted that the loss of the object can be known, for reality itself is, in this case, the lost object and so cannot serve as the testing principle for its own loss. The project of verifying the lostness of the lost object, as a consequence, must be elevated from the status of a preliminary clause (as in Freud's sentence) and made the main work of New Historicist mourning.

Thus it is, we can conclude, that the most basic task of the New Historicism as a work of mourning is simply to verify the possibility of loss in an otherwise closed, lossless, posthistorical universe. The New Historicists say, in essence: "We recognize that we live in a lossless world in which beneath every poetic denial the object denied can still be found, waiting to be unpacked by the analyst. But *even yet* we wish to believe that something significant is lost in the act of denial. For only if we conserve the possibility of real loss can we also hold the world open to the notion of real, and miraculous, gain. Thus shall we exaggerate the fiction of all-or-nothing, present-versus-absent history as an illusion saving the possibility that there can *be* absolute losses and absolute gains. This is the hope, the prophecy, of our elegy."

It remains to be seen whether the posture of mania or that of mourning—the grand and the abject poles, respectively, of the sublimity that postmodern theory has lately resumed—is the most ethical, political, and artistic stance to take in the face of the postmodern loss of loss.

Or, less agonistically, we need not overdramatize the choice between these two postures because each draws secretly on the other as its interior resource. Instructive in this regard is Lyotard's refusal to periodize the distinction between "regret" and "assay" in his "Answering the Question: What Is Postmodernism?" Modernism is that which expresses nostalgic "melancholia" in its sublime effort to present the "unpresentable," while postmodernism expresses "jubilation," Lyotard posits, but the *modern* versus *postmodern* pairing here is structural rather than diachronic: the two stances coexist in the same condition of postmodernity.[19] Moreover, they coexist, not just on a global scale (the globe on which I crudely mapped a French sensibility alongside the Anglo-American-Germanic), but locally: *within* the work of each theorist of postmodernity. Thus, if the major key of such mourners of postmodernity as the New Historicists, Jameson, or Habermas is melancholia, their minor key is clearly a mania that keeps them skipping like weightless stones across vast reaches of historical material. (The New Historicists study Napoleon *and* gypsies *and* family history *and* economics *and* . . . *and* . . . *and*, while Jameson studies postmodern architecture *and* video *and* painting *and* film *and* literature etc.) And, antithetically, if the major key of such maniacs of postmodernity as Lyotard is jubilation, their minor key is clearly and keenly mourning—as in the paradigm of Auschwitz on the first page of Lyotard's *The Differend*.

To vary Lyotard's phrase, in short, it may be that melancholic regret and jubilant assay are the two faces of a single meditation on loss and history. Assay is haunted by regret, and regret finds itself open to assay—to a sublime effort to imagine the perdurance of loss. For us—here and now—it is loss that is the unpresentable. "The nuance which distinguishes these two modes may be infinitesimal; they often coexist in the same piece, are almost indistinguishable; and yet they testify to a difference (*un différend*) on which the fate of thought depends and will depend for a long time, between regret and assay."[20]

We certainly would not say that discipline is what defines a war machine: discipline is the characteristic required of armies after the State has appropriated them. The war machine answers to other rules. We are not saying that they are better, of course, only that they animate a fundamental indiscipline of the warrior, a questioning of hierarchy, perpetual blackmail by abandonment or betrayal, and a very volatile sense of honor, all of which, once again, impedes the formation of the State. . . . And each time there is an operation against the State—insubordination, rioting, guerilla warfare, or revolution as act—it can be said that a war machine has revived, that a new nomadic potential has appeared, accompanied by the reconstitution of a smooth space or a manner of being in space as though it were smooth.

DELEUZE AND GUATTARI, *A THOUSAND PLATEAUS*

6/

The Interdisciplinary War Machine

I wish in this essay to undertake a salutary critique of interdisciplinarity in the humanities. The critique occurs in two steps. The first is to probe a particular cluster of interdisciplinary works that for some time was near to the heart of my own applied research: French Revolution studies in its recent postmodern historicist inflections. This first step of criticism has a satiric edge to it congruent with that of Stanley Fish's important 1989 essay in *Professions*, "Being Interdisciplinary Is So Very Hard to Do." Like Fish, I question whether the interdisciplinary effort (except in the context of the fully plural, collaborative, team research that some have called *polydisciplinary*) can, in fact, do more than project an überdiscipline of interdisciplinarity. The second step, however, is redemptive. Leaving behind the particular example of French Revolution studies, I offer an apology for the interdisciplinary concept as a whole. In my view, there is something precious about the concept, however impossible (to use Fish's epithet) it may be.

Saluting the Interdisciplinary

To begin with, we review some of the studies of the French Revolution period published at the zenith of the New Cultural History and the New Historicism, which I present under a metaphor that is deliberately antithetical to the interdisciplinary ethos. The metaphor is martial discipline. Here is a parade of quotations—almost military in their basic uniformity—that we can review to mark the New Historicist vanguard of inquiry into the French Revolution.

First, line up the historians. Here is Mona Ozouf, in her now classic *Festivals and the French Revolution*:

> Symbolism reigned supreme. Most of the demands concerned various symbols: the kiss, the weathercock, the cockade. The violence itself was often entirely symbolic.[1]

François Furet, from his crucial *Interpreting the French Revolution*:

> The Revolution marks the beginning of a theatre in which language freed from all constraints seeks and finds a public characterised by its volatility. . . . [The Revolution] ushered in a world where mental representations of power governed all actions, and where a network of signs completely dominated political life. . . . The Revolution was a collectively shared symbolic image of power.[2]

Lynn Hunt, in *Politics, Culture, and Class in the French Revolution*:

> Rather than vertically peeling away the layers to get at what revolutionary language "really" meant, I propose to look at language more horizontally, that is, in terms of its internal patterns and its connections to other aspects of political culture. . . . Revolutionary language did not simply reflect the realities of revolutionary changes and conflicts, but rather was itself transformed into an instrument of political and social change. . . . I propose to treat revolutionary rhetoric as a text in the manner of literary criticism.[3]

And one last example, Keith Baker, in "Memory and Practice":

I hope also to throw some light on the more general question of the ideological origins of the French Revolution—understood, that is, as the emergence of the symbolic forms that defined the meaning of the events of 1789 and gave them their explosive force as revolutionary action.[4]

Now line up the literary critics. Here is Marie-Hélène Huet, from her *Rehearsing the Revolution*:

The Revolution operated as well, perhaps primarily, in the order of language. Names were so many signs having the force of law. . . . The relationship, during the French Revolution, of death to writing and writing to logos—or, inversely, of word to law, and law to execution—not only underlay the revolutionary practice of justice, its obsession with legitimacy, but, conversely, underlay the theatrical practice of the Revolution.[5]

Mary Jacobus, from her "'That Great Stage Where Senators Perform'":

The Macbeth allusion [in bk. 10 of Wordsworth's *Prelude*] is the nearest we come to a sense of Wordsworth's complicity—if only the complicity of sympathy—in [the execution of Louis]. . . . Wordsworth was a typical moderate in turning to "tragic fictions" as a way to make sense of frightening reality when a predominantly humanitarian commitment to the revolutionary cause found itself faced by the bewildering ferocity of revolutionary practice. The appropriation of tragedy by the troubled consciences of men like Wordsworth gave them a potent language in which to describe their own powerlessness.[6]

Reeve Parker, in "Reading Wordsworth's Power":

Passionate action is spectacular action; as theater it is political in its use—or abuse—of power over others. Perhaps that is the lesson Wordsworth read in Paris.[7]

Julie Carlson, in "An Active Imagination":

Primarily devised to contravene the recent examples of France, Coleridge's plan for reform stresses the theoretical centrality—and the contemporary absence—of imagination in the public mind. To remedy this situation, Coleridge looks to the theater to revive the British public's imaginative powers.[8]

Theresa M. Kelley, in *Wordsworth's Revisionary Aesthetics*:

> As Wordsworth turned against revolutionary France, the revolutionary
> sublime became a major vehicle for his investigation of what is at stake in
> all contests for power over language—whether those contests take place in
> political centers of power like the French senate, or in poetic speech.[9]

Steven Blakemore, from *Burke and the Fall of Language*:

> Revolutionary and counterrevolutionary writers . . . knew that the linguis-
> tic, ideological war was an extension of the military war—they sensed
> that language and ideology are intimately intertwined and that whoever
> controls language controls not only the terms of "war" but the terms of
> "reality" itself.[10]

And, finally, from my own *Wordsworth: The Sense of History*:

> In approach, [this chapter draws] seminally upon recent studies of the
> French Revolution by François Furet, Marie-Hélène Huet, George Arm-
> strong Kelly, Richard Cobb, and others—studies whose common trait
> (applied most recently by Lynn Hunt) has been a rejection of the divide
> between historical action and representation. "Discourse" is taken to be an
> indispensable agency in both actions and their representations.[11]

Such is the march of interdisciplinarity in historiography and literary criticism of the French Revolution during our contemporary era of
postmodern historicism. To take one side of the equation, historians have
adventured into literary criticism, Foucauldian or Geertzian cultural reading, and semiotics to bring home such shibboleths as "symbolic system,"
"discursive strategy," "rhetoric," "genre," "theater," "metaphor," "motif,"
and, above all, "representation." As we may read in Lynn Hunt's introduction to the collection *The New Cultural History*, such adventuring registers
a fascinated belief in literary and symbolic analysis, and the motive is active *unbelief* in two older modes of explanation that had exerted an especially powerful hold over French historiography: Marxism and the *Annales*
school.[12] In regard to the former, it is telling that Furet's *Interpreting the
French Revolution* (originally published 1978) punctuates its prosecution
of Marxist histories of the French Revolution with such anticipations of
perestroika as the following: "Today the Gulag is leading to a rethinking
of the Terror."[13] The New Cultural History is what might be called *sans-
sansculotte*: it returns to a specifically political history but rejects the thesis

that political experience must be subordinated to the social in its material and class formations. Politics should, instead, be cosigned *culture* (the preferred subject of the New Cultural History being the hybrid concept *political culture*) to distinguish it from the traditionally sociopolitical. Similarly, the New Cultural History contests its antecedent *Annales* history, which, in Fernand Braudel's scheme of undergirding *longue durée*, intervening social rhythms or cycles, and uppermost short-term event, was partly congruent with a classically layered Marxism of infra- and superstructure. *Annales* history invented a *histoire de mentalités* able to face toward culture but—as the New Cultural History perceives it—then segregated such mentality together with short-term political experience on Braudel's uppermost tiers, submitting both to determination by deeper geologic, economic, demographic, and social substrata to be mined through serial statistical operations.

The overall result of thus repudiating both Marxist and *Annales* school approaches is that the New Cultural History—which also includes such notable scholars outside French Revolution studies as Darnton, Chartier, and the authors collected by Hunt and Wilentz—has decapitated politics from the social body.[14] Political experience floats free, we might say, with allusion to a famous sentence in Braudel, much like the "surface disturbances, crests of foam" that overlie the seas and tectonics of the world.[15] Specifically (and my overt literary drift here is leading), politics floats free like an Orphic head singing. How to cosign politics *culture*? If politics is no longer grounded credibly on socioeconomic determination alone, then it must, in part, be regrounded on a culture of *language* whose very essence is its arbitrary (in the Saussurean sense) suspension between determinacy and indeterminacy: that polymorphous, undecidable, and yet all-deciding language of "opinion," for example, that Furet makes the leading agency of the Revolution. Here, we descry the central novelty of the New Cultural History. Rather than read *through* language to underlying social meaning, Hunt observes, it reads language's "patterns" as if close-reading. It defers social reference, establishing instead an unfixable reciprocation between the politics of discourse and the conditions of society according to which *both* the discursive and the social share in causal power. As Hunt puts it: "A better metaphor for the relationship between society and politics is the knot or the Möbius strip, because the two sides were inextricably intertwined, with no permanent 'above' or 'below.'"[16] Or as Chartier says succinctly: "The representations of the social world are themselves the constituents of social reality."[17]

Such, in quick summation, is the recent adventure of the historians. For reasons of space, I do not here provide a proportionate recitation of the adventure of the literary critics. Let me simply review the argument offered in chapter 1 above. The literary-critical return to history of the past decade, I have argued, is, in the end, at once a repudiation and a deep acknowledgment of the older turn *from* history. The New Historicism, of course, characteristically signs itself by swerving aggressively away from formalism—from what Greenblatt (in a variant of antimonarchist discourse) calls literature as "self-regarding, autonomous, closed system."[18] Unfulfilled by Cleanth Brooks's textual well-wrought urn, the New Historicism excavates the "Sylvan historian" Keats had buried in that urn. Yet, if the New Historicism thus swerves away from formalism, it at last does so only in a mode that might be called, in Harold Bloom's vocabulary, *apophrades*, or the return of the dead.[19] Every particle of the New Historicism—from its habitual vocabulary of ambiguity, irony, contradiction, paradox, and so on, to its timelessly framed narrative anecdotes and its chiasmatic patterning of syntax and argument—confesses a remembrance of formalism deep as bone. Authored originally by scholars trained during the twin climax of formalism and political activism in the academy of the late 1960s and early 1970s, the New Historicism cannot think the formative processes of society without also saturating those processes with old formal assumptions.

Nor, it may be added, just assumptions. In the hands of its most intense practitioners, the New Historicism does not simply rehearse the theory of formalism; it becomes in itself an art of formalism. There is thus little in recent literary criticism more essentially avant-garde in the high old modernist sense than the deft cuttings and tessellations required to create the New Historicism's contextual/textual paradigms. The particular principles of tessellated form may be new: if this is art, this is clearly the postmodern art that Fredric Jameson, in his discussion of the New Historicism, calls the "elegance" of pastiche, collage, or—in a phrase drawn from Sergei Eisenstein's film writings—"montage of historical attractions."[20] But, as the allusion to Eisenstein might indicate, the basic practice of making such montages is at least as old as the forms first inspiring formalist theory: *The Battleship Potemkin*, for instance, or T. S. Eliot's "heap of broken images" in *The Waste Land*.[21]

There is a sense, then, in which the New Historicism is really New Critical and deconstructive formalism amplified to the scale of the world. New Historicists close-read history, conferring on materiality the complex grace of the "thickest" (Geertzian) description they know: literariness. The very history of the world thus becomes subversive in the way in which a poem is ambiguous, paradoxical, ironic, tense, and indeterminate. And so the dead return: formalism comes back with ghostly power to speak through historicism as its medium. Not surprisingly, therefore, the conclusions that New Historicists reach bear a striking resemblance to those of the New Cultural History. For the New Historicism, texts are also embedded within social reality such that the arrow of reference is reversible: if society is the ground of the literary text, then the text is also a ground of society. In a standard turnabout formulation, Montrose writes: "To speak, then, of the social production of 'literature' or of any particular text is to signify not only that it is socially produced but also that it is socially productive."[22] Or, again, with a similar chiasmatic twist (as Brook Thomas analyzes it), Greenblatt concurs: "Language, like other sign systems, is a collective construction; our interpretive task must be to grasp more sensitively the consequences of this fact by investigating both the social presence to the world of the literary text and the social presence of the world in the literary text."[23]

To return to my martial parade, then, what we see in reviewing French Revolution studies is an emergent uniformity where historical and literary disciplines cross. There is no better way to call the march of that uniformity than by remarking three power words in the historiographic/literary-critical reinterpretation of the French Revolution period: *representation, action, plot*. Each of these words is now undecidable in reference. Each cleaves between historical action, on the one hand, and symbolic discourse, on the other, such that *representation*, for example, becomes at once a political and a linguistic phenomenon, at once a matter of the vote and of the symbol. So too *action* becomes agency and dramaturgy, a doing and a hollywooding; and *plot* becomes conspiracy–cum–Aristotelian mythos, political plot with a good script. When the actors of the French Revolution—as Furet and others call them with mise-en-scène in mind—spread dark rumors about aristocratic "plots" against the new state of "representation," we no longer know whether we are on the boards of the revolutionary theater or the stones of the revolutionary street. As understood by historians and literary critics schooled by Paris 1968, the street demonstrations of Paris 1792 seem both a course of action and a discourse of placards.

Beyond the Impossible

What do I intend by surveying interdisciplinary French Revolution studies as if saluting military uniformity? The first answer is that the salute signals my assent to the critique of the interdisciplinary humanities marking the maturity of the first generation of interdisciplinary theory. The generation I denominate may be dated roughly from the early 1970s, which initially saw a burst of explicit, sustained discussions (beginning in Europe) focused primarily on pedagogy and task-oriented team research in the physical and social sciences.[24] By the late 1970s and the 1980s, such discussions evolved not only into broadly synthetic and reflective studies but also into—my special concern here—a number of highly aggressive criticisms of the interdisciplinary concept. The latter include, for example, Fish's "Being Interdisciplinary Is So Very Hard to Do," Guy Palmade's *Interdisciplinarité et idéologies*, and Vincent C. Kavaloski's "Interdisciplinary Education and Humanistic Aspiration."

These critical works suspect the ideology of the interdisciplinary agenda, which they see as promising cryptorevolutionary freedom but yielding only a new tyranny: what Fish calls the "imperialist" appropriation of fields within a hegemonic überdiscipline and Palmade the "imperialistic" "conglomeration" of disciplines under such standards as structuralism.[25] And they prosecute that charge through what must be acknowledged to be a devastating cross-examination of the basic integrity of interdiscipline as a method of knowledge. Thus, Palmade observes interdisciplinarity's "confused" and "contradictory" emergence; Kavaloski targets what he calls the recalcitrant "objectivist epistemology" of interdisciplinarity making it no different from older disciplines; and Fish, in a maneuver complementary to Kavaloski, targets the "epistemological" impossibility of interdisciplinary studies. "Being interdisciplinary is more than hard to do," he says; "it is impossible to do."[26]

To recapitulate Fish's take-no-prisoners thesis more fully: interdisciplinarity, he argues, pursues its variously implicit or explicit agenda of freedom by proposing a pedagogy of "antiknowledge." Pedagogy in this mode prompts students to see the historically determined boundaries that construct traditional human knowledge by occluding other territories of human possibility. The assumption, as it were, is that simply seeing such constraining constructions will lead to emancipatory disbelieving or, again, that remarking will lead to remaking: open the eyes of the students now being constructed by knowledge disciplines to the very *fact* of discipline, and freedom of mind will be enabled. Students will come to share the interdisciplinary researcher's goal of freely crossing, blurring, melding, and otherwise reconstructing the world of knowledge.

To this "stirring vision" and "heady prospect," Fish sternly says no.[27] The interdisciplinary agenda, he argues, is fatally contradicted by the epistemology allowing it to frame the project of seeing through historically constructed disciplines in the first place. According to this underlying epistemology, knowledge is all constructed, with the consequence—if we extend the line of thought far enough—that we can never really even *see* the disciplinary boundaries that construct us as knowing subjects precisely because we *are* constructed by those boundaries. If we think we spy a constricting boundary, that can only be because some other, still-hidden construction of knowledge with its own boundaries has made it possible for us to do so. Only some god with transcendental perspective could discover where the disciplinary firmaments really lie and, thus, overreach them in an all-creative interdisciplinary moment akin to revelation. But, for humans, the god's view is impossible. "From what vantage point will the 'structures that organize how we know' be revealed?" Fish asks. His answer: only "from the vantage point of a structure that is at the moment *un*revealed."[28]

The conclusion Fish reaches, therefore, is that interdisciplinary studies is only fooling itself when it seeks to "know" the configuration of disciplines in order to transcend that configuration. This conclusion is not a benign one. For Fish predicts that ideological illusion built on epistemological bad faith can herald only a return of the repressed by which disciplinary enclosures reemerge with a vengeance. Interdisciplinarity, he says with unsparing rigor, will turn out to be either the appropriation of other disciplines by the home discipline, the capture of other disciplines by an emerging, hegemonic discipline, or *itself* a new discipline, a synthetic metadiscipline of interdisciplinarity, a sort of specialization in generalization, we might say, akin to the superdisciplinary project of Destutt de Tracy and the French Ideologues that provoked Napoleon, reacting against abstraction, to invent our now suspicious sense of the word *ideology* in the first place.[29] In short, there is no such thing as a truly interdisciplinary, free, or open mind. "The American mind, like any other, will always be closed," Fish concludes in a memorably isolationist bumper sticker.[30]

In the face of such a rigorously argued assault on interdisciplinarity, especially as formulated in epistemological terms by Fish and by Kavaloski before him, one can only assent.[31] Thus, the satirical quality of the salute to interdisciplinarity with which I began. What we witness in recent New Cultural Historians and New Historicists of the French revolutionary period (to resume my example) is a group of freethinkers all marching to the same drum of pantextualist language, all—that is—enlisting in a super- or metadisciplinary army that just happens to loft as its banner the motto *interdisciplinarity*. Indeed, the metaphor of militancy, which I initially presented in an extraneous manner, turns out to be an especially telling one because it touches on a secret allegory interior to interdisciplinarity itself. On the one hand, interdisciplinarity often compares itself to democratic or leveling freedom. In his much-remarked essay "Blurred Genres," for example, Clifford Geertz argues: "There has come into our view of what we read and what we write a distinctly democratical temper. The properties connecting texts [from different fields] with one another, that put them, ontologically anyway, on the same level, are coming to seem as important in characterizing them as those dividing them."[32] But, just as often, interdisciplinarity recruits its comparisons from another kind of allegory oddly tangent to that of revolutionary or democratic freedom: military action, which we can spy, for example, in Richard Macksey's idiom of "breaching disciplinary boundaries" and "sorties into alien territory," Roland Barthes's insidious litotes that "interdisciplinary work is not a peaceful operation," Fish's gloss of interdisciplinary teaching as a "guerilla warfare," or Nancy F. Partner's observation that "language-model epistemology" has been "smuggled out of linguistics and philosophy departments by literary critics and free-ranging or metacritics, and lobbed like grenades into unsuspecting history departments."[33] In her book *Interdisciplinarity: History, Theory, and Practice*, Julie Thompson Klein fills an even fuller portfolio with such war metaphors. "Claims are 'indefensible,'" she notes, "criticisms land 'right on target,' positions are wiped out by 'strategy,' arguments are 'attacked,' 'demolished,' 'won,' or 'shot down,'" and "disciplines have become 'warring fortresses between which envoys are sent and occasional temporary alliances formed.'"[34]

The significance of these pervasive military figures is that they are at once incommensurable *and* complicit with the interdisciplinary program of freedom—much in the oxymoronic spirit, we may note, of the French revolutionary wars of liberty. Attached to the ideology of liberty by an unthought association, the figure of militancy opens to view, not just interdisciplinarity's ethos of freedom, but also its deep dependence on a counterethos of regulation, uniformity, absolute *discipline*. And the sure sign of that contradiction—rooted, if Fish is right, in epistemological paradox—is the instability of the metaphor of militancy itself. As is true of the postcolonial understanding of war generally, interdisciplinary encroachment across borders seems undecidably an action of conventional and of irregular forces, of disciplined armies and adisciplinary guerrillas or terrorists (where terrorism itself, of course, now splits connotatively between anti- and ultradiscipline).

By trumpeting the metaphor of militancy, in sum, I call to attention within interdisciplinary discourse precisely the master disciplinarianism that Fish locates by epistemological critique: if interdisciplinary study is an urge toward freedom conducted by raids across borders of knowledge, that urge is tainted by old disciplines of national, colonial, and imperial hegemony.

But perhaps I had better at last say that I acquiesce rather than assent to the epistemological critique. For, as I earlier indicated, my ultimate project here is, not only to criticize or satirize interdisciplinarity, but also to apologize for it—*apologize* in the strong sense of such precedents as Sidney's *Apology for Poetry* or Shelley's *Defense of Poetry*. Interdisciplinary studies, it is true, must accept the full brunt of the epistemological critique. But, just as Sidney in the *Apology* accommodated the *mysomousoi* or poet-haters *within* his defense (and just as this classic strategem of *refutatio* set the mold for intellectual defense right up through de Man's total internalization of *refutatio* in "The Resistance to Theory"), so it seems to me that the true use of the *resistance to interdisciplinarity* (as the epistemological critique may be called) is to be incorporated within interdisciplinarity itself as a necessary moment of self-refutation, self-irony, and abjection.[35] The gain to be sought in such self-critique is, not freedom from impossible epistemological boxes, but, rather, useful reflection *on* impossibility, allowing us to refuse what is finally the artificial polemics of a debate between knowledge and antiknowledge, possibility and impossibility, freedom and constraint.

For the great shortcoming of the Fishean critique, it may be suggested, is, not that it is wrong, but that it stops where it does in an artificially neat, Q.E.D. demonstration of epistemological fallacy. To quote the last sentence of Fish's essay in full: "The American mind, like any other, will always be closed, and the only question is whether we find the form of closure it currently assumes answerable to our present urgencies." To my mind, this should be the beginning of an essay, not the end. Everything depends on that latter question regarding "whether we find the form of closure" now limiting us "answerable to our present urgencies." Some closures are better than others, which is to say that they make available new areas or formulations of knowledge previously barred off by some other configuration of closure. Some reconfigurings of closure, indeed, might even goad us, not to assume that the closed American mind is "like any other" (an assertion that would surely have different reverberations elsewhere in the world), but to ask more usefully whether there might not be other minds a bit more open than home knowledge or, more accurately, closed in directions and configurations still unknown to the American mind.[36]

Nor is it only in the arena of globalism—and of varying regional, national, social, and cultural views of the relation between isolationism and globalism, closed and multiculture—that interdisciplinarity plays out differentially. Some of the most crucial problems in interdisciplinary studies now bear on the differential relations between such *institutions* as corporate business, science, the health industry, the legal profession, media, the government, the military, and education. In varying ways, interdisciplinarity has recently been central to all these institutions. But the interdisciplinary practices of some institutions have exerted an overpowering, normative influence over those of others—to the extent that we may say that we are now threatened by a monoculture of interdisciplinarity. The current hegemon, clearly, is corporate interdisciplinarity. In the corporate sphere, interdisciplinarity is a function of the elementary social unit of the New Economy: the team (a phenomenon I have discussed in greater detail in *Laws of Cool*).[37] One of the most important kinds of corporate teams is the interdisciplinary team (including the "tiger team" outside the normal chain of command) created to address particular problems or opportunities by assembling experts from across departments (e.g., design, engineering, manufacturing, marketing). And paralleling corporate interdisciplinarity is the model of big science, which at least since the Manhattan Project has had remarkable success in convening similar multidisciplinary research teams (composed, e.g., of physicists, mathematicians, chemists, and computer scientists). Furthermore, in just the single decade from the popularization of the Internet in the early 1990s through the rise of the "Web 2.0" or "user-created content"/"Web services" era in the early years of the twenty-first century, the corporate and the scientific practices of interdisciplinarity have been reinforced by collaborative information technologies (e.g., collaboration programs, "extranets," "Web services," "content-management systems," blogs, wikis, and, in general, fuller implementations of the principle of networking). Such technology both allows work teams to interoperate seamlessly across corporate information systems and geographic borders *and,* as in the case of social networking or folksonomic-tagging sites, disseminates an uncannily similar model of teamwork to popular culture.[38] The crucial point is that, while in the past most social institutions improvised their own protocols, practices, and conventions of interdisciplinarity, the current domination by big business and big science abetted by Web 2.0 has the potential to impose an ultimately impoverished uniformity of interdisciplinarity—a state in which even popular knowledge pantomimes neocorporate knowledge work by flowing through standard Web templates to standard databases "mashed up" interoperably with others through standard application programming interfaces (APIs).

After all, one might admire the innovative, interdisciplinary work processes of New Economy firms and their Web 2.0 look-alikes but still inquire critically about the sufficiency of the general model for society as a whole. By what historically meaningful (as opposed to short-term, market- or popularity-driven) measure, for example, can it be judged that the team model of interdisciplinarity is necessarily more rewarding to society than that of lone individuals engaged in interdisciplinary research? The latter model—still the norm in the humanities despite an increasing number of collaborative, grant-driven projects in recent years—seems the poorer cousin of the richly endowed business and science practices, let alone the Wikipedias of Web 2.0, until we remember the results of such notably interdisciplinary individuals as Leonardo da Vinci, John von Neumann, or Tim Berners-Lee (to name just a few examples from distinct historical epochs). Might a hybridization of the two models be possible?[39] Closure, to recur to Fish's term, may be a limitation of individual epistemology, but it is just as assuredly, if not more so, a phenomenon of institutional epistemology—of what our most influential social institutions ("learning organizations," as they have been idealized) do, or can, know.[40]

In short, the Q.E.D. of the epistemological critique easily punctures the idea of interdisciplinary studies to show that such ideation is only illusory ideology. But it doesn't even begin to offer terms of analysis adequate to what might be called the *pragmatics* (as opposed to *neopragmatics*) of inter-disciplinarity—everything about interdisciplinarity that aims not so much for absolute freedom of mind as for explorations of alternative forms of closure, alternative ways to make the shape of limitation "answerable to our present urgencies"; everything about interdisciplinarity, in other words, that escapes an epistemology able to sort out only two categories of knowledge, the possible and the impossible. It is no accident, we notice, that, just before leaving his critique hanging on the question about present urgencies, Fish gropes for some alternative to epistemology by which to evaluate what interdisciplinarity is doing *well* if not *possibly* and comes up with only a dead-end analytic of personal pleasure. "For my own part," he says in the sentences before his closing dictum, ". . . I find the imperialistic success of literary studies heartening and the emergence of cultural stud-ies as a field of its own exhilarating. It is just that my pleasure at these developments has nothing to do with the larger claims—claims of libera-tion, freedom, openness—often made for them."[41]

Only reflection on the deeper significance of epistemological impossi-bility, I suggest, will allow us to move beyond the finally unpragmatic (i.e., useless) analytic of knowledge versus antiknowledge to other frameworks able to discriminate between better and worse "impossible" interdisciplin-ary attempts.

Apology for Interdisciplinarity

I would like to close, then, by offering in sketch form a defense of interdisciplinarity in the humanities that incorporates the epistemological critique but then rethinks the terms of that critique. As an indication of argument to come, let me return momentarily to the case of the New Cultural History and the New Historicism in the French revolutionary field to notice one anomaly in what I previously saluted as superdisciplinary pantextualism.[42] I refer to the imperative in both the New Cultural History and the New Historicism to outflank the *reading* of cultural and literary representations by acts of *seeing*. Thus, for example, Hunt's *Politics, Culture, and Class in the French Revolution* includes abundant pictures as well as a chapter on revolutionary imagery, while, in the field of romanticism, Ronald Paulson's, Theresa Kelley's, Mary Jacobus's, and my own work turned increasingly to visual means of reading history.[43] This imperative to see as well as to read is general in interdisciplinary study. It is not accidental that Foucault's *The Order of Things*, for example, begins with a meditation on a Velázquez painting or that Greenblatt's *Renaissance Self-Fashioning* hinges on a Holbein painting.[44] Within the seeming uniformity of pantextualism, we glimpse a vision.[45]

How to understand that window of vision left open within the closed superdiscipline of pantextualist interdisciplinary studies? Here is a four-stage defense of interdisciplinarity that will at last bring me to that window.

The first step, as indicated above, is to accept the accusation of epistemological impossibility. As a means of opening up knowledge, we can agree, interdisciplinary studies is (in a strict sense) unthinkable.

The second step is then to unthink *thinking*, or, more precisely, a too-narrow version of thought and knowledge. There is no out from the epistemological critique so long as we grant that epistemological consistency is the index of possibility and that, therefore, Fish's own überdiscipline lurking in the background, philosophy, is the final arbiter of disciplines. Which is the more philosophical, after all (to reask the classic question), history or poetry? It is striking the extent to which Fish's critique is bound up within an empiricist/skeptical project of pre-Kantian epistemological inquiry. The Kantian question, What are the conditions of possibility? founding much Foucauldian interdisciplinary work is, thus, defined as out of bounds by an analytic that, as Fish's rejection of any transcendental vantage point indicates, is precisely nontranscendental.[46]

How to rethink *thinking* in a way that incorporates the epistemological critique usefully within a working theory of interdisciplinary study? I suggest the following formulation: interdisciplinarity is an epistemological impossibility only because it is primarily what my emphasis on such metaphors and allegories as that of militancy has already implied, a *tropology*. Tropology, after all, is the very art of doing an end run around epistemological closure in order to say the impossible or (in the broad, Yale school sense) catachrestic—to say of truth, for example, that it is a sun. Interdisciplinarity-as-trope is part of the general rhetoric that hollows out logic and grammar in the trivium as interpreted by de Man in "Resistance to Theory" (his meditation, especially in its discussion of the trivium and quadrivium, on interdisciplinarity). Thus, it makes perfect sense, for example, to say that literary critics who talk beyond their practical knowledge of history utter, not any logic at all, but a *rhetoric* of historicity. So too historians who speak indiscriminately of symbols, metaphors, and signs are engaged in a manner of sophistry.

The precise manner in which interdisciplinarity is really a rhetorical tropology may be unfolded as follows. In interdisciplinary studies, I suggest, the relation between the home discipline and the other or exotic discipline is really the relation between what might be termed a *convention* and a *figure* for knowledge.[47] The home discipline offers a convention of systematic knowledge that is arbitrary insofar as it *is* a convention. It therefore craves some more absolute validation—some faith that its configuration of knowledge is grounded on truth. But such validation can be satisfied only in shadow form through practices that establish rigorous *internal* standards of truth—for example, protocols for documentation, peer review, hiring, evaluating graduate students, and so forth. It is these practices, we know, that provide home disciplines with a sort of surrogate feeling for validity, screening it from deeper worries about essential truth. By contrast, the beautiful other discipline is *never* imported home with comparable systemic and practical knowledge. This is because its allure lies, not in knowledge at all, but in the new paradigms—which is to say, tropological figures rather than protocols—that it offers for *representing* the validity of home knowledge to itself.

The purpose of that representation is single in what I presume to call the *thin* interdisciplinary studies model and twofold in the *thick*—categories of evaluation, I should add, that separate out not so much camps of interdisciplinary scholars as aspects within any work of scholarship. On the one hand, the representation of knowledge embodied in the other discipline is simply compensatory: it confers extra validity on home knowledge because it seems to represent an infusion of intuitive or natural truth. Thus, for example, we eventually detect in even the most sophisticated New Historicist literary criticism a romance of empirical history: to the jaded eyes of textualists, history is, at some level, intuitively more immediate or real. The very fact that mandarin literary criticism now soils its hands once more in dusty historical documents seems to reaffirm its validity—to allow it a sort of "my literary criticism is more real than yours because it has history in it" one-upmanship. So too New Cultural Historians betray a romance of symbolic or allegorical language: to investigators who actually have experience with the broken, missing, myriad, scattered, and hard-to-interpret archives of history, the "language" learned secondhand from New Critics or deconstructionists seems so much more *there*. If such language is full of absence in a theoretical sense, then at least all that absence is there, gathered visibly in what—by comparison with the archives—seems just a few books (Rousseau's, e.g., as deconstructed by Derrida or de Man). The thinner the interdisciplinary project, I hypothesize, the more home knowledge is content to see in the other discipline *only* such a deictic, "there-it-is" representation of truth—only, that is, a romance of the other.

On the other hand, the thicker or deeper the project, the more it will also discover that romance is a dark interpreter. As told in such poems as Keats's "La Belle Dame sans Merci," we remember, romance sustains the feyness of the figural other only by at last making the home world itself a cold hill's side, itself other. The representation of knowledge glimpsed in other disciplines, that is, can have the uncanny or unhomely effect of utterly *hollowing out* the home field's sense of valid knowledge. The moment when a discipline is entranced by the knowledge of other disciplines, after all, is also the moment when its own knowledge dissolves into a centerless relativism of paradigms, methodologies, theories. As in the Keats poem, the home world becomes merely an interminable *approach*. Put in academic rather than poetic terms, few of us today have any knowledge anymore; we all have approaches instead. The thicker or deeper the interdisciplinary work, I suggest, the more it will signal this latter, dark side of the romance of the other—and in ways more substantive, for example, than a preface confessing that the subsequent book is merely a preliminary, cursory, or fragmentary attempt to comprehend a vaster topic.

What could such a substantive signal be?

Of course, it would be possible to ratchet up the Fishean critique one notch here and say that, in redefining interdisciplinarity as rhetoric, I have so far merely confirmed its status as a pantextualist superdiscipline. To an extent, such a charge is deserved. Pantextualism and interdisciplinarity are homologous: textualism is the inner form of a currently widespread rethinking of knowledge whose outer form is interdisciplinarity. Yet, in another sense, the charge is moot. *Rhetoricity* is not exclusively a textualist label for the interdisciplinary process I sketch by which other disciplines both validate and undermine home knowledge. It would be possible at this point to go deconstructive and read de Man's "Shelley Disfigured," for example, on the way rhetorical tropology occupies an unknowable rift between sight and sound. But, instead, I draw the same lesson of *inter-mediation* (as it might be called) by citing a number of interdisciplinary texts.[48] The works I have in mind are just some of those that, despite all our doubts about the interdisciplinary hype of recent years, indicate that there is still a remainder, an excess in the rhetoric that is more than hype. I think, for example, of such intensely interdisciplinary works in the history of science as Paul Feyerabend's *Against Method*, in anthropology as Lévi-Strauss's "The Science of the Concrete" with its meditation on a painted lace ruff, in art history as Ronald Paulson's literary-cum-psychoanalytic work on the paintings of J. M. W. Turner and John Constable, in environmental or geographic approaches to the arts as Jay Appleton's *The Experience of Landscape* or Yi-Fu Tuan's *Segmented Worlds and Self*, and in such jack-of-all-trades fields as Deleuze and Guattari's remarkable *A Thousand Plateaus* (readers are here invited to make up their own list).[49] By no stretch of credibility can all these interdisciplinary works—some quite wild in spirit and execution—be called *only* disciplinary in disguised form. Even more compelling examples might be drawn from works of new media art, literature, and theory—that is, born-digital works in which text and graphics evolve from the same primordial soup of bits and algorithms.[50]

What is missing in the picture? What is missing in our consideration of interdisciplinarity so far is precisely the *picture*, which, in these works as well as those I cited earlier, provides the signal I am calling for—the signal that the interdisciplinary effort creates, not only an alluring rhetoric for knowledge, but also a rhetoric that senses, without being epistemologically clear about it, that it has yet further limitations to reconfigure, further forms of closure to try out. There is nothing magical, I hasten to add, about pictures in themselves (and, insofar as the visual medium *does* seem magical, then it is simply part of the compensatory interdisciplinary romance). Rather, what is significant about the use of pictures in pantextualist interdisciplinary works is that it signals that a bridge already established between two such disciplines as literary criticism and history must be further reconfigured to take account of a whole other kind of gap to span. The more satisfying the interdisciplinary work, I suggest, the more it will be aware that the interdisciplinary problem is always at some level coextensive with an intermedia (and, increasingly, new media) problem. In the last analysis, that is, interdisciplinary rhetoric leads to a rethinking, not only of the idea- and language-oriented branches of epistemology, but also of the perceptual base.

Thus I arrive on the final step in my apology for the interdisciplinary. If epistemological impossibility makes interdisciplinarity really a rhetoric, then the fate of that rhetoric is to lead the more interesting sorts of projects to awareness of the impossibility even of rhetoric. There is no moment quite as compellingly vulnerable in a New Historicist or New Cultural History project, it may be noted, as that in which the literary critic wishing to be a historian, or vice versa, confronts the task of talking about a picture. The very language that allows the scholar to make of his or her "other" discipline a rhetorical trope now falls mute or proves woefully inadequate. More accurately, scholars who concentrate on bridging literary-critical and historiographic approaches (to continue with my example) *could* certainly discuss pictures intelligently but, characteristically, are aware that they *won't* because there simply is no space, time, or desire left to develop a whole, third methodology inscribing visual artifacts. Thus, the total effect is a feeling of wordlessness akin to what Lyotard calls the "differend" between language games—in this case, between one set of language games and another so different it is not even language anymore.

I know two names for this moment of impossible rhetoric. One is the *sublime*. The other is what the sublime in its Longinian, Burkean, Kantian, and Lyotardian modes always includes as its other face: *dejection* or (as it may also be called) *abjection*. In the moment when we rise up most high before that for which we have no words, sublime theory tells us, then are we cast down in utter humility, and vice versa. Only the mute signaling of such dejection and abjection, I believe, testifies to the continued openness of interdisciplinarity to new forms of closure, new realms of understanding beyond what it presently "knows"—even new intimations of what Lyotard calls the "unpresentable" beyond knowledge forms themselves. We might here aptly misquote Lyotard on the postmodern sublime by substituting our cardinal terms for his (such that *postmodern* and *unpresentable* become *interdisciplinary* and *intermediated*, while *modern* and *presentable* become *disciplinary* and *media*): "The interdisciplinary would be that which, in the disciplinary, puts forward the intermediated in presentation itself; that which denies itself the solace of good forms, the consensus of a taste which would make it possible to share collectively the nostalgia for the unattainable; that which searches for new media, not in order to enjoy them but in order to impart a stronger sense of the intermediated within the interdisciplinary."[51]

Why do I close so abjectly (or, in the inverted tonal register of the French postmodern theorists, jubilantly)?[52] As my vocabulary declares, here we might begin a turn toward what has lately impressed me as one of our most powerful (if indirect) meditations on the boundaries of disciplinary subjects and the impurity of interdisciplinary crossings: Julia Kristeva's *Powers of Horror: An Essay on Abjection*. Indeed, here could begin a cultural extrapolation of Kristeva's meditation centered on another trope of interdisciplinary discourse: the crossing of disciplinary borders. I take another page from Klein's book on interdisciplinarity: everywhere we look, Klein says, we see "the 'breaching' of boundaries, 'cross-cultural exploration[s],' 'floundering expeditions' into other disciplinary territories, and excursions to the 'frontiers' of knowledge, . . . 'alien intrusion[,]' . . . 'border traffic,' 'intellectual migration,' and 'transient authorship.'"[53] What does it mean in interdisciplinary discourse of the postmodern age to be an alien or transient crossing borders? It means to be free and enlightened but also—in that blinding moment of enlightenment when the border or Coast Guard patrol turns its light on us—to be utterly abject in the face of an unknown world that we can only *strive* to reshape so that closure is kinder.

In summary response to the epistemological critique: the epistemology of interdisciplinarity is not a closed box because interdisciplinary knowledge is really a rhetoric, and the essence of that rhetoric is at last to arrive on an abject wordlessness that is *not* the same as closure. It is a striving to reconfigure—refigure and reenvision—the forms of our closure so as to make it answerable to present urgencies.

I started by saluting the war machine in interdisciplinary studies. Let me add a last word that will reconfigure that machine so that it is not just a regime of superdiscipline. Pictured another way—as a line of flight from knowledge through rhetoric at last to an unclosed otherness—the interdisciplinary war machine can also become what Deleuze and Guattari make of it in *A Thousand Plateaus*. There, the war machine is an originally nomadic horde of border peoples antithetical to the modern state. It has as its object "not war but the drawing of a creative line of flight, the composition of a smooth space and of the movement of people in that space."[54]

A poet participates in the eternal, the infinite, and the one; as far as relates to his conceptions, time and place and number are not. . . . And the choruses of Aeschylus, and the book of Job, and Dante's "Paradise," would afford, more than any other writings, examples of this fact, if the limits of this essay did not forbid citation.

PERCY BYSSHE SHELLEY, *A DEFENSE OF POETRY*

7/

Sidney's Technology

A Critique by Technology of Literary History

1

Imagine that "technological rationality" or the total life of "technique"—as Herbert Marcuse and Jacques Ellul, respectively, conceived it in the mid-twentieth century—is constituted, not as a monolithic condition of modernity, but, instead, as a perpetual slippage between two domains of *technē*.[1] One domain is that of machinic practices, or technology proper. The other is that of bodily, social, and organizational practices, or technique. Technology enables, and is enabled by, technique. Yet these two domains do not evolve in lockstep; nor do their interior structures always align. Technology and technique slip against each other because the fit between them is never determined all the way down. At some level, the flow between the two becomes unpredictable, turbulent. *Technē* enters a zone of chaos. Or, rather, to translate explanation by chaos into socially meaningful terms, let us say that in these zones of "misfit" irrationality between technology and technique—of what seems forced, inefficient, atavistic, plural, diverse, or even contestatory in the way people use machines—signals are being received from distant or alternative zones of *technē* (present, residual, or emergent) that cannot here and now be acknowledged except as "noise."

The signs of such irrational, unacknowledged slippage between technology and technique are at least two—first, the invention of forced, catachrestic metaphors to paper over the misfit (we "scroll" down a Web "page," e.g.); and, second, the convention that such metaphors as *scroll*, *page*, and even *Web* register a specifically temporal sense of slippage: the experience of a *lag* between advancing technology and residual techniques instantiating that greatest noise in our postindustrial New Economy: obsolescence.

Any technological society, that is, must have its poetics. And that poetics, I will argue, must also be a poetics of historicity, which is how we imagine a world big enough to hold all the "downsized" and (in Evan Watkins's phrase) "throwaway" populations living in a state of historical obsolescence *within* the new.[2]

2

This is an essay that seeks to characterize the project of literary history as a technical practice that is part of the broader poetics of contemporary *technē*. My aim will be to bring us to the point—though here *just* to the point—of seeing the difference between the technical ethos of past literary history and that of the so-called new literary history (the anthologies, literary histories, and readers published since ca. 1985).[3] The best way to make this difference clear is to review the older literary history from a perspective designed to force the issue. In order to clarify the technical difference I indicate, this essay submits the literary historical practices of the past to a critique by technology—specifically, to critique from the anachronistic perspective of contemporary technology. What do past practices of literary history look like as a communications, media, and information system? And how is the new literary history different?

The materials to be considered here will include only the following works representing certain shared elements of literary-historical explication from the sixteenth century through modernity: Sidney's *Apology for Poetry* (which will be my main example), Gray's "The Progress of Poesy," Shelley's *Defense of Poetry*, Taine's *History of English Literature*, Eliot's "Tradition and the Individual Talent," Harold Bloom's *Anxiety of Influence*, and formalist literary history spanning from the Russian Formalist thesis of "systemic evolution" (Shklovsky, Eichenbaum, Tynjanov, Jakobson) to later hermeneutical and genre-study variants (e.g., Hans Robert Jauss and Ralph Cohen, respectively). I will also invoke one representative anthology: the *Norton Anthology of English Literature*.

The literary history represented by such works, we can define, is the *management and socialization of representations of literature*. This definition can be analyzed into two component axioms.

Literary history is the management of presentations of literature. The great threat to literary history, we observe, has always been the literal presentation of literature, by which I indicate, not the kind of literalness that in the fourfold scheme of biblical exegesis shared the universe of understanding with higher allegories, but a much more uncontrolled habit that does not even perceive the possibility of plural understandings and so simply presents its chosen view—whether literal or allegorical in the exegetical frame—as the transparent truth of "the text itself." Literal presentation is the attempt to give a sense of the essence of the text as if there were no gap between perception and intuition. What is the spirit, truth, or beauty of a text, in other words? Why, it is *this* spirit, truth, or beauty that I sense here.

At an elementary level, this is the kind of interpretation engaged in by the student who, when asked to talk about a text, answers with a recital or close paraphrase—as if to say indexically, "There it is." At a more advanced level, literal presentation is the interpretive mode that has most exercised such defensive literary histories as Sidney's and Shelley's. The challenge posed by Sidney's "poet-haters" or *mysomousoi*, we can thus say, is that they view literature as something that need only be perceived for its essence to appear. The realization that textual sense and essence might differ can then come only in the form of the basic Platonic accusation: literature lies. One kind of literalness (the sensory form constructed by figure, meter, rhyme, and so on) misleads us from another (the intuitive or Platonically transcendental truth).

It is precisely such literalization that Sidney counters when, in answering the charge that poetry lies, he infantilizes the *mysomousoi* as too literal minded: "What child is there that, coming to a play, and seeing *Thebes* written in great letters upon an old door, doth believe that it is Thebes? If then a man can arrive, at that child's age, to know that the poets' persons and doings are but pictures what should be, and not stories what have been, they will never give the lie to things not affirmatively but allegorically and figuratively written."[4] Nor, we should note, is it only explicitly defensive literary histories that are activated by the challenge of literal presentation. In one way or another, all the works in my paradigmatic set of literary histories could be said to revolve around the need to refute the unmediated reading that characterizes, if not *mysomousoi*, then superficial readers. Thus, the primary mission of Taine's *History* is to differentiate between the literature one can actually read and something invisible to perception: what in the introduction he calls the life of the "man," "psychology," and, ultimately, "Idea" within literature's "shell." And so too Eliot's gaze past individual talent to the mysteries of tradition or Bloom's past the errors of the author to the foreauthor differentiates between the shell and the core.

Such repudiation of the presentable, we may speculate, is what starts literary history on the task of translating the textual spirit, truth, or beauty of the literalizer into the specifically literary-historical version of essence: history. This is because history (as I have argued more fully in *Wordsworth: The Sense of History*) is the unpresentable that is there at the foundation. It is the hollowing out of the here and now that paradoxically founds all that we are in the name of all that we are not or are no longer. And a further speculation: if historical consciousness in literary history can, indeed, repudiate literal presentation by subordinating the sense of the text to an invisible historical essence, then—in a secondary operation—it will be able to open the eyes of literalizers to the fact that literature itself has always been only literary history. Literature is the repudiation of literal truth that Sidney and Shelley celebrated as "prophecy" but that literary history calls *history*.

Technical Corollary A

The full interest of viewing literary history as a management of presentation appears when we then identify the technique of such management. Indeed, it is only at the level of its *technē* that we perceive literary history to *be* a management of literalism at all rather than a blunt denial. As in the case of any strong denial or defense, the difficulty is that the object of negation is also part of the positive identity of literary history. Even the most sophisticated differentiation of textual essence from sense, after all, must at some point fall back into the habit of literal presentation to make its case—if for no other reason than to ballast the argument with "intuitive" examples that seem to say, "*This* is what I mean." Or, more simply and profoundly, consider the expression *see* in literary history, as in a citation like "see Sidney's *Apology*, 153." However complex the passage referred to in such instances, it is presumed in the fiction of the citation that simply going to the proper page will allow us to perceive something essential to the present argument. No more need be said: "There it is." Literal presentation, in short, cannot be wholly expunged from literary history: it must, instead, be technically contained, screened, or—in a word—managed.

What are the techniques by which literary history manages literal presentation? There are many ways, of course, to approach the techniques of literary history as they exist in tandem with underlying language technologies. In studying Sidney's *Apology*, for example (as Margaret Ferguson has suggested), we might do well to begin with the techniques of classical rhetoric.[5] Literary history as Sidney practiced it was a *dispositio* or arrangement of literature. But I will assimilate rhetorical analysis to a technical approach suggested by modern structural semantics and pragmatics—specifically, semiotic narratology—together with the metaphor of modern industrial communication systems that underlies such narratology. From this perspective, literary history manages presentation by means of a communication system in which narrative speech acts redirect the dangerous immediacy of citation-as-seeing into a long distance of citation-as-calling.

We can start our technical analysis at the macro level by noting that the ubiquitous surface form generated by many older literary histories is recognizable as what we would today call *anthology discourse*. Consider the pattern of a typical literature anthology: a work of literature appears under the management of a narrative headnote and a complementary set of citations (the latter a formalization of references scattered through the headnote itself). Or, again, observe that the anthology pattern is the basic discursive unit, not just of anthologies, but of literary-historical exposition generally. Surveying the genres, for example, Sidney finishes with a flourish on the epic. It will be useful to quote at length:

> There rests the heroical, whose very name (I think) should daunt all backbiters; for by what conceit can a tongue be directed to speak evil of that which draweth with it no less champions than Achilles, Cyrus, Aeneas, Turnus, Tydeus, and Rinaldo? Who doth not only teach and move to a truth, but teacheth and moveth to the most high and excellent truth; who maketh magnanimity and justice shine throughout all misty fearfulness and foggy desires; who, if the saying of Plato and Tully be true, that who could see virtue would be wonderfully ravished with the love of her beauty— this man sets her out to make her more lovely in her holiday apparel, to the eye of any that will deign not to disdain until they understand. . . . For as the image of each action stirreth and instructeth the mind, so the lofty image of such worthies most inflameth the mind with desire to be worthy, and informs with counsel how to be worthy. Only let Aeneas be worn in the tablet of your memory, how he governeth himself in the ruin of his

country, in the preserving his old father, and carrying away his religious ceremonies, in obeying the god's commandment to leave Dido, though not only all passionate kindness, but even the human consideration of virtuous gratefulness, would have craved other of him; how in storms, how in sports, how in war, how in peace, how a fugitive, how victorious, how besieged, how besieging, how to strangers, how to allies, how to enemies, how to his own; lastly, how in his inward self, and how in his outward government, and I think, in a mind not prejudiced with a prejudicating humor, he will be found in excellency fruitful, yea, even as Horace saith, *"melius Chrysippo et Crantore"* [better than Chrysippus and Crantor].[6]

What comes clear in this passage is the artfulness with which Sidney— much like Pugliano managing horses in the opening anecdote of the *Apology*—manages the *Aeneid* by anthologizing it. He prefaces his digest of the poem with a narrative headnote about the epic genre bristling with citations to other epics as well as to secondary authorities (Plato and Tully). Then a citation to Horace closes off the unit with epigrammatic finality.

Generating such anthology discourse is a technical apparatus that may be disclosed by improvising on narratology as follows. My particular guide is Greimasian semantic or structural narratology, according to which stories consist in a transmission act conceived along the lines of the information-theory model that came out of Bell Labs in the late 1940s in the well-known work of Claude Shannon and Warren Weaver (figure 7.1).[7]

Narrative action, in this view, is a communications transmission. In particular, the heart of action is the predication by which a heroic subject (located at the site of the "information source" or "transmitter," in Shannon's vocabulary) takes its quest object, which is to say, transmits itself to that object. But, in Greimas's scheme, the predicative transmission is only part of a larger structure of narrative communication. By deploying frame figures, narrative configures action within a communications system in which it is the sender who, together with a helper, codes the hero with competence and transmits him (a monarch, e.g., sets a knight a task). It is then the receiver who, once the heroic signal passes an interfering opponent (Shannon's famous "noise"), reaps the communion of subject and object that predicates happiness ever after (examples of receivers: another monarch, the knight's lady, or perhaps even the knight himself).

To apply this schema to literary history requires two progressively more structural steps. One is to recognize that the Greimasian design indeed describes the stories literary history tells about authors, works, corpuses, genres, and periods—and with no more stretching of narrative concepts

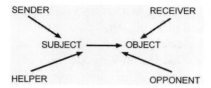

Figure 7.1. Narrative action as a communication transmission. (Adaptation of visualization in Prince, *A Dictionary of Narratology*, 2.)

than Greimas himself tolerates when sketching, for example, the ur-plots of philosophy or Marxism.[8] To illustrate, we can look again at Sidney's anthologization of the *Aeneid*. The generative core of the passage, we can now see, is precisely a story:

Subject	"Heroical" poetry
Object	"Truth"
Sender	[God, inspiration]
Receiver	Humanity
Opponent	Human "mind"
Helper	Literary form

The subject of Sidney's story is "heroical" poetry, and the object of that poetry is "truth" (epic characters, Sidney says, "teacheth and moveth to the most high and excellent truth"). The implicit sender is God or inspiration, an identification we can make with some assurance on the basis of Sidney's earlier discussion of the poet as prophet. The receiver is humanity. And shepherding the whole transmission is the great helper of the *Apology*: literary form. It is poetry's form or "holiday apparel" that allows it to overcome its perennial, noisy opponent: the dull human "mind." When Sidney rallies "images" to "stir" and "inflame" the mind, he is recalling his earlier praise of poetry's ability to seize the mind with "perfect pictures"; and, when he opens his digest of Virgil with the phrase, "Only let Aeneas be worn in the tablet of your memory," he anticipates his ensuing discussion of verse as the prompt of memory.[9] Similar narratives generate the anthology discourse of other literary histories. Without going into detail, for example, it is clear that the headnote to Sidney in the *Norton Anthology of English Literature* constructs a narrative of "influence" in which the hero is Sidney, the object great literature, the sender the spirit of the Elizabethan Age (the historicist version of inspiration), the receivers genres started by Sidney, the helper Protestantism, and the opponent early death.[10]

If anthology discourse in literary history is the parole, in sum, then narrative structure is the underlying langue. Nor should we be surprised that literary history can be locked into the grid of structural-linguistic assumptions underlying the Greimasian appropriation of information theory. Whatever the fate of structuralism after poststructuralism, it is clear that, in this case, the heavy-handed element of control that structural models of communication project is exactly the point. Literary history, after all, tells relatively naive, sparse, or (in Lévi-Strauss's sense) mythic stories about literature's rise, quest, rebellion, triumph, and (in recent years) "death" whose power depends on eschewing complexity and cleaving to the essential, controlling structures of narrativity.[11] Without retreating from structuration, then (at least for the moment), it will repay us to press our model of literary history home by delving down one further layer: to the microtechnique of its structure.

It is here that we come squarely on the device of citation, whose ubiquitousness in anthology discourse follows from the fact that it must be considered to be the elementary structure of literary history. Like binaries in structuralist decision trees (left / right, raw / cooked, bear clan / eagle clan, and so on), citational devices are the microcomponents—the transistor switches—that steer narrative signals as they course down the literary-historical version of decision trees (the plot of romanticism, e.g., with its sequential forks: French Revolution / or nature, nature / imagination, imagination / love, and so on).[12] To understand where their controlling power comes from, we need to look past specific devices of citation— namings, titlings, allusions, epigrammatic quotes, bibliographic references—to the basic contradiction implicit in all of them: the tension between seeing authority and calling (or summoning) authority. The danger of literal presentation in citation, it may be suggested, can be suppressed only by redirecting *seeing* into *calls* to remote sources—when immediate inspection, that is, defers to something like an apostrophe to the invisible gods ("O Hermes!"). Or, in the spirit of Industrial Age messenger systems, we might borrow Avital Ronell's explicitly telephonic vocabulary and say that literary history is a communications system in which the narrative subject can never call its object on the predicative line without the interruption of remote and usually more powerful or elevated authorities (the sender, receiver, helper, and opponent) calling in on auxiliary lines.[13] The function of these latter lines is to switch the circuit of the predicative line to its proper destination when called on by the subject in an inquiry loop.

"Which object should I seek?" we can thus hear heroes asking, requesting a direction to be relayed from the sender. Or, again, a call inquiry of the sort, "Which path should I take?" solicits helpers to relay tactics and craft.

"Stand or flee!" calls out an opponent in the way a bullfighter's "citar" (in Roland Barthes's fanciful meditation on "citation") summons the bull.[14] And, "Wilt thou receive me, lady?" the hero solicits of his receiver in order to switch at last into happiness mode. Only after all the connections to auxiliary parties are completed can the fatal call then be placed allowing the subject to communicate directly with the object of quest—grail, gold, secret, whatever. Literary-historical narratives connect in exactly the same way to remote authorities to switch their heroic authors, periods, and genres along forking decision trees. Thus the prevalence of inquiries of the type, "Who were the ancestral senders?" (in one version of the romanticism story: Milton/or Spenser); "Who the ephebe receivers?" (Eliot/Stevens); "Who the helpers?" (Coleridge/Dorothy); "Who the opponents?" (French Revolution/nature). Transposed into the declarative, such calls on remote authority become citations of the standard sort: "According to Coleridge"; "Burke wrote"; "See Hartman on romantic nature"; and so forth.

There is one crucial relay, as we will see, left to close. But at least in principle we can now understand the circuit-switching mechanism by which literary history manages literal presentation. Literary history cites remote information about its heroic authors, works, corpuses, genres, and periods that can be used to switch any literal presentation of these heroes away from "intuitive" objects to ever more abridged and nonintuitive objects. Abridged because each fork in the decision tree cuts off yet another portion of relevant material, and nonintuitive because the final object of literary history is, not what can be seen on the page at all, but, rather, something invisible: that gigantic communications switchboard (as monopolistic in its way as the prebreakup AT&T) called *tradition*.

Thus, we can add a further elaboration to our speculations about history in literary history. It is no accident that history as understood by older literary history has generally emerged from the unpresentable into manifest, citable form precisely as *tradition*. Tradition is historical consciousness managed by citations. Done well, such citation has a deus ex machina effect that confers on narratives of literature the seemingly *necessary* contingency of history itself. Whether literary history tells stories of continuous tradition or of its revolutionary reversals, in other words, it creates a story in which the ordering of cited information about a work appears identical with the very evolution of historical action—a fusion of the concepts of reception and evolution nowhere more programmatic than in Jaussian hermeneutical literary history.[15] Thus, what is the object of imagination in the Simplon Pass episode of Wordsworth's *Prelude*? Recent "operators" of romantic literary history tell us: "Please hold that call from Wordsworth's mind; I have another call coming in from Napoleon."[16] The call from Napoleon is the apparent voice of history. It is the voice of the seemingly necessary contingency that interrupts the call placed by the imagination to self-consciousness (the "poet's calling" that the poem literally celebrates) in the service of citing a more remote political context capable of usurping self-consciousness in the name of history.

Technical Corollary B

But perhaps we have too prematurely subordinated citation-as-seeing to citation-as-calling. One relay in the system, as I indicated, is still open. To locate this relay, we can make yet another pass through Sidney's paragraph on the *Aeneid* with the question in mind: What in the passage is barely under control?

The answer, clearly, is the digest of Virgil, which paraphrases the plot so fulsomely that it not only threatens to suspend Sidney's narrative argument about epic but strains even his syntax. The digest opens by marshaling events in parallel subordinate clauses: "how [Aeneas] governeth himself in the ruin of his country, in the preserving his old father, . . . in obeying the god's commandment to leave Dido. . . ." But once Sidney reaches Dido, we notice, a miniature epyllion starts up requiring a digression into further subordination: "though not only all passionate kindness," the sentence adds, "but even the human consideration of virtuous gratefulness, would have craved other of [Aeneas]." And, with this digression releasing more of Virgil's original narrative than the sentence can easily subordinate, syntax begins to founder. "How in storms, how in sports, how in war, how in peace, how a fugitive, how victorious," and so on, Sidney continues, eliding predication in each clause so severely that the "tablet" of our "memory" can barely recover in time for the sentence to close. We might be reminded here of Odysseus's scar as studied by Auerbach: Sidney's mention of Dido, like the servant's touch on the scar, suddenly calls up a whole prior tale usurping the control of the main tale.[17]

The relay still open, of course, is the one at the very heart of literal presentation inspiring us to explore narrative management in the first place. I refer to what has so far remained invisible in my schematization: the contact that literary-historical narrative must at some point make with the original narratives of primary literature, the wires, as it were, that conduct from such stories as "the development of epic" to full-bodied stories on the order of "arms and a man" (the *Aeneid*). Literary history, as we have seen, is a system of remote citations designed to control the connection between literary-historical subjects and objects. But how does primary literature get fed into the system in the first place as a subject able to be distributed and, thereby, abridged and steered? What if the initial charge of literature were simply too large to be handled by the literary-historical circuits and could discharge only in a lightning strike of literal presentation?

By *initial charge*, I mean roughly something like the effect of Milton on a student who either "loves" or "hates" him—*all* of him. *Paradise Lost* is a great (or terrible) poem; each individual book or line is great; even single words "rebound" on us as if we too were belated peasants surprised by the "joy and fear" of the essential Miltonic voice (reduced in its reception to "joy *or* fear"). Put quantitatively, the problem such charge poses for literary history is that there is a perennial imbalance of force making even the slenderest conduit leading from literary history to primary literature potentially a source of overload. With the possible exception of such especially compulsive literary histories as Harold Bloom's, after all, literary history's tales of "rises," "declines," "revolutions," and so forth tend to be far weaker in realization than the primary literary narratives they manage. What they gain in mythic or schematic clarity they lose in the felt allure, complexity, suspense, and, ultimately, deep pathos that make us "read for the plot." Without some impedance or, better, buffer (in current technologese: *flow control*) able to compensate for this imbalance, all the delicate narrative forks of literary history would be flooded by an initial surge of primary narrative that becomes unmanageable simply because it saturates *all* the forks in the literary-historical decision tree, making the object of the *Aeneid*, for example, both Sidneyan truth *and* deceit, love and hate, honor and dishonor, public identity and privacy, and so on or that of *Paradise Lost* (contrary to the hoary gambit of asking which is Milton's real hero) all the following: God, man, woman, *and* Satan (not to mention, on the plane of influence, Virgil, Moses, *and* Spenser). Indeed, we see such saturation beginning to work in the *how* clauses of Sidney's digest, which increasingly occupy both poles in a series of binaries: war/peace, allies/enemies, inward self/outward government.

The qualitative aspect of the problem is just as telling. This is because the truly insidious character of literal presentation, we can now realize, is that it is *not* just an unfocused discharge like lightning. Rather, it is itself a technique of citation—a whole, uncanny *countertechnique* emphasizing citation-as-seeing rather than citation-as-calling. However intuitive it may seem, that is, literal presentation of literature is really a full-blown communications system whose microdevices of paraphrase, long quotation, transcription, facsimile, and so on travesty the citation function in literary history. Rather than being managerial, these citational devices are reproductive. Even the most muted among them (paraphrase, e.g.) calls on the original work so as to regenerate within the space of literary history a potentially ungovernable literature, and such more elaborate devices as long quotation or transcription create monsters.

Primary literature, we can say, is a vast generator of information linked to a reproductive technology and (my focus at present) reproductive technique. Literary history is a much less robust apparatus whose specialized technique would tap that generator delicately. At the moment when literary history necessarily engages in literal presentation—however briefly or subtly—to quote or paraphrase the primary text, its citational apparatus becomes perilously vulnerable to a massive incursion of information that shorts out all the fine interpretive relays to the sender, receiver, helper, and opponent. Or, to bring the conceit home in familiar terms, one false or badly phrased question by the teacher, and the student responds to a citation calling on traditional authorities by objecting obstreperously, "But if we *look* at the text, it says . . ." (followed by a long, unmanageable paraphrase).

How can the citational connection between literary history and primary literature be monitored, therefore, so as to control the entry of reproductive citations into the network of managerial citations? Indeed, how are managerial citations themselves controlled so that they do not suddenly turn reproductive and ask us to see too much of the remote authority? If each relay in a literary-historical narrative is a sentry controlling the actions of literature as "hero," in short, what prior sentry with a master on/off switch can from the first either cut literature down to size (phrased qualitatively: limit and organize the use of reproductive devices) or buffer it with flow-control techniques (storing the signal in the cache of history and tradition) so that it becomes narratively tractable?

The answer, I suggest, must be located in a secondary, institutionally specific technique of management: a second-order narrative monitoring literary-historical narrative itself. To sketch this supervisory apparatus, it will be useful to vary the Greimasian approach by raising it fully from semantics to pragmatics. As we have so far sketched it, literary history is a communicational situation whose pragmatics are restricted to the plane of the narrative. Senders, receivers, and so forth are frame figures peripheral to, but still signally *in*, the story. To observe the second-order monitoring apparatus, we need now to step off the narrative plane to the institutional situation in which literary history functions. The apparatus I have in mind can be visualized as a communicational situation superimposed over literary-historical narrative as shown in figure 7.2.

This is the pragmatic situation that adds to literary-historical narrative the specific managerial techniques of the institution we know as the

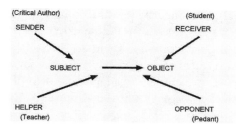

Figure 7.2. Monitoring apparatus of literary-historical narrative.

academy. It is not accidental that it has been so easy above to reach for examples from the scene of instruction (a student reciting a text, a typical teaching anthology, and so on). Nor is it incidental that Sidney's *Apology* so consistently honors literature on the point of learning. "Heroical" poetry "teacheth and moveth," we heard Sidney say in one of many variants on the Horatian "delight and instruct" dictum. Throughout the *Apology*, *teaching* and *learning* are privileged terms—even to the point of acquiring specifically academic connotations under the titles of "learned men," "learned Hebricians," "scholar," or school-"master." (In his opening anecdote, Sidney figures his relation to Pugliano tongue in cheek as "scholar" to "master.") Just so, Shelley—antipedagogical as he could be in other contexts—deploys a version of the Horatian dictum ("the beautiful and the true") when he closes an extraordinary paean to literature by granting teachers the last, best place next to God: "But poets, or those who imagine and express this indestructible order, are not only the authors of language and of music, of the dance, and architecture, and statuary, and painting; they are the institutors of laws, and the founders of civil society, and the inventors of the arts of life, and the teachers, who draw into a certain propinquity with the beautiful and the true, that partial apprehension of the agencies of the invisible world which is called religion."[18] And, if it is not too perverse, we could move at this point directly from Shelley to Eliot, whose "Tradition and the Individual Talent" is uncomfortably aware of the "usual objection" that Eliot's view of poetry "requires a ridiculous amount of erudition (pedantry)." Eliot's response is to save the phenomena of knowledge by expanding the schoolroom to the scale of the world: "It is not desirable," he says, "to confine knowledge to whatever can be put into a useful shape for examinations."[19]

The exact manner in which the pragmatics of the academy—that is, the communicational situation of the classroom—metamanages the literary-historical management of narrative can be elucidated as follows. It may be noticed that, in my discussion so far, I have slighted remote citations to critical or secondary literature: what Plato, Tully, or Horace have to say in the Sidney passage, for example (or what Castiglione, Fulke Greville, Spenser, and others have to say in the *Norton* headnote on Sidney himself). I have also elided certain crucial citational devices with a strong figurative component: namings-by-address, apostrophes, invocations, personifications, and sometimes full-scale impersonations. In classically rhetorical terms, the latter *personating* citations (as they may be called) manage *dispositio*. The distribution of argument in the *Apology* into *narratio*, *explicatio*, *partitio*, *refutatio*, and so forth depends on a series of callings by which Sidney makes spokesmen of differing views appear—and then quickly disappear—in clever concatenation. We can instance such Sidneyan personations as the following:

> I will give you a nearer example of myself, who . . . in these my not old years and idlest times [have] slipped into the title of a poet.

> And first, truly, to all them that professing learning inveigh against poetry. . . .

> And even historiographers . . . have been glad to borrow both fashion and perchance weight of poets.

> But truly now having named him [David], I fear me I seem to profane. . . .

> As principal challengers step forth the moral philosophers, whom, me thinketh, I see coming towards me with a sullen gravity. . . .

> The historian scarcely giveth leisure to the moralist to say so much, but that he, laden with old mouse-eaten records . . . denieth, in a great chafe, that any man for teaching of virtue . . . is comparable to him.

> First, truly I note not only in these *mysomousoi*, "poet-haters," but in all that kind of people. . . .[20]

It is possible to project all these secondary and personating citations on the primary plane of literary-historical narrative. Sidney's impersonated moral philosophers, historiographers, and poet-haters, for example, could be seen as noisy opponents supplementary to the dull mind. But I have not utilized these citations in this way because it is important to see that they are only partly rooted on the plane of literary-historical narrative. Their larger function is to serve as relays outward from that narrative to the institutional communicative situation. Citations that personate a narrator on the narrative plane (e.g., the self-aware "I think" at the end of Sidney's paragraph on the *Aeneid*) thus project on a different plane an author super-imposed over the sender position. In a specifically academic or pseudoaca-demic institutional setting, that author is the literary historian or scholar, critic, and/or theorist. So too citations that personate a narratee map over the receiver an implicit reader whose academic embodiment is the stu-dent. When at the end of his paragraph Sidney addresses the "mind not prejudiced with a prejudicating humor," he in effect invokes the character of a receptive student. In a similar vein, citations that personate or call on secondary authorities (Horace, Plato, and Tully in the Sidney passage) map over the helper an implicit didact or teacher. Finally, citations that personate moral philosophers, historiographers, and other falsely learned *mysomousoi* (e.g., the "backbiters" at the head of the passage on epic) su-perimpose over the opponent position a character familiar to Eliot: the pedant (or in neoclassical terms, dunce).

Once this monitoring apparatus grounded in the institution is set in place, then the technology of management is complete. How to prevent literal presentation from overloading the narrative switches when literary history, as it must occasionally do, cites its primary literature? The answer is to counter the deictic or firsthand forcefulness of reproductive citation with the even more coercive citational technique that is pedagogy. The reason, of course, is that the elementary switch or control mechanism by which pedagogy communicates its narrative arguments in the class-room is a particularly potent form of citation—an "interpellation" de-signed to enforce the laws of narrative citation. According to the standard teaching format, a student calls on the teacher (who, in turn, calls on the scholar-critic-theorist) to solicit a lesson. But, when it is the teacher who calls on the student (in the way that an Althusserian policeman "hails" or cites a man in the street), then the result is the inverse of a lesson: a test.[21] (Teacher: "What is the *Aeneid* about?" Student: [narration]. Teacher: "Identify this quotation." Student: [citation].)

One further dimension of the history in literary history can now be noticed. If such history begins in the need to deny literal presentation, as I suggested, and if it first emerges into manifest form as tradition, then the institution in which we learn the tradition that denies us our present is education. Put simply, historical consciousness—whether deployed in literary or other kinds of study—is now what we *mean* by education in the humanities. When the student presents the literal text as if it were self-evident, education responds: look at the text in such a way as to see through it to its tradition of texts and contexts, to everything, in short, that manages the text by precedence, parallel, or interpretation. Such is one reason, as John Guillory's work on the literary canon so incisively argues, that an adequate discussion of literary history must at some point cite the history of the academy.[22]

Literary history is the socialization of representations of literature. But the academy, of course, is not the ultimate ground of the pragmatics allowing literary history to manage literal presentation. There is still one more step to take in modeling traditional literary history, a step that we can accomplish in much more abbreviated fashion because the territory is so familiar in older literary histories and so reconfigured in the new literary history.

The step is from literature—through the intervening technique of literary-historical narrative and pedagogy—to the general pragmatics of culture. At this point, it is more sensible to speak of the management of representations of literature rather than of presentations. The total intent of the techniques of management we have observed, it may be said, is to regulate presentations of literature to the point where there are effectively *no* presentations at all, only apparent representations. All good academic technique thus triggers a representation effect. Good teaching in a seminar, for example, depends in part on the ability of the instructor to transform student presentations into self-aware "views." After a student presents a particularly aggressive reading, a teacher can turn to the class and say something like, "Would you agree with Melissa's view?" At that moment, presentation becomes representation: a "view," "interpretation," "argument," or "narrative" in quotation marks. The effect is roughly the same when Sidney figures a moral philosopher or historian offering his view of literature. At the moment Sidney displaces our attention to the presenter (through devices of impersonation), we no longer directly perceive the presentation; we watch representation in quotation marks.

Given that academic literary history ultimately resolves all presentations into representations of literature, then the question becomes, What to do with plural, alternate, or incommensurable representations? We can take a quick inventory of representations of literature to indicate the scope of the problem. In my paradigmatic set of literary histories, for example, we hear spokesmen tell literary-historical tales according to which the object of literature is lying (Plato), abuse (the *mysomousoi*), ornament (Sidney), knowledge (Sidney, Shelley), imaginative prophecy (Sidney, Shelley, Bloom), delight or pleasure (Sidney, Shelley), therapeutic "music" (Gray, Shelley), "catalysis" (Eliot), and "defamiliarization," changing "expectations," or "innovation" (Russian Formalists, Jauss, Cohen). How can academic literary history sort out such multiple stories, rejecting some representations of literature, and linking others together in an overarching hierarchy? How, in other words, can it compose all its *petits récits* into a metanarrative?

The key to the dilemma lies in realizing that the many alternate stories of literature available to academic literary history do not simply come from left field. Rather, they become materials for literary-historical synthesis because from the first they are profoundly and intimately known to the academy. In particular, we can hypothesize that the majority of literary-historical *récits* have derived from scenes of instruction related in some way—psychologically, socially, or institutionally—to formal education itself. Thus, for example, representations of literature as lyrical music, pleasure, or (for Bloom) psychorhetorical agon hark back to an explicitly childish or primitive social kindergarten. ("In the youth of the world, men dance and sing," Shelley imagines. "In climes beyond the solar road, / Where shaggy forms o'er ice-built mountains roam," Gray concurs.)[23] And the scene of instruction traditionally responsible for such childishness is familial domesticity. Whatever its purport, we might thus say, Shklovsky's exemplum of literature as the defamiliarization of a household parlor (the room being "habitually" cleaned in the Tolstoy passage he quotes) is actually not so unfamiliar: we are still at home.[24] Or, again, representations of literature as prophecy invoke the religious adjuncts of the academy. Given that the pragmatics of literary-historical instruction involve cross-institutional affiliations and competitions, then, our question about metanarrative can be refashioned as follows: What larger or überinstitution monitors the whole complex of related scenes of instruction such that the institution of formal education is legitimated? What institution of institutions, that is, adjudicates and privileges the very notion of education in the fractious context of its domestic, religious, and other institutional kin?

The answer most often has been national culture. The recourse of the literary-historical instructor charged with the many unruly narratives of domestic, religious, and other regimes, in other words, is to convene them in a classroom administration that looks outside itself for final legitimation to the management regime that is society at the state level—in particular, to the "England," "America," "France," or other state or imperial civilizations that have been the predominant metaheroes of literary histories (as in *The Norton Anthology of English Literature*). In this regard, the vast bulk of literary histories are really nation or area studies, whether British, American, French, or otherwise. All, that is, socialize competing

narratives of literary history by convening them in an academy imaging a
larger national or imperial administration, a more authoritative template
for socialization.

We can thus add a last speculation about the history in literary history.
Literary history, we recognize, achieves its fullest form when historical
consciousness progresses from the sense of the unpresentable through the
sense of tradition to an explicit historiography and sociology of nation
(or, inseparably bound up with nation, a "national literacy"). I refer to
the imperative in most of the literary histories in my paradigmatic set to
map the tradition of literature over the development of civil society. The
relation between literature and state civility is variously conceived such
that one or another is causally prior to the other (or, sometimes, the two
are simply parallel), but the effect in all cases is to organize competing
representations of literature into a metanarrative functioning as a sort of
Aeneid of literary history: the story of a nation's founding. The full result
of thus mapping the history of literature over the social, economic, and
political condition of the state is the long roll call of explicit civil histories
in literary history. Sidney traces the connate rise of literature and classical civilization at the beginning of the *Apology*, goes on in the middle to
match literature to the history of empire (in the section on "poetry . . .
the companion of camps"),[25] and then delineates the history of literature
in the context of the English nation. Shelley surveys the parallel rise of
poetry and civilization in prehistoric times, extends that survey in a long
history of the relation between literature and societies, and, of course, at
last gives literature a place in the legislature of the world. Gray's "Progress
of Poesy" follows the migration of literature from nation to nation in the
wake of freedom ("When Latium had her lofty spirit lost, / They [the
Muses] sought, oh Albion! next thy sea-encircled coast").[26] Taine charts
his literary history infamously over the coordinates of "the race, the sur-
roundings, and the epoch."[27] Eliot seeks a literary "main current" that is
also the spirit of nation-state Europe ("the mind of Europe—the mind
of [a poet's] own country").[28] And, to take just one more instance, the
Russian Formalists in their late period desperately sought to correlate the
theory of evolving literary systems with Soviet social dialectics.

It is a fallacy, we can conclude, to say that even the most rigorously
formal literary history does not contextualize. All literary histories have
completed themselves explicitly or implicitly by mapping the history of
texts over the history of peoples as those peoples have been organized
since early modern times in national cultures. All manage *and* socialize
representations of literature.

3

How do we turn the page, then, to the new literary history? This is not a question I can address here in more than telegraphic form (to revert to a communications technology even older than telephony). But terse telegraphy of the sort that helped control the railroads—and so assisted the rise of the first great, modern corporate organizations (as studied in the work of Alfred D. Chandler Jr. and James R. Beniger)—may be useful.[29] Just as the telegraph signaled "collision impending," we might say, so I must now do the Morse for "paradigm change impending."

For the peculiar feature of telephony as a paradigm, of course, is the thoroughness with which its phenomenology—originating in centralized, circuit-switched, and master-slave relations (whereby a higher authority, the sender, redirects the circuit in toto between the transmitter and the receiver)—began to convert since the 1970s to the new god of decentralized, packet-switched, and (the key word here) networked relations: to what is now called, not telephony at all, but *voice networking*. The appropriate metaphor for the new literary history that currently displays the deconstructive, culturalist, and multiculturalist research agendas of the past few decades, I suggest, is *networking*. However variously these several research agendas have described their project, from the point of view of a critique by technology—that is, of a critique of the changed position of literary-historical knowledge in a world dominated by information culture—they must all also be described as just another interface for new technologies and techniques governed in the last instance by the "learning organization" now contending with the academy for lordship over knowledge. I refer to the postindustrial corporation. Poststructuralism and its sequelae share an office with distributed networking, packet switching, subnets, "virtual corporations," flexible work teams, "just in time," "chaos management," and so on through all the litany of terms invented by that great contemporary imagination of *technē*: knowledge work.[30]

But there is a difference, and it is this difference that a fully critical engagement between academic knowledge and knowledge work—one in which the critique runs in both directions—must grasp. I can do no more here to suggest that difference than to advert to a single, dominant metaphor in the new literary history—not networking, not telephony, not even telegraphy, but an even older technology of work and communication that poses (besides its more explicit poststructural, multicultural, and gendered meanings) a certain kind of historicizing *stance* toward technology capable of saving a space in the new for the old. The metaphor is one about which there is much more to say: *patchwork quilting*. Why so many of the volumes of the new literary history have cover illustrations evoking patchwork—and equivalent tropes such as the mosaic and the kaleidoscope—is a question worth technical investigation.[31]

Any technological society, in short, must be a poetics. And that poetics must also be a poetics of history, which is our only way to imagine a world big enough to hold all of us.

8 /

Transcendental Data

Toward a Cultural History and Aesthetics of the New Encoded Discourse

\<preface type="general"\>

Whether one writes fiction or business reports, prepares lectures or sales presentations, publishes works stored in a library or a commercial database—whatever, in fact, one's domain of authoring might be—the chances are that one is already producing content that somewhere along the route of its transmission takes the form of a uniquely contemporary kind of discourse: encoded or structured discourse, in the technical sense of digital text encoding and structured markup.[1] At its most local, such encoding or markup shows up in the copyedited manuscripts that authors now see from publishers, which, instead of notes to the designer in the old style of "18 pt. heading" (and so on), provide pure logical descriptors or "tags" keyed to house style—for example, the title of this chapter would appear as "\<ct\>Transcendental

Data</ct>."[2] More globally, a bewildering variety of the world's documents and media have in the recent past been encoded in, or are managed by, standardized text-based markup schemes (especially XML, or Extensible Markup Language) that include descriptors for everything from textual or multimedia content to such metadata as author, date, section, and so on. Alternatively, such documents and media have been entered in databases that hold content in tables, records, and fields exportable into XML.

This entire collection of databases and markup languages has so far remained largely hidden from individual writers and readers because it is first being implemented at the institutional level. An increasing number of businesses, publishers, booksellers, university libraries, and digital text archives now use databases and XML to manage the jostling, dynamic bundle of data objects we once called *books, articles, reports,* or *songs.* But, now that XML is being integrated into standard enterprise and personal-productivity software (including well-known proprietary as well as open-source office suites), ordinary authors and readers—especially those working in institutional settings—will be influenced as well.[3] Authors and readers will join with their institutions to complete a new discursive circuit we might call, updating Friedrich Kittler's media analysis, *discourse network 2000.*[4]

Though the problem of reading the new discourse—browsing, searching, annotating or tagging, and so forth—is intriguing in its own right,[5] I concentrate in this essay on the originating end of the transmission act—authoring. What will discourse network 2000 mean for the act of authoring?

A critical analysis of the new discourse first requires that we unfold its logic in its own terms, which is to say, the technological terms of the postindustrial institutions led by knowledge-work business. But it also requires that we view such techno-logic through the lens of other participating institutions that, while increasingly colonized by postindustrial principles, offer an alternative perspective. The specific institutional perspective I bring to bear is that of the humanities and arts in the academy, which have, in their own way, begun exploring discourse network 2000. Members of the Association for Computers and the Humanities (ACH) and the Text Encoding Initiative (TEI), for example, have long had a hand in developing or adapting text-encoding standards, and, in the last decade, major digital text and image archives at East Coast centers of humanities computing in the United States (such as Brown University and the University of Virginia) have proved the sophistication and robustness of text encoding for literature.[6] In a logically similar move, some of the most advanced humanities computing projects on the U.S. West Coast—for example, those associated with the University of California's Digital Cultures Project and Digital Arts Research Network (DARnet)—have pursued the complementary paradigm of database technology.[7] Seen one way, such projects make the transmission of academic knowledge more efficient and flexible and, thus, enroll the humanities and arts in the techno-logic of discourse network 2000. But, viewed differently, they also prepare the academy to refract such techno-logic through its own values, which are not always on the same page with the business master plan. After all, while the technological measure of the new discourse paradigm is postindustrial efficiency coupled with flexibility, that is, the ability to say anything to anyone quickly, the measure of academic knowledge is also historical, social, philosophical, artistic, and public (nonproprietary) diversity, for example, the ability to say anything to anyone fully, richly, openly, differently, kindly, or slowly.

Because one of the emphases in the humanities in the past two decades has been cultural studies, there is special interest at this juncture, I believe, in seeing what a cultural-history approach might tell us about the structured encoding of knowledge.[8] My first critical question will thus be: *What is the social logic that underlies the techno-logic of discourse network 2000?* With specific reference to authoring: *How is an author now a postindustrial producer?* But social history alone is not cultural for the humanities and arts unless it also treats representation, expression, and style, especially as these are now understood to extend beyond the canvas of form onto such subjective and/or material registers of experience as identity or body. My final critical question will open a preliminary speculation into aesthetic logic: *What are the aesthetics of encoded or structured discourse or, as I will term it, of* postindustrial dematerialization? And: *How is it possible for writers or artists to create in such a medium?*

</preface>

<preface type="technical">

But, first, what exactly is encoded or structured discourse? Consider the problem of sending a poem over the Internet to a distant computer without knowing exactly what program will receive it, the nature of the processing or display technologies at the other end, or even the remote user's purpose. The poem is as follows:

The SICK ROSE

O Rose thou art sick.
The invisible worm,

That flies in the night
In the howling storm:

Has found out thy bed
Of crimson joy:
And his dark secret love
Does thy life destroy.[9]

What is the best way for the author to send, not just the content of the poem, but also the exact instructions for processing that content? The general goal is to enable the greatest number of machinic idiots savants at the other end—by turns dumb and brilliant in ways the author cannot predict—not just to receive the poem, but also to do something intelligent with it, whether reproducing the original or something else.

A poor solution, it turns out, is to transmit procedures. A procedural instruction for the display of the poem, for example, might say in essence: "Display the first line beginning at screen position 400 pixels on the x-axis, 500 pixels on the y-axis." Such instructions tell the machine exactly what to do but, for that reason, are not readily adaptable when circumstances vary. (What would a small cell phone screen, e.g., do with a line of text offset 400 pixels to the right?) Procedural instructions also allow for little use of intelligence by the receiving machine to adapt the content to local needs—for instance, to the needs of a hypothetical poem aggregator that looks only for poetry related to disease or written in quatrains (analogous to one of the RSS news aggregator sites that use XML to pull together syndicated news articles from all over the Web).[10] The procedural approach, in other words, addresses only the idiot, not the potential savant that is inhumanly good at filtering, searching, aggregating, transforming, or otherwise processing communication for its own (sometimes unforeseen) purposes.[11]

A better solution, then, is to break the circuit of transmission and reception into two independent parts assisted in their mating by a common standard. On the transmission end, the author can use a logically descriptive rather than a procedural approach to define the elements of the poem—for example, line and stanza—so that they fit within an overall conceptual structure for the parts of a poem. The structure either is implied in a common discursive standard (a set of specifications) that all participants in the discourse network understand or, for customized needs, can be stated explicitly as a set of subordinate, extended standards to be sent along with the content in definitional statements. At the receiving end, the particular program then allows the standard to guide it in using its own procedures for processing or display. A single description of content at the source can in this way be molded in typically postindustrial fashion to a decentralized variety of consuming programs, formats, and usages.

One common implementation of such an approach is the database solution I previously mentioned. A modern relational and SQL (Structured Query Language) database holds its content descriptively in tables, records, and fields.[12] For example, a set of interrelated tables might contain information about a poem in fields labeled *title, author, publication_date, line_number,* and (for the actual content of a particular verse) *line.* Such a database could be "queried" (through a search for *Blake* together with *rose,* e.g.) so as to produce a nicely formatted version of "The Sick Rose." The pure-database approach works best when both the sending and the receiving computers run the same database program, sharing a common discursive standard built into the workings of the software itself. But, for wider compatibility, databases can also present their content on the Web (more precisely, through the Web's HTTP transmission protocol) by means of middleware programming or scripting that shuttles content into HTML (Hypertext Markup Language) or, as we will see below, XML. The rules of HTML or XML, established by the World Wide Web Consortium (W3C), then serve as the common standard that the browser or some other program uses to process the material. A distributed network of users connected by the Web can thus access database content and use Web forms to search or edit that content.

The other major implementation (used by itself or, as suggested above, with databases) is text encoding or markup, whose most current common standard is XML. Developed by the W3C beginning in 1996 as a subset of the older SGML (Standard Generalized Markup Language), XML is designed to be far more capable than HTML (the previous subset of SGML) at sharing information over the Internet in a manner at once uniform and customizable (extensible).[13] XML is human readable in the sense that its descriptive code consists of plain-text tags in angle brackets residing at the same level as the content they encode (i.e., in the same document). These tags, which thus accompany the content wherever it goes, serve the same descriptive function as fields in a database. In XML, for example, our poem might be marked up:

```
<anthology>
    <poem><title>The SICK ROSE</title>
        <stanza>
            <line>O Rose thou art sick.</line>
            <line>The invisible worm,</line>
```

```
        <line>That flies in the night</line>
        <line>In the howling storm:</line>
    </stanza>
    <stanza>
        <line>Has found out thy bed</line>
        <line>Of crimson joy:</line>
        <line>And his dark secret love</line>
        <line>Does thy life destroy.</line>
    </stanza>
  </poem>
</anthology>
```[14]

Each pair of open and close tags (e.g., <stanza> </stanza>) describes its enclosed content as an element of the discourse (sometimes supplemented by an attribute or more precise specification of that element). The logical consistency of the whole set of descriptions is guaranteed by a common set of XML rules specified by the W3C such that, to take a simple example, each open tag must be followed by a matching close tag. In addition, the descriptive vocabulary for a particular kind of document—poem, prose, business card, and so on—can be specified in an accompanying DTD (document type definition) or, better, XML schema that explicitly defines, for instance, <line> and <stanza> so that the former can be nested validly within the latter, but not vice versa. The computer receiving the transmission would then use an XML-processor program working in league with a server application (e.g., a database) or user application (e.g., a browser) to handle the poem appropriately according to the standards.[15]

The overall morphology of discourse network 2000 can thus be outlined as three functionally independent strata, each comprising a set of functions enacted by a variable assemblage of machines, programs, people, and institutional support structures:[16]

> *Content Management.* This stratum of discursive activity feeds content into a database or XML source document in structured form, where *structured* means a format able to differentiate and relate such logical units as paragraph, quotation, and title.
>
> *Transmission Management.* This discursive layer exports or sends content over the Internet in the intervening form of XML (together with such supporting standards governing the manipulation or sending of XML as XSLT, SOAP, and so on). Underlying this layer of discourse are the Internet's TCP/IP (Transmission Control Protocol/Internet Protocol) and related

protocols, responsible for transmitting, not documents per se, but their constituent files and data packets.

Consumption Management. Consumption management is the stratum of discursive activity that receives the XML transmission and absorbs, reformats, filters, edits, or otherwise *actively* consumes it for local purposes. To use Alvin Toffler's term in his description of postindustrialism, it is productive consumption or "prosumption."[17]

</preface>

<argument title="techno-logic" subtitle="the blind spot on the page">

On the early world "wild" Web, one corporation's or library's idiosyncratic database might not have been able to send its contents to any other database or end-user program through equally idiosyncratic HTML code. And the gap between ordinary word processing and the Web—let alone the so-called Deep Web of underlying databases—was even wider. But now thick, pliant strands of XML are girding the wilderness (and even tying in word-processor documents) to enable a new order of knowledge. Discourse network 2000 is a step in the direction of what Tim Berners-Lee, the Web's founder, has envisioned as a future "Semantic Web"—a Web that will understand something about the nature of the discourse it is being asked to communicate and, thus, be able to process that discourse more intelligently and automatically.[18]

The techno-logic that informs this vision may be stated in the form of three powerful needs that have converged in contemporary business and other institutions that value the efficient and flexible, which is to say, postindustrial, transmission of information.

The first is the need to make discourse as *transformable* as possible between varying technological and social conventions so that identical content might flow just as easily, for example, to a printed page, a Web page, or a cell phone display.

The second is the need to make discourse *autonomously mobile* in a way that updates Claude Shannon's transmission model of communication (with fixed points of sender and receiver separate from the logic of the message itself). Just as data packets in the Internet's TCP/IP protocol are atomistic parts of a file each with just enough microintelligence about source, destination, and position in the overall file to fly solo like a carrier pigeon and reassemble in proper order with its flock, so in loosely analogous fashion XML elements such as <line> and <stanza> are what might be called *document packets* with just enough logical autonomy—assisted by the common XML standard—to know where and how they should be processed relative to the document as a whole. It's like writing a novel on index cards and throwing them out of an airplane at thirty thousand feet. When the cards land, somehow they line up in the right order or—even more uncannily—in someone else's searched, sampled, remixed, summarized, and aggregated order.

The third is the need to *automate* such discourse so that a proliferating population of machinic servers, databases, and client programs can participate as cyborgian agents and concatenated Web services facilitating the processing and reprocessing of knowledge.[19] In the case of an RSS news aggregator, for example, humans no longer need to take many of the intervening steps necessary to find and filter articles residing on different servers and databases. They become just the last of many agents automatically negotiating with each other on the Web to perform the transaction of reading, or browsing, for us.

These cardinal needs of transformability, autonomous mobility, and automation resolve at a more general level into what may be identified as the governing ideology of discourse network 2000: *the separation of content from material instantiation or formal presentation.* Endorsed explicitly or implicitly by the standards-setting bodies (e.g., the TEI, which declares: "XML focuses on the meaning of data, not its presentation"), the ideology of the separation of content from material or formal presentation is the deep logic behind the discursive morphology outlined earlier in which the intervening layer of transmission management serves as something like a secret-agent cutout allowing content management at the source and consumption management at the terminus to be double-blind to each other.[20] From the author's viewpoint, therefore, a poem can now be written free of commitment to, or even knowledge of, the formal or material conventions for receiving the poem.[21] Just as striking is the inverse of the double-blind relation: an author can now create the formal or material conventions for receiving a poem (epitomized in what we now call *interface design*) free of any specific knowledge about what actual source content will be delivered into that frame.

Witness, therefore, the phenomenon of the so-called data island now apparent to Web authors and, with the new generation of XML-based word-processing systems, soon likely to influence the psychology even of mainstream authoring in institutional contexts. Data islands, or, more generally, what I will call *data pours*, are places on a page—whether a Web page or a word-processing page connected live to an institutional database or XML repository—where an author in effect surrenders the act of writing to that of parameterization.[22] In these topoi, the author designates a zone where content of unknown quantity and quality—except as parameterized in such commands as "twenty items at a time" or "only items containing 'sick rose'"—pours into the manifest work from databases or XML sources hidden in the deep background. Content, in other words, becomes semiotically transcendental (in the sense of what Derrida, in "Structure, Sign, and Play in the Discourse of the Human Sciences," called the "transcendental signified"). The transcendental signified of discourse network 2000 is content that is both the center of discourse and—precisely because of its status as essence—outside the normal play or (as we now say) networking of discourse.

Here are two examples of data islands or data pours from my own past online projects.[23] The first is code from a Web page that draws its content dynamically from a relatively simple database to create a gallery of images for a course on romantic landscape art (figure 8.1).[24] The page initially establishes a connection with the database (liu-images.mdb) and then uses SQL to select all fields from a particular table in that database (the table called *Artists*). Subsequent code on the page requests the content of specific database fields/records and displays it in HTML format for the Web. Records are poured automatically from the database onto the Web page one at a time, but, because the data pour is nested within a repeat statement (which can be variously parameterized), the operation generates a cumulative list or table containing all relevant items in the database even though the author may not know what is in the database or may have ceded control of the database to someone else. The second example represents a data pour implemented through a simple XML document that I created for pedagogical purposes to manage a work of Web-based fiction (Edward Falco's powerful but technically simple *Self-Portrait as Child with Father*), together with an associated XSLT stylesheet (which transforms XML content into some other format, in this case HTML for the Web). As seen in the XSLT stylesheet, content moves from the XML document to the Web through "select" statements roughly analogous to the select statements used to query SQL databases (figure 8.2).[25]

As a result of such data pours, the interface of the contemporary Web increasingly differs from that of first-generation Web work, where most substantive content was there on the page together with formatting code and other elements under the direct, often idiosyncratic control of the author. Now Web pages increasingly surrender their soul to data pours that throw transcendental information onto the page from database or XML sources reposed far in the background, yet in a manner manifestly different from the thrownness (in Heidegger's phrase) or, more simply,

Code Excerpt 1

Code from a simple database-driven Web site showing the method by which a Web page calls for content from an underlying database (highlights indicate code discussed in essay):

```
//Connects the Web page to an Access database named "liu-images.mdb,"
//Creates data object through a SQL query "Select" statement

<%
var Recordset1 = Server.CreateObject("ADODB.Recordset");
Recordset1.ActiveConnection = "Provider=Microsoft.Jet.OLEDB.4.0;
Data Source=E:\databases/liu-images.mdb";
Recordset1.Source = "SELECT * FROM Artists ORDER BY LastName, FirstName, Dates, Nation";
Recordset1.CursorType = 0;
Recordset1.CursorLocation = 2;
Recordset1.LockType = 3;
Recordset1.Open();
var Recordset1_numRows = 0;
%>

//HTML table whose data is pulled through the data connection from records in the database
//The table is set within a Repeat procedure that repeats the process for every record in the database

<% while ((Repeat1__numRows-- != 0) && (!Recordset1.EOF)) { %>
<TABLE width="95%" border="0">
<TR valign="top">
    <TD width="40%">
        <A HREF="directory-page.asp?<%= MM_keepNone + ((MM_keepNone!="")?"&":"") + "Artists.ArtistsID="
        Recordset1.Fields.Item("ArtistsID").Value %>">
        <B><% if (Recordset1.Fields.Item("LastName").Value !== "") %>
        <%=(Recordset1.Fields.Item("LastName").Value)%>
        <%if (Recordset1.Fields.Item("FirstName").Value !== "") %>,
        <%=(Recordset1.Fields.Item("FirstName").Value)%>
        <% if (Recordset1.Fields.Item("MiddleName").Value!== "") %> 
        <%=(Recordset1.Fields.Item("MiddleName").Value)%></B></A>
    </TD>
    <TD width="20%"><%=(Recordset1.Fields.Item("Dates").Value)%></TD>
    <TD width="20%"><%=(Recordset1.Fields.Item("Nation").Value)%></TD>
    <TD width="25%"><A href="<%=(Recordset1.Fields.Item("InternetSite").Value)%>">Suggested
Site</A></TD>
    <TD width="5%"><%=("ArtistsID").Value)%></TD>
</TR>
</TABLE>
<% Repeat1__index++; Recordset1.MoveNext(); }%>
```

Figure 8.1. Code from a simple database-driven Web site showing the method by which a Web page calls for content from an underlying database (highlights indicate code discussed).

rendered thereness of the rest of the page.[26] I refer to the complex phenomenology of dissonance that appears most visibly, for example, in the telltale way in which data-pour pages eschew "cool" Web design in favor of regular, minimalist, or modernist page layouts with simple geometries (what Lev Manovich calls the "Bauhaus filter" that is surprisingly prevalent in contemporary information aesthetics).[27] It is only a simpler list or table structure on a Web page, for instance, that can easily receive the serial repetition of an unpredictable number of structurally similar items—that is, the kind of items thrown forth automatically from databases or

Code Excerpt 2

Code for the XSLT stylesheet "Hypertext_Fiction.xsl" (from my "Hypertext Fiction Tracker" demo) showing the method by which a Web page calls for content from an underlying XML document. (Highlights indicate code discussed above.)

```
// Called by the XML document "falco_instance.xml" to transform XML into HTML for Web;
// Uses <SPAN> tags to format for HTML the content found in "nodes" in the XML document;
// Note the analogy between the XPATH language "select" statement that locates nodes (e.g.
// "select="REGISTER/WORK" and the SQL "select" statement

<?xml version="1.0"?>
<!-- File Name: Hypertext_Fiction.xsl -->
<xsl:stylesheet version="1.0" xmlns:xsl="http://www.w3.org/1999/XSL/Transform">

<xsl:template match="/">

<HTML>
    <HEAD>
        <TITLE>Hypertext Fiction Tracker</TITLE>
    </HEAD>
    <BODY>
        <SPAN STYLE="font-family:arial, Helvetica, sans-serif; font-size:14px">
        <DIV align="center">
            <FONT size="+4">Hypertext Fiction Tracker</FONT><BR/>
            <FONT size="+3">Conceptual Demo of XML Application</FONT><BR/>
            <FONT size="+2">(Alan Liu; last rev. Feb. 18, 2002)</FONT>
        </DIV><BR/>

    <xsl:for-each select="REGISTER/WORK">

        <SPAN STYLE="font-size:130%; font-weight:900">
        Title of Work:
        </SPAN>
        <SPAN STYLE="font-size:130%; font-weight:900; color:red">
            "<xsl:value-of select="WORK_TITLE"/>"
        </SPAN><BR/>
        <SPAN STYLE="font-size:130%;font-weight:900">
        Author:
        </SPAN>
        <SPAN STYLE="font-size:130%; font-weight:900; color:red">
            <xsl:value-of select="AUTHOR"/>
        </SPAN><BR/>
        <SPAN STYLE="font-size:130%;font-weight:900">
        Date of Publication:
        </SPAN>
        <SPAN STYLE="font-size:130%; color:red">
            <xsl:value-of select="DATE"/>
        </SPAN><BR/>
        <SPAN STYLE="font-size:130%;font-weight:900">
        Media Format:
        </SPAN>
        <SPAN STYLE="font-size:130%; color:red">
            <xsl:value-of select="MEDIA"/>
        </SPAN><BR/>
        <SPAN STYLE="font-size:130%;font-weight:900">
        URL:
        </SPAN>
        <SPAN STYLE="color:red">
            <A><xsl:attribute name="href">
                <xsl:value-of select="WORK_URL"/>
            </xsl:attribute>
            <xsl:value-of select="WORK_URL"/>
            </A><BR/>
        </SPAN><BR/><BR/><HR/>
        <SPAN STYLE="font-size:130%; font-weight:900; color:red">
        Plot Strands:
        </SPAN><HR/><BR/>

    <xsl:for-each select="/REGISTER/WORK/PLOT/STRAND">

        <SPAN STYLE="font-size:130%; font-weight:900; color:blue">
            <xsl:value-of select="STRAND_TITLE"/>
        </SPAN><BR/><BR/>

    <xsl:for-each select="LEXIA">

        <TABLE width="80%" border="1" align="center" bordercolordark="FFFFFF" bordercolor="#999999">
        <TR>
            <TD width="15%"><SPAN STYLE="font-weight:800; color:blue">Lexia Title: </SPAN></TD>
            <TD><SPAN STYLE="font-weight:800; color:blue">
            <xsl:value-of select="LEXIA_TITLE"/></SPAN></TD>
        </TR>
        <TR>
            <TD><SPAN STYLE="font-weight:800">Characters: </SPAN></TD>
            <TD><xsl:value-of select="CHARACTERS"/></TD>
        </TR>
        <TR>
            <TD><SPAN STYLE="font-weight:800">Mode: </SPAN></TD>
            <TD><xsl:value-of select="MODE"/></TD>
        </TR>
        <TR>
            <TD><SPAN STYLE="font-weight:800">Description or Keywords: </SPAN></TD>
            <TD><xsl:value-of select="KEYWORDS"/></TD>
        </TR>
        <TR>
            <TD><SPAN STYLE="font-weight:800">Lexia URL: </SPAN></TD>
            <TD><A>
                <xsl:attribute name="href"><xsl:value-of select="LEXIA_URL"/></xsl:attribute>
                <xsl:attribute name="target">"2"</xsl:attribute>
                <xsl:value-of select="LEXIA_URL"/>
            </A></TD>
        </TR>
        </TABLE><BR/><BR/>

    </xsl:for-each>
    <HR/>
    </xsl:for-each>
    </xsl:for-each>
    </SPAN>
    </BODY>
</HTML>
</xsl:template>
</xsl:stylesheet>
```

Figure 8.2. Code for the XSLT stylesheet "Hypertext_Fiction.xsl" (from my "Hypertext Fiction Tracker" demo) showing the method by which a Web page calls for content from an underlying XML document. (Highlights indicate code discussed.)

XML documents that are like volcanoes able to hurl forth only identically shaped rocks.[28] An example would be an RSS news-aggregator site or any of the Internet radio (e.g., SHOUTcast) or streaming/on-demand music sites (e.g., Rhapsody or MusicMatch), where a request for an artist or a kind of music produces a page with a geometrically simple list. In the academic domain, my own *Voice of the Shuttle* throws forth the content of its underlying database in list structures.[29]

In sum, data pours open the prospect of a new model of authoring predicated on technologies enforcing ever more immaculate separation of content from presentation. Or, rather, the term *technology*—along with its whole complement of undecidably objective/social complements (technique, procedure, protocol, routine, practice)—is too narrow. What is at stake is the very *ideology* (as I called it) of strict division between content and presentation—the religion, as it were, of text encoding and databases. Indeed, while I earlier constrained transcendence to semiosis, it would not be inappropriate to inflate semiosis (in the manner of Derrida himself in his discussion of the transcendental signified) to the scale of metaphysics and, in the limit case, religion. Discourse network 2000 is a *belief*.[30] According to its dogma, true content abides in a transcendental logic, reason, or noumen so completely structured and described that it is in and of itself inutterable in any mere material or instantiated form. Content may be revealed only through an intermediary presentation that is purely interfacial rather than, as it were, sacramental—that is, *not* consubstantial with the noumenal. Unless content is hacked, therefore (which is how our most extreme protestant reformers of information technology today attempt to transcend the interfacial to experience direct revelation), it is to be rendered only through GUIs (graphical user interfaces) that are defined as ipso facto superficial rather than—in the original Orthodox rather than Apple or Microsoft sense—iconic.[31] Unlike an Orthodox icon, which embodies inextricably in its beaten gold the very particles of transcendence, in other words, our interfaces today are ever more transparently just what are termed *skins* or, put technically, *templates, schemas, stylesheets*, and so on designed to *be* extricable.

Behold, then: there is now a great blind spot on the page that authors, artists, and designers of the interface no longer directly control but can only parameterize. (Much of the early debate in hypertext theory about the reversal of roles between the author and the newly empowered reader now seems obsolete precisely because *both* the author and the reader are disempowered. Authors and readers become operators of black-box machinery who select criteria for prescripted actions.) In an earlier time, this blind spot through which data floods from transcendental sources might have been called *the sublime*. Even earlier in the history of transcendence, it was *God*.[32] But now we pray in SQL or XML. *Not* "Our Father, who art in heaven . . . Give us this day our daily bread," but, instead, the select statement that is the soul of data islands—for example, "SELECT * FROM Artists ORDER BY LastName, FirstName, Dates, Nation" (in SQL) or "<xsl:value-of select = "LEXIA_TITLE"/>" (in XML).[33] Not "give us," in other words, but "select from." Not the Lord's Prayer, but our great contemporary prayer, the query.

</argument>

<argument title="sociologic" subtitle="rifles, bricks, and forms">

Of course, the religious analogy *is* inappropriate to the extent that it misdirects us from the particular church now spreading the discursive Word: postindustrialism. If the principles of transformability, autonomous mobility, and automation that separate content from presentation—and, thus, the juggernaut of databases and XML—currently seem to go without question, then such fatefulness is symptomatic of the exquisitely tight, even supple fit between this rationale and the combined values of industrial efficiency and postindustrial flexibility now responsible for managing our new world order.[34] Such a fit did not arise from above or, what amounts to the same thing, as an entelechy unfolding as progress from the universal reason of humanity. Rather, a cultural-studies approach might show that the alignment of the new discourse with our New Economy is the result of a historical process of *making* things fit. That process we now call *management*, the modern theory of civilization. God begat Enlightenment reason, which begat industrial scientific management, which in turn begat postindustrial management theories that synonymize the progress of civilization and management without any remainder. In the words of Peter Drucker, the scholar who helped found management studies in the United States: "Management . . . converts a mob into an organization, and human efforts into performance."[35]

My thesis is that the postindustrial techno-logic of encoded or structured discourse dates back—with a signal difference I indicate later—to nineteenth- and early-twentieth-century industrialism. In particular, the mold was set by John Hall and Frederick Winslow Taylor. In regard to Hall, first of all, I am influenced by Wendell Piez, a professional XML developer, theorist of markup languages, and humanist who participates in the ACH.[36] Piez argues that Hall's now-famous interchangeable-part manufacturing process of the 1820s and 1830s (at the U.S. armory in Harpers Ferry, Virginia) was the predecessor to the logic of separating content from presentation that ultimately triggered not so much databases and XML as the exact social, economic, and technical *need* for databases and XML. We can set the scene by witnessing the increasing complexity of gun manufacture prior to Hall as the Harpers Ferry armory ramped up production to meet new, industrial age demands. As described in Merritt Roe Smith's detailed historical study, guns at the armory were still being manufactured as late as 1807 in a pure artisan system. Each craftsman performed all six types of work needed to create a composite product: "barrel making, lock forging, lock filing, brazing, stocking, and finishing."[37] But, when in 1808 the U.S. government dramatically increased its demand to fifteen thousand muskets annually, Harpers Ferry could not muster the necessary number of skilled craftsmen. It thus modified the artisan system by decomposing gun manufacture into separate tasks (soon numbering fifty-five for muskets), each of which could be assigned to a lesser-skilled workman needing to know only, for example, how to make a barrel as opposed to a stock.[38] The composite product was thus dispersed among a network of occupations. Still, the new system left intact the original artisanal method of allowing each worker, no matter how much his task had been simplified, to craft his own gun part. While production numbers went up, therefore, the new system did nothing to prepare for the next demand (in 1815) from the U.S. Ordnance Department: that musket parts be uniform enough so that individual guns could be repaired in the field with parts from other guns made by that same armory and even by the other government armory in Springfield, Massachusetts. Two years of effort dedicated to solving the standardization problem failed to redress what the Ordnance Department called "a total disagreement" between muskets at the two U.S. armories.[39]

It is into this situation that Hall stepped in 1819 when he was appointed the director of the Rifle Works, a new, semi-independent unit at Harpers Ferry designed to manufacture his superior, breech-loading rifle.[40] Importantly, Hall was not just an inventor of the rifle but an indefatigable innovator of the machines, tools, and work processes needed to build rifles. Hall's renovation of the overall system of manufacture ultimately made the difference in the armament industry and U.S. manufacturing as a whole. "At his Rifle Works," Piez observes, "Hall developed a system by which guns could be made without the hand-crafting traditionally required of them. . . . Instead, the parts were all made to more-than-humanly possible close tolerances by machine, and then assembled not by piece, but by type. That is, any barrel could fit on any stock, with any receiver, any lock, etc. This required a rigid adherence to standards, enforced by the use of machine tools fitted with jigs, and by a careful regimen of testing with gauges."[41] These "gauges," in fact, were the essence of Hall's new system. Enabling a rigorous method of parts inspection, Hall's case-hardened gauges—distributed in duplicate sets to workmen and to inspectors—soon far outnumbered the inspection devices used for traditional muskets (over sixty-three gauges for one of Hall's breechloader models, e.g.).[42] As Piez argues, in other words, the real proof of quality in Hall's manufacture of a gun was not that the gun fired but that its parts—tested separately in disassembled form—fit against the gauges, which thus became the "Platonic form" of the gun. In the language of XML rather than of Plato, the gauges were the equivalent of a DTD or, better, schema used to validate the particular instance of an XML document against strict standards of complete, consistent, and lawful data structure.[43] "Shades of text-encoding, anyone?" Piez asks.

The crucial point to be made is not that there are particular technical analogies between Hall's rifle manufacture and discourse network 2000, though there are a surprising number of such correspondences—for example, Hall's use of "bearing points" on each rifle part to determine "its relative position for all subsequent machining operations," which might be likened logically to XML namespaces and XPATH nodes that determine, respectively, the bearing of XML tag vocabularies relative to a specific vocabulary set and of the branches of an XML document relative to nodal points in the document structure.[44] The deeper correspondence lies at the level of the overall system of standardization that Hall introduced.[45] While different in the way it creates composite products, postindustrialism starts on the same fundamental requirement of standardization, only its standards are housed, not in gauges, but in an ever more fulsome complement of standards, specifications, DTDs, schemas, and the like.

My own addition to Piez's argument extends the thesis with variation to Taylor, who, at the beginning of the twentieth century, added to Hall's standardized production the management model that takes us a step closer to postindustrialism and what I called *content, transmission,* and *consumption management.* We might take our example from any of Taylor's case studies of pig-iron handling, shoveling, the manufacture of bicycle bearings, and so on.[46] But perhaps the clearest exemplum is bricklaying as it was studied and reformed by another member of the American Society of Mechanical Engineers, Frank B. Gilbreth, whose work Taylor discusses at length in his *Principles of Scientific Management.* Prior to Gilbreth, bricklayers had built walls in a style akin to that of the traditional armorers we saw making muskets at Harpers Ferry: they decided ad hoc or by custom how many bricks to cart over, how close to place the pile, how many bricks to lift at one time, how to tamp the bricks down, and so on. But, after reengineering bricklaying (including, e.g., formulating "the exact position which each of the feet of the bricklayer should occupy with relation to the wall, the mortar box, and the pile of bricks"), Gilbreth reduced the motions required to lay each brick from eighteen "to five, and even in one case to as low as two motions."[47] Bricklaying was standardized for efficiency.

Or, rather, standardization was just one of the principles necessary to efficiency in Taylor's system.[48] New in Taylorism was the additional principle that decisions had to be extracted from the embodied work of the laborer and described on instruction cards as procedures that could be optimized, reprogrammed, distributed, and otherwise mediated. The instruction card, Taylor explains in *Shop Management*, specifies, for instance, "the general and detail drawing to refer to, the piece number and the cost order number to charge the work to, the special jigs, fixtures, or tools to use, where to start each cut, the exact depth of each cut, and how many cuts to take, the speed and feed to be used for each cut, and the time within which each operation must be finished."[49] With the introduction of instruction cards (and the Taylorist planning departments that stood behind them), work became the structured, modular, and algorithmically manageable process by which—again translating prophetically into XML—each individual element <BRICK> was nested within the larger element <WALL>. That is, each node or field in the work process (in XML-speak and database-speak, respectively) became part of a programmatic description of wall building that allowed the content (actual bricks lifted by embodied workers) to be separated from the presentation of the wall. Though only superficially akin to modern database forms or XML documents, Taylor's instruction cards might thus be said to be the first economically and socially significant form of programming—of a piece both logically and chronologically with Herman Hollerith's tabulator punch cards.

The mediation of work was, in turn, the platform for another principle of efficiency that became Taylor's greatest contribution to industrial history: modern management. In this light, twentieth-century management may be parsed into two correlative ideas. One is that management is management of, and through, media. It is management as document processing or, as JoAnne Yates calls it in her study of document management in the era of Taylor and other systematizers, "control through communication."[50] Once all work decisions were extracted from the laborer and mediated through instruction cards, planning-room diagrams, time-study charts, and all the other paper apparatuses of Taylor's system, manufacturing could be controlled as if through the revision and rearrangement of documentation alone. The other management idea to emerge in step with mediation is distributed management or what Taylor called "functional foremanship." When manufacturing could be charted out on paper as an interlocking sequence of operations, operators, locations, and resources, then responsibility for the entire plan could be distributed piecemeal to an organization chart of managers that broke the gang-boss mold of management, according to which individual managers directly oversaw platoons of workers. Managers matched up instead with discrete, transposable, and reprogrammable functions that bore no necessary relation to individual workers or work-group formations, which, in turn, could be restructured piecemeal as needed. Workers, in other words, no longer had a boss per se; they were minded instead by a buzzing hive of "order of work and route clerks," "instruction card clerks," "time and cost clerks," "shop disciplinarians," "speed bosses," "inspectors," "repair bosses," and so on who bossed them by bossing around pieces of paper.[51] Freed of the need to be directly bossy, indeed, managers, in Taylor's argument, could even be "friendly," or what we might today call *user-friendly systems of management*.[52] In short, Taylor's functional foremanship was the origin of today's professional-managerial or professional-technical-managerial "new class."[53] Or, perhaps, the real new class to come will not need human managers at all to oversee their user-friendly systems. It is symptomatic that the software client program through which one today administrates a Microsoft SQL Server database is named Enterprise Manager while similar interfaces in the Oracle9i database are called Management Server, Enterprise Management Console, Change Manager, Performance Manager, and so on.[54] Databases and XML are now our ultimate functional managers. They are the automatic mediators of the work of contemporary knowledge.

The missing link between Taylor's paper-pushing managers on the factory floor and today's dedicated document handlers (a.k.a. knowledge workers) in the office can subsequently be found in the books of the Taylorist missionary of clerical and white-collar work William Henry Leffingwell—for example, *Scientific Office Management* (1917) or, with Edwin Marshall Robinson, *Textbook of Office Management* (1932). Leffingwell's time-motion approach to tasks performed on particular kinds of office equipment or in variable lighting and ventilation environments might provide many examples.[55] But the most telling phenomenon is Leffingwell's codification of Taylor's instruction card into the modern "form" (and such related document genres, as Yates calls them, as tables and reports). Near the beginning of their *Textbook of Office Management*, Leffingwell and

Robinson compare forms to jigs to show how well-designed documents facilitate the factory-like standardization of office work: "The preparation of a form, for example, was in reality nothing more than the devising of a standard way of recording information. A form, properly designed, enabled the office manager of that day to get the desired information recorded exactly in the shape he wanted it and without the use of personal instructions. Such a form might be regarded as analogous to the 'jig' used in factories, which enabled a 'machine hand' to perform work which otherwise could have been done only by a skilled mechanic."[56] But the use of standard forms also reinforced the specifically Taylorist innovation of mediated management. As Yates points out, printed forms and tables—especially when they began to converge on a companywide "general logical rule for all forms"—"facilitated the comparisons of data so critical to systematic managers."[57] Leffingwell thus says: "All reports made by one office should follow certain rules devised for that office . . . to the end that all who have occasion to work upon or with the reports, or who use them, may contract uniform and desirable habits of work and thought in relation to this activity."[58] When columns, rows, and fields in one form or table lined up visually with those in other forms, in other words, then not only could information be managed across time and organizational space (e.g., comparing last year's accounting figures against this year's sales figures), but information management became ipso facto worker management as well—a discipline of management powerful enough to be interiorized as a kind of bureaucratic conscience within the psychology of work ("uniform and desirable habits of . . . thought," as Leffingwell says). As Yates observes, organizational communication at the time circulated in a general, upward and downward system of information that helped sustain managerial oversight.[59] Such synoptic management mediated by forms would culminate in the computer era, when, as Shoshana Zuboff studies in *In the Age of the Smart Machine*, the first instinct of both managers and workers on exposure to a firm's computer system was a phenomenology of super-vision. The computer lets them "see" it all.[60]

The upshot of such a social history of databases and XML is that the common presumption of business writers, technologists, and others that there was a sharp break between industrialism and postindustrialism is historically too shallow.[61] There was, indeed, a break, but its distinctive nature cannot be appreciated without first recovering archaeologically the surprising bandwidth of connection between the two epochs. In light of the capitalism underlying both, after all, the separation of content from presentation now being mandated by business-oriented information technology is a profound euphemism. From a historical perspective, knowledge (the great value of postindustrialism) is being separated or extracted from what presentation really means: labor. What Marx called "surplus labor value" is in the post-Marxist, postindustrial world nothing other than the programmability of work—a programmability that can be functionally managed, extracted, mediated, optimized, and distributed (e.g., licensed to other companies or the end user) for what, in a classically Marxist view, is excess gain.[62]

Premonitions of database- or XML-like features in industrialism are one clue to this congruence between the past and the present. But they are not important in themselves. My historical argument is not one of linear evolution or typological anticipation. Rather, I would deploy a reversed-time variant of the idea of the skeuomorph that N. Katherine Hayles uses to explain the history of technological change in *How We Became Posthuman*. Hayles borrows the term *skeuomorph* from archaeological anthropology to describe retro features of the present (like simulated stitching in vinyl molded plastic or, in my context, document forms akin to jigs) that negotiate a comfort zone between the past and the present.[63] Reversing the time arrow, we can say that the database- or XML-like features that we have noticed in the past are a kind of prophetic relic or reverse skeuomorph. In their own time, they were proposed as instrumental to the progress of industrialism. But, seen from our perspective, they are epistemological rather than instrumental stitches between past and present. They are an index or a placeholder (rather than a cause or an antecedent) of the future. If such devices as Taylor's instruction cards or Leffingwell's forms (and many other devices that now seem to us merely odd or quaint) did not exactly carry forward to the future, then something else would have been invented to do so—that is, databases and XML.

Only by understanding the deep connection between industrialism and postindustrialism are we now prepared to discern the great difference of the latter. Both epochs, as we have seen, share the projects of standardization and management. But only postindustrialism saw these projects through to their radical conclusion, which might be called *metastandardization and metamanagement*. When Hall standardized the modern rifle, we note, he did so by creating or implementing a host of one-off, stand-alone, ingenious second-order machines for making rifles that were themselves anything but standard. Craft, we might say, merely retreated to the artisanship of Hall himself as the standardizer of craft. So too, when Taylor and Leffingwell brought scientific management to bricklaying or form writing, they only partly regularized the processes of standardization and management themselves. Some actual human being—much more unpredictable than a machine in aptitudes, skills, and personality—still had to fill the role of the professional-technical manager creating the instruction cards, forms, and so on.[64] The insight of postindustrialism is that there can be metastandards for making standards. XML, for example, is, technically, not a standard, but a metastandard, a family of standards that governs the extensible creation of specific vocabularies of XML tags and their rule sets (such as the TEI guidelines designed for the encoding of scholarly humanities and social-science documents). Similarly, as shown in the massive purge of middle managers in the last few business cycles, postindustrialism is all about the metamanagement of management—the flattening of management layers and the concomitant increase in managerial spans of control made possible by information technologies that transume management through common standards for the transformation, autonomous mobility, and automation of knowledge work. A better name for postindustrialism, we may say, is *metaindustrialism.*

The main point is that a historically deep investigation of discourse network 2000 would inquire into, not just the purpose of data-driven documents (standardization, flexibility, speed, interactivity, collaboration, and so on), but the purpose of that purpose: the foundations of the programmability that today facilitates networked production and consumption. In the context of my specific inquiry, authors are, indeed, postindustrial producers.

Where in the world of rifles, brick walls, and office forms might there still be room for a poem about a sick rose printed in a nonstandard manner and then hand-watercolored by a poet and his wife?

</argument>

<argument title="aesthetics" subtitle="data sublime">

Finally, then, what are the aesthetics of discourse network 2000? Of course, new media studies—which conjoins humanities computing, social-science computing, and the digital arts (including "network art")—has just recently emerged as a coherent, if not wholly unified, field able to address digital, networked communications at the point of intersection between its technology, society, history, philosophy, and aesthetics. Only after ca. 2000, for example, was it possible for new media studies programs to be formed around a more or less shared set of theoretical or other field-defining texts along the lines of books by Espen Aarseth (*Cybertext*), Katherine Hayles (e.g., *My Mother Was a Computer*), Jerome McGann (e.g., *Radiant Textuality*), Willard McCarty (*Humanities Computing*), and Lev Manovich (*The Language of New Media*), supplemented by an ever richer set of studies by younger scholars marking out new directions of research. (Especially germane among the latter are books such as Matthew G. Kirschenbaum's *Mechanisms* and Rita Raley's *Tactical Media* (and in-progress *Reading Code*) that specifically address the evolution of textual discourse amid the material, code, and interface forms of new media.)[65] Also arriving roughly in the same years were surveys and readers of new media—for example, Noah Wardrip-Fruin and Nick Montfort's important *The New Media Reader*, Stephen Wilson's *Information Arts*, Christiane Paul's *Digital Art*, and the Electronic Literature Organization's *Electronic Literature Collection* series. Taken together, this ensemble of creative, research, and pedagogical materials supporting new media studies can now supply the cross-disciplinary principles and methods that allow us to explore how aesthetics contributes to the total social and historical fact of discourse network 2000.

But in lieu of any attempt at a programmatic synthesis of such principles and methods at the end of this essay, I close simply by mounting a gallery show of past and present art that bears on the theme of data transcendence (what Julian Stallabrass calls the data "sublime") and its impact on the relation between content and presentation.[66] After all, if postindustrial ideology mandates the separation of content from formal presentation or material instantiation, then the arts offer a uniquely critical perspective on this ideology because, in their practice, such separation—however possible as a goal (as demonstrated by some conceptual, digital, or network art)—never goes without saying. The tight, tense marriage between content and materiality/form that the arts witness is at least as powerful as the tight fit between encoded discourse and postindustrialism that divorces content from presentation.

The following is a small gallery of artistic data pours, past and present.

The first instance is a late painting by J. M. W. Turner, *Light and Colour (Goethe's Theory): The Morning after the Deluge* (1843), in which Turner's characteristic vortex of energies, focused on a potent blank spot or white mythology on the canvas, marks a romantic prefiguration of the data pour (figure 8.3). Out of this data pour emerges what seems to be the first record of a transcendental database: an image of Moses writing the Pentateuch. Yet what necessary quantum of aesthetic experience, we may ask, is added by Turner's distinctively formal and material signatures—his rough yet limpid handling of oils and his very imposition of the vortex form?

The second instance is a passage from William Gibson's *Neuromancer*

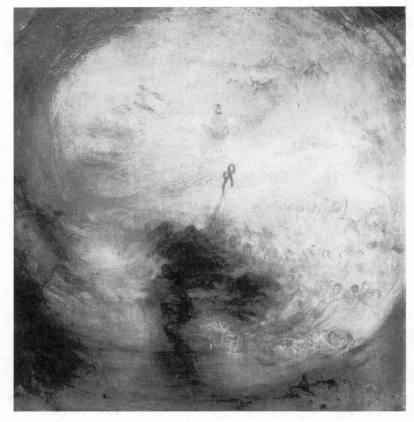

Figure 8.3. J. M. W. Turner, *Light and Colour (Goethe's Theory): The Morning after the Deluge* (exhibited 1843).

depicting the indescribable, shifting needle of the Kuang virus at the climax of the novel:

> Something dark was forming at the core of the Chinese program. The density of information overwhelmed the fabric of the matrix, triggering hypnagogic images. Faint kaleidoscopic angles centered in to a silver-black focal point. Case watched childhood symbols of evil and bad luck tumble out along translucent planes: swastikas, skulls and crossbones, dice flashing snake eyes. If he looked directly at that null point, no outline would form. It took a dozen, quick, peripheral takes before he had it, a shark thing, gleaming like obsidian, the black mirrors of its flanks reflecting faint distant lights that bore no relationship to the matrix around it.[67]

The "null point" of hypnagogic imagery here is the injection point of Gibson's neuromantic rather than romantic data pour (with strong intimations of Thomas Pynchon in the background).[68] Yet what material and formal instincts—coded, if not in the reptile brain, then at levels of culture far deeper than today's knowledge work—imagine this null point specifically as swastikas, skulls and crossbones, dice flashing snake eyes, and shark thing?

The third instance is an image by Marcos Novak representative of his "transarchitecture" and "liquid architecture" (figure 8.4). Among his other projects, Novak programs four-dimensional, algorithmic architectural shapes that mutate in time, then extracts from the unimaginable four-dimensional matrix three- or two-dimensional snapshots (through 3D rapid prototyping or 2D imaging). The result is a reduced-dimension data pour from a higher-dimensional reality designed to elicit what Novak terms "allogenetic," truly alien aesthetics beyond the ken even of neuromantic notions of transcendence.[69] Yet what instinct compels Novak to materialize and form his unimaginable 4D shapes in 3D or 2D at all? Why is that stepping down of the dimensional plenum necessary? Moreover, what criteria motivated this *specific* presentation of the unimaginable out

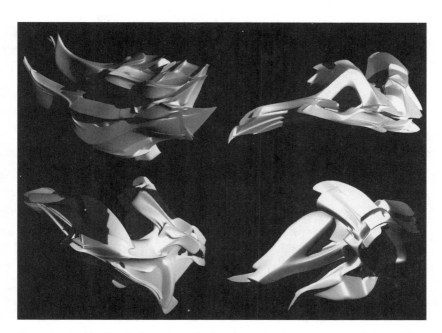

Figure 8.4. Marcos Novak, four views of a four-dimensional transarchitectural shape (2001). Reproduced by permission of the artist.

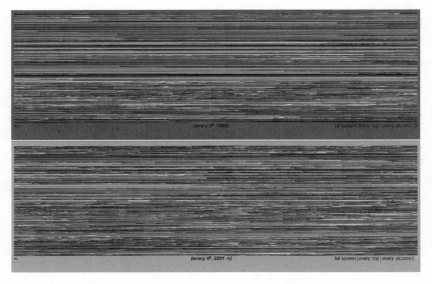

Figure 8.5. Lisa Jevbratt, *1:1*, *"Every"* interface. Reproduced by permission of the artist.

of all the algorithmic possibilities? Why choose this image as especially interesting?

The fourth instance is a now-already-classic work of net art by Lisa Jevbratt that is, perhaps, the epitome of the data sublime. Titled *1:1*, the work consists of a net crawler programmed by Jevbratt to access IP addresses on the Internet, a database to hold the addresses together with information about their status (e.g., accessible, inaccessible, returning a server error), and a set of graphical interfaces to display the results while maintaining live, clickable interactivity with the sites behind the IP numbers. The *"Every"* interface, for example, represents every IP address on the Internet in 1999 and then again in 2001 (figure 8.5).[70] In an astonishing enactment of a data pour, it is a portrait of the Internet in toto (actually, a reduced sampling generated by the crawler) done on an apparently 1:1 scale of correspondence. Yet why did Jevbratt, who started out as a painter, arbitrarily choose particular colors to represent particular aspects of the IP information so as to create a "postphotographic" interface, as the prologue to the project calls it, that may also be appreciated as a recurrence of such painterly postphotographisms as abstract art?[71] Moreover, why did she also make such alternative interfaces for *1:1* as *"Migration"* (using different colors to track the drift of live addresses on the Internet between 1999 and 2001) that have an even stronger resemblance, not only to the media-specific form of abstract expressionism, but also to the embodied form of DNA gel or stain sets (figure 8.6)?[72]

Finally, the fifth metainstance is the well-known theoretical prescription from Lyotard's "Answering the Question: What Is Postmodernism?" on the postmodern sublime: "The postmodern would be that which, in the modern, puts forward the unpresentable in presentation itself; that which denies itself the solace of good forms, the consensus of a taste which would make it possible to share collectively the nostalgia for the unattainable; that which searches for new presentations, not in order to enjoy them but in order to impart a stronger sense of the unpresentable."[73] The questions we can ask Lyotard in the present context are why "new presentations" are necessary at all and what forms such presentations should take. What is it that makes certain presentations, if not "good," then what Lyotard elsewhere in *The Postmodern Condition* calls "paralogically" interesting?

In the early years of the Web, when data transcendence was presented in piecemeal ways that could still be manually supervised and activated (e.g., hypertext links invoking CGI scripts) or in automated ways that were still relatively crude (e.g., so-called push processes), cool was the dominant aesthetic of the interface.[74] Cool as rendered in HTML, we may say, was the archaic barbarian in the church of the separation of content from presentation. It was the secret adherent of nonstandard, proprietary, hand-coded, and other clearly infidel (or, what is the same in industrial

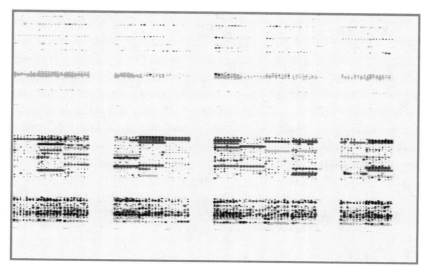

Figure 8.6. Lisa Jevbratt, *1:1*, *"Migration"* interface. Reproduced by permission of the artist.

history, artisanal) practices of embodying content inextricably in presenta-tion (e.g., through pages with so-called dynamic HTML layers that work only in a particular browser or pages with fixed-width tables sized exactly to match a particular graphic image). But, in today's world of massive, automatic data pours through untouchable data islands embedded within retro-Bauhaus rather than cool formalisms (i.e., the regularism of the lists and tables mentioned earlier), what can still be cool?

Here is a first attempt at an analytic of the aesthetics of data transcen-dence in the age of discourse network 2000. Modern art and literature at the beginning of the twentieth century apprehended the spirit of industri-alism in the formalist credo that form is integral to content or, transmuted into the new idiom of process, function. The avant-garde of the time could be famously perverse or obtuse in implementing that formula—offering up everything as art from a Duchamp ready-made to a New Critical ver-bal icon. Indeed, as I and others have argued, cool in its earlier, Jazz Age usage arose precisely in an orthogonal relation to technological and other functionality.[75] But the avant-garde conviction that there *was* a necessary relation between form and content, nevertheless, reflected industrial stan-dardization and management. Modernists had their gauges too; in their unforgiving manifestos they were faux managers akin to Taylor's shop dis-ciplinarians. Jan Tschichold on the New Typography, for instance, twisted Leffingwellian office forms along the diagonal to stress asymmetry, but the very rigor of his twisted symmetry betrayed that he was still filling out a form (a method later extended into what post-Bauhaus typography called *grid design*).[76]

Postindustrialism, however, shows that there was a third term in the modernist equation of form and content that had not been expressed and that the mere deletion of this term made possible the most far-reaching efficiency-cum-flexibility. That third term is materiality, the implicit sub-strate of a New Typography poster, imagist poem, or artifact of Bauhaus architecture or furniture design that absolutely fixed the relation between form and content for any one mass-production run. While modernism was the era that first lived with telemedia (telegraphy, telephony, radio), it nevertheless did not grasp the full implications of telepresence. In adapting itself to distributed presence on the Internet, postindustrialism removed the substrate of materiality to allow form and content to be equated in the oxymoronic relation of standard variation or uniform flexibility. When the material substrate was removed to allow for Internet transmission, that is, *variable* methods of standardization—for example, XML documents governed by a common standard but adaptable to undetermined kinds of hardware, software, and usages—could suddenly be imagined. Material embodiment—in the substrate of a work and the bodily practices of the artisanal artist both—was now immaterial to the full, independent expression of content and form.

Is the writer or artist any longer an author in such circumstances, let alone a creative one? Earlier I said that I would concentrate on authoring in discourse network 2000 as the originating end of the transmission act. The key to the problem of the status of the author, perhaps, lies in the very limitations of that formulation. The origin of transmission in discourse network 2000 is not at the cursor position of the author. Indeed, the heart of the problem of authorship in the age of networked reproduction is that there is no cursor point. We might put the case by updating Kittler's argument about the difference between the 1800 and the 1900 discourse networks in the following fashion. In the romantic era ca. 1800, Kittler observes, the hermeneutical discourse network began when a source of meaning located in nature or the mother called to poets to transmit its transcendental essence through language conceived as a mere channel of translatability. In the modernist era ca. 1900, by contrast, mother nature was a faint echo. The true source of the signal, Kittler argues by recounting psychophysical nonsense reading and speaking experiments of the time, was an apparently random, senseless, automatic, untranslatable, and, thus, nonhermeneutical noise inherent in the channel of transmission itself—like tuning your radio to a Pynchonesque channel of revelation indistinguishable from utter static.[77]

The distinctive signal of 2000, by contrast, synthesizes 1800 and 1900. In 2000, the channel is just as seemingly senseless, random, and automatic as in 1900. (Take a cross section of a document transmission over the Internet at any moment, e.g., and witness a dispersion of atomistic file packets and molar document elements.) But the source point of the transmission is phase-shifted so that phenomenally senseless automatism follows from a precursor act of sense making in the databases and XML repositories outside the direct control of the author. Where the author was once presumed to be the originating transmitter of a discourse next sent for management to the editor, publisher, and so on through all the other positions in the discursive circuit, now the author is in a mediating position as just one among all those other managers looking upstream to previous originating transmitters—database or XML schema designers, software designers, and even clerical information workers (who input data into the database or XML source document). Random and senseless those precursor transmissions may seem (in the way we often feel that overwhelming data is meaningless), yet—in a curious reversion to 1800—that content held in databases and XML now sets the very standard for an ultrastructured and ultradescribed rationality purer than any limiting instantiation of the *Ding an Sich*. And so what Kittler calls the "mother's mouth"—now the discourse of the motherboard, of the matrix itself—seems to return. Only it is alienated from the romantic-era voice of inspiration issuing from the unstructured life that Wordsworth or Blake called "childhood."

Such a reflection on aesthetics 2000, I think, is the harbinger of a new, but also very old, front for the humanities and arts. The core problem is what I have in my *Laws of Cool* called the "ethos of the unknown"—of the unencoded, unstructured, unmanaged—in human experience. In our current age of knowledge work and total information, what experience of the structurally unknowable can still be conveyed in the structured media of knowledge (databases, XML, and so on)? Perhaps the arts—if they can just crack the code of ordinary cool and make it flower—know.

</argument>

Escaping History

The New Historicism, Databases, and Contingency

In 1982, he lined the walls of a room with floor-to-ceiling panels of cardboard and poster board on which he carefully inscribed the events of William Wordsworth's life and times until he was encircled by an intricate, seething web of dates threaded with colored strings pinned from node to node. Sometimes when he stood back, he could almost make out the whole pattern there. Something immanent—not the portrait of an author or his age, perhaps, yet more than just a pulsing circuitry of convergences and divergences—seemed to bulge across the interface into the room. But it always retreated. There was too much imprecision, white space, noise in the panels—too much that could not be known or inscribed except through imprecision, white space, noise.[1]

In 1989, he wrote an essay on the fascination of postmodern cultural criticism with "local knowledge," "the massive fact of cultural and historical particularity," "the concrete, the material, and the particular," "the details of disposition and empirical contingency," the "picture of great detail," "etc." "Media-oriented readers," he wrote, "may wish to view this matrix [of detail] as if with remote control in hand—flitting from channel to channel and sentence fragment to sentence fragment in a hallucinatory blur of strangely continuous discontinuity." Perhaps detailism, he thought, could be immersion in history. But, in the end, he found himself again writing about the retreat of the presence. Immanence became detachment. The pictures of great detail dissolved into simulations whose hyperresolution was somehow the same as background noise, a mere texture or decor of history.[2]

Then, in the 1990s, he thought he had found the medium of capable imagination for these slippery encounters with history: not cardboard or television channel, but network and database. Some years after collaborating to build the Romantic Chronology *on the Web, he rebuilt the site in a database that dynamically generated lists of events, each flanked by a "Details" link that convened related resources automatically.[3] As in the case of other database-to-Web projects he experimented with at the time (culminating in the migration of his* Voice of the Shuttle *into a database), he felt that the* Romantic Chronology *might thus offer a fuller, livelier picture of great detail.[4] Yet, the more he learned about the workings of databases, the more he woke to the fact that the great, digitally sharp massifs of detail they rendered only set off by contrast all the presence not there—whatever could not be cut up and cut down to fit the granular structures of databases, whatever could appear only as a ghost limned in the ceaseless froth of redundant or contradictory entries, overlapping dates, null values, and other database noise attesting to the pressure of the unstructured and unknown. That part of history that was by nature blurred, messy, and contingent (adaptation of* contingent-em, *Latin for "touching together or on all sides, lying near, contiguous, coming into contact or connexion, befalling, happening, coming to pass"; from* con + tangere, con-touch) *could not otherwise manifest in databases of fine, digital touch.[5] Only some grosser, whole-body, ambient touch, he thought, could make contact with the ghost.*

This final essay speculates at once retrospectively and prospectively on the function of the New Historicism in the age of the database. In the New Historicism and other postmodern cultural criticisms, history both emerges from the buzzing, blooming swarm of events caught in the great matrix of detail and escapes in the noise of that detail. Similarly, history both manifests and sublimes in databases, both emerges in the tables, records, fields, and joins that are the structure of the modern relational database (implemented in SQL, or Structured Query Language) and escapes all such holding structures. Whether in the form of the New Historicism or of a database, contemporary postmodern historicism is an escape structure. As they say, it is the "end of history."[6]

Yet the New Historicism does not just accompany data on the great escape of random access. Its specific function in the age of the database, I believe, is to bind that escape to the escape structures of the past that might be called *the beginning of the end of history.*

I start with a note (no more than an anecdote) recounted by Charles Babbage, go on to consider the relational database (epitomized in a recent database project at the Microsoft research labs), and conclude by reflecting, once again, on the New Historicism.

The Chains of History

In the 1838 second edition of his *Ninth Bridgewater Treatise: A Fragment* (original edition, 1837), Charles Babbage added a remarkable anecdote to the end of his chapter on historicity.[7] To discern how singular this anecdote is, we need to read it within the series of nested frames—almost like nested instructions in a modern computer program—in which it is recursed.

The main frame of Babbage's treatise is natural theology. Offered as an uninvited, unsanctioned sequel to the eight previous Bridgewater Treatises, which had been endowed by the Earl of Bridgewater to demonstrate the "Power, Wisdom and Goodness of God, as manifested in the Creation," Babbage's *Ninth* (as we might call it for short) sought to make deductive mathematics as relevant to the problem of natural theology as the physical, geologic, biological, astronomical, and other natural sciences. It did so, in essence, by calculating the existence of God.[8] Nature is a calculating machine, Babbage analogizes, and God is its programmer (where analogy, of course, was the norm of proof in natural theology, with such mechanically simpler analogies as that of a watch or a clock serving as the precedent).[9]

Specifically, Babbage drew on the contrast between his partially built Difference Engine (which generated mathematical tables based on polynomial functions through straightforward, if mechanically complicated, algorithms) and his recently conceived Analytical Engine (the predecessor of today's logically general, stored-program computers that can be programmed to change their own programming depending on previous calculations).[10] We can paraphrase—and mathematically simplify—Babbage's God proof as follows. Imagine first, Babbage says in his second chapter, that the world is a Difference Engine running the same, predictable algorithm forever unless a change in the program (i.e., a miracle) is effected ad hoc by the programmer. Such was the world in the age of miracles. But imagine instead, Babbage continues, that the world is an Analytical Engine programmed from the first to change its own programming from epoch to epoch—that is, the discontinuous epochs of geology and biology then being discovered by the sciences—such that what once seemed a natural law as predictable as the series 1, 2, 3, 4, 5, . . . could be wrenched into a new series (e.g., 1, 2, 3, 4, 5, 16), not through the direct intervention of the programmer, but merely through the operation of a higher-order, humanly incalculable algorithm governing the succession of lower-order algorithms. Such is the world in the age of natural theology, where God as programmer sets nature in motion with a single, all-creative code.[11] As it were, not "Let there be light," but, on the command line, "execute." "Which of these two engines," Babbage asks, gives "the higher proof of skill in the contriver?" Unequivocally, he answers, the universe–as–Analytical Engine.[12] The only real questions that remain concern the trustworthiness of the evidence that humans, as reverse engineers of creation, require to deduce the design of the original program (an issue Babbage takes up both directly, in applauding the empirical evidence of geology at the end of his second chapter, and indirectly, in regard to testimonial evidence in his later chapters on Hume and miracles) and the possibility of free will in a preprogrammed universe (a topic he addresses in his final chapter, "Reflections on Free Will").

Nested one level down in Babbage's calculation is then the chapter on historicity that is our particular concern.[13] Entitled "On the Permanent Impression of Our Words and Actions on the Globe We Inhabit," this ninth chapter in Babbage's *Ninth* calculates the time arrow of the universe in reverse as a sort of check-sum verification of the progress of the God program. Borrowing with attribution from the French mathematician Pierre Simon de Laplace, whose *Philosophical Essay on Probabilities* (1812) had envisioned a universe of atomistically precise causal determination, the chapter projects Babbage's version of what has come to be known as the Laplace Demon.[14] Babbage imagines a "Being" of enormous calculating powers who can, not only foresee the future trajectory of every particle of nature, but also review the vectors of quanta back to their sources as if reading in a perfectly lossless, infinitely detailed library of history. "What a strange chaos is this wide atmosphere we breathe!" he exclaims:

> Every atom, impressed with good and with ill, retains at once the motions . . . imparted to it. . . . The air itself is one vast library, on whose pages are forever written all that man has ever said or woman whispered. . . .
>
> No motion impressed by natural causes, or by human agency, is ever obliterated. The ripple on the ocean's surface caused by a gentle breeze, or the still water which marks the more immediate track of a ponderous

vessel gliding with scarcely expanded sails over its bosom, are equally indelible. The momentary waves raised by the passing breeze, apparently born but to die on the spot which saw their birth, leave behind them an endless progeny, which, reviving with diminished energy in other seas, visiting a thousand shores, reflected from each and perhaps again partially concentrated, will pursue their ceaseless course till ocean be itself annihilated.

The track of every canoe, of every vessel which has yet disturbed the surface of the ocean, whether impelled by manual force or elemental power, remains for ever registered in the future movement of all succeeding particles which may occupy its place.[15]

Three paragraphs later, this line of thought brings Babbage to the following moral:

If the Almighty stamped on the brow of the earliest murderer—the indelible and visible mark of his guilt—He has also established laws by which every succeeding criminal is not less irrevocably chained to the testimony of his crime; for every atom of his mortal frame, through whatever changes its severed particles may migrate, will still retain, adhering to it through every combination, some movement derived from that very muscular effort, by which the crime itself was perpetrated.[16]

Here the chapter had closed in the 1837 first edition. But, as if prompted by the drift in his media substrate from "wide atmosphere" to the "ocean's surface" inscribed by "the track of every canoe, of every vessel," Babbage at this point adds in the 1838 second edition one further paragraph that drives the moral home through the then topical example of slave ships. The new paragraph reads:

The soul of the negro, whose fettered body surviving the living charnel-house of his infected prison, was thrown into the sea to lighten the ship . . . will need, at the last great day of human account, no living witness of his earthly agony. When man and all his race shall have disappeared from the face of our planet, ask every particle of air still floating over the unpeopled earth, and it will record the cruel mandate of the tyrant. Interrogate every wave which breaks unimpeded on ten thousand desolate shores, and it will give evidence of the last gurgle of the waters which closed over the head of his dying victim: confront the murderer with every corporeal atom of his immolated slave, and in its still quivering movements he will read the prophet's denunciation of the prophet king.[17]

Now we come to the singular anecdote I mentioned, which is remarkable because it is nested within this final, moral codicil as a footnote
whose further level of recursion—intended to clinch the point—proves
in the end not to be recursive at all. The anecdote (cited by Babbage from
a section of the *Parliamentary Papers* quoted in the *Quarterly Review* for
December 1835) is "from a report by Captain Hayes to the Admiralty, of a
representation made to him respecting one of these vessels in 1832." Babbage quotes Hayes:

> "The master having a large cargo of these human beings *chained together*,
> with more humanity than his fellows, permitted some of them to come on
> deck, but *still chained together*, for the benefit of the air; when they imme-
> diately commenced jumping overboard, hand in hand, and drowning in
> couples; and, continued the person (relating the circumstance), **'without
> any cause whatever'** [emphasis added]. Now, these people were just brought
> from a situation between decks, and to which they knew they must return,
> where the scalding perspiration was running from one to the other, covered
> also with their own filth, and where *it is no uncommon occurrence for women
> to be bringing forth children, and men dying at their side,* with full in their view
> *living and dead bodies chained together*; and the living, in addition to all their
> other torments, labouring under the most famishing thirst (being in very
> few instances allowed more than a pint of water a day)—and, let it not
> be forgotten, that these unfortunate people had just been torn from their
> country, their families, their all! Men dragged from their wives, women
> from their husbands and children, girls from their mothers, and boys from
> their fathers; and yet in this man's eye (for heart and soul he could have had
> none) **there was no cause whatever** [emphasis added] for jumping over-
> board and drowning. This, in truth, is a rough picture; but it is not highly
> coloured. *The men are chained in pairs*; and, as a proof they are intended so
> to remain to the end of the voyage, *their fetters are not locked, but rivetted by
> the blacksmith*, and as deaths are frequently occurring *living men are often for
> a length of time confined to dead bodies*; the living man cannot be released till
> the blacksmith has performed the operation of cutting the clench of the
> rivet with his chisel; and I have now an officer on board the *Dryad*, who,
> on examining one of these slave vessels, found *not only living men chained to
> dead bodies, but the latter in a putrid state*. And we have now a case reported
> here, which, if true, is too horrible and disgusting to be described."[18]

The interest of this anecdote—an anamorphic paratext that does not,
and cannot, fully fit within the nested structures of Babbage's main argument—can be stated in this way. Let us accept for the sake of argument

Babbage's premise that there is a great chain of determination by which history, slaved to natural determination, can be read forward and backward all along the illimitable tracks of the great program until the alpha and omega of existence—the outermost open and close parentheses in the God program—at last come into view to guarantee closure, correctness, justice. Edmund Burke's variant of this premise is instructive. We remember that, just before the passage in the *Reflections on the Revolution in France* on society as a "great primaeval contract of eternal society, linking the lower with the higher natures" and "those who are living, those who are dead, and those who are to be born," Burke speaks of "the whole chain and continuity of commonwealth."[19] Babbage, as it were, did the code for that, rescuing chain and contract from the messy imprecision of Burke's "custom" or "prejudice" (all so many tangled, unclosed loops of code) to make the "primaeval" program calculable. Processed through Babbage's interpreter, God's high-level source code—whose compiled form is nature—might be rendered as follows: *Do not weep, ye enchained slaves crossing the watery deep of nature's indifference and human cruelty. There is a greater chain, not just of being, but of calculability, in which the links that bind you even as they so cruelly sever you from your country, your families, your all ("Men dragged from their wives, women from their husbands and children, girls from their mothers, and boys from their fathers") will be redeemed in the eyes of God. In the calculation of the final account, positive must balance out negative, and there will be no remainder.*

In the ethical calculation that Babbage runs on top of the primary program of natural and historical determination, in short, there is no remainder—except, of course, for what remains after we have processed Captain Hayes's anecdote and found a bug in the program. Everything in the anecdote between the statement by the anonymous witness quoted by Hayes that the slaves jumped "without any cause whatever" and the damning recapitulation of that phrase by Hayes ("and yet in this man's eye . . . there was no cause whatever")—everything, in other words, framed by the open and close statements in the algorithm of moral judgment being run here—is designed to output a determinate cause. But neither the witness nor Hayes can compute the cause—the witness because the action of the slaves undermines the very premise of rational calculation underlying slavery's (and not just slavery's) regime of force (namely, that human beings will suffer utmost pain and degradation rather than die), and Hayes because, when put to it, he cannot quite come out and declare his alternative theory of rational choice, that pain and degradation *cause* humans to prefer death. Except for the most heartless necessitarian, perhaps, that conclusion is unspeakable and, truth be told, unknowable. "Who are those that are *born to poverty?*" Dr. Johnson had asked in his critique of Soame Jenyns's theory of social determination.[20] A variant of that question applies here: Who is to say *which* humans *must* be driven by *what degree* of suffering to step overboard?

In any case, what emerges at this point instead of rational statement is an incalculable loop of figuration seeming at once to affirm the slaves' determination by slavery *and* their freedom, not just from that system, but from the entire chain of calculation—rational, economic, moral—in which exploiters and redeemers alike try to link them. Witness, therefore, the weirdly revealing way in which, on the one hand, Hayes's imagery of chains (a metonymic figure of thought for slavery) stands paradoxically for the inhumane *dis*concatenation of "men . . . from their wives, women from their husbands and children, girls from their mothers, and boys from their fathers," while, on the other hand, his aggregative or anaphora-like *and*'s (a figure of speech) stand for a grotesque *re*concatenation of human society: "It is no uncommon occurrence for women to be bringing forth children, *and* men dying at their side, with full in their view living and dead bodies chained together; *and* the living . . . —*and*, let it not be forgotten . . . [and so on]."[21] *And* here (and throughout this passage) marks both a cruel syntax of utterly associative, arbitrary, and, thus, fractured causality *and* a powerful, redemptive figure of inalienable sociality—of a society whose continuity somehow survives, not just despite, but *in* externally caused fractures of pain and degradation. *And* projects the vision of a humanity that, chained side by side as if in an exploded diagram of all the stages of generation, forms a society of life in death literalizing (and ironizing) Burke's chain of the living and the dead. Such is the unspeakable allegory of painfully broken yet redeemed society hidden within Hayes's discourse—otherwise too explicit and reticent both, in strange measure, to look past the naked, embodied hurt of inhumanity to the *subject* of humanity that survives precisely because it needs no assigned cause. It is its own cause. And, at the end of the anecdote, therefore, no conclusion is possible except through an inexpressibility topos (the quit statement in the program) introduced by another *and* marking at once a link and a break in the link of determinate logic: "And we have now a case reported here, which, if true, is too horrible and disgusting to be described." Such is the open-ended close of this unthinkable train, or chain, of thought.

In the very process of imagining a cosmic system of determination that would account in the last days for human beings lost in unutterable abjection, in sum, Babbage counterimagines through the medium of Captain Hayes an undecidable reversal between his thesis and his empirical example that is incalculable within tidily closed, nested programming

Figure 9.1. J. M. W. Turner, *Slavers Throwing Overboard the Dead and Dying—Typhon Coming On* (exhibited 1840).

structures of the sort that makes slavery just a subroutine framed between the *begin* and *end* statements of divine right. Just as free will is a profound problem in the larger argument of the *Ninth Bridgewater Treatise* about the calculability of the universe, so is the event of the slaves jumping overboard "without any cause whatever." At this point in Babbage's argument, calculability reaches an impasse where one of its functions seems to be precisely incalculability, or the determination to escape determination.

If Babbage's *Ninth* were scored to Beethoven's Ninth, we might say, the anecdote of the slaves leaping overboard would be a somber version of the "Ode to Joy"—the climax of the opus of freedom that is actually not part of the symphonic structure of that opus. Or we might allude to Wordsworth's and Coleridge's notion of the One Life. All things touch on, and are codetermined by, all things in the round of nature, but, somehow, there is one thing (not slave, perhaps, but Wordsworthian child or subject) left free to imagine.[22] Or, again, if the "Ode to Joy" and the One Life seem too pretty a comparison, we might look for a more exact analogy to J. M. W. Turner's *Slavers Throwing Overboard the Dead and Dying*, exhibited at the Royal Academy in 1840 just two years after Babbage published his anecdote (figure 9.1). In the painting, Turner's characteristically orbicular or vortex

Figure 9.2. J. M. W. Turner, *Slavers Throwing Overboard the Dead and Dying* (detail).

Figure 9.3. J. M. W. Turner, *Slavers Throwing Overboard the Dead and Dying* (detail).

composition frames the scene of horror between the twin arcs of the sky (especially at the topmost right) and the sea (especially in the swirling patterns at the lower left). But the closure of these transcendental parentheses is violently quartered by the grid imposed by the x-axis of the horizon and the y-axis of the cleft of light centered on the sun. And, in the exploded quadrants of the composition thus formed, we see in the lower-left and -right foreground a drama of isolated human limbs whose hyperrealistic chains—seeming almost to be inscriptions added with a detail brush— limn their essential disconcatenation from any transcendental, unifying composition (figures 9.2–9.3). The limbs, the fish, the birds, the chains, the froth: it is as if some great database underneath the sea were throwing forth images ("and . . . and . . . and") organized by random access.[23]

MyLifeBits

To update Babbage's "one vast library" of history from the age of mechanical calculation to that of digital computing, we might next proceed through a series of well-established relays in the history of computing. One such relay, for example, is the Memex machine imagined by Vannevar Bush in 1945 whose repository of codable microfilm was to have been interlinked in random-access "trails" of associations. A second is the Xanadu project that Ted Nelson started in the 1960s and 1970s. The random-access "docuverse" that Nelson dubbed *hypertext* was to have included, among other features, "historical backtracking" or time-based "intercomparison" between earlier and later assemblages of linked documents.[24] And a third relay, of course, is the Internet and World Wide Web, which followed up on the hypertext vision.

I will concentrate, however, on a fourth relay in the digitization of the "one vast library" that is less well-known in the humanities but equally crucial (and, in computer science, canonical): E. F. Codd's work at IBM on the theory of relational databases, most influentially in his 1970 "A Relational Model of Data for Large Shared Data Banks." Codd's formalization of high-level, logically general, and consistent database structures—together with later work by others at IBM on the SQL language that (partially) implemented Codd's theory—brought into being the modern relational database.[25]

Before Codd, we know, databases in the 1960s and 1970s followed the so-called hierarchical or network paradigms, according to which information was logically organized in single-root or multiroot tree structures such that finding anything required traversing a so-called pointer (like running one's index finger down a branching diagram) to the appropriate logical location.[26] The disadvantage, of course, was that changing the structure at a later date—for example, adding a new branch or level—scrambled up all the pointers. It was like giving someone elaborate, procedural directions to retrieve a book from the library by taking the elevator to the fifth floor, turning left, going down four aisles (and so on), only to find that someone had added an extra aisle or even a whole floor. Fundamentally, such lack of logical *independence*, as it is called, was symptomatic of an underlying lack of physical independence. A system of traversing pointers was premised at base on needing to know exactly how the bits were organized in hard storage. In the early years, when limited computing power rewarded those who kept an eye out for what the machine was actually doing, database science was more an empirics than a theory.

The first true *theory* of the database appeared in Codd's work in 1970, though it would be a decade before computers came up to the speed needed to implement his notions. By the 1980s, Codd's relational model had made the hierarchical and network models obsolete, and it is now so dominant that it is staving off even the newer object-oriented model that claims to be better aligned with recent programming philosophy. This dominance ensued from the clean break that Codd's relational concept made with both physical and logical data dependency.

An example will be expedient. Consider the following data: "Alan Liu, customer 5643289, of [such and such an address], orders from an online vendor on May 1, 2004, a book by E. F. Codd entitled *The Relational Model for Database Management, Version 2* (Addison-Wesley, 2000, ISBN 0201141922)."[27] In a relational database, this proposition would be recorded as a set of data known technically as a *relation* or *relational variable* (more colloquially, a *table* consisting of individual *records* or *rows*, each holding data in discrete *columns* or *fields*). A first draft of a book-order table in which the above example is the most recent entry might appear as in figure 9.4. Each record in this table consists of a set of entities whose interrelation the database describes through the table structure alone, independent of any awareness of the underlying physical data model and even of the locational order of records (which can be entered in any order). Instead—and this is the heart of Codd's theory qua theory—data are related through a pure mathematics of value comparison and manipulation based on set theory and its database variant, relational algebra. By parsing, transforming, and cross-referencing data tables (individually or in combination) through computable set operations named *restrict* (or *select*), *project*, *product*, *union*, *intersect*, *difference*, *join*, and *divide* (akin to arithmetic addition, subtraction, multiplication, and division), relational algebra does all the origami trick of folding and unfolding data tables into derivative tables showing

Book Order Table

Order_No	Customer_No	Date	C_First_Name	C_Last_Name	Street	City	State	Zip	ISBN	A_First_Name	A_Last_Name	Title	Publisher	Year Published
3587849	5643289	5/1/04	Alan	Liu	[Street address]	Santa Barbara	CA	93117	020114 1922	E. F.	Codd	Relational Model for Database Management, Version 2	Addison-Wesley	2000
3587898	5643289	4/10/04	Alan	Liu	[Street address]	Santa Barbara	CA	93117	851960 058	Charles	Babbage	Ninth Bridgewater Treatise	Pickering	1989

Figure 9.4. Book-order table.

information exactly as the user wants. Thus, a *restrict* (or *select*) operation, for example, might convert our book-order table into a derivative table showing just records in which the customer last name field is "Liu" (in SQL: "SELECT * FROM Book_Order_Table WHERE C_Last_Name = 'Liu'"), or, again, a *join* operation might produce a derivative table linking Liu to another table containing credit card information. The basic idea is that data can be broken down into members of a logical set whose permutations can be manipulated free of the restrictions imposed by the "real" concatenations of data in the internal program or physical system.

Nor does the drive toward data independence stop there. Any database programmer today would shudder at the book-order table instanced above, which is only a first, untidy approximation of the pristine state of data freedom. Programmers would know that this table is unclean because it exhibits the very anathema of good relational database design: redundancy. Whether in its most dangerous form, duplicate records, or in the lesser form exhibited here of information tediously repeated from record to record (e.g., the repetition of the customer name and mailing address), database redundancy is inherently bad because it inevitably leads to inconsistency or ambiguity—for instance, when some, but not all, instances of a customer's credit card number are updated in a large, complex, and evolving database maintained by multiple operators over many years. At base, redundancy is a symptom of incomplete data *atomization*—a term with multiple meanings in database theory that applies from the level of individual fields (e.g., the need to atomize names into separate first and last names) all the way up to that of whole "transactions" (involving multiple records and tables) that must complete as discrete, bounded, and self-consistent events without any possibility of partial or double completion.

The problem with our book-order table in figure 9.4, we may say, is that it is molecular rather than atomic: it is really several tables living together in unclean cohabitation and generating data redundancy among them. Specifically, if we think of the ideal table as a proposition about one, and only one, subject (the "primary key," unique identifier, or, more loosely, *identity* of a record), then our book-order table is abnormal because it is about at least three different subjects: the book order (identified by order number), the customer (identified by customer number), and the book (identified by ISBN number).[28] In an actual database, our book-order table would thus likely undergo a process that database theory calls *normalization*. It would be decomposed into at least three, separate tables: one holding just data about the customer, a second holding just data about the book, and a third holding the actual event of the order itself with the customer number, ISBN number, and date (see figure 9.5). In this revised

Customer Table

Customer_No	C_First_Name	C_Last_Name	Street	City	State	Zip
5643289	Alan	Liu	[Street address]	Santa Barbara	CA	93117

Book Table

ISBN	A_First_Name	A_Last_Name	Title	Publisher	Year Published
0201141922	E. F.	Codd	Relational Model for Database Management, Version 2	Addison-Wesley	2000
851960058	Charles	Babbage	Ninth Bridgewater Treatise	Pickering	1989

Order Table

Order_No	Date	Customer_No	ISBN
3587849	5/1/04	5643289	0201141922
3587898	4/10/04	5643289	851960058

Figure 9.5. "Normalization" of book-order table (decomposition into independent tables). *a*, Customer table. *b*, Book table. *c*, Order table.

scheme, customer and book tables are independent of each other, yet convene in the order table through the propinquity of their primary keys. It is like isolating the intercourse between one body of material and another to a single Michelangelesque, God-to-Adam point of indexical contact. A new god of random access thus arises—more Maxwell's Demon than Laplace Demon—for whom creation is a return to the state of entropy where any one atom can again be free to touch any other.

Or, at least, such is the theory. We have still to account for a crucial remainder not accounted for by database theory. To do so, we must now recognize—as database programmers in fact do all the time—that data independence is in real life not so pristine. First, the normalization process that decomposes data tables almost never proceeds to its conclusion— often stopping at the so-called third normal form—because logical and physical efficiency *does* matter beyond a certain point (data independence is purchased at the expense of extra operations that the machine must perform to interpret the pure concept). Second, the SQL language that allows users to manipulate and query databases is, from the point of view of relational purists, a compromised, even bastardized implementation of the theory—failing, for example, to interdict duplicate records.[29] And, third, there is the enormous compromise represented by so-called three-value logic or, in a word that makes some database theorists almost cross themselves, *nulls*. In theory, every value in a database should be evaluated as true or false (e.g., either a year is or is not 2000). But, in the real world, there is enormous pressure to enter records into a database even if some of the values in a record are either unknown or nonexistent (e.g., no declared publication date for a book). The result is that major database programs today contravene the purity of database theory by allowing the option of null values, which are neither true nor false but instead a third computational value of *unknown*.[30] By the mathematical logic of relational algebra, however, *any* comparison operation that involves a null results in a null (akin to multiplying by zero), with the consequence that the null state, unless carefully controlled, propagates outward across ever vaster, more distant reaches of the database, shadowing knowledge in a cone of night within which all things, again, are indistinguishably concatenated.[31]

This part of the discussion has been technical, but the important point to retain is not. Babbage sought total data determination, but wrestled with an incalculable remainder of independence called *free will*. Inversely, relational databases quest for total data independence but grapple with an incalculable remainder of dependency called, among other bad words, *redundant* and *null*. (Indeed, there is a whole other class of databases called *knowledge bases*, *data warehouses*, or *decision support databases* that are anti-

thetical to data independence because they present agglomerated historical data for the purpose of managing enduring patterns.)[32] If Babbage had
his "chains" and database theory has its "relations," in other words, then
the weak link in both systems—indeterminability for Babbage, concatenation in databases—is the common link that joins them in a conterminous,
if inverse, meditation on the way human history is ordered.

We can thus at last close all the historical relays mentioned above to
watch the signal of random—but not random enough—access surge into
the present in "one vast library" projects like MyLifeBits, a software application under development in the early years of the twenty-first century
by Jim Gemmell, Roger Lueder, and Gordon Bell of the Media Presence
Group at the Microsoft Bay Area Research Center. While explicitly inspired by Bush's Memex and Nelson's docuverse, MyLifeBits is grounded
in practice on Codd's relational database.[33]

MyLifeBits is a personal history system whose true intention (as in the
case of such other recent projects as Total Recall, LifeLog, Memories for
Life, Time-Machine Computing, and Shoebox) is total history.[34] The premise is that advances in storage media will soon enable users to have, not just
gigabytes, but terabytes of personal storage—more space, in fact, than can
easily or even feasibly be filled.[35] In such an abundant-resources environment, therefore, why not save everything? "MyLifeBits is a lifetime store of
everything," the project's homepage declares in its first sentence. As defined
in the group's paper "MyLifeBits: Fulfilling the Memex Vision," *everything*
means that "users will eventually be able to keep every document they
read, every picture they view, all the audio they hear, and a good portion
of what they see."[36] Or, again, as Bell chants the mantra in an interview:
"everything you read, every picture you've ever taken, everything you've
said." Indeed, as the project's designated guinea pig, Bell is personally practicing the art of everything. Assisted by such aide-mémoire as scanners,
recorders, and "cameras mounted on his hat and glasses" that save "the
previous 30 seconds of video when a button is pressed," he is embarked on
a hyper-Shandyan enterprise of recording all that crosses his sensorium,
past or present: "The system now captures everything that you see that
comes to you electronically. You've got all that. I'm capturing phone con-
versations, so those are available. I've got a Sony voice recorder . . . so in
principle every conversation you have could be captured there. The TiVo
capability could get you all the TV you'd ever watched."[37]

But, of course, omnistorage is not the same as omniscience. Given "all
that," the specific research problem of MyLifeBits becomes *finding* things
in life's everything.[38] This problem has two aspects, which we can call the
blob and the *tree*:

Problem. Text can be searched in relatively well-understood ways, but the ever-burgeoning stream of images, video, and audio entering into people's life stores cannot because they are technically "blobs." Blobs are binary large objects stored in databases as wholes of raw, binary data without any innate features or internal structure apparent to the storage system.[39] To be made tractable, they must be annotated in some way, whether with textual descriptors or through the intelligent juxtaposition of neighboring data related by time, place, or some other criterion important to human experience.[40]

Solution. MyLifeBits is developing various ways to "gang" annotate large batches of multimedia so that they can be poured automatically or semiautomatically *with* descriptions into the relational database that undergirds the system (in this case, Microsoft's SQL Server).[41] Users will then be able to search both text and blobs through the database's built-in query functions. "Everything," truly, will be random accessible.

Problem. Besides searching, users also want to assemble, navigate, browse, and mine their life data in configurable ways—all of which requires organizing information so that its multiplex relations can be presented through what the project calls flexible "views" or visualizations (including detail, thumbnail, timeline, story, and other views).[42] But the hierarchical tree method of organization that currently rules is hopeless because, above a certain scale, it always degrades into *dis*organization (data isolated in ill-sorted, arbitrary, cryptically named or forgotten folders).

Solution. Here, MyLifeBits's profound reliance on the relational database paradigm is clearest since, of course, it was precisely the tree that Codd set out to hew. MyLifeBit's organizational solution is the particular design of its SQL Server database, whose highly modular, pliant table structures are designed to be preadapted to human experience—allowing loose organization in some circumstances, imposing tight organization in others, and never constraining information to hierarchical logic. In the vocabulary of the project, users need be aware of only two genres of structure: "resources" and "links." Resources are documents, e-mail, contacts, events, images, music, and so on, while links relate those resources either polymorphously (when all that is required is to stuff things into such all-purpose structures as "collections" and "annotations") or semantically (through so-called strong typing imposing finer relations so that, for instance, a person can be associated with a document through an "author of" link but not an "attendee of" link).[43] The actual work of organization is then performed in the background by the table schema of the MyLifeBits database, which the group diagrams as in figure 9.6. As a consequence, users will be able to view their life through the full

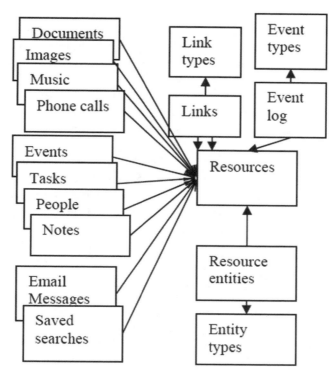

Figure 9.6. "Key Elements of the MyLifeBits schema. Each box is a database table. Arrows indicate foreign keys." (Diagram and caption from Gemmell et al., "Living with a Lifetime Store.") Reproduced by permission of Jim Gemmell.

repertory of database-query operations and not just the narrow-purpose, text-string operation we normally call *search*. "Everything" will be an even richer experience of random access.

Only, we note, there is one revealing anomaly, almost a regression, in the way MyLifeBits exploits its database. Consider the MyLifeBits "pivot by time" feature, a last-measures function designed to allow users who have exhausted all other search strategies to cast a very wide net into the sea of data. A user, for example, might remember nothing about a document or Web page (not the author, title, URL, or even precise topic) except that it must have been encountered sometime around the date of a phone call to a particular person who recommended it. In that case, the MyLifeBits team proposes, the user can ask the system for "everything with a timestamp close to that of the object" or, again, for "everything in the database with a time falling inside the span of the phone call."[44] The return of the repressed here, of course, is "everything." "Everything in the database" is the frightening, final threat of the MyLifeBits system. In the case of the most difficult or desperate queries, we are invited to revert our life to a gigantic blob or, more uncanny still, the database simulation of a blob: thousands of e-mails, appointments, files, images, and so on exploding into view in their original chronological order around a point in time. The most advanced, random-access digital technology, in other words, is dedicated to reproducing exactly the concatenated mess that was life in the first place.

And so the blob comes back to life. Where Babbage's *Ninth* focused on programming the concatenation of things but discovered a disturbing remainder of unprogrammability epitomized in the slaves, MyLifeBits reverses the dilemma. It focuses on freeing things from each other, which is to say, random access, but in the end rediscovers the everything that cannot be disconcatenated. The alter ego of MyLifeBits is MyLifeBlob.

\ Escaping History: The New Historicism Reconsidered

> The format for parameter expansion is as follows:
>
> ${expression}
>
> where expression consists of all characters until the matching '}'. Any '}' escaped by a backslash or within a quoted string . . . shall not be examined in determining the matching '}'.
>
> **from the Open Group and IEEE specification for a standard operating system interface and environment**

Think of it this way: we want to live in history, where our ancestors and all our brethren live and die in common. Those are the expanded parameters of our community (Burke's contract and chain). But, however expansive such parameters may be, we also desire to escape from history. No one, after all, actually wants to live in history if there is no escape from its chains. To adapt Nietzsche's argument of purposiveness in his *Use and Abuse of History*, that is not what history is *for*. We want to be chained in history, but we also want to be unlinked via an escape character (in programming: a backslash, quote sign, comment tag, and so on) that allows us the freedom to be a link unto ourselves or to whom and what we choose.[45]

Now we are ready to reconsider the New Historicism. Since the 1980s, we know, the New Historicism has blurred somewhat into the larger scene of postmodern cultural criticisms. Insofar as it remains distinctive, it is often because of the keepsake we call the *anecdote*—a silhouette of its best, and worst, features. Yet, in the age of the database, I think, the

New Historicist anecdote may well be our best clue to the general relation between postmodern historicism in the academy and postindustrial
technologism everywhere else. After all, anyone other than a cutting-edge
cultural critic (and even the latter when engaged in the act of querying a library database or quickly verifying a date via Google or Wikipedia) knows
what the anecdote really is. It is random access. If the New Historicism is a
kind of relational database, then the anecdote is its query. As it were: *Here
is a key incident. It has a microdesign that feels like it may be part of a broader
pattern. What does the whole data set of history look like if we filter it through
that microdesign (in SQL, e.g., "SELECT author, work FROM history WHERE
keyword = 'nature' OR keyword = 'Napoleon' AND year > '1802'")? What other
"hits" might be returned leading toward pattern recognition—that is, the recognition of "episteme," "mentality," "structure," "power," etc.?*

As a touchstone, we can consult the eulogy for the New Historicism
(already referred to in the introduction to this volume) that appeared in
2000, Catherine Gallagher and Stephen Greenblatt's *Practicing New Historicism*, where the anecdote is characterized first of all as what amounts to
random access. Indeed, one of Greenblatt's chapters in the book describes
anecdotes in faux-technical terms uncannily reminiscent of Codd hewing
hierarchical trees (or, the equivalent of the tree in Renaissance studies, the
chain of being in the book the New Historicists loved to hate, E. M. W.
Tillyard's *Elizabethan World Picture*). Anecdotes, Greenblatt says, "subvert
a programmatic analytical response, a fully systematized methodology."
The "unfamiliar cultural texts" they mark are "marginal, odd, fragmentary,
unexpected, and crude."[46] Or as Gallagher elaborates in one of her chapters: "outlandish and irregular . . . heterogeneous . . . askew . . . accidental,
suppressed, defeated, uncanny, abjected, or exotic."[47] More subversively,
as the New Historicism likes to say, anecdotes do not just atomize history
analytically; they are atomization as ontology. "Random" (analogous to
the universal, even metaphysical implications of entropy in modern physics) is the ground state of being. In other words, the random anecdote's interior contradiction, irony, or aporia (a whole Foucauldian heterocosm in
microcosm) exposes the fault lines in the "reality" of history itself, which
is thus revealed to be the primordial disjoint structure—no less than an
ironic New Critical or poststructuralist *literature* of ontological being (all
paradox, *différance*, and so on). Phrased somewhat differently in romantics
New Historicism, but no less ironically, the anecdote is (as noted in chapter 5 above) what shows history to be "'displaced,' 'erased,' 'suppressed,'
'elided,' 'overlooked,' 'overwritten,' 'omitted,' 'obscured,' 'expunged,' 'repudiated,' 'excluded,' 'annihilated,' and 'denied'" (160–61). In part, such
displacement is a perspective effect imposed by somebody with a par-

ticular, angled view of reality—state official, poet, critic, or anyone else. It is akin to anamorphosis as discussed in Greenblatt's *Renaissance Self-Fashioning*: a fracturing of history into partial, contradictory, ideologically blindered views that can be manipulated with imaginative legerdemain to conceal and, more rarely, to reveal.[48] But, more deeply, the displacement effect runs deeper—all the way to the default mode of historical reality. Random-access details (e.g., Wordsworth's image of "wreathes of smoke" at Tintern Abbey) are only apparently random. Like Freud's puns, they are apparitional. They make appear the truth that history qua history is the original agent of reality displacement—of erasure, exclusion, annihilation, denial, and all the other precious and dreadful mobilities of human desire, all the perpetual fragmentations and remixings we call *war, revolution, poverty, diaspora, terror,* and so on that break open the solid facade of reality to reveal its radically atomic form, free and cruel at the same time.[49]

This is to say that the seeming levitas of the New Historicism's random anecdotalism (what I labeled *why not?* in chapter 1) is counterbalanced by a profound gravitas: no less than the pull of the real itself. As the vocabulary of denial in my own *Wordsworth: The Sense of History* perhaps too aggressively suggests, the New Historicism is overdetermined (dealing in *denial* rather than just displacement).[50] Random access in the New Historicism is the very mark—like a brand on flesh—of the forces of historical determination that break up bodies, lives, families, villages, nations, and so on to make both tyranny and recuperative freedom possible. In short, the New Historicism is the intuition simultaneously of random access (an atheist transcendence) *and* determination (a bowing down or conviction). Greenblatt thus witnesses in his chapter in *Practicing New Historicism* entitled "The Touch of the Real": "We wanted to recover in our literary criticism a confident conviction of reality, without giving up the power of literature to sidestep or evade the quotidian and without giving up a minimally sophisticated understanding that any text depends upon the absence of the bodies and voices that it represents. We wanted the touch of the real in the way that in an earlier period people wanted the touch of the transcendent."[51] Participating fully in the emancipatory program of random access, the New Historicism nevertheless acknowledges its overlap with older philosophies of determination—including the nineteenth-century historicisms that originally credited determination by climate, zeitgeist, modes of production, ideology, and, yes, Analytical Engines too.

In sum, the New Historicism wants a paradox of random determination or determined randomness (Greenblatt: "We wanted to recover . . . a confident conviction of reality, without giving up the power of literature to sidestep or evade"). This want, I wager, is more than just greed, a matter of wanting to have one's cake and eat it too. It is the want for a very notion of human want or desire unconstrained by our contemporary master verbs *search* and *query*, with their carefully metered promise of *more* ("next 10 results") indicated by the link at the bottom of any Web-search results page. It is the want for the combined substance and freedom of history that, as I intimated earlier, Babbage's and Codd's worldviews could not individually acknowledge as more than their weak link, their unconscious. The New Historicism wants the determination *and* the random access it believes make up the whole span (always both enslaved and free) of human life.

The function of the New Historicism in the age of the database, then, is to declare our hope for both a significant history and the end of history. Where better to look for such hope, the New Historicism argues, than to history itself, which—in something like the function calls of contemporary object-oriented programming—can be called on to show that the past is the exact precursor of our own determination to be free of the past. All the New Historicism's anecdotes of subversions, displacements, denials, and so on: what are they but stories of how dearly people have always wanted both determination and freedom, both their history and the end of their history? The function of the New Historicism in the age of the database is to define the function of the past as the beginning of the end of history.

Postscript: The Poetics of Contingency

Is the New Historicism, therefore, a continuation of the project of the Enlightenment, which named the paradox of determination and freedom *reason* (a progressive, irresistible tide of reason that could free humanity from the dark chains of its past)?

A final thought—one that might well serve as an epitaph for the movement—is that the New Historicism is, ultimately, not a project of the Enlightenment because it is devoted to the romance of irrationality that postmodern cultural criticism calls *contingency*. As Gallagher says in one of her chapters in *Practicing New Historicism*, the attraction of representing history as akin to texts is that "'history' could be imagined as part of [textual] contingency."[52] The anecdote is the form of contingency.

Widely espoused in contemporary cultural criticism and epitomized in the New Historicism, contingency is a philosophy of compromise between determination and random access. It is both a "touching together or on all sides, lying near, contiguous, coming into contact or connexion, befalling, happening, coming to pass" according to which nothing can act but in lockstep with everything (see *OED* etymology for *contingent*) and an aleatory slippage within the consistency of everything that allows some things to slip free.[53] As Elena Esposito writes in "The Art of Contingency," we are today witnessing a "general reassessment of the relationship of the necessary and the contingent, of the stable and the mutable, of redundancy and variety." We desire "loosely coupled elements" in which "data represent a set of elements whose bonds are loosened in order to be available for new recombinations."[54] Or as Esposito once put it more succinctly to me in a personal communication: "Constraint is not the same as determination."[55] Indeed, constraint may even be the very ground of creativity—as formulated in Jon Elster's rational choice theory definition of creativity as "maximizing aesthetic value under constraints."[56]

We might visualize it as follows. Imagine that each particle of existence is constrained within its immediate historical context so that the whole weather cell of history moves together or not at all. But also imagine that, beyond a certain distance, the constraint of any local cell of action ends at its interface with another cell. The result is a world of contingency in which particles may be chained to contexts but where contexts themselves perpetually slip along their interfaces in sudden, unpredictable shifts evincing unknown metaconstraints beyond the reason of local maximization. And this is not even to reckon the full epistemological as well as ontological force of the unknown in its contemporary guise as the science, philosophy, and literature of contingency. I refer to the epistemology of "emergence," according to which (as in complexity theory) deterministic local systems yield unpredictable results when seen as part of a higher-level, emergent system.[57] Contingent history is like code "escaped" with a backslash (or some other escape character) in programming: the escaped material is embedded in the local routine but lives a different life.

The function of the New Historicism in the age of the database is to declare that the past determines us to be free, and the name of that radically determined freedom is *contingency*, the form of our near escape.

Notes

Introduction

1. U.S. patents may be invalidated if the patent office finds that there has been relevant "prior art" that undermines the claim of a patent to uniqueness and innovation. The relevant portion of U.S. patent law begins: "Any person at any time may cite to the Office in writing prior art consisting of patents or printed publications which that person believes to have a bearing on the patentability of any claim of a particular patent. If the person explains in writing the pertinency and manner of applying such prior art to at least one claim of the patent, the citation of such prior art and the explanation thereof will become a part of the official file of the patent" (35 U.S.C. 301; U.S. Patent and Trademark Office, "Appendix L: Patent Laws").

2. Schumpeter, *Capitalism, Socialism and Democracy*, 83–84. For a discussion of the way the late twentieth and early twenty-first centuries adopted Schumpeter's phrase as the unofficial motto of postindustrialism, see Liu, *Laws of Cool*, 2.

3. It is instructive to contrast with Schumpeter Jürgen Habermas's "Modernity—an Incomplete Project." Habermas's essay remembers just how old the idea of a modern "new" breaking with the past actually is before then

focusing on the span of modernity between the Enlightenment and postmodernism that is also my temporal domain in this book.

4. *Just in time* (JIT) is a catchphrase in postindustrial business theory that originally referred to new ways of managing inventories so that the parts and supplies necessary for manufacturing flowed adaptively to the point of assembly "just in time"—thus eliminating the need for larger, inflexible "just-in-case" stores of materials. The phrase has since widened in usage to refer to many other processes and trends of business that depend on quick-response, networked information technology. In the Internet's transmission protocol, "Time to Live," or TTL, is a counter set in the header of an individual data packet that defines how long (or how many hops between routers) the packet lives before it stops circulating and an error message is returned to the sender.

5. These concepts are associated with, respectively, David Harvey's *The Condition of Postmodernity* and Francis Fukuyama's *The End of History and the Last Man* (and Fukuyama's earlier "The End of History?"). In a different sense of *end of history*, Fredric Jameson speaks in his work on postmodernism of "the disappearance of the sense of history, the way in which our entire contemporary social system has little by little begun to lose its capacity to retain its own past, has begun to live in a perpetual present and in a perpetual change that obliterates traditions of the kind which all earlier social formations have had in one way or another to preserve" ("Postmodernism and Consumer Society," 125).

6. Liu, *Laws of Cool*, 76. For a definition of *ethos* in relation to *cool*, see ibid., esp. 71–72.

7. The iPod is a particularly appropriate emblem of the paradoxical phenomenon I address here. Its iconic, originally "white," no-fuss design (like that of many of the Apple products of the 1990s and 2000s) bespeaks the entire lineage of design from Bauhaus through minimalism that created the profession of "design" in the first place as the fusion of modern art with industrial modernization. The iPod is a retro icon of the modern: its plastic white front (and chromed metal back) a tabula rasa of history on which any patina of historical experience can seem only a greasy fingerprint, to be wiped clean. Yet its use to restore a sense of community and identification ("my music") places the emphasis on the *i* in *iPod*. This lowercase *i* perhaps accurately measures how tall personal identity and communitarian identity now stand among the modular organizations (corporations, cubicles, pods) of the postindustrial age.

8. See, e.g., *Sid Meier's Civilization IV* in the *Civilization* series of games. In this turn-based, simulation-style game, the player grows a civilization from a prehistoric village to an advanced society.

9. For Fredric Jameson's well-known critique of postmodern pastiche and the loss of history, see his "Postmodernism and Consumer Society" (as well as his later *Postmodernism*). Peter Krapp speaks of similar phenomena as a contemporary, media-based "déjà vu" (see his *Déjà Vu*).

10. On the crisis of historicism in the early twentieth century, see, e.g., Iggers, "Historicism." In referring to the *complex, interpretive knots of hermeneutics* that characterized advanced historicist thought in that period, I am thinking in particular of the works of Wilhelm Dilthey and R. G. Collingwood.

11. Benjamin, "The Work of Art in the Age of Mechanical Reproduction."

12. In this book, I capitalize *New Historicism* to designate the specific movement in literary criticism that arose ca. 1980, as opposed to a more generic sense of *new historicism* that includes the closely related movements in other disciplines mentioned here.

13. See, e.g., the work of Friedrich A. Kittler and Lisa Gitelman.

14. "From ca. 1980," of course, is a loose chronology, and there is some argument that

"from ca. 1970" would be more accurate since the 1970s first witnessed the combined social and intellectual ferment released in the season of May 1968 or, in the United States, May 1970. The advantage of speaking of 1980 as the onset date, however, is that it more clearly differentiates cultural criticism from the poststructuralist theories of the 1970s that faced more explicitly toward the scene of language rather than that of culture.

15. For a fuller exposition of the relation between historicism and informationalism—and between the New Historicism and the age of the database—see esp. chapter 9 below. Of course, my stress at this point on the way both cultural criticism and information technology subverted hierarchy can also be inverted to stress the containment of such subversion. Just as in the New Historicist argument "subversion" is ultimately "contained" (see chapter 2 below), so in information technology "decentralization" is at last "managed" (see chapter 7 below as well as the discussion of the relation between information decentralization and "recentralization" in my *Laws of Cool*, 144–50).

16. Clayton, *Charles Dickens in Cyberspace*, 5, 7.

17. I allude to Stephen Greenblatt's *Renaissance Self-Fashioning*.

18. As attested by such metaphors as *bombardment* in Schumpeter's work on creative destruction (originally published in the years of the Second World War), creative destruction—the inheritor of romantic Sturm und Drang—ineluctably witnesses history. A passage such as the following from Schumpeter's *Capitalism, Socialism and Democracy*, it seems to me, refers to the temper of its times. Creative destruction, Schumpeter writes, is "competition which commands a decisive cost or quality advantage and which strikes not at the margins of the profits and the outputs of the existing firms but at their foundations and their very lives. This kind of competition is as much more effective than the other as a bombardment is in comparison with forcing a door" (84).

19. As the *OED* indicates, *critique* began to be used in the eighteenth century.

20. Gallagher and Greenblatt, *Practicing New Historicism*, 1.

21. Colebrook, *New Literary Histories*, 23–24. Colebrook is quoting Greenblatt, "Towards a Poetics of Culture," 1. Chapter 1 of *New Literary Histories*, "History, Historicism and New Historicism," is an excellent, ambitious attempt to sketch an extensive genealogy of contemporary new historicisms. Especially resonant with my argument is Colebrook's discussion of eighteenth-century, romantic, and nineteenth-century understandings of history within that genealogy.

22. Colebrook, *New Literary Histories*, viii.

23. Gallagher and Greenblatt, *Practicing New Historicism*, 2. Compare also Greenblatt, "Towards a Poetics of Culture": "One of the peculiar characteristics of the 'new historicism' in literary studies is precisely how unresolved and in some ways disingenuous it has been—I have been—about the relation to literary theory. On the one hand it seems to me that an openness to the theoretical ferment of the last few years is precisely what distinguishes the new historicism from the positivist historical scholarship of the early twentieth century. . . . On the other hand the historicist critics have on the whole been unwilling to enroll themselves in one or the other of the dominant theoretical camps" (1).

24. Clover, *Their Ambiguity*. The second page of the poem (an unpaginated chapbook published in 2003) begins: "Against things made things, new desires. But I had wanted to tell you about my town and already we have reached the problem of the new. . . . New every day! Adrift in Late Contingency. . . . "

25. Ross, "Contingent Predilections," 510, 497. Where I have imagined a zigzag path of method through a minefield, Ross takes a more organic metaphor from the following comment by Kenneth Burke: "We could state the principle of the laboratory in this proposition: Every machine contains a cow-path. That is: there are embodied somewhere

in its parts the variants of a process that remains simply because the originators of the machine embodied this process in their invention" (Burke, *Attitudes toward History*, 228 [quoted, as an epigraph, in Ross, "Contingent Predilections," 485).

In general, Ross's rich, deep essay—one of the finest on the New Historicism to appear in the 1990s—is an estimable companion to this introduction. Especially important is his discussion of the following paradox:

> On the one hand, contingency means that which may or may not happen; it means a sort of accidental touching or chance happening, without design, without foresight. On the other hand, it means, as its derivation indicates, to touch together; a happening dependent upon another happening. The latter meaning has become especially germane in the study of logic, where a contingency denotes that which is true only given certain specific conditions; it means conditional, as opposed to categorical. On the one hand, the anecdote serves to display the new historicist's awareness that writing history is a chancy business, that the peregrinations of the unconscious self and the arbitrariness of language are always involved. On the other hand, the anecdote functions as a kind of causal logic, indicating how everything is conditional, how everything is dependent on everything else. . . . The anecdote gives the aura of accidental contingency needed for a method that claims to take into account the limited perspective (methodical self-consciousness) of the historian while at the same time it provides the conditional contingency (the making of explanatory connections) that every historical method needs in order for history to get written (491).

Or, as Ross also puts it: "The anecdote joins the *eventuality* of the historical structure (what happened when) to the *structure* of the historical event (why did it happen in this way) so that structure and event can reflexively explain each other without being interrogated by each other" (492).

The following sections amount to an attempt to think a way out of this paradox. How can historicism as theorized/practiced by recent cultural criticisms be both accidental and causal and, therefore, both free of method and prone to method?

26. Wordsworth, *The Prelude: 1799, 1805, 1850*, 452, 454, 456 (12.312–53 [1805]).

27. Jones, "Virtual Sublime."

28. Shakespeare, *Richard the Second*, 66 (2.1.40–43); Churchill, speech to House of Commons, 20 August 1940.

29. For the French revolutionary context of Wordsworth's experience of Salisbury Plain, see chapter 2 below.

30. On the Druids as perceived in Wordsworth's time, see the discussion of *Salisbury Plain* in Liu, *Wordsworth: The Sense of History*, chap. 5. See also chapter 2 below.

31. Chance is one of the rarest, most problematic concepts in Wordsworth's poetry, where all accidents seem, ultimately, to derive instead from what "Resolution and Independence" calls a "peculiar grace, / A leading from above, a something given" (Wordsworth, *William Wordsworth*, ed. Gill, 262 [lines 50–51]). In general, the problem of accidentality in romanticism—as differentiated from eighteenth-century associationism, the picturesque, and other forms of adventitiousness—is a deep one. Or, rather, depth may be precisely the problem since the romantics' phenomenology of inner or profound experience conflicts with their attention to the minute surface and boundary conditions (e.g., reflective, glimmering effects of light, water, or atmosphere) that nurture "accident" into a fuller sense of contingency. John Constable's cloud studies are a case in point, as are any of the improvisational or sketch-like forms that the romantic poets, artists, and musi-

cians unfurled like sails to catch the breeze of contingent events that, just by accident, happened to contain the "spirit" of the age.

32. Benjamin, "Theses on the Philosophy of History," 257–58.

33. See, e.g., Nicolis and Prigogine, *Exploring Complexity*.

34. De Landa, *A Thousand Years of Nonlinear History*.

35. As mentioned by Momme Brodersen (*Walter Benjamin*, 120), Benjamin purchased Klee's *Angelus Novus* in spring 1921. A year earlier, Brodersen adds, he had received from his wife another Klee, *Vorführung des Wunders* (Performance of the miracle), for a birthday gift. Brodersen also quotes the following from a letter Benjamin wrote in 1920: "I am coming more and more to the realization that I can depend sight unseen, as it were, only on the painting of Klee, Macke and maybe Kandinsky. Everything else has pitfalls that require you to be on guard" (120 [caption]).

36. On the Menger sponge, see Weisstein, "Menger Sponge."

37. Simpson, "Is Literary History the History of Everything?" par. 17; Jameson, *The Political Unconscious*, 9; Benjamin, "Theses on the Philosophy of History," 254.

38. Nietzsche, *The Use and Abuse of History*. Contrast, however, the subtle argument in Anne-Lise François's *Open Secrets* that the domain of what simply is—the given of experience—also invites an expansive rather than a minimal ethics, and aesthetics, of commitment.

39. Jesus, Elizabeth I, and Patton, e.g., are some figures from the past who have been written about in business books as types of the effective executive. For a discussion of this phenomenon, see my *Laws of Cool*, 302.

40. The spirit of this paragraph, of course, is largely post–May 1968. The flowering of cultural-critical theory coincided initially with the May 1968 season of protest in France (May 1970 in the United States) but really came into its own only in the aftermath of that revolution manqué with the realization that freedom from the condition of history was not going to be a linear, direct process. On the intellectual significance of the events of May 1968, see, e.g., Ferry and Renaut, *French Philosophy of the Sixties*.

41. Just as Picasso's *Guernica* was a commentary on the Spanish Civil War, so implicitly was the New Criticism a commentary on the collision between Northern industrial and Southern agrarian lifestyles after the American Civil War. John Crowe Ransom and others in the agrarian movement antecedent to the New Criticism directly editorialized against creeping "Northernism" in *I'll Take My Stand* (1930).

42. Fineman, "The History of the Anecdote," 57.

43. MacLeish, *Collected Poems*, 107 (lines 17–18).

44. Fineman, "The History of the Anecdote," 61.

45. Ibid., 61. The full sentence, one of the most complex in Fineman's essay, develops the notion of the anecdote being both inside and outside history (as my paraphrase simplifies it) in the style of a specific form of paradox: infinite recursion or *mise-en-abyme*. The sentence reads: "Further, I want further to maintain, still speaking formally, that the opening of history that is effected by the anecdote, the hole and rim—using psychoanalytic language, the orifice—traced out by the anecdote within the totalizing whole of history, is something that is characteristically and ahistorically plugged up by a teleological narration that, though larger than the anecdote itself, is still constitutively inspired by the seductive opening of anecdotal form—thereby once again opening up the possibility, but, again, *only* the possibility, that this new narration, now complete within itself, and thereby rendered formally small—capable, therefore, of being anecdotalized—will itself be opened up by a further anecdotal operation, thereby calling forth some yet larger circumcising circumscription, and so, so on and so forth."

46. Compare Ross's comment in his explanation of the New Historicist anecdote that "accidents limit the ways we can act in history, but they also enable us to act in ways that go against our conditioning, against behavior that has been conditioned by genetics, systems, institutions, practices, and historical events themselves" ("Contingent Predilections," 495).

It may be noted that the controversy in literary circles about New Historicist anecdotes has, by and large, left out of consideration the fact that the anecdotal approach is of much broader application across a spectrum of disciplines, including history, anthropology, and others. Typical of New Historicist anecdotes themselves are the openings of several chapters in Greenblatt's *Renaissance Self-Fashioning*—e.g., the recursive anecdote (an anecdote about an anecdote) that begins the chapter on Thomas More: "A dinner party at Cardinal Wolsey's. Years later, in the Tower, More recalled the occasion and refashioned it in *A Dialogue of Comfort Against Tribulation* as 'a merry tale,' one of those sly jokes that interlace his most serious work. The story reaches back to a past . . ." (11). (For examples from other New Historicists, see n. 1, chapter 1, below.) But a proper sense of perspective requires that such anecdotes be set alongside the microhistorical narratives of such new cultural historians as Robert Darnton (e.g., *The Great Cat Massacre*), Natalie Zemon Davis (*The Return of Martin Guerre*), and Carlo Ginzburg (*The Cheese and the Worms*). So too the anecdotal method might be compared to that of such a canonical essay of cultural anthropology as Clifford Geertz's "Deep Play: Notes on the Balinese Cockfight," which also starts with a recursive anecdote (the anthropologist's anecdote about fleeing a police raid that includes a discussion of the Balinese villagers' requests for his very anecdotes of that event: "They asked us about it again and again [I must have told the story, small detail by small detail, fifty times by the end of the day]" [416]). Anecdotalism is a general method of postmodern historicism.

Chapter 1

This essay was presented in early versions in 1986 and 1987 at Northwestern University, the University of California, Los Angeles, and the University of Wisconsin, Madison. I am grateful to my audiences on these occasions for more than normally searching discussion periods and have incorporated some of this experience. Between the completion of this essay and its original publication, several articles appeared that reflect on the New Historicism and bear on concerns I share, including Walter Cohen's "Political Criticism of Shakespeare"; Joseph Litvak's "Back to the Future"; Carolyn Porter's "Are We Being Historical Yet?" and Don E. Wayne's "Power, Politics, and the Shakespearean Text." I regret that I was unable to incorporate these works in more than passing mentions. All touch at some point on formalist or deconstructive traits in the New Historicism. Litvak's well-informed study of the complex affiliation between the New Historicism and deconstruction is especially insightful in this regard.

1. Howard, "The New Historicism in Renaissance Studies," 39. For examples of such paradigmatic or anecdotal openings, which since the time of Howard's essay have become a favorite stalking horse for readers critical of the New Historicism, see Greenblatt, *Renaissance Self-Fashioning*, 11–12, 74, 193, and "Invisible Bullets" (1988), 21 (see also the original opening to this essay: "Invisible Bullets" [1981], 40–41); Goldberg, *James I and the Politics of Literature*, 1–2; Mullaney, *The Place of the Stage*, 26, 60, 88, 116, 135; and Fumerton, "'Secret' Arts," 57.

2. On the relation between Renaissance New Historicism and E. M. W. Tillyard's *Elizabethan World Picture*, see Howard, "The New Historicism in Renaissance Studies," 14, 18; and Wayne, "Power, Politics, and the Shakespearean Text," 48. In general, Renaissance New Historicism has enjoyed knocking the Elizabethan world picture off its hook. See,

e.g., Montrose, "The Purpose of Playing," 54, and "The Elizabethan Subject," 303–4. (The reference to "the now-tarnished 'world-picture' approach" in "The Elizabethan Subject" was originally worded to specify the "Elizabethan world picture" ["Renaissance Literary Studies," 6]. With some variation, the short "Renaissance Literary Studies" is repackaged as the theoretical opening and closing of the longer, more substantive "The Elizabethan Subject." I will, in the main, cite from the latter, but it will sometimes be useful to recover the wording and emphases of the former.) See also Dollimore, *Radical Tragedy*, 6–8, and "Introduction: Shakespeare, Cultural Materialism and the New Historicism," 5–6; Richard Helgerson, review of *Language as Ideology, Language and Control,* and *Literature, Language and Society in England*, 362; and Cartelli, "Ideology and Subversion in the Shakespearean Set Speech," 1.

3. Greenblatt, *Renaissance Self-Fashioning*, 17–26.

4. To conserve space, I have excised what was originally an appendix to this essay documenting the critical vocabulary of the New Historicism. In the main, the method bears the imprint of a massive borrowing from the New Criticism (*paradox, irony, ambiguity, tension, contradiction, fusion*), from deconstruction (*play, vertiginous, deferral, absence, abyss, mise-en-abyme*), from "dialectic" and its components (*antithesis, affirmation/effacement, submission/negation*), and from complementary terminologies in Foucault, Geertz, and Althusser. Most germane to my purposes in this essay is the influx of the formalist vocabularies (cf. Litvak, "Back to the Future"; and Porter, "Are We Being Historical Yet?" 779–80).

For the influx of the New Critical idiom, see Greenblatt, *Renaissance Self-Fashioning*, 26, 30, 54, 57, 58, 63, 65, 72, 110–11, 152, 154, 192, 195, 254, "Invisible Bullets" (1988), 30, 35, 52, 62–63, 65, "*King Lear* and Harsnett's 'Devil-Fiction,'" 241, and "Murdering Peasants," 11–13, 20–21; Montrose, "'Eliza, Queene of shepheardes,'" 155, 159, 162, 166, 168, 169, 170, 171, 179, 180, "The Purpose of Playing," 57, 61, 64, 66, 71, "'Shaping Fantasies,'" 64–65, 74, 75, 82, 85, and "The Elizabethan Subject," 309, 322, 330, 332; Goldberg, *James I and the Politics of Literature*, xi, xiii; Orgel, "Making Greatness Familiar," 44–45, and "Prospero's Wife," 3, 8; Tennenhouse, "Strategies of State and Political Plays," 113, 118, 122, 125 (this essay has since been included in revised form in Tennenhouse, *Power on Display*); Helgerson, "The Land Speaks," 51–52; and Mullaney, *The Place of the Stage*, 62, 63, 64, 69, 72, 74, 85–86. (For a thematization of "amphibology" or "ambiguity" as the language of treason in the Renaissance, see also Mullaney, *The Place of the Stage*, chap. 5 ["Lying Like Truth: Riddle Representation, and Treason"].)

For borrowings from deconstruction, we can look first of all to the massive co-optation of *play*, a concept mapped over culture, as I discuss below, through the paradigms of theatricality and the carnivalesque. See also such terms as *vertiginous, deferral, absence, abyss,* and *mise-en-abyme* in Greenblatt, *Renaissance Self-Fashioning*, 25, 58, 220, 224, and "Invisible Bullets" (1988), 63; and Goldberg, "The Politics of Renaissance Literature," 530. Goldberg (530–31) discusses the relation between Greenblatt's approach and Derridean deconstruction. On the interface between the New Historicism and deconstruction or intertextuality, see also Litvak, "Back to the Future"; Cohen, "Political Criticism of Shakespeare," 29, 32–34; and Wayne, "Power, Politics, and the Shakespearean Text," 60–61.

The imprint of the New Criticism and deconstruction in particular (and to some degree also of dialectic) gives New Historicist discourse what I here characterize as its obliqueness—its combined theme and air of paradox, contradiction, vertiginous regress, and dialectical reversal. Such obliqueness is magnified by the method's habit of enacting paradox, contradiction, etc. in a theory-speak that is self-consciously oxymoronic in effect (e.g., "pastoral power," "*otium* and *negotium*," "holiday and policy," "awesome intimacy," "sophisticated quaintness") and heavily predisposed to chiasmus or reversal of subject and object (e.g., "The Historicity of Texts and the Textuality of History," "The Forms of Power and the Power of Forms," "the power of virginity and the virginity of power," "creates the culture by which it is created, shapes the fantasies by which it is shaped, begets that by which it is begotten"; "The king who ruled by contradiction was also ruled by contradiction"; "if the traitor abuses words, he is also abused by them"). (For the above examples, see, respectively, Montrose, "'Eliza, Queene of shepheardes,'" 169, 172, 180, "'Shaping Fantasies,'" 86, and "The Elizabethan Subject," 305; Greenblatt, ed., "The Forms of Power and the Power of Forms in the Renaissance"; Goldberg, *James I and the Politics of Literature*, xiii; and Mullaney, *The Place of the Stage*, 119.) At times, the result is a scholastic discourse as tightly self-knotted as Montrose at his best, e.g., in the opening sentence of his "'Eliza, Queene of shepheardes'" ("Pastoral power might seem an oxymoronic notion, for pastoral literature is ostensibly a discourse of the powerless in dispraise of power" [153]) or in such subsequent sentences in the essay as the following: "Pastorals that celebrate the ideal of content function to articulate—and thereby, perhaps, to assuage—*discontent*" (155); "The charisma of Queen Elizabeth was not compromised but rather was enhanced by royal pastoral's awesome intimacy, its sophisticated quaintness. Such pastorals were minor masterpieces of a poetics of power" (180).

5. I have included in this book illustrations that were not included in this essay's original publication because of considerations of space. Such images also give evidence of the pictorial imagination so central to New Historicist works. Following such precedents as Foucault's meditation on *Las Meninas* at the opening of *The Order of Things*, the New Historicism characteristically looks to pictures for initiatory emblems of argument. Pictures function in the method as the quintessence of paradigmatism. Their seeming concreteness and relative muteness (from the perspective of the verbal realm) emblematize the *otherness* of history that the obsessively textual imagination of the New Historicism seeks to interview. In pictures, the methodology of "discursive formations" glimpses its imago. (See also my argument about the use of pictures in interdisciplinary studies in chapter 6 below.)

6. For Orgel's discussion of *Florimène*, see *The Illusion of Power*, 27–36, and "The Royal Theatre and the Role of King," 266–71.

7. Greenblatt, *Renaissance Self-Fashioning*, 5.

8. Theater and the theatrical paradigm in the New Historicism are so pervasive that in most cases individual page references are not useful. My samples in the Renaissance field include Bristol, *Carnival and Theater*; Dollimore, "Transgression and Surveillance in *Measure for Measure*," 72–87; Goldberg, *James I and the Politics of Literature*; Greenblatt, *Renaissance Self-Fashioning*, "Invisible Bullets," "*King Lear* and Harsnett's 'Devil-Fiction,'" and the introduction to "The Forms of Power and the Power of Forms in the Renaissance"; Montrose, "'Eliza, Queene of shepheardes,'" and "The Purpose of Playing"; Moretti, "'A Huge Eclipse'"; Mullaney, *The Place of the Stage*; Orgel, *The Illusion of Power*, "The Royal Theatre and the Role of King," and "Prospero's Wife," esp. 7; and Tennenhouse, "Strategies of State and Political Plays." (See also other essays [besides Dollimore's and Tennenhouse's] in Dollimore and Sinfield, eds., *Political Shakespeare*; the essays in Howard and O'Connor, eds., *Shakespeare Reproduced*; and Weimann, "History and the Issue of Authority in Representation.") Romantics studies that draw on the paradigm include Carlson, "An Active Imagination"; Jacobus, "'That Great Stage Where Senators Perform'"; Jewett, "'Action' in *The Borderers*"; Liu, *Wordsworth: The Sense of History*, esp. chaps. 4 ("The Poetics of Violence") and 6 ("The Tragedy of the Family"); and Parker, "Reading Wordsworth's Power," and "'In some sort seeing with my proper eyes.'" Much of this body of work is influenced explicitly or implicitly by the new wave of French Revolution studies that "dramatized" history as part of their interpretation of the Revo-

lution as symbolic display; most important are Furet, *Interpreting the French Revolution*, esp. 46; Huet, *Rehearsing the Revolution*; Hunt, *Politics, Culture, and Class in the French Revolution*, esp. 19–20, 34–38; Kelly, *Mortal Politics in Eighteenth-Century France*, esp. 304–7; and Ozouf, *Festivals and the French Revolution*, esp. 79–82. The alliance between the literary study of the romantics and the historical study of the French Revolution may be usefully likened to the alliance of Renaissance New Historicists with such interpreters of Continental early modern culture as Natalie Zemon Davis and Emmanuel Le Roy Ladurie.

9. Orgel, *The Illusion of Power*, and "The Royal Theatre and the Role of King"; Huet, *Rehearsing the Revolution*, esp. 1–25, 47–69 (on the symbolic relation between the theatrical justice that condemned the king and the judgmental theater that beatified the Friend of the People [Marat]).

10. *Power* has been discussed by proponents and critics of the New Historicism to such an extent that it perhaps now needs no documentation. For a particularly concise generalization of the concept, however, see Montrose: "My argument is that the symbolic mediation of social relationships was a central function of Elizabethan pastoral forms; and that social relationships are, intrinsically, relationships of power" ("'Eliza, Queene of shepheardes,'" 153). In a note to this sentence, Montrose then points to Abner Cohen's definition (in *Two-Dimensional Man*, xi) of *power*: "'Power' is taken to be an aspect of nearly all social relationships, and 'politics' to be referring to the processes involved in the distribution, maintenance, exercise and struggle for power. . . . Power does not exist in a 'pure form' but is always inherent in social relationships." For a collection of essays centered on the anthropology and cultural history of power, see Wilentz, ed., *Rites of Power*.

11. Jurij Tynjanov: "Since a system is not an equal interaction of all elements but places a group of elements in the foreground—the 'dominant'—and thus involves the deformation of the remaining elements, a work enters into literature and takes on its own literary function through this dominant. Thus we correlate poems with the verse category, not with the prose category, not on the basis of all their characteristics, but only of some of them" ("On Literary Evolution," 72–73). Roman Jakobson: "The concept of the *dominant* . . . was one of the most crucial, elaborated, and productive concepts in Russian Formalist theory. The dominant may be defined as the focusing component of a work of art: it rules, determines, and transforms the remaining components. It is the dominant which guarantees the integrity of the structure" ("The Dominant," 82). Tynjanov's and Jakobson's essays originally appeared in 1927 and 1935, respectively. Compare Montrose's Marxist-based usage of *dominance*: "I construe ideology not as a monolith but rather as a shifting complex of components, including what Raymond Williams calls 'interrelations between movements and tendencies both within and beyond a specific and effective dominance'; these include the residual and emergent, oppositional and alternative values, meanings, and practices which are always creating potential spaces from which the dominant can be contested, and against which it must be continuously redefined and redefended" ("Renaissance Literary Studies," 10–11). (For Montrose's reapplication of the quote from Williams and reworking of this thought, see Montrose, "The Elizabethan Subject," 331, 339 n. 48.) Montrose's "shifting complex of components," we can see, is mappable over the early structuralism of Tynjanov's evolving system, with the consequence that the New Historicism can be seen to incorporate elements not only of Marxism and structural Marxism (in "Renaissance Literary Studies" Montrose immediately goes on to instance "relative autonomy") but also—as I go on to argue—of a formalism as pure as that which momentarily coexisted with Marxist thought after 1917.

12. Orgel, *The Illusion of Power*, 27–29, and "The Royal Theatre and the Role of King," 266; Huet, *Rehearsing the Revolution*, 2–4.

13. I adapt here Orgel's comments about Elizabeth I and James I (see *The Illusion of Power*, 9, 16).

14. Ibid., 10–16.

15. *Richard the Second*, 119 (4.1.200). Anamorphosis is a concept precisely suited to *Richard II*. At one point, Bushy paints for Richard's queen a trick "perspective picture" of her fears (in the specialized sense of the day) analogous to Holbein's *Ambassadors*:

> For Sorrow's eye, glazèd with blinding tears,
> Divides one thing entire to many objects,
> Like perspectives which, rightly gazed upon,
> Show nothing but confusion; eyed awry,
> Distinguish form. (ibid., 77 [2.2.16–20])

16. *Annual Register . . . for the Year 1793*, 220. For another allusion in the press linking Louis to the scene of the English Revolution, see *The Times*, 25 January 1793, 2.

17. See Fumerton, *Cultural Aesthetics*, 5–9. I am indebted to Fumerton for a prepublication glimpse of her book when I was writing this essay. I am also indebted to her for sustained conversation on the New Historicism.

18. Liu, *Wordsworth: The Sense of History*, 147–48.

19. Wayne, *Penshurst*, 81–115.

20. See the discussion of the Fra Angelico *Annunciation* in the Diocesan Museum, Cortona, in my *Wordsworth: The Sense of History*, 72–74. My present allusion to the Fra Angelico is prompted in part by Wayne's discussion of Penshurst's own symbolic garden.

21. Goldberg, *James I and the Politics of Literature*, 30–54; Belsey, *The Subject of Tragedy*, 2–4; Fumerton, "'Secret' Arts"; Mullaney, *The Place of the Stage*, chap. 3 ("The Rehearsal of Cultures") and passim. Goldberg's discussion makes an especially suitable companion piece to Wayne's since it recognizes in James's triumphal arches (a motif also imitated on title pages of books) an invocation of classical authority akin to Penshurst's invocation of the baronial past. In Mullaney's book, the paradigm of the wonder cabinet is minor compared to the preoccupation with theatricality. I include the wonder cabinet here because it provides a convenient link between the several modes of interiority—theatrical and architectural/inventorial—occupying the imagination of Renaissance studies. It is thus clear in Mullaney's work that theatricality is a paradigm that can be expanded or collapsed, seen through a telescope or a microscope, at will. Thus, "The Rehearsal of Cultures" collates the theater of Shakespeare's *Henriad* between the landscape-size mise-en-scène at Rouen reenacting Brazilian tribal life for the French king (the central episode in the chapter) and the inscape of curios that was the wonder cabinet. Whether sized to fit landscape or chamber, the curiosity shop in which the Renaissance accommodated otherness was a oneness that rehearsed *within* itself the supplement of otherness—a thesis that finds equivalent expression in Wayne's study of the baronial manor house embedded within Penshurst Place or Fumerton's of the foreign ambassadors that Elizabeth entertained in her private chamber.

One other qualification of my present use of Mullaney is in order: the wonder cabinet belongs here under my rubric of the governing line only insofar as it is cognate with the mock-Brazilian scene at Rouen as viewed by the French king. Imagining that act of viewing with the aid of a contemporary picture of the mock scene, Mullaney (*The Place of the Stage*, 67–68) conceives the king as looking out from a stationary vantage point (precisely, we might say, as if on a masque in which all the scene unfolds to the royal eye); and what the king sees in particular is the vignette of a Brazilian king and queen in their hammock, which Mullaney makes the "dominating" center of the picture. Thus is a perfect line of governance drawn between the French king and the vanishing point of otherness. However, from a different perspective, the wonder cabinet could just as well be cataloged within my later category of the disturbed array or the carnivalesque, in which the governing line turns into the disturbed array. Poking among the wonder cabinets of the time, Mullaney observes: "These are things on holiday, randomly juxtaposed and displaced from any proper context. . . . Taken together, they compose a heteroclite order without hierarchy or degree, an order in which kings mingle with clowns . . ." (62). (In the same way, Belsey's view of Felbrigg Hall images what is essentially a heteroclite architecture, which I have labeled a *split representation* in allusion to Claude Lévi-Strauss's thesis [see *Structural Anthropology*, chap. 13 ("Split Representation in the Art of Asia and America")].) What Mullaney points out, in sum, is that the house that Jack built in which I am presently locking all the paradigms of the New Historicism is also inevitably a wonder cabinet—a dissolve structure from which beasts and curios are always escaping.

22. Fumerton, "'Secret' Arts," 57–71.

23. Bender reproduces section and elevation plans for the Panopticon prison based on Bentham's proposal (see *Imagining the Penitentiary*, 25, 209). He gives a succinct sketch of his own application of the paradigm: "[Bentham] suspended inmates in a transparent medium dominated by a hidden omniscient authority. Bentham fused narratively structured reformative confinement with the principle of supervision" (23). On the visitor's gallery in the projected Panopticon prison, which Bentham added to his proposal in a postscript on finding that the plan drawings had inadvertently left unused a large space in the chapel, see Himmelfarb, "The Haunted House of Jeremy Bentham," 212. On Bentham's intention to display prisoners theatrically before visitors in the chapel, see Bender, *Imagining the Penitentiary*, 202. Also relevant to the paradigm of the Panopticon is, of course, Foucault's *Discipline and Punish*.

24. See Liu, *Wordsworth: The Sense of History*, esp. 61–65, 80–84, 88–90. Wordsworth's passage on the Falls occurs in the 1793 version of *An Evening Walk*, lines 53–84.

25. On royal progresses and entry pageants, see Montrose, "'Eliza, Queene of shepheardes,'" 168–80; and Breitenberg, "'. . . the hole matter opened.'"

26. For sources and a fuller discussion relevant to this and the next paragraph, see my *Wordsworth: The Sense of History*, 61–137.

27. My thanks to Frederick Badger, who—before I was able to visit Lower Rydal Falls myself—took the photograph of the summerhouse and waterfall that appears in my *Wordsworth: The Sense of History*, 89. For the present discussion, I have provided my own photograph from a trip to the Lakes in 1990.

28. Castle, *Masquerade and Civilization*, 17; Ozouf, *Festivals and the French Revolution*, 46. (Ozouf's work was originally published in French in 1976.) For contemporary pictures of the Champ-de-Mars during the fête, see the citations in my *Wordsworth: The Sense of History*, 16, 517 n. 16.

29. On pigs and authorship, see Stallybrass and White, *The Politics and Poetics of Transgression*, 27–79. On butchers and fishmongers, see Bristol, *Carnival and Theater*, 72–87. Stallybrass and White carry their study of the carnivalesque, the grotesque body, and dirt from the Renaissance through the nineteenth century.

30. Haynes, "Festivity and the Dramatic Economy of Jonson's *Bartholomew Fair*"; Helgerson, "Inventing Noplace," 112–16; Tennenhouse, *Power on Display*, esp. 17–71; Marcus, *The Politics of Mirth*. For a theoretical discussion of the carnivalesque and recent critical and philosophical developments, see Wilson, "Play, Transgression and Carnival."

31. Levinson, *Wordsworth's Great Period Poems*, 93–94. See also the discussions of Wordsworth and fête in Liu, *Wordsworth: The Sense of History*, esp. 15–18, 163, 165–66; and Simpson, *Wordsworth's Historical Imagination*, 53.

32. Wordsworth, *William Wordsworth*, ed. Gill, 299–300 (lines 85–107).

33. Castle, *Masquerade and Civilization*, esp. 1–109.

34. An event sometimes called *la journée des brouettes*. See Liu, *Wordsworth: The Sense of History*, 16; and Ozouf, *Festivals and the French Revolution*, 45–47.

35. Montrose, "Gifts and Reasons"; Fumerton, "Exchanging Gifts"; Greenblatt, *Renaissance Self-Fashioning*, 180–94, and "Invisible Bullets" (see also his "Murdering Peasants," which addresses the analogous suppression of peasants); Helgerson, "The Land Speaks"; Levinson, *Wordsworth's Great Period Poems*, esp. chap. 2 ("Spiritual Economics: A Reading of 'Michael'"); Heinzelman, *The Economics of the Imagination*; Simpson, *Wordsworth's Historical Imagination*; Eilenberg, "'Michael,' 'Christabel,' and the Poetry of Possession," and "Wordsworth's 'Michael.'" The chapter on *The Ruined Cottage* in my *Wordsworth: The Sense of History* (chap. 7, "The Economy of Lyric: *The Ruined Cottage*"), as well as the two sessions of the Wordsworth-Coleridge Association titled "The Value of Romanticism" at the Modern Language Association convention, 28 December 1987, can also be cited as part of the turn of romantic studies to issues of property, money, credit, and other species of romantic speculation (together with its inverse, the discourse of poverty). At the time this essay was written, I was aware of recent dissertations in the romantics field that continued the trend and have since been published as monographs—e.g., Harrison's "Wordsworth and the Itinerant Poor," which appeared in revised form as *Wordsworth's Vagrant Muse*, and Schoenfield's "Wordsworth, Law, and Economics" (esp. chap. 6 ["An Incursion into a Theory of Property: Wordsworth's *Excursion*"]), which appeared in revised form as *The Professional Wordsworth*.

36. For the consistent dependence of the New Historicism on an often ideal, abstract, or merely shorthand concept of *dialectic* and its elements (e.g., *antithesis, reversal* or *cancellation, affirmation/effacement, submission/negation*), see, e.g., Greenblatt, *Renaissance Self-Fashioning*, 9, 36, 77, 110, 156, "Invisible Bullets" (1988), 41, and "Murdering Peasants," 12; Montrose, "'Eliza, Queene of shepheardes,'" 168, 171, "The Purpose of Playing," 53, 68, 70, "Gifts and Reasons," 448, 453, and "'Shaping Fantasies,'" 61–62, 65–66, 86 (on Montrose's work, see also Goldberg, "The Politics of Renaissance Literature," 525–26); Orgel, "Prospero's Wife," 1; Mullaney, *The Place of the Stage*, 69, 79, 123, 125–26; Helgerson, "The Land Speaks," 64, 75, 77; Marotti, "'Love Is Not Love,'" 422; and Bristol, *Carnival and Theater*, 124–39. Compare such full-scale inquiries into dialectic and Renaissance literature as McCanles, *Dialectical Criticism and Renaissance Literature*; and Wells, *The Dialectics of Representation*.

37. Foucault, *The Order of Things*, xv. For an uncanny analogue of this laugh (and its Bakhtinian version) in the New Historicism, see Greenblatt's meditation on "strange laughter—not belly laughter, not even the laughter that accompanies a sudden release from menace, but a taut, cruel laughter that is at once perfectly calculated and, as in a nightmare, out of control" ("Murdering Peasants," 15 [see also 17–18]).

38. Bakhtin, *Rabelais and His World*, and *The Dialogic Imagination*, esp. 259–422 ("Discourse in the Novel"). For Bakhtin on laughter, see esp. *Rabelais and His World*, introduction and chap. 1.

39. I conflate here the harem or bathhouse scene, in which the descent of the Valkyries turns into a circus (as so often in Fellini), and the final scene, in which the hero joins the ring of characters from his life. Fellini's emphasis on carnival coupled with theatricality, together with his concern with autobiographical or pseudo-autobiographical

subjectivity, makes his work an excellent analogue to the New Historicism's vision of exaggerated play.

40. Bakhtin, *The Dialogic Imagination*, 270–72.

41. E. H. Gombrich: "It was Wölfflin who gave art history the fateful tool of systematic comparison; it was he who introduced into our lecture rooms a need for two lanterns and two screens, for the purpose of sharpening the eye to the stylistic differences between two comparable works of art. . . . It is a pedagogical device that has helped many teachers to explain to their students certain elementary differences, but unless it is used with care it subtly but decisively falsifies the relationship between the two works" (*Norm and Form*, 90).

42. On the link between Wölfflin and Russian Formalism, see Eichenbaum, "The Theory of the 'Formal Method,'" 104; and Victor Erlich, *Russian Formalism*, 59–60, 274.

43. I refer to Wölfflin's concept of *die typischen Motive* or *Hauptmotive* (see *Kunstgeschichtliche Grundbegriffe*). For the Russian Formalist usage of *motive* and *motif*, see Eichenbaum, "The Theory of the 'Formal Method,'" 119–22; Shklovsky, "Sterne's *Tristram Shandy*," esp. 40; and Tomashevsky, "Thematics," esp. 78–87. See also Vladimir Propp's related usage of *move* in *Morphology of the Folktale*, chap. 9. Tomashevsky's explanation of *motive* is especially useful: "The system of motifs comprising the theme of a given work must show some kind of artistic unity. If the individual motifs, or a complex of motifs, are not sufficiently suited to the work, if the reader feels that the relationship between certain complexes of motifs and the work itself is obscure, then that complex is said to be superfluous. If all the parts of the work are badly suited to one another, the work is *incoherent*. That is why the introduction of each separate motif or complex of motifs must be *motivated*. The network of devices justifying the introduction of individual motifs or of groups of motifs is called *motivation*" ("Thematics," 78). In light of my discussion of motive, subject, and hero that follows, Tomashevsky's comments on the narrative hero are also suggestive: "The usual device for grouping and stringing together motifs is the creation of a character who is the living embodiment of a given collection of motifs" (ibid., 87–88). (There is an intriguing resonance between my discussion here and Litvak's "Back to the Future." Litvak titles one of his sections on the New Historicism's relation to deconstruction "Motivating the Arbitrary.")

44. Other studies in the Renaissance field that might be cited include Reiss, "Montaigne and the Subject of Polity"; and Fumerton, "'Secret' Arts." Related inquiries include Helgerson's study of the "identity" of the British "land" (see "The Land Speaks") and the widespread interest in Renaissance "authorship" and "authority" (e.g., Stallybras and White, *The Politics and Poetics of Transgression*; Bristol, *Carnival and Theater*, 111–24; Montrose, "The Elizabethan Subject," 318–32; Goldberg, *James I and the Politics of Literature*, 17–27; and Haynes, "Festivity and the Dramatic Economy of Jonson's *Bartholomew Fair*," 662–63). Helgerson relates authorship and authority in his formulation of "the twin emergence" of "the author and the land, of the self and the nation" ("The Land Speaks," 67 [see also 64–65]). As regards romantic studies, subjectivity is the donnée of the field. The whole field at one point seemed to pivot around the imaginative "self," which faces both toward the transcendental and—as historicizing romanticists increasingly pointed out—toward the material. Thus, e.g., Simpson's *Wordsworth's Historical Imagination* places the poet's unstable subjectivity within the field of contemporary historical instabilities. See also my *Wordsworth: The Sense of History*, which is similarly preoccupied with historicizing the poet's egotistical sublime.

45. I allude particularly to the inquisition of *man* in Foucault, *The Order of Things*, chaps. 9 ("Man and His Doubles") and 10 ("The Human Sciences"). The modern anthro-

pological and psychoanalytic inquisitions of the subject are, of course, very relevant as well.

46. Dilthey, *Pattern and Meaning in History*, 89.

47. Collingwood, *The Idea of History*, 282–302. On historical understanding as costume drama, cf. Belsey, *The Subject of Tragedy*, 2.

48. See the following Renaissance scholars for discussion or application of the subversion/containment dilemma (with such associated ambivalences as "oblique resistance," "ironic dissent," "domination/submission," "domination/subordination," "domination/dependency," "opposition/submission," "content/discontent," "consolidation/resistance," "containment/expression," "adoration/contestation," "legitimacy/challenge," "enablement/constraint"): Cartelli, "Ideology and Subversion in the Shakespearean Set Speech," esp. 1–4, 21–22; Dollimore, *Radical Tragedy*, 109–19 and passim, "Introduction: Shakespeare, Cultural Materialism and the New Historicism," 7–15, and "Transgression and Surveillance in *Measure for Measure*"; Greenblatt, *Renaissance Self-Fashioning*, 61, 63, 71, 120, 203, 214, 254, "Invisible Bullets," and "Murdering Peasants," 9, 11, 13; Helgerson, "The Land Speaks"; Marcus, *The Politics of Mirth*, 6–9; Montrose, "'Eliza, Queene of shepheardes,'" 155, 177, "'Shaping Fantasies,'" 64–65, 74, and "The Elizabethan Subject," 309–10, 322–23, 330–31; and Tennenhouse, "Strategies of State and Political Plays," esp. 111–12, 125. See also the discussion of the subversion/containment problem in Goldberg, "The Politics of Renaissance Literature," 528–29; and Howard, "The New Historicism in Renaissance Studies," 29–30, 34–37, 39–40. For a discussion of the older debate on whether the romantics were actors of "romantic revolt" or of archconservatism, see Woodring, *Politics in English Romantic Poetry*, 24–48. For an extension of the Renaissance subversion/containment debate into the romantics field, see chapter 2 below. For a slightly fuller bibliography of subversion, see n. 2, chapter 2, below.

49. See Greenblatt, "Invisible Bullets" (1981). I discuss "Invisible Bullets" further at the close of this essay. Particularly relevant to my discussion here is the way in which the essay implicates the undecidability of the subversion/containment problem in the general undecidability of hermeneutics, of modern interpreters reading the past.

50. Marcus (*The Politics of Mirth*, 6) defines the escape-valve theory of festival as "the view that holiday inversions of hierarchy are essentially normative and help to perpetuate a preexisting system by easing, at regular, predictable intervals, tensions that might otherwise build to a full-scale challenge of the system" (see also her note to this sentence [ibid., 267 n. 8]). For other references to the escape- or safety-valve theory of subversion/containment, see Bristol, *Carnival and Theater*, 27; and Stallybrass and White, *The Politics and Poetics of Transgression*, 13–14. On the "material bodily lower stratum," see Bakhtin, *Rabelais and His World*, 368–436.

51. I think here especially of Lévi-Strauss's speculations on the static quality or reversibility of mythic thought and its relation to time and history (see *The Savage Mind*, 230–44, 263–69, *Structural Anthropology*, 209–12, and *Structural Anthropology, Volume 2*, 137–38).

52. Smith, "Critical Opinion," 275.

53. Althusser, "Ideology and Ideological State Apparatuses."

54. Compare Montrose's excellent "The Elizabethan Subject," which explores the flexibility of this core sentence of subjection by showing that it may also be read in reverse.

55. I draw here on Hayden White's distinction between historical annals and higher-order narratives of history (see *The Content of the Form*, chap. 1 ["The Value of Narrativity in the Representation of Reality"]). In the date and event lists of annals, White observes, there is no "notion of a social center" allowing the annalist to organize events along a narrative line (11). He then meditates on a passage from Hegel to formulate the

distinguishing feature of annals: lack of a "rule of law" and, therefore, of a legitimized "subject" capable of having a narrative line of events (12–13). In essence, we may say, the New Historicism to date has been a method preoccupied almost exclusively with the status, not of annals imagination, but of its narrative legitimation: variously legitimate or illegitimate subjects who may be recognized/discovered only in story form. One way in which to approach the problem of New Historicist paradigms might thus be to recognize that they are, first and foremost, highly sophisticated exercises in storytelling. Indeed, it often seems that the most successful New Historicist works are those that form a sustained sequence of tales akin to an updated hagiography. Whatever else it is, e.g., Greenblatt's *Renaissance Self-Fashioning* is a moving tale of the passion and blindness of intellect in its fatal dance with authority. Each chapter is a critical biography that could be titled "More," "Tyndale," and so on. By corollary (though I can here attest only my own experience), the most difficult and rigorously worked sections of a New Historicist study are those that may seem most naive and transparent: the narratives of "events" or "facts." The difficulty lies, not in practicing the art of narrative in itself, for which our available schema are many, but in contouring the narrative so that it contains as an entelechy the development of the proper thematic "subject": an interpretive line of argument formed as a second-order or metanarrative. The implication of this corollary is that any radical recovery of an annals imagination innocent of the processes of narrative legitimation must contest the dictates of our critical form itself. Criticism is that which converts annals (or any mere chronology of life or textual events) into what might be called *mediated annals* (collections or structurations of "themes," "motifs," "images," "figures" already big with argument) before using the mediation to create its thesis narratives of beginning-middle-end (e.g., the end of neoclassicism and the growth of romanticism). For a discussion of narrative vs. nonnarrative critical forms, see McGann, *Social Values and Poetic Acts*, 132–51.

    56. Rimbaud, *Rimbaud: Complete Works, Selected Letters*, 251.

    57. En route to his definition of art as defamiliarization, Shklovsky begins by setting aside Alexander Potebnya's influential thesis that art is "thinking in images" designed to economize "mental effort" (Shklovsky, "Art as Technique," 5–13). Particularly apropos in our current context is Shklovsky's placement of Potebnyaism in literary history: "Potebnya's conclusion, which can be formulated 'poetry equals imagery,' gave rise to the whole theory that 'imagery equals symbolism'" (ibid., 8). On Potebnyaism, Russian Symbolism, and the origins of Russian Formalism, see also Eichenbaum, "The Theory of the 'Formal Method,'" 105–6, 111–15; and Erlich, *Russian Formalism*, 23–26, 33–69.

    58. A useful line of inquiry would be to compare what Shklovsky ("Art as Technique," 12) calls the "difficult" "feeling" of art at the moment of defamiliarization (especially when "we can define poetry as *attenuated, tortuous* speech" [23]) with the agony of Aristotelian discovery and reversal. In Russian Formalist poetics, defamiliarization is also a discovery and reversal in the order of the known, but the attendant pain of agon seems somehow anesthetized or shunted aside (e.g., into the erotics and suppressed violence of the dirty folk story that then preoccupies Shklovsky in "Art as Technique").

    59. As I clarify below, I use the period term *romantic* here semielastically to designate both the age of the French Revolution and the immediately subsequent revolutionary period that saw the advent of high historicism on the Continent—especially in French and German historiography, legal theory, and philology. By broadening the chronology of romanticism in this way, we can include, not only the two generations of literary romantics, but also an analogous span of generations in historiography (thus, not only Herder, e.g., but also Ranke).

60. Empson, *Seven Types of Ambiguity*, 153–54.

61. For a fuller discussion of the relation between the abyss of deconstructive vision and cultural history, see chapter 2 below. The concept of deep play alludes to Geertz's "Deep Play: Notes on the Balinese Cockfight."

62. There is an intriguing resonance between my characterization of the New Historicism as "embarrassed" of the historicist spirit and Litvak's sustained description of it (in "Back to the Future") as "anxious" over deconstructive undecidability. The razor edge on which the New Historicism balances between embarrassment about too-determinative *Geist* (and/or the "people") and anxiety over too-indeterminate textuality is the space of an acute fastidiousness. Fearing total commitment to either contextual or textual understanding, it pauses nervously in between. Seen in this light, the relative shallowness of New Historicist theorizations to date ("simultaneous fascination with theory and resistance to it," as I discussed with reference to Gallagher and Greenblatt's phrase in the introduction to this book, and as I will advert to below) is a sign of perhaps too much self-consciousness on the part of practitioners who fear that theorization will expose nakedly the method's affiliations to established methods of contextual or textual study that have not been so squeamish in promulgating doctrine. As I go on to argue, however, anxious/embarrassed self-consciousness is also a potential resource of strength in the New Historicism.

63. See Brooks, *The Well Wrought Urn*, chap. 8 ("Keats's Sylvan Historian: History without Footnotes").

64. For the New Critical notion of ironic or conflicted unity, see, e.g., Brooks: "[Poetic] structure] unites the like with the unlike. It does not unite them . . . by the simple process of allowing one connotation to cancel out another nor does it reduce the contradictory attitudes to harmony by a process of subtraction" (ibid., 195 [from chap. 11 ("The Heresy of Paraphrase")]). For the New Critical notion of "resistance" (and such affiliated ideas as "local resistance," "irrelevant local texture," "tension," and so forth), see also Brooks's valorization of "the resistance which any good poem sets up against all attempts to paraphrase it" (196).

65. I draw here on Mink, "Change and Causality in the History of Ideas."

66. See Stewart, *The Burden of Time*, 107–71 and passim. In general, Stewart is highly informative about the early milieu of the New Criticism.

67. Lovejoy, *Essays in the History of Ideas*, 8–9 (the statement on unit ideas that I cite was first published in 1938). The essay "On the Discrimination of Romanticisms" (included in ibid., 228–53) first appeared in 1924.

68. Boas, *The History of Ideas*, 22–23.

69. Relevant here is the history of the "field-coverage" principle in the academy that Gerald Graff tells in *Professing Literature*.

70. On the formative but now invisible influence of Hirsch, see Stewart, *The Burden of Time*, esp. 3–35.

71. The contestatory origins of the New Criticism may also be confirmed by attending to the history of its institution as a pedagogy. In a local-history version of Graff's *Professing Literature*, I had occasion to compile a history of introductory English courses at Yale University ("Toward a Theory of the Prerequisite"). What came to light in interviewing emeritus Yale faculty and reading back through the century in the university's course descriptions was the intense controversy surrounding the introduction of the "too analytical, theoretical, intellectual" approach of the New Criticism (Chauncey Brewster Tinker, as paraphrased by Richard Sewall). It was only after heated debate in the department that a group of junior faculty, fascinated by Cleanth Brooks and Robert Penn Warren's new anthology, *Understanding Poetry*, won the sanction in the academic year 1940–41 to reorient

Yale's freshman English course wholly around the "poem itself" and such leading concepts as "irony" and "ambiguity." Eventually, the premises of this very early precedent of the New Critical seminar determined what became (and continues to be) the archetypal New Critical course at Yale: Major English Poets.

72. The one term in my series that may not seem to belong is *longue durée*. However, see the attempts Braudel makes to link his concept with that of structure in *On History*, 31.

73. On borrowings from deconstruction in the New Historicism, see n. 4 above.

74. See the fuller discussion of interdisciplinary study in chapter 6 below.

75. See Foucault, *The Order of Things*, chap. 2 ("The Prose of the World").

76. Greenblatt, "Invisible Bullets" (1988), 65; Montrose, "'Shaping Fantasies,'" 85. For a fuller list of borrowings from the New Criticism in the critical vocabulary of the New Historicism, see n. 4 above.

77. Foucault, *The Order of Things*, 23.

78. Althusser, "Ideology and Ideological State Apparatuses," e.g., 130.

79. Relevant here is the reaction to a suggestion I made in the discussion period after the conference "Romanticism, Politics, and the New Historicism" at the University of California, Los Angeles, November 1986. Thinking of the locale of some of the major practitioners of the New Historicism and of the journal *Representations*, I remarked what had seemed to me a commonplace (at least on the East Coast, where I was situated at the time): that campus events of the early 1970s, especially in California, had much to do with the advent of the New Historicism. The collective resistance of the audience to any such attempt to localize the New Historicism was memorable.

80. Montrose, "The Elizabethan Subject," 332.

81. Montrose, "Renaissance Literary Studies," 11.

82. Sidney, *An Apology for Poetry*, 154.

83. Montrose, "The Elizabethan Subject," 332–33.

84. Greenblatt, *Renaissance Self-Fashioning*, 36.

85. Greenblatt, "Invisible Bullets" (1988), 39. Greenblatt slightly revised this important passage after earlier appearances of "Invisible Bullets."

86. Compare Meaghan Morris: "In the end, the aim of analysis [in cultural and popular studies] becomes to generate ['negotiated,' 'resistant,' and 'oppositional' readings], thus repeatedly proving it possible to do so. Since there is little point in re-generating a 'dominant' reading of a text (the features of which are usually pre-supposed by the social theory which frames the reading in the first place), the figure of a misguided but on-side Other is necessary to justify the exercise and guarantee the 'difference' of the reading" ("Banality in Cultural Studies," 21). My thanks to Lindsay Waters for bringing Morris's essay to my attention.

87. Howard, "The New Historicism in Renaissance Studies," 15, 17.

88. Ibid., 43.

89. On the New Cultural History, see the essays in Hunt, ed., *The New Cultural History*, esp. Hunt's "Introduction: History, Culture, and Text."

90. Montrose ("Renaissance Literary Studies," 6n) notes that Greenblatt debuted the term *New Historicism* in 1982 in his introduction to "The Forms of Power and the Power of Forms in the Renaissance."

91. For a particularly intriguing history of the interdisciplinary development of historicism, see Kelley, *Historians and the Law in Postrevolutionary France*, esp. 3, 13, 18, 20–21 (on the old "new history").

92. On the crisis of historicism, see n. 10, introduction, above.

93. Montrose, "The Elizabethan Subject," 305.

94. Compare Porter on "colonialist formalism": "To be sure, from the vantage point of a traditional formalist criticism, to appeal to extraliterary discourses . . . is by definition to attend to the 'marginal' realm of the nonliterary in a new and important way. . . . But the anecdotalization of the discursive fields now opened for interpretation works only to expand the range of the very formalism from which new historicists manifestly wish to escape" ("Are We Being Historical Yet?" 779–80).

I owe the word *imperialism* here to Montrose, who, after presenting a version of his "The Elizabethan Subject" at Yale University in 1986, began answering a question that I put (quoting from memory: "Does the New Historicism diminish formalism, or does it amplify it—to the scale of the world?") by remarking that he detected a preoccupation with disciplinary imperialism in the question. Antithetical to my point about the implicit formalism of the New Historicism is Edward Pechter's thesis in "The New Historicism and Its Discontents" that the method is primarily a Marxist mode of historical determinism. As he puts it at one point: "An absolute parity of literary and social texts is a will-o'-the-wisp. More important, even if parity were possible, it is not what the new historicists really want. Their whole endeavor is to situate the literary text in social history and thus to see it in a determined or secondary position" (295). Any such attempt to label the New Historicism primarily determinist or materialist, it seems to me, is wholly wrong. So too the claim that the method is essentially or primarily Marxist is far from secure. (Compare Porter's discussion of Pechter in "Are We Being Historical Yet?") Many critics associated with the New Historicism do draw extensively from Marxist criticism whether or not their own stance is recognizably Marxist. Not to do so would be to ignore the most sustained body of work on the link between history and form in the twentieth century. However, there is no settled consensus between historicist critics who are more or less deconstruction oriented, those who locate materialism primarily in acts of language, and those who are committed to a more classically firm materialist base (for a provocative effort to discern a "deconstructive materialism," see Levinson, *Wordsworth's Great Period Poems*, 1–13)—a lack of consensus that will require further exploration if the curious alliance between American-style New Historicism and British-style cultural materialism is to be understood. In any case, the massive investment of Marxist criticism in formal and/or structural study (both in its traditional inquiries into the genre of the novel and in newer approaches to genre, style, and language) cuts the ground out from under any too-simple effort to single out Marxism as the absolute mark of difference between mainstream literary formalisms and historicism.

To extend the context of debate: it now appears that the "resistance to history" (to vary on Paul de Man's "The Resistance to Theory") initiated its counterattack against the New Historicism on the basis of a massive misreading. One might instance here many full-scale attacks on the New Historicism in the romantics field on the assumption that the method is necessarily determinist in the "necessary" link it makes between history and literature. What such attacks show is too-little reading in the New Historicism. Perhaps my own voice grows counterpolemical here in engaging with more dedicated acts of polemic, but it can, nevertheless, be stated that such missives in the resistance to history are fighting old specters.

95. Litvak's "Back to the Future" provides an excellent reading of the New Historicism in light of de Man's work. Particularly apropos here is Litvak's speculation, based on a passage in de Man, that "critics who widen their scope to include the fictiveness of all discourse are merely engaged in a mystified allegorizing of linguistic structures: 'history'

would be nothing but an immense catachresis, an illusion produced by the unwitting projection of narrative figures onto the absent ground of reality" (124).

96. In alluding to Sidney together with classical rhetoric in this essay, I am influenced by Margaret W. Ferguson's study of the rhetorical structure of Sidney's *Apology for Poetry* (see *Trials of Desire*, 137–62). In essence, my present essay is an apology or apologetics for the New Historicism complete with incorporated criticisms.

97. Orgel, *The Illusion of Power*, 5, 17ff.; Frow, *Marxism and Literary History*, esp. 234–35. For a short bibliography and discussion of what might be called a *new rhetorical historicism* now making its advent, see chapter 2 below.

Chapter 2

My thanks to Alan Bewell for his detailed reading of an early version of this essay (first presented as a paper in 1987) and to the Romantics Study Group at the University of California, Los Angeles, for their probings in response to another version. I am also grateful to R. A. Foakes for discussion and correspondence that, in their critical examination of my colonial discourse thesis, provoked me to sharpen and expand.

1. Mullaney, *The Place of the Stage*. Mullaney's intriguing book may be read as a sustained exploration of the subversion/containment problem with its non-Euclidean geography within/without the boundaries of established culture. The Liberties of London, Mullaney argues, "served as a transitional zone between the city and the country, various powers and their limits, this life and the next—as a culturally maintained domain of ideological ambivalence and contradiction, where established authority reached and manifested, in spectacular form, the limits of its power to control or contain what exceeded it" (viii–ix). Or again: "London's Liberties were places of exile, yet the banishment enacted in them was of a more ambivalent order. What was lodged outside the city was excluded, yet retained; denied a place within the community, yet not merely exiled" (22). At the limits of the city walls, in other words, literature began on a stage both subversively enactive of dominance's own excesses and "maintained," "retained," and contained by dominance.

2. Gaudibert, *Action Culturelle*, 116. See the following for enactments or discussions of the subversion/containment problem (also coded as "oblique resistance," "ironic dissent," "domination/submission," "domination/subordination," "domination/dependency," "opposition/submission," "content/discontent," "consolidation/resistance," "containment/expression," "containment/intervention," "adoration/contestation," "legitimacy/challenge," "enablement/constraint"): Bristol, *Carnival and Theater*, 27; Paul Brown, "'This thing of darkness I acknowledge mine'"; Cartelli, "Ideology and Subversion in the Shakespearean Set Speech," esp. 1–4, 21–22; Cohen, "Political Criticism of Shakespeare," 35–37; Dollimore, *Radical Tragedy*, 109–19 and passim, "Introduction: Shakespeare, Cultural Materialism and the New Historicism," 7–15, and "Transgression and Surveillance in *Measure for Measure*"; Greenblatt, *Renaissance Self-Fashioning*, 61, 63, 71, 120, 203, 214, 254, "Invisible Bullets" (1988), and "Murdering Peasants," 9, 11, 13; Helgerson, "The Land Speaks"; Marcus, *The Politics of Mirth*, 5–8; Moisan, "'Which is the merchant here? and which the Jew?'"; Montrose, "'Eliza, Queen of shepeardes,'" 155, 177, "'Shaping Fantasies,'" 64–65, 74, and "The Elizabethan Subject," 309–10, 322, 330–31; Mullaney, *The Place of the Stage*, 19, 131, and passim; Stallybras and White, *Politics and Poetics of Transgression*, esp. 13–14; and Tennenhouse, "Strategies of State and Political Plays," esp. 111–12, 125–26. See also the discussion of the subversion/containment problem in Goldberg, "Politics of Renaissance Literature," 528–29; and Howard, "The New Historicism in Renaissance Studies," 29–30, 34–37, 39–40.

In thinking through my issues, I have learned most from the essays by Brown and Cohen as well as from Greenblatt's "Invisible Bullets"—all of which take a hard look at the subversion/containment analytic. I return to these essays below.

For our present purposes, it is a secondary issue that the bulk of the subversion/containment criticism occurs in Renaissance New Historicism. The Renaissance constructed by the New Historicism, as I have speculated in chapter 1 above, stages not just the historical Renaissance but also our sense of the history spanning from romanticism through the postmodern scene. In this sense, the movement is not really a field apart. Some secondary features, however, do set it off from its counterparts in such fields as romanticism. In romantics New Historicism, e.g., the focus has been not so much on subversion or resistance as on the related concept of displacement, a sidestepping of contestation leading to the interiorization of subversive energies in the conflicted romantic self (see my review of Simpson's *Wordsworth's Historical Imagination*).

3. For an intriguing meditation on this intersection, see Wayne, "Power, Politics, and the Shakespearean Text," esp. 56–62. See also Cohen, "Political Criticism of Shakespeare," 18–19. A confirmation of the generational basis of the New Historicism may be found in Helgerson's informal census of the Renaissance arm of the movement. As he puts it: "The return to history in American literary criticism has a generational basis. Its main contributors were all born in the late thirties or early forties, came of age in the sixties, emerged from graduate school and took their first jobs around 1970, and began publishing in the mid-seventies" (review of *Language as Ideology, Language and Control*, and *Literature, Language and Society in England*, 363).

4. I allude to J. Hillis Miller's advertisement of the *mise-en-abyme* by means of a cocoa box. Taking up a passage from Michel Leiris's *L'âge d'homme* ("One side of this box was decorated with an image representing a peasant girl with a lace headdress who held in her left hand an identical box decorated with the same image and, pink and fresh, offered it with a smile. I remained seized with a sort of vertigo"), Miller articulates *mise-en-abyme* as a subversion, undermining, or abyssing of the icon: "The paradox of the *mise en abyme* is the following: without the production of some schema, some 'icon,' there can be no glimpse of the abyss, no vertigo of the underlying nothingness" ("Stevens' Rock and Criticism as Cure [Part I]," 12 [reprinted in Miller, *The Linguistic Moment*, 399–400]). In light of Gaudibert's critique of subversions that end up bought and sold ("marchandise, décor, gadget culturel, icône inoffensive"), what may be noticed about Miller's paradigm is its underlying economic vision: a smiling, pink, and fresh "peasant girl" offers a consumable, boxed image of herself to a consumer of icons able at last to reap the benefit of the "production" of the *mise-en-abyme*. The benefit is vertigo, a sort of cocoa rush. What is exceedingly strange about Miller's paradigm, in other words, is the manner in which a radically subversive and iconoclastic concept such as *mise-en-abyme* ends up so contained (by the cocoa box, by industrial economy, by advertising iconology) that it is indistinguishable from exploitation. Of course, the paradox of such subversion/containment is part of the declared dynamics of deconstruction, which inhabits what it deconstructs. Thus, Miller goes on in the same paragraph to speculate that the deconstructive experience is no sooner opened to view than it is shut again within the confectionary containers allowing logocentrism to rationalize its universe: "Any such schema [i.e., an icon that reveals the abyss] . . . both opens the chasm . . . and at the same time fills it up. . . . [It] almost instantaneously becomes a trivial mechanism, an artifice. It becomes something merely made, confected, therefore all-too-human and rational" ("Stevens' Rock and Criticism as Cure [Part I]," 12). In short, the deconstructive experience is confessedly a consumable and must be constantly renewed (as in Miller's description [ibid., 13] of the constantly rebeginning *mise-en-abyme* in Stevens's poem).

But, when such dynamics are shifted to cultural criticism, they inhibit rather than complement the latter movement's enabling ideology (of engagement, committedness, liberalness, etc.). To confess the containment of cultural subversion is to know subversion to be only a confection for which the consumer/producer of criticism acquires a taste. It is to admit an essential aestheticism about cultural criticism, as if what we seek in the past is something like a perfume or a rare taste of subversiveness not to be enjoyed except after being bottled up within containment structures. Freighted across the centuries by middlemen-historians, these containment structures at last open for the benefit of discerning cultural-critical palates. The subversion/containment controversy within cultural criticism is, in part, a guilty acknowledgment that the movement is a consumer of history.

5. As opposed to the more politically activist style of British cultural materialism. On the differences between American and British new historicisms, see Helgerson, review of *Language as Ideology, Language and Control,* and *Literature, Language and Society in England;* Wayne, "Power, Politics, and the Shakespearean Text"; and Cohen, "Political Criticism of Shakespeare," 21, 26–38.

6. The phrase *interpretation of cultures,* which I make a general descriptor here of the New Historicism and related cultural criticisms, is taken from Geertz's book of that title.

7. I explore more fully the New Historicism's emphasis on the subject and its favored realm of theatricality in chapter 1 above. For a brief bibliography of the subject in the New Historicism, see n. 44, chapter 1, above.

8. Coleridge, *Biographia Literaria,* 1:189.

9. Wordsworth, *The Prelude: 1799, 1805, 1850,* 370, 372 (10.229–74 [1805]).

10. On the date and place of this incident, see Moorman, *The Early Years,* 224; and Reed, *Wordsworth: The Chronology of the Early Years,* 148 and 148n. If Moorman's dating by reference to the Battle of Hondeschoote is correct, the church service occurred while Wordsworth was finishing up his visit at Jones's house and just before his possible third trip to France in October to witness the execution of Gorsas. Regardless of the exact date, however, her attribution of the service to North Wales and the visit with Jones is almost certainly accurate. As Moorman notes, Wales was the only place at the time where Wordsworth would have attended a service offering prayers for the country. For the fact that Jones had been ordained, see Moorman, *The Early Years,* 224.

On the Anglican-led Welsh counterrevolution from 1793 on (with its blend of anti-Jacobinism, antiatheisism, and anti-Methodism), see Evans, *A History of Wales,* 221–30. On the social changes prompting the Welsh Anglican clergy to reaction—including the explosive growth of Methodism and a Welsh cultural revival peaking in the Jacobinism of Welsh intellectuals in the 1790s—see my argument below.

11. Hayden, *Wordsworth's Travels in Wales and Ireland,* 3–6.

12. Wordsworth, *The Salisbury Plain Poems,* 27, 35.

13. I cannot here fully explore the humor that attends the telling of this incident. Such humor is a *power laughter,* as it might be called, putting people in their place. It would seem to be the inverse of a Foucauldian or Bakhtinian laughter disordering social and epistemological place. However, the whole subject is characterized by reversal and involves an uncanny resemblance between those with place laughing to keep others in their place and, inversely, those without place laughing to displace higher-ups. In the analogous case of laughter in the French Revolution, e.g., it is not clear that the extravagantly Bakhtinian festivity of the people (involving a literal slapstick at the expense of aristocratic heads and other body parts) differs from the repressive joke work of British counterrevolutionary caricature, lampoons, savagely vulgar broadsheets, etc. In short,

what we encounter here is a historical expression of humor over which the entirety of the subversion/containment problem—with its similar reversibility—could be mapped.

On the appropriateness of the epithet *racial* to describe Wordsworth's humor in this instance, see below. Certainly, Coleridge read the incident as an example of racial (and national) bigotry. In his notebooks, he associates "Wordsworth & the Welshman" with a parallel episode of anti-German humor during his own adventures. For Coleridge, humor of this sort provokes conscious inquiry into the "ludicrous" and the operations of "laughter." See Coleridge, *The Notebooks of Samuel Taylor Coleridge*, vol. 1, text entry 1586, notes entry 1586.

14. On the date of the incident recounted in the letter, see Reed, *Wordsworth: The Chronology of the Early Years*, 316–17.

15. For an estimation of Pennant's importance to the Welsh cultural revival of the eighteenth century, see Morgan, "From a Death to a View," 52, 81–82. Pennant lived only some fifteen miles from Robert Jones's house (Reed, *Wordsworth: The Chronology of the Early Years*, 317).

16. On the charged issue of language in the history of Welsh cultural decline, revival, and nationalism, see below. For an example of alcoholic boasts and curses against Englishmen, see Davies, "Race Relations in Post-Conquest Wales," 48. (Compare the drunken Vortigern in the Geoffrey of Monmouth myth, discussed below.) For an example of another "red-hot Welshman" in Montgomeryshire at the time who hated the English and whose identity was much invested in his language, see Williams, "Montgomeryshire Worthies."

17. Wordsworth, *The Letters of William and Dorothy Wordsworth*, 5:77–79. Reed (*Wordsworth: The Chronology of the Early Years*, 316) corrects the "William Thomas" noted in the *Letters* to "Thomas Thomas."

18. The Welsh used *treason of the Blue Books* to describe the defamatory report of three government commissioners surveying the culture of Wales in 1846 (see Morgan, "From Long Knives to Blue Books," 199–215). On the treason of the long knives itself, see ibid.; Morgan and Thomas, *Wales*, 138–39; and Kendrick, *The Druids*, 4–7.

As Francis Celoria shows, Wordsworth's allusion to the long-knives legend was influenced by Chatterton's story of Stonehenge in "The Battle of Hastings II" ("Chatterton, Wordsworth and Stonehenge"). See Chatterton, *Poems, Supposed to Have Been Written at Bristol, by Thomas Rowley*, 265. See also Chatterton, *The Complete Works of Thomas Chatterton*, 2:830–32; and the discussion of Wordsworth's use of the ancient Britons and Druids in my *Wordsworth: The Sense of History*, chap. 5. The legend is not necessarily connected with Stonehenge.

19. William Hutchinson, *The History of the County of Cumberland*, 1:234n. Hutchinson's work originally appeared in four parts (later bound into two volumes) from 1793–96. It is unclear whether Wordsworth would have been able to see the relevant portions of vol. 1 in time for *Salisbury Plain*; however, Hutchinson's discussion of the "Druid's Monument" or "Long Meg and Her Daughters" (which prompts the inclusion of the Monmouth tale) may be directly relevant to Wordsworth's imagination of prehistoric Britons near Penrith in the 1794 revisions to *An Evening Walk*. These revisions, it may be noted, first occurred on pages facing *Salisbury Plain* in DC MS 10 (see below on the 1794 revisions). For a modern translation of the Monmouth legend, see Geoffrey of Monmouth, *The History of the Kings of Britain*, 164–66, 196. Monmouth was himself drawing on an earlier and less well-known version of the story in Nennius's *History of the Britons*.

The treason of the long knives is an excellent context in which to think about subversion because the story is double-edged. On the one hand, the story helped foster Welsh pride. But, on the other, it also cut deep into Welsh pride itself since it was only the complicity of the Britons under the intemperate and power-hungry Vortigern (who invited the mercenary Hengist into Britain in the first place, to help defend against Irish and Pict invaders) that allowed the Saxons to gain their foothold. The true treason, according to the story, was a subversion originating at once outside and inside the camp. Or, as I put it below, the intentionality of subversion has no clear-cut inside differentiated from outside.

Given the recent focus of romanticists on the "Vaudracour and Julia" (i.e., Wordsworth and Annette Vallon) episode in bk. 9 of the 1805 *Prelude*, the treason of the long knives is also noteworthy for its sexual understory. (For examples of revived interest in the story of Vaudracour and Julia, with its testament to confused politics-cum-sexuality in Wordsworth's own life, see Erdman, "Wordsworth as Heartsworth"; and Jacobus, "The Law of/and Gender.") The knives "long as their thies" in the Monmouth legend point an exaggeratedly Oedipal tale centering on the daughter of Hengist, Renwein (also Rhonwen, Rowena, and, later, Alice), after whom the British king Vortigern lusts. Hengist immediately "gives" Renwein to Vortigern, who marries her "that very night and she pleased him beyond all measure" (Geoffrey of Monmouth, *The History of the Kings of Britain*, 160). After Vortigern loses the throne of Britain to his eldest son, it is Renwein who regains it for him by poisoning the son. The symmetry of the tale is then closed when Vortigern summons the mercenary Saxons under Hengist back from Germany and suffers the treason of the long knives (ibid., 161–66). (On Renwein, see also Morgan, "From Long Knives to Blue Books," 200–201.) For Wordsworth scholars, this will appear a larger version of the Vaudracour and Julia story, one in which Vortigern plays the part of both Vaudracour's oppressive father and Vaudracour himself. Thus, the relation between Vortigern and his son is analogous to that between Vaudracour's father and the unmanned and essentially castrated Vaudracour, while the relation between Hengist and Vortigern makes Vortigern himself the castrated son. The guillotines of the French Revolution, we may say, affected Wordsworth's heart and mind, but the long knives of Celtic contest may have touched him more viscerally because they expressed that part of his personal involvement in the Revolution (i.e., Annette/Renwein) that could not be told except in fabular form. The fable of the broken truce between Saxons and Britons in *Salisbury Plain* is a precedent of the fable of broken love at the end of bk. 9 of the 1805 *Prelude*.

20. Hengist began the series of intrigues leading to the treason of the long knives by distracting the British Vortigern with his daughter Renwein, who literally intoxicated the British king (Geoffrey of Monmouth, *The History of the Kings of Britain*, 159–60).

21. For the imagination of a tumulus and giant warrior near Penrith in the 1794 revisions, see Wordsworth, *An Evening Walk*, 143–44. For Wordsworth's bibliography of readings in Druidism, see the facsimile reproduction and transcription in Wordsworth, *The Borderers*, 420–21. See also Wordsworth, *The Salisbury Plain Poems*, 35n. On the incidence of recusancy in Denbigh and Llandaff during the Renaissance, see Thomas, ed., *The Welsh Elizabethan Catholic Martyrs*, 25–26.

22. Compare Nicholas Roe's argument that Wordsworth's acquaintance with radicals, "his two visits to France, the closing lines of *Descriptive Sketches*, the manuscripts of his pamphlet [*Letter to the Bishop of Llandaff*] and of *Salisbury Plain*," and his letter of 8 June 1794 to William Mathews on the proposed magazine the *Philanthropist* all "would have been hard evidence of 'seditious' inclinations" ("Citizen Wordsworth," 26). On Price's sermon and its impact in England as well as its selective dissemination through Wales by means of the Dissenting community, see Evans, *A History of Wales*, 215–16.

23. On the spy sent to watch Wordsworth and Coleridge, see Moorman, *The Early Years*, 329–31; Reed, *Wordsworth: The Chronology of the Early Years*, 204–5; Eagleston, "Wordsworth, Coleridge, and the Spy"; Roe, "Who Was Spy Nozy?" Johnston, "Philan-

thropy or Treason?" 406–7. On the ludicrously failed French landing in Pembrokeshire in February 1797 and its exaggerated impact on the British imagination of threat, see Emsley, *British Society and the French Wars*, 56–58; and Evans, *A History of Wales*, 226–27. Evans notes: "The assumption behind the landing must have been that the Welsh would rise spontaneously although no previous contacts were made by the French as they did in Ireland. Nevertheless, suspicion rested on the locality which had its sequel in local men being charged with treason. Eight were imprisoned but only two stood trial" (226–27). Emsley adds: "These fears help to explain why, some months later, the people of Alfoxton assumed from the antics of Wordsworth and Coleridge that they were French spies and Portland was sufficiently impressed to direct an agent to investigate. The west coast of England and Wales was the last area where the government and its military advisers had expected an invasion attempt" (56–57). On the French Revolution's watch committees with their charge to "redouble surveillance" of all foreigners in 1793, see Stewart, *A Documentary Survey of the French Revolution*, 412–14.

24. On "Huns within our gates," see Roosevelt, *The Foes of Our Own Household*, excerpted in Davis, ed., *The Fear of Conspiracy*, 214–16. In general, Davis's anthology of the American imagination of conspiracy provides a fascinating—and also fascinatingly repugnant—inside look at the politics of bigotry. The mood of "scholarship" is difficult to maintain when reading such material because, in the very act of understanding what is meant, we collaborate unwittingly with the terms of discussion and thus find ourselves being drawn into a dramaturgy of antipathy / sympathy.

25. Howell and Howell, eds., *A Complete Collection of State Trials*, 22:909.

26. Dollimore, "Introduction: Shakespeare, Cultural Materialism and the New Historicism," 12–13.

27. Brown argues about *The Tempest*: "There seems to be a quality in the island beyond the requirements of the coloniser's powerful harmonics, a quality existing for itself, which the other [i.e., the colonized other, or Caliban] may use to resist, if only in a dream, the repressive reality which hails him as villain. . . . This production of a site beyond colonial appropriation can only be represented through colonialist discourse, however, since Caliban's eloquence is after all 'your language,' the language of the coloniser. Obviously the play itself, heavily invested in colonialist discourse, can only represent this moment of excess through that very discourse: and so the discourse itself may be said to produce this site of resistance" ("'This thing of darkness I acknowledge mine,'" 65–66). (Compare the Foucauldian notion of "productive" containment I draw on below.)

28. Howell and Howell, eds., *A Complete Collection of State Trials*, 22:909.

29. On the formal requirements of relevancy in sedition trials, see Cockburn, *An Examination of the Trials for Sedition Which Have Hitherto Occurred in Scotland*, 1:96–97. Cockburn comments about the Scottish sedition trials of 1793: "It was the fashion of those days to object to the relevancy of almost every indictment. . . . Whether the charge was really liable to challenge or not, [the prisoner's] counsel would have been thought deficient in zeal if he had allowed it to pass without some objection or other" (ibid.). In general, Cockburn's work is an excellent analysis of due and undue process in the Scottish sedition trials.

30. In his "On Reading Wordsworth's *Lyrical Ballads*," Abrams made a memorably strong attack on the New Historicism in romantics studies (particularly in its materialist expressions). The core of the attack was that the New Historicism is at once too deterministic in its insistence that texts are "necessarily" grounded on history and too indeterminate in its dependence on purely negative or silent evidence (i.e., the history that the poem displaces or refuses to talk about). I return to this subject below.

31. On the paradigm of displacement, particularly in romantics New Historicism, see my review of Simpson's *Wordsworth's Historical Imagination*.

32. For a fuller explanation of the New Historicism's emphasis on the *subject*, see chapter 1 above, esp. 45–47 and n. 44.

33. Relevant to my argument here about the underresearched containment side of the subversion / containment dialectic is the insightful analysis in Cohen, "Political Criticism of Shakespeare," 35–37. Cohen observes that, despite its strong notice of subversion, American New Historicism (in Renaissance studies) paradoxically ends up reaffirming the totalitarianism of containment: "Though new historicists know that the theater was at times subversive, and though they argue that it was inherently ambivalent, their readings of individual Shakespearean plays almost always demonstrate the triumph of containment. . . . This *non sequitur* involves a certain fidelity to Foucault, whose political activity was often aimed at encouraging resistance and whose theoretical formulations allowed scope for both power and resistance, but whose historical analyses revealed the unconstrained victory of power" (35). Such one-sided reaffirmation of containment, Cohen continues, is, in part, facilitated by a lack of contemporary evidence about containment or, even when such is presented in full, by elision of the evidence from later history necessary to judge whether an act of subversion was, in effect, contained (36). In short, the dependence of the New Historicism on a sort of slice-of-life paradigm of the text in its immediate contexts of containment creates a tendency merely to model containment by gesture. The oppressive or recuperative power of the "Establishment" thus gestured has the epistemological validity of cliché; and the result is that subversion appears doomed because it is difficult for concrete historical acts of subversion to resist ubiquitous cliché (clichés about the celebration of royal power, the recuperation of popular culture, etc. [on the latter, see ibid., 36]). Only a formulation of the contexts of containment equal in range and detail to our present formulations of subversive texts (in their most immediate, most eye-catching, or otherwise most alluring contexts) could allow a fair fight.

34. For examples of the expansion of deconstruction, deconstruction-influenced thought, and language theory into cultural criticism, see the essays gathered in a special issue of *Diacritics* titled "Marx after Derrida"—including Lewis, "Reference and Dissemination"; Parker, "Futures for Marxism"; Spivak, "Scattered Speculations on the Question of Value"; Terdiman, "Deconstructing Memory"; and Weber, "The Intersection." See also Attridge et al., *Post-Structuralism and the Question of History*; Frow, *Marxism and Literary History*; and Ryan, *Marxism and Deconstruction*. The New Historicism, of course, is not without its deconstructive borrowings. But, as I document in chapter 1 above, these borrowings tend mostly to be superficial uses of deconstructive vocabulary unaware of the deeper congruencies between the cultural-critical representation of history and de Manian allegory. Thus, in romantics New Historicism, e.g., what Levinson (*Wordsworth's Great Period Poems*, 10) perceptively calls "deconstructive materialism" has been more an engagement than a marriage between deconstruction and materialism (though the fine texture of Levinson's own readings perhaps comes closest to fulfilling the deconstructive vow).

35. Miller, *The Linguistic Moment*, 419.

36. I abbreviate Miller's manifold speculations about the meaning of *cure* in Stevens. The whole passage of etymological speculation (*The Linguistic Moment*, 396–97) is of interest in our context because its arc from cure-as-"caring for" through cure-as-"covering" (and onward to other possibilities) incorporates a subversive cure-as-"scouring" (in the sense of clearing away all the covers).

My language of "deep romantic chasms" at this point (as well as of "opium" allegory below) alludes to Coleridge's "Kubla Khan."

37. *Joy* here alludes to Miller's columns as president of the Modern Language Association in the 1986 *MLA Newsletter* on "Responsibility and the Joy of Reading," "Responsibility and the Joy (?) of Teaching," and "The Obligation to Write." I originally started the present essay during my (and Miller's) last year on the Yale faculty in 1986. I still remember walking down Elm Street in New Haven by Old Campus buoyed by the sense of wonder that reading one of his "joy" columns had brought that day to the gritty, numbing professional routine of an ordinary evening in New Haven.

38. Althusser, "Ideology and Ideological State Apparatuses."

39. Althusser has been particularly useful to the New Historicism because the whole effort of "Ideology and Ideological State Apparatuses"—despite its brief and disjointed genuflections before materiality and repressive state apparatuses—is to spotlight the subject and its representations. Althusser's definition of *ideology* ("Ideology represents the imaginary relationship of individuals to their real conditions of existence" [153]) has thus been received so enthusiastically by literary criticism in part because the definition translates the whole problem of ideology into terms supremely comfortable to literary thought.

40. See Foucault, *Power/Knowledge*, esp. 118–19, 139–42. It may be especially recommended to the New Historicism that it read the more politicized works in Foucault's corpus in tandem with the familiar tributes to static discursive systems and containment structures. Compare Walter Cohen's statement about the selective New Historicist use of Foucault quoted in n. 33 above.

41. Frow, *Marxism and Literary History*, 231.

42. Three of these are covered in Helgerson, review of *Language as Ideology, Language and Control*, and *Literature, Language and Society in England*.

43. See the excellent concluding chapter in Frow, *Marxism and Literary History*, esp. 234–35.

44. Liu, *Wordsworth: The Sense of History*, chap. 7.

45. Stephen, *A History of the Criminal Law of England*, 2:248. See also *Sources of English Constitutional History*, 227.

46. *Sources of English Constitutional History*, 668.

47. Compare LaCapra, *Rethinking Intellectual History*, 47: "One important area for the study of impact that has not been sufficiently investigated is that of the readings texts receive at trials. The trial serves as one instance of social reading that brings out conventions of interpretation in an important social institution. It is significant that in their basic assumptions about reading, the prosecution and the defense may share a great deal, and what they share may be quite distant from, or even placed on trial in, the work itself."

48. Cockburn, *An Examination of the Trials for Sedition Which Have Hitherto Occurred in Scotland*, 1:162.

49. The legal battles pertaining to copyright (with its underlying basis in the economics of intellectual property) are an excellent analogue to those concerning sedition and treason: both were scenes on which the nature of an author and of authorship was being defined. For a study of copyright law complementary to my briefer look here at sedition law, see Rose, "The Author as Proprietor."

50. A celebrated example of Erskine's efforts to redefine the law in the courtroom is his important speech in the 1792 trial of Thomas Paine for libel (see Howell and Howell, eds., *A Complete Collection of State Trials*, 22:357–472). On this trial, see also Stephen, *A History of the Criminal Law of England*, 2:363–64. For an example of the many contemporary, politicized publications of the trials, see *State Trials for High Treason*, esp. the editorializing advertisement and the epilogue celebrating the cause of liberty.

51. For an example of the complex dialectic of subversion/containment—or, in Coleridge's case, "oscillation" of principles—in the press of the 1790s, see Erdman's introduction to Coleridge's *Essays on His Times in "The Morning Post" and "The Courier."* Erdman recounts the incident in which a too-detailed report in the *Morning Post* of the arrests for treason of John Binns, James Coigley, and Arthur O'Connor in 1798 landed the paper's editor, Daniel Stuart, in Privy Council. Immediately after this summons, as Erdman shows, the *Post* and the paper's lead essayist, Coleridge, were effectively contained (ibid., lxxvii–lxxix).

52. The fragmentary poem on the fleet was titled by Ernest de Selincourt "At the Isle of Wight. 1793" (Wordsworth, *The Poetical Works of William Wordsworth*, 1:307–8).

53. Helgerson, "The Land Speaks."

54. On the map, this orbit appears roughly as a clockwise circling of the boundaries of Britain. A more detailed charting of the poet's movable residence in these years may be gleaned from Reed, *Wordsworth: The Chronology of the Early Years*, and *Wordsworth: The Chronology of the Middle Years.*

55. *The Tempest* is a commonplace paradigm in works addressing the issues of colonialism (see the works cited in Cartelli, "Prospero in Africa").

56. Wallerstein, *The Modern World-System II*. Wallerstein's Braudelian or *Annales* historiography in this important work (and its preceding, first volume)—i.e., his explanation of political and other organizations on the basis of *longue durée* organizations of raw materials and patterns of production and transport—leads to a classification of the world in terms of core/semiperiphery/periphery. The precedent of this thesis is the metropolis vs. satellite classification of Frank's *Capitalism and Underdevelopment in Latin America.* The tripartite classification has facilitated the growth of the internal colonialism explanation of underprivileged regions or population sectors in the United States, Latin America, Africa, and, recently, Wales. For Hechter's use of the core and periphery concepts, see *Internal Colonialism*, esp. 9–10, 18. (See also Brown, "'This thing of darkness I acknowledge mine,'" 51–52.) For a résumé of the core/semiperiphery/periphery and internal colonialism theses, see Khleif, *Language, Ethnicity, and Education in Wales*, 15–17, 317; Hechter, *Internal Colonialism*, 8–9, 30–33 and notes; and Williams, *The Welsh in Their History*, 196.

57. Wordsworth, *The Excursion*, in *The Poetical Works of William Wordsworth*, 5:102 (3.753–54), 102 (3.760–67), 103 (3.812–15), 104 (3.821–22), 107 (3.953).

58. The precedents are González-Casanova, "Internal Colonialism and National Development"; and Stavenhagen, "Classes, Colonialism, and Acculturation." See also n. 56 above. For a skeptical view of the applicability of the internal colonialism premise to Wales, see Williams, *The Welsh in Their History*, 196–97.

59. Works on Wales are cited as drawn on below. A more precise statement of methodology here would need to indicate that the *Annales/histoire de mentalités* approach provides a more or less thematically neutral frame of presentist inquiry buffering our object of study from any too-quick fusion of horizons with the more prejudicial presentism (in our context) of the internal colonialism thesis. *More or less* means that Braudelian historiography is not wholly neutral with regard to the internal colonialism concept. Rather, it makes a fusion between the internal colonialism thesis and past historical perspectives possible because it intersects with both. For Hechter's use of Braudel, see *Internal Colonialism*, 32, 47, 49. For Wallerstein's Braudelianism, see n. 56 above.

60. The most influential exponent of the connection between the Druids and the ancient Hebrews, and between the Welsh language and the kabbalah, was the vicar Henry Rowlands, whose *Mona Antiqua Restaurata* (1723) was known to the early Wordsworth (evidenced by its inclusion in a brief, handwritten bibliography of Druid lore he drew

up [see Wordsworth, *The Borderers*, 421]). On Rowlands's thesis, see Owen, *The Famous Druids*, 73–82; and Piggott, *The Druids*, 148–49.

61. Compare also Morgan, "From a Death to a View."

62. Compare Jenkins, who notes that Welsh revivalists fostered "a renewed sense of patriotism" and, to press home the point that "Welsh history was a tale of repeated injuries, usurpations, and conquests," "strove to shore up rickety Welsh legends and fables" (*The Foundations of Modern Wales, 1642–1780*, 406).

63. For a convincing argument that the many social and caste differences between the Welsh and the English in earlier Wales may best be understood in terms of race, see Davies, "Race Relations in Post-Conquest Wales." Davies is especially insightful with regard to the intricate ways in which issues of "blood" circulated through more easily defined issues of Welsh vs. English land tenure and law. From early times on, of course, racial discourse was coded, not only into property, legal, and other institutions, but also into the language of abuse and prejudice. Particularly telling was cross-cultural figuration. An Englishman could, thus, observe: "We have Indians at home, Indians in Cornwall, Indians in Wales, Indians in Ireland" (quoted in Mullaney, *The Place of the Stage*, 71). For the resemblance of Welsh nationalism to other ethnic renascences and comparisons of the Celts to American Indians and Afro-Asians, see Khleif, *Language, Ethnicity, and Education in Wales*, 4, 20. The notion of race and ethnic identity is also prominent in Hechter's *Internal Colonialism*, e.g., xvi–xvii, 30, 39–43.

64. Compare Hechter, *Internal Colonialism*, xvi.

65. On the geographic distinctions that shaped Welsh history, sometimes literally through the creation of boundary walls, see Rees, *An Historical Atlas of Wales*. On the tenor of relations between the Welsh and the Englishries, see Owen, "The Englishry of Denbigh." On Welsh vs. English law and customs of land tenure and inheritance, see Davies, "Race Relations in Post-Conquest Wales"; and Williams, *When Was Wales?* 90–93.

66. Gwyn A. Williams is especially penetrating on the intricate and contradictory process of acculturation between the Welsh and the English. Discussing the use by the English of Welsh law to protect their holdings, e.g., he comments: "The ultimate caricature of colonialism in Wales is the spectacle of a colonial people clamouring for the law of the colonists in the face of resistance from colonial authorities stubbornly maintaining native custom to stop themselves going bankrupt!" (*When Was Wales?* 92).

67. See the chart comparing Celtic and English systems of land use that Hechter (*Internal Colonialism*, 58) draws from Thirsk's "The Field Systems in England."

68. For the ironic possibility that the Welsh borrowed the story of the treason of the long knives from the Saxons (for whom the tale applied to events in Germany), see Morgan, "From Long Knives to Blue Books," 201.

69. Williams, *When Was Wales?* 90.

70. Ibid., 143–45. On the economic and industrial history of the Celtic fringe, see also Hechter, *Internal Colonialism*, 47–95.

71. On the changing economic understructure of Wales, see Williams, *When Was Wales?* 143–50, 159–61. On the economic renovation or "Americanization" of Wales, see Williams, *The Welsh in Their History*, 196–97.

72. Williams, *The Welsh in Their History*, 11. Williams is drawing on Hobsbawm's *Primitive Rebels*.

73. Williams, *When Was Wales?* 159.

74. On the forms of Old Dissent, see Williams, *When Was Wales?* 151–52. On Method-

ism in Wales, see ibid., 155–59; and the excellent, vividly detailed account in Jenkins, *The Foundations of Modern Wales*, 342–85.

75. Williams, *When Was Wales?* 158–59.

76. Morgan, "From a Death to a View," 54.

77. Williams, *When Was Wales?* 155.

78. Williams notes that the term *gwerin* was applied nostalgically to the lower classes after their shift of allegiance to Nonconformity (ibid., 152).

79. Evans, *A History of Wales*, 210–11.

80. See ibid., 211. On the conservatism of Methodism, see Jenkins, *The Foundations of Modern Wales*, 369.

81. On the perceived connection between revolution and Methodists, see the report of a curate quoted in Williams, *When Was Wales?* 162. On the radicalism of Glanmorgan, see ibid., 149. On that of Denbighshire and Flintshire, particularly during the mob actions of the famine years in the 1790s, see ibid., 145–46, 163, 169.

82. In this synopsis of Welsh Associations, I draw throughout from Evans, *A History of Wales*, 212–14.

83. In the following discussion, I draw particularly from Williams, *When Was Wales?* 159–72, and *The Welsh in Their History*, 11; Evans, *A History of Wales*, 215–30; and Morgan, "From a Death to a View," 56–69.

84. See esp. Williams, *When Was Wales?* 163, and *The Welsh in Their History*, 11; Morgan, "From a Death to a View," 58–59; Evans, *A History of Wales*, 221; and Jenkins, *The Foundations of Modern Wales*, 321–23, 388–92.

85. On these London clubs and the Welsh corresponding societies, see Evans, *A History of Wales*, 220–21.

86. I cull my list from ibid., 216–18; and Williams, *When Was Wales?* 140, 163–64.

87. On the Primrose Hill ceremony, see Piggott, *The Druids*, 164–66. On Iolo's adaptation of Druidic grottoes set in gardens for his rituals, see Morgan, "From a Death to a View," 65–66.

88. A useful aid in grasping the extent, form, and geographic location of British popular protest in the 1790s (as well as other periods) is Charlesworth, ed., *An Atlas of Rural Protest in Britain*. The maps of protest in the *Atlas* document the fact that Wales, and particularly north Wales, participated in the intense and widely spread disturbances of the 1790s.

89. Monoglot Welsh speakers made up some 90 percent of the population earlier in the eighteenth century. Most of Wales was still monoglot at the century's end (Jenkins, *The Foundations of Modern Wales*, 220–21, 397–99).

90. Ibid., 400. On the deep-rooted contest of language throughout Welsh history and in the 1790s, see ibid., 219–25, 397–401; Davies, "Race Relations in Post-Conquest Wales"; Evans, *A History of Wales*, 231–33; Khleif, *Language, Ethnicity, and Education in Wales*; and Morgan, "From a Death to a View," 48.

91. On Dissent and language, see Williams, *When Was Wales?* 152–55. On the circulating schools in part associated with Methodism, see Jenkins, *The Foundations of Modern Wales*, 370–81. Jenkins observes that these schools "were the chief means by which the native tongue was strengthened and preserved during the eighteenth century" (ibid., 380).

92. On Denbighshire printers in London, see Williams, *When Was Wales?* 163.

93. Morgan, "From a Death to a View," 69–79; Jenkins, *The Foundations of Modern Wales*, 400–404; Williams, *When Was Wales?* 140, 163–67.

94. Williams, *When Was Wales?* 167.

95. Evans, *A History of Wales*, 218–20, 233–34; Williams, *When Was Wales?* 140–41.

96. Evans, *A History of Wales*, 223–26; Williams, *When Was Wales?* 170.

97. For this discussion of the first wave of Welsh emigration to America and of Welsh sympathy with the American Revolution, I draw from Evans, *A History of Wales*, 207–10; Williams, *When Was Wales?* 156–57; and Jenkins, *The Foundations of Modern Wales*, 316–20. On the concept of a second Wales, see Evans, *A History of Wales*, 207.

98. Williams, *When Was Wales?* 157.

99. Evans, *A History of Wales*, 207.

100. Williams, *When Was Wales?* 170.

101. Ibid., 170, 124–25; Morgan, "From a Death to a View," 84.

102. For this résumé of the Madoc legend and its ramifications in the 1790s, I draw on Williams, *When Was Wales?* 140–41, 170–72; and Morgan, "From a Death to a View," 83–85. For the date of Southey's early manuscripts of *Madoc* (including the first complete draft of 1797–99), see Jarman, "Madoc, 1795." Jarman also discusses the contemporary interest in Madoc and the sources that influenced Southey (362–63).

103. Khleif, *Language, Ethnicity, and Education in Wales*, 11. For a historical study of early colonialism in Wales, see Davies, "Colonial Wales."

104. Charlesworth, ed., *An Atlas of Rural Protest in Britain*, 127–30. The militia riots were also economically motivated.

105. Williams, *When Was Wales?* 169.

106. Evans, *A History of Wales*, 225.

107. Johnston, "Philanthropy or Treason?" For the dates and circumstances of Wordsworth's meetings with Godwin and his circle, see Reed, *Wordsworth: The Chronology of the Early Years*, 164–66, 182–83, 211.

108. Everest, *Coleridge's Secret Ministry*, 127–29.

109. I borrow here from my review of Simpson's *Wordsworth's Historical Imagination*.

110. Douglas, *Purity and Danger*.

111. Mullaney, *The Place of the Stage*, 77.

112. Chandler, *Wordsworth's Second Nature*.

113. In the long letter to William Mathews of 8 June 1794, in which he sketched the idea of the *Philanthropist*, Wordsworth declines to come to London to help his proposed partners actually set the enterprise afoot. He cites Raisley Calvert's promise of a legacy and adds: "It would be using him very ill to run the risque of destroying my usefulness by precipitating myself into distress and poverty [by coming to London] at the time when he is so ready to support me in a situation wherein I feel I can be of some little service to my fellowmen" (Wordsworth, *The Letters of William and Dorothy Wordsworth*, 1:126–27). We should note, however, that some revolutionary sentiment did appear in print at the close of *Descriptive Sketches* (published on 29 January 1793, just a week after the execution of Louis XVI).

114. On 19 December 1791, Wordsworth wrote his brother from France: "I am not yet able to speak french with decent accuracy but must of course improve very rapidly" (Wordsworth, *The Letters of William and Dorothy Wordsworth*, 1:70).

115. Moorman, *The Early Years*, 602–3.

116. On Catholic resistance in Renaissance Wales and the pipeline for Welsh priests (particularly of north Welsh origin) from the Continent back into Wales, see Thomas, ed., *The Welsh Elizabethan Catholic Martyrs*, esp. 31ff.

117. Wordsworth, *The Prelude: 1799, 1805, 1850*, 380 (10.381–93 [1805]).

118. On the martyr literature of the Welsh Catholics, see Thomas, ed., *The Welsh Eliza-bethan Catholic Martyrs*, 71–78. The source material Thomas presents (ibid., 85ff.) makes for a wrenching reading experience.

119. Wordsworth, *The Prelude: 1799, 1805, 1850*, 434, 430, 432 (11.341–42, 11.293, 11.305–7 [1805]).

120. Peek, *Wordsworth in England*, 101–40.

121. For details, see my *Wordsworth: The Sense of History*, chap. 8.

122. Wordsworth, *The Prelude: 1799, 1805, 1850*, 460, 462 (13.39–40, 69–79 [1805]).

123. Greenblatt, "Invisible Bullets" (1988), 39.

Chapter 3

1. Besides *Neuromancer*, see also Gibson's later novels, e.g., *Count Zero* and *Mona Lisa Overdrive* as well as his collection of stories, *Burning Chrome*. For other authors associated with the cyberpunk movement, see, e.g., Sterling, ed., *Mirrorshades*. For a report on early attempts to define cyberpunk at the conference "Fiction 2000" at the University of Leeds in 1989, see *The J. Lloyd Eaton Collection Newsletter* 1, no. 2 (Fall 1989). (My thanks to Frank McConnell for directing me to this source.)

Since this essay and, in particular, the present note were originally written in the late 1980s, of course, cyberpunk has become more widely known and has been discussed more extensively in scholarship—partly owing to the popularizing influence of films such as *The Matrix* molded directly or indirectly by the worlds created by Gibson and other writers in this subgenre of science fiction.

2. Hartman, *Wordsworth's Poetry*.

3. Wordsworth, *The Prelude: 1799, 1805, 1850*, 460, 464 (13.69, 111–19 [1805]).

4. I have not been able to find a better word than *banal* for my purposes, though the term has been complicated by Jean Baudrillard. See the critical discussion of Baudrillard in Morris, "Banality in Cultural Studies." My use of the term *simulation* in this essay, of course, is Baudrillardian.

5. For examples of these terms, see Gibson, *Mona Lisa Overdrive*, 247, 308, and *Neuro-mancer*, passim; and Shirley, *Eclipse Corona*, 33–34, 279.

6. Wordsworth, *The Prelude: 1799, 1805, 1850*, 50 (1.421 [1805]). Gibson, *Neuromancer*, 4, 51 (see the epigraphs to this chapter).

7. I choose the term *high postmodern* by analogy with *high modernist* or *high romantic*. Gender, ethnic, area (including postcolonial), and cultural-materialist cultural criticisms, of course, can overlap with high postmodern sorts—thus, e.g., the relation between cultural-materialist "conjuncturalism" and the contextualist "detailism" I will come to. But there is a palpable difference: the degree to which the alternative cultural criticisms speak from, to, for, or in the midst of discrete population bases. In this regard, Richard Rorty's "liberal community" and other such high postmodern "interpretive communities" may be "specific," "local," and "parochial" in principle, but they are clearly "meta-" by comparison with the countercultural youth, biker, and other subcultures, e.g., that were the early stomping ground of conjuncturalist research in the 1970s. It would be unwarranted, however, to exaggerate the divergence between high and alternative cultural critics. A fairer statement would be that each individual postmodern cultural critic, precisely to the extent of his or her postmodernity, moves *between* high and alternative, generalist and population-dedicated, modes.

8. I should emphasize that my priority in this essay is scope: I show the *similarity of*

contextualist discourse among many authors who in other ways are strikingly disparate. The reason that close readings in difference must be secondary here is not only limitation of space but also the complicity of any streaks-in-the-tulip approach with the rhetoric of detailism that is my topic. Focus on similarity, in other words, is critical in function. The first task of any criticism of high cultural criticism must be to suspend the postmodern dogma of difference in order to see it from a new angle. I say *suspend*, of course, because difference—as deconstruction teaches—inevitably catches up with discourses of similarity. But there is something to be learned in not too quickly allowing our criticism to coalesce with its topic in a common discourse of difference, *différance*, and differends.

9. Schor, *Reading in Detail*, 3. Since the present essay was originally written, other studies of detail have appeared—e.g., Massey, ed., "Particularism," a special issue of *Criticism*. Included in the special issue is Schor's essay "Rereading in Detail," which begins by summarizing the main argument of pt. 1 of her *Reading in Detail*.

10. Though Schor sometimes invokes the postmodern, her basic paradigm for current detailism is high modernist and poststructuralist (with Barthes serving as the terminus ad quem). According to this paradigm, the detail emerged in the twentieth century from past aesthetic regimes—Hegelian and realist—that had subordinated it to transcendental sublimity or (what Schor considers its equivalent) brute immanence. Liberation from such aesthetics came through a "desublimation" of detail or Barthesian valorization of "truly inessential" particulars (*Reading in Detail*, 79–80, 84–85, and passim). I use the designation *postmodern* rather than *high modern* or *poststructuralist* in order to address cultural criticisms that range widely beyond literature and the arts. But certain of my conclusions about cultural criticism are consonant with Schor's about aesthetics. What I call *detachment* in cultural criticism is analogous to what Schor calls "aesthetic desublimation." *Detachment* or *desublimation* names the moment when the perceiver suddenly sees, not reality, but the simulation that Barthes calls the "reality effect." And what I call the *immanental* Schor names the "return" of the real, especially in her discussion of late Barthes and the *punctum* (ibid., 88–97). The discrimination of a returned-real within the reality effect contributes to Schor's critical questioning of high modernist and post-structuralist aesthetics (e.g., ibid., 86–95). Similarly, it is the discernment of a nostalgic, immanental sense of reality within cultural criticism's detached or simulated visions that will enable my own critical interrogation. I would point even more emphatically than Schor to the haunt of older, specifically nineteenth-century regimes of detail within the postmodern—much in the manner that the celebration of modernity that opens Schor's last paragraph ("Doubtless, it has taken our modernity to shake the hegemony of the sublime") finishes by remembering the precedent of the Balzacian detail (ibid., 147). In my view, "our modernity" has *not* shaken "the hegemony of the sublime."

11. Geertz, *Local Knowledge*, 232.

12. Rorty, *Consequences of Pragmatism*, 173.

13. McGann, *Social Values and Poetic Acts*, 7, 122, 124. McGann quotes the phrase from Parry, *The Making of Homeric Verse*, 411. On this quote, see also McGann's pseudonymous essay, Mack and Rome, "Marxism, Romanticism, and Postmodernism," 615.

14. On criticism as array, see McGann, *Social Values and Poetic Acts*, 132–51. As already prefaced in my excursus on cyberpunk science fiction, I emphasize the concept of the matrix in this essay to foreground one of postmodernism's most common motifs: the image of a world structured at both infra- and superstructural levels as labyrinthine network or grid—a sort of deconstructive structure or what in chapter 1 above I have called the *disturbed array*. Thus, to recur to science fiction, we might witness such instances as the intricate circuitries of cities, biocyber hardware, "wetware," software, and cybernetic

minds in Gibson's fiction or, again, the claustrophobic array of high-tech/low-life streets, corridors, and air ducts in the *Blade Runner* and *Alien* films (or, more recently, the gigantic, microchip-like cube of the Borg ship in television's *Star Trek: The Next Generation*). I privilege the word *matrix* in particular because it is a fixation, not just in science fiction, but in virtually all the branches of high postmodern cultural criticism. (This essay was originally published before the Wachowski brothers' *Matrix* films, which since 1999, of course, have reinforced the phenomenon I describe.) *Matrix* is the most frequent of a whole brood of similar grid words recited so often that they acquire a fetishistic quality. Indeed, an analysis of "grid fetish" from the perspective of feminism or of the history of sexuality would need to address the psychosocial dimensions of matrix worship (*matrix*: from *māter*, "mother"). (Foucault's *The History of Sexuality* is itself replete with the vocabulary of *matrices*, *grids*, *networks*, *arrays*, and *manifolds*.) Phrased ontologically rather than sexually, *matrix* is what postmodern cultural criticism now has instead of *matter* (both words, of course, born of the same "mother"). Though still instinctively empirical, as I go on to argue, cultural criticism has learned to merge materialism with the purely informatic (and/or ideological) by detaching *matter* from any premise of absolute, physical ground. Matter is now a structure akin to transistor circuitry implemented in a variety of materials—i.e., a *pattern* that may be facilitated by, but is logically independent of, the substratum that carries it. Rendered essenceless, the substratum becomes, not a ground at all, but—and this is a concept that complements *matrix* in postmodernism—the *medium* of the pattern. Media is the universe of depthless, essenceless pure surfaces (screens, displays, facades) on which matrices play out their representations of matter.

15. This matrix is culled from a larger database that I will at times draw on to supplement the discussion below. Two general qualifications: First, the categories of the matrix are flexible. Some authors broadcast on two or more channels, and the channels themselves are intermixed or internally split in complex ways. (Thus, e.g., Lentricchia is as much a critic as an associate of the New Pragmatism; and, in general, the neo-Marxist, -historicist, and -pragmatist elements participate nervously in each other.) Second, the matrix quotes what Lyotard calls "phrase universes" without context or full syntax. When clarity or fairness demands, I restore matrix quotations to their context in my ensuing discussion.

A more specific qualification is that my selection of New Historicist authors from Renaissance and romantics studies is not meant to exclude such other fields as eighteenth-century, Victorian, or American literature. The reason I pair the Renaissance field (where the New Historicism most famously arose) only with romantic studies for present purposes is that stressing romanticism conforms to my overall hypothesis about the onset of critical historicism (set forth in the introduction to this book) as well as prepares for specific argument below. Of course, a full disclaimer would acknowledge that such an emphasis undoubtedly also reflects my original training in the literature and culture of the romantic era.

A further specific qualification is that, since this essay was originally written, my awareness of the fuller dimensions of pragmatist thought has broadened, primarily under the influence of my colleague at the University of California, Santa Barbara, Giles Gunn. In retrospect, it should be clarified that my argument alludes to contemporary pragmatism as a whole but, in fact, focuses in particular on just the two variants most visible across disciplines roughly at the time of the other postmodern cultural criticisms I study: the against-theory movement and Rorty's work (see the discussion below).

16. Sources in order of citation: Geertz, *Local Knowledge*, 167 and passim, 48, 69, and *Interpretation of Cultures*, 363; Chartier, *Cultural History*, 9, 14; Darnton, *The Great Cat Massacre*, 23, 94, 107; Davis, *Society and Culture in Early Modern France*, 132, 193, 266, 225; Ginz-

burg, *The Cheese and the Worms*, xiv, xx; Le Roy Ladurie, *Love, Death, and Money in the Pays d'Oc*, 158, 509; Greenblatt, *Shakespearean Negotiations*, 1, 4, 16, 19; Helgerson, "The Land Speaks," 65, 68, 73; Marcus, *Puzzling Shakespeare*, 31, 36, 165; Montrose, "The Elizabethan Subject," 305, 306; Mullaney, *The Place of the Stage*, 68, 69, 116; Klancher, *The Making of English Reading Audiences*, 11, 81, 82; Levinson, *Wordsworth's Great Period Poems*, 1–3, 12, *The Romantic Fragment Poem*, 8, and "Back to the Future," 649; Liu, *Wordsworth: The Sense of History*, 47, 245, 465; McGann, *Social Values and Poetic Acts*, 55, 33, 29, 63, 125, 126, 63, 127; Simpson, *Wordsworth's Historical Imagination*, 13, 16, 212; Fish, *Is There a Text in This Class?* 109, 318, and "Consequences," 110; Lentricchia, *Criticism and Social Change*, 7, and "The Return of William James," 176, 177, 180, 191, 193; Rorty, *Philosophy and the Mirror of Nature*, 179, 387, *Consequences of Pragmatism*, 165, 168, and *Contingency, Irony, and Solidarity*, 16, 17, 77; Althusser and Balibar, *Reading Capital*, 15, 42, 58; Althusser, *Lenin and Philosophy and Other Essays*, 136; Jameson, *The Political Unconscious*, 18, 22, 25, 56, and "Postmodernism and Consumer Society," 119; Macherey, *A Theory of Literary Production*, 51, 92; Baudrillard, "The Structural Law of Value and the Order of Simulacra," 65–66, 69, and "Fatal Strategies," 189; Bourdieu, *Outline of a Theory of Practice*, 95, 105, 110; de Certeau, *The Practice of Everyday Life*, ix, xiv, 48, 68, 96, 125; Lyotard, *The Postmodern Condition*, xxiv, 15, 60, and *The Differend*, 155; and Foucault, *Discipline and Punish*, 139, 307, *Power/Knowledge*, 82, 126, 142, and *History of Sexuality*, vol. 1, *An Introduction*, 96, 97.

17. Rosen, "Taming the Detail." My thanks to the author for a copy of the manuscript.

18. Of course, Barthes's structuralist analysis of detail in "The Reality Effect" (originally published in 1968) is relatively early in his corpus. His poststructuralist discussions of detail could even more plausibly be said to be relevant to the argument offered below. But I have not foregrounded Barthes because his detailism is so fully explored by Schor.

19. For Geertz on functionalist sociology, see, e.g., *The Interpretation of Cultures*, 206, 448. For the effort of the New Historicism to distance itself from formalism (in some regards counterfactually), see, e.g., Howard, "The New Historicism in Renaissance Studies," 14–15. For the complex reaction of the New Cultural History against *Annales* historiography (particularly its sociological tendencies), see Furet, "Beyond the *Annales*"; Hunt, "French History in the Last Twenty Years," esp. 213ff., and "Introduction: History, Culture, and Text," 6–7; and Chartier, *Cultural History*, 19–52. (*Reaction* against the *Annales* movement could also be called *revisionism* since Chartier and others descend with variation from the *mentalités* side of *Annales* method.)

20. The phrase about how things "hang together" derives from a saying of Wilfrid Sellars's that Rorty quotes and alludes to several times (see e.g., *Consequences of Pragmatism*, xiv). My analogy to history painting alludes by contrast to the tradition of pictorial *istoria*: the "great pictures" of Old Master art (descended paradigmatically from Renaissance Italian painting) that were the visual equivalent of epic. Such "story/history" works depicted pivotal episodes of classical or biblical narrative (later, such secular equivalents as a major land or sea battle) big with institutional meaning, as in the founding/instituting of a nation or a religion. They were all about how things came to hang together, but with a doctrinal rather than a pragmatist purpose.

21. The deep influences (or, perhaps, confluences) on my discussion of the rhetoric of detail in this essay include de Man, Barthes on the reality effect, Baudrillard on hyperreality and simulation, and Lyotard on phrase universes. An interesting thought experiment, e.g., would be to read de Man together with Barthes's discussion of rhetoric and reality's "resistance to meaning" ("The Reality Effect," 14). So too Baudrillard on "the rhetoric of the real" ("The Structural Law of Value and the Order of Simulacra," 70), hyperreality, and simulations could be read in proximity both to de Man and to Barthes. The notion

of simulation, e.g., resonates against that of imposition in de Man's "Shelley Disfigured" (esp. 63–64) as well as against the idea of imitating "what is already the simulation of an essence" in Barthes's "The Reality Effect" (13). Finally, Lyotard on phrase universes, on the contingent "linking" of phrases, and on the "name" that can link only because it is an "empty and constant designator" (*The Differend*, 44) would make a fitting reprise of the themes of rhetoric, imposition, and simulation, respectively. Lyotard's vision of phrase universes, we may say, amplifies the reality effect into a "universe effect."

22. On elsewhereness, see my *Wordsworth: The Sense of History*, 5, 467, 497, and passim.

23. I refer especially to the last two sections of Geertz's "Deep Play: Notes on the Balinese Cockfight" and to the chapters on Vladimir Nabokov and George Orwell in the last part of Rorty's *Contingency, Irony, and Solidarity*. A passage such as the following (from the introduction to *Contingency, Irony, and Solidarity*) epitomizes the linear trajectory I indicate: "This process of coming to see other human beings as 'one of us' rather than as 'them' is a matter of detailed description of what unfamiliar people are like. . . . This is a task not for theory but for genres such as ethnography, the journalist's report, the comic book, the docudrama, and, especially, the novel" (xvi).

24. McGann, *Social Values and Poetic Acts*, 82 (see also 9, 91–92, 114, 246). On this point, see Fischer, review of *Social Values and Poetic Acts*, 35–37.

25. It would be ideal to read within cultural criticism both the history of thought and more primary historical determinants—economic, social, political, etc. But I have found it more important to restrict myself here to the history of thought. Historicizing projects such as my book on Wordsworth plunge into domains of primary history partly because they wish to use such history to revise an established intellectual history (e.g., romanticism as conceived by historians of ideas from Lovejoy through Abrams or, with a visionary twist on *idea*, Hartman; or, again, the Elizabethan world picture as conceived by Tillyard). A historicizing criticism of postmodern cultural criticism such as the one I embark on here must thus articulate the still largely amnesiac intellectual history of the method. High postmodern cultural criticism has so far tended either to repudiate or simply to elide the influence of any history of thought older than modernism. The New Historicism, e.g., is thus aggressively oblivious of its many sediments of formalist, original-historicist, and romantic thought. (See chapter 1 above; cf. the linkage of the New Historicism to *Historismus* and traditional American pragmatism in Thomas, "The New Historicism and Other Old-Fashioned Topics." My thanks to Thomas also for a prepublication look at the first chapter of his *The New Historicism and Other Old-Fashioned Topics* [subsequently published in 1991], which shares some of the concerns of the present essay.) Such amnesia is symptomatic of postmodernism at large, which characteristically attempts to find its identity by asking the claustrophobic, historically foreshortened question, Is postmodernism continuous or discontinuous with modernism?

26. I am simplifying, obviously, on several fronts. Most basically, a sufficient mapping of the intellectual history of cultural criticism would need to be nonlinear. A particularly vexed instance is the complex, multilinear modernist moment. Take the case of early-twentieth-century American pragmatism: not only would the relation of such pragmatism to the aesthetics, formalism, history of ideas, Marxism, and other aspects of the modern moment need further thought, but so too would the relation of such pragmatism to its own nineteenth-century or turn-of-the-century precedents and to nineteenth-century historicism. Or, to enter the problem through the alternative gateway of the New Criticism, one of the great underexplored connections in intellectual history is the link of similarity/difference between the New Criticism and the American pragmatic tradition. With its worry over the use of poetry, its hands-on praxis of close

reading, its ambiguous understanding of literature as fluid experience, and its very style of argumentative (and often polemical) discourse, classical New Criticism at times bears an uncanny resemblance to classical pragmatism. In short, each historical moment in my fiction of intellectual history is crisscrossed in synchronic and temporal directions by multiple links with other developments. The use of a fiction such as the one I am generating is to make imaginable a research agenda that would otherwise be prevented by the posthistorical ethos of postmodernism. What can research tell us about the history of the posthistorical? Or about how that history extends beyond the confines of the normal controversy about postmodernism: its relation to the postindustrial present and/or to modernism?

27. Mink, "Change and Causality in the History of Ideas."

28. As I suggest in n. 14 above, the matrix form is also finally a hollowing out of matter. Matrices in cultural criticism are at last undecidable: at once full of matter and outside matter. They are a kind of hyperspace.

29. Rorty, *Contingency, Irony, and Solidarity*, 23–27. Compare Barthes on "the blazon" in *S/Z*, 113–14.

30. Darnton, *The Great Cat Massacre*, 20.

31. Geertz, "Deep Play: Notes on the Balinese Cockfight," 427 n. 13. In general, Geertz's notes to this essay are intriguing: they insert under the argument of cultural interpretation a semifoundational respect for scientific objectivity and completeness (coupled with a consciousness of the inability to fulfill such standards). Note 14, thus, begins, "For purposes of ethnographic completeness, it should be noted . . ." (427), while n. 15 ends, "But a detailed understanding of the whole process awaits what, alas, it is not very likely ever to get: a decision theorist armed with precise observations of individual behavior" (428). The critique of Lévi-Strauss's pseudoempiricism that Derrida prosecutes in "Structure, Sign and Play in the Discourse of the Human Sciences" would apply to Geertz as well.

32. Althusser, "Ideology and Ideological State Apparatuses," 136–37.

33. Lyotard, *The Differend*, 67.

34. For economy, I have used lists of categories or concepts as my examples. The point would also be true if Darnton and Geertz were (as they do elsewhere) to itemize, not categories, but factual particulars ordered by number, dimension, location, or chronology. For a splendid thematization (but also enactment) of the problem of matrix making and listing, see Darnton, *The Great Cat Massacre*, chap. 4 ("A Police Inspector Sorts His Files").

35. Althusser, "Ideology and Ideological State Apparatuses," 138.

36. The *etc.*, we may say, is where cultural-critical "thought" becomes what Barthes calls mere "pensiveness," a discourse that signals rhetorically that its "head is heavy with unspoken language." Cultural criticism (in Barthes's words about pensiveness), "having filled the text but obsessively fearing that it is not *incontestably* filled, [insists] on supplementing it with an *et cetera* of plenitudes" (*S/Z*, 217). Barthes's improvisation on the rhetoric of the blazon is also apropos: "Striptease and blazon refer to the very destiny of the sentence. . . . The sentence can never constitute a *total*; meanings can be listed, not admixed: the total, the sum are for language the promised lands, glimpsed *at the end* of enumeration, but once this enumeration has been completed, no feature can reassemble it—or, if this feature is produced, it too can only be *added* to the others" (ibid., 114).

37. On synecdoche and detail, cf. Schor, *Reading in Detail*, 28–29.

38. On the relation between the detail and the microcosmic fragment, see Schor, *Reading in Detail*, 28. On "fragmented transcendence," see Adorno, *Aesthetic Theory*, 184.

Levinson's reading of romantic fragment poems as sites of collision, contradiction, and internal divisiveness points, by contrast, to what might be called a *digital, binary,* or *differential* understanding of the fragment (see *The Romantic Fragment Poem,* e.g., 13, 27, 85, 204). If in its immanental aspect cultural criticism speaks of the fragment as microcosmic, in its commitment to praxis and its adversarial stance it speaks of the fragment as faction.

39. See Ransom, *The New Criticism,* chap. 4 ("Wanted: An Ontological Critic"). Fischer compares Ransom on "local details" to McGann on particularity (see his review of *Social Values and Poetic Acts,* 36). For prominent examples of the semitechnical imagination of literary "devices" in Russian Formalism, see Shklovsky, "Art as Technique," and Tomashevsky, "Thematics."

40. Keats, *Complete Poems,* 345 (lines 35–37).

41. See n. 36, chapter 1, above.

42. For Greenblatt's strongly antithetical outline of Renaissance self-fashioning, see the introduction to his *Renaissance Self-Fashioning,* esp. 9. For a comparison of Greenblatt and Hartman, see my review of Simpson's *Wordsworth's Historical Imagination,* 180. Some of my ideas on details were initially sketched out there.

43. McGann, *Social Values and Poetic Acts,* 207.

44. See my review of Simpson's *Wordsworth's Historical Imagination,* 177–79. On my selective look just at Renaissance and romantics New Historicism, see n. 15 above.

45. Knapp and Michaels confine themselves to literary theory. But I include "Against Theory" in my discussion of cultural criticism both as a cause célèbre of the New Pragmatism and as a lead-in to Rorty's cultural criticism. (On the parameters and limitations of my discussion of the New Pragmatism in this chapter, see n. 15 above.)

A fuller consideration of "Against Theory" could usefully set its "intention" or "squiggles in the sand" vs. "meaning" issue side-by-side with analogous ghost-in-the-machine problems in other work by Knapp and Michaels. Most germane is Michaels's own cultural-critical book: the New Pragmatist/New Historicist *The Gold Standard and the Logic of Naturalism.* Here, Michaels discusses much the same squiggles in the sand vs. meaning problem (more generally: "material and representation, hard money and soft, beast and soul" [173]) under the topics of commodity value, money, corporations, bodies vs. persons, automatic writing, gambling, and photography. However, the historicist medium in which Michaels's book embeds the problem makes a qualitative difference in the felt outcome of the discussion. "Against Theory," we note, reductively collapses the binary terms of the ghost/machine controversy to leave us in pragmatism's characteristically flat, leveled world: in its view, to see a meaningful text in squiggles in the sand just *is* to see a ghost of authorial intention; otherwise, we would not see a text in the first place. Or as Knapp and Michaels put it flatly: "We have argued that what a text means and what its author intends it to mean are identical and that their identity robs intention of any theoretical interest" ("Against Theory," 19). But *The Gold Standard and the Logic of Naturalism* delays the collapse of the terms, allowing them to interfere, reverse, and complicate each other in an "antithetical" fashion (for "antithetical," see ibid., 173).

Delay, indeed, could here be elevated into a critical concept. It might be said that the contribution of the New Historicism to such New Pragmatism—movements that are otherwise uncannily alike in their assumptions—is precisely to introduce a salutary *delay* not unlike deconstructive "deferral." Delayed by the necessity of finding, reading, revising, and being fair to historical examples with all their messy imprecision (as opposed to the "pure" philosophical examples I discuss below), the doctrine of antitranscendence and local belief encounters a resistance it is forced to internalize. In the process, it becomes more truly interesting.

It is thus telling to calibrate *The Gold Standard and the Logic of Naturalism* against "Against Theory" precisely on the score of what I have called *delay* and its use. Logical analysis in "Against Theory," we observe, habitually occurs along a hypothetical temporal axis: "In one moment he identifies meaning and intended meaning; in the next moment he splits them apart"; "Hirsch is imagining a moment of interpretation before intention is present"; "Intention . . . must be present from the start"; "The moment of imagining intentionless meaning constitutes the theoretical moment itself"; "One might ask whether the question of intention still seems as irrelevant as it did seconds before" (13–16). And the use of catching the essay's many antagonists in an inconsistency framed by the split-instant shift between one thought "moment" (or even "second") and another, of course, is to prove a "mistake" (one of the essay's key words, e.g., 12–14, 18, 22, 23). The general argument of "Against Theory" is that any temporal break interposed between always-already-identical concepts is instantly fallacious (the spatial version of this argument is the vaunted, all-or-nothing New Pragmatist distinction between being "in" one's context of belief and transcendentally "outside" it).

  The Gold Standard and the Logic of Naturalism, however, has to locate the delay of fallacy in more or less thickly described contexts of historical controversy and fiction. The following, e.g., is essentially a temporal analysis realized in a particular milieu: "The subject of naturalism . . . is typically unable to keep his beliefs lined up with his interests for more than two or three pages at a time" (177). As a result, the delay of fallacy is embedded in historical time, and finding a slip between one instant in an author's text and another leads, not to the shrill "aha!" tone of "Against Theory," but to the bass chord of *historical understanding*. Witness, e.g., the cherish with which Michaels treats the "mistakes" of naturalism: "But can economies be subjects? Can they have intentions, desires, beliefs? Can they have interests? . . . From [a certain] standpoint, the ascription of interests to a money economy . . . is only a figure of speech or a mistake. . . . At the same time, however, as literary critics—and as critics in particular of naturalism—we can hardly dismiss this mistake, this particular figure, as merely one among others. For according to the logic of naturalism it is only because we are fascinated by such mistakes—by natural objects that look as if they were made by humans—that we have any economy at all. The foundation of our economy, the primitive desire to own, is nothing but our response to these mistakes, our desire to own the mistakes themselves" (178–79 [for a complicated treatment of "mistakes," see also 171]). Mistakes such as these are part of history (and of our participation in history); and history—given the pragmatist respect for contingency— is not as easily dismissed as theory. According to the overall argumentative paradigm of *The Gold Standard and the Logic of Naturalism*, therefore, the use of discovering mistakes in history is, not to prove or disprove fallacy, but to "exemplify" a historical "network of related contradictions and controversies" (174–75). The authors that Michaels discusses "exemplify" the logical tensions of naturalism in all its literary, intellectual, economic, and social complexity (on exemplification, see also 27).

  (I do not discuss here Knapp's *Personification and the Sublime* because it has less obvious connection to the New Pragmatism, the New Historicism, or cultural criticism generally. But its central issue—the unstable interface between the literal and the figurative in extreme personifications—is deeply congruent with the ghost/machine problem in both Knapp and Michaels's "Against Theory" and Michaels's *The Gold Standard and the Logic of Naturalism*; cf. the mention of "personification" in *The Gold Standard and the Logic of Naturalism*, 178–79.)

  46. Waismann, *The Principles of Linguistic Philosophy*, 326; Searle, *Intentionality*, 62; Austin, *Philosophical Papers*, 186; Carnap, "The Elimination of Metaphysics through Logical Analysis of Language," 67, and "Psychology in Physical Language," 179. For the

purpose of making my present, limited point, I have simply run together analytic and ordinary-language philosophy. A sharper focus on the philosophical precedents of the New Pragmatism would differentiate the two and concentrate on the latter (whether in the work of Austin and Searle or its parallels in the later Wittgenstein). It may be speculated that it was Austin's scrupulously *detailed* attention to language, coupled with his basic enterprise of describing language as *usage* (as opposed to the Carnapian task of analyzing language as logical truth statement), that provided the perfect filter through which original pragmatism could pass to the New Pragmatism.

47. Knapp and Michaels, "Against Theory," 15 (the full example runs to 17).

48. A discussion of the Preface to *Lyrical Ballads* in light of twentieth-century British philosophy would be instructive. Wordsworth's philosophy of language, if it may be so-called, blends the compulsions of analytic and ordinary-language philosophies. Thus, rural discourse is at once a "more permanent, and a far more philosophical language" and "a selection of language really used by men" (Wordsworth, *The Prose Works of William Wordsworth*, 1:125, 123).

49. Wordsworth, *The Prelude: 1799, 1805, 1850*, 172 (5.389–413 [1805]).

50. Shelley, *Shelley's Poetry and Prose*, 213 (lines 104–5).

51. In this regard, Knapp and Michaels's note is misleading: "Wordsworth's lyric has been a standard example in theoretical arguments since its adoption by Hirsch; see *Validity in Interpretation*, 227–30 and 238–40" ("Against Theory," 15n). As specified in the pages cited here, Hirsch was himself improvising on earlier theorizers of the Lucy poem, including Cleanth Brooks (see n. 53 below). And, once we reach back to the New Criticism, we must attend to the strongly overdetermined presence of romanticism in modernist aesthetics. It is no accident, e.g., that the first poems mentioned in Brooks's *The Well Wrought Urn* are two Wordsworth sonnets, that Ransom spent so much time deriding the romantics (see *The New Criticism*, e.g., 304–6), and, of course, that such high old modernists as T. E. Hulme and T. S. Eliot were so archly postromantic. Knapp and Michaels's claim that they are following a "standard" example does not register the overdetermination that made the example standard in the first place (or, it must be said, the sheer bizarreness of their own improvisation on the example).

(Highly relevant to my comments on "Against Theory" in this essay is the excellent discussion of Knapp and Michaels's use of "A Slumber Did My Spirit Seal" in Kamuf, *Signature Pieces*, 177–200. Thanks to Cynthia Chase for pointing me to Kamuf's essay, which, unfortunately, I did not discover until after originally writing this essay.)

52. Wordsworth, *William Wordsworth*, ed. Gill, 132 ("Tintern Abbey," lines 16–17).

53. Knapp and Michaels, "Against Theory," 12. Compare Cleanth Brooks's discussion of "A Slumber Did My Spirit Seal": "Yet to intimate that there are potential ironies in Wordsworth's lyric may seem to distort it. After all, is it not simple and spontaneous? . . . Are the terms *simple* and *ironical* mutually exclusive? What after all do we mean by *simple* or by *spontaneous*? We may mean that the poem came to the poet easily and even spontaneously. . . . What is likely to cause trouble here is the intrusion of a special theory of composition. . . . A theory as to how a poem is written is being allowed to dictate to us how the poem is to be read" ("Irony as a Principle of Structure," 737).

54. Wordsworth, *The Prose Works of William Wordsworth*, 1:125.

55. A final comment on "Against Theory": whether Knapp and Michaels's argument about intentionality is correct or useful we will never know from their example. To discover a Lucy poem at the heart of an argument that is otherwise numbingly clear (in the New Pragmatist style) is to come on something like a Zen koan: we may or may not be enlightened, but not by way of understanding. To invoke a standard Blake koan:

Knapp and Michaels "stain the water clear." If we read the line "stain'd the water clear" in Blake's "Introduction" to the *Songs of Innocence* (Blake, *Complete Writings*, 111) to mean that the water ends up stained, is the other possible meaning (according to which Blake stains the water *clear*) intended? Or is it just a squiggle? What Blake's verse or Wordsworth's Lucy poems indicate, I suggest, is that Knapp and Michaels's analysis rests on an antithesis whose very precision makes it inadequate to the task of mapping objects (literature, language) akin to those defined by fuzzy set theory. The sets of language and squiggles are not mutually exclusive. Everything interesting in a literary text has to do with the fact that texts can seem both artifacts of language and squiggles simultaneously.

56. Chandler, *Wordsworth's Second Nature*, 216–34.

57. On Rorty and romanticism, see Lentricchia, *Criticism and Social Change*, 17–19.

58. Rorty, *Philosophy and the Mirror of Nature*, 105, 190, *Consequences of Pragmatism*, 67, 149, and *Contingency, Irony, and Solidarity*, 97, 109.

59. Dewey, *Experience and Nature*, 270; James, *Essays in Pragmatism*, 11. Many other examples of Dewey's and James's explicit use of romanticism could be cited.

60. Rorty, *Consequences of Pragmatism*, 142, 67, 91, 148, 153, and *Contingency, Irony, and Solidarity*, 25.

61. Bloom is important throughout Rorty's *Contingency, Irony, and Solidarity*, e.g.: "In my view, an ideally liberal polity would be one whose culture hero is Bloom's 'strong poet' rather than the warrior, the priest, the sage, or the truth-seeking, 'logical,' 'objective' scientist" (53).

62. A variant example here would be Jean Baudrillard, whose controversial "silent majority" thesis has been called a "populist neo-romanticism" (Ryan, "Postmodern Politics," 566). To read Baudrillard and Lyotard together in the context of romanticism may well require thinking the relationship between the former's "silent majority" and the latter's "silent" "feeling of the differend" (see below).

63. For the connection between Lyotard's semiotic pragmatics and the tradition launched by Peirce and Morris, see Lyotard, *Postmodern Condition*, 9, 87 n. 28.

64. Lest there be any unclarity, I am here ventriloquizing Lyotard, who is himself ventriloquizing an investigator skeptical of the facticity of the gas chambers. On Auschwitz and the Final Solution as verification problem, see Lyotard, *The Differend*, 3–4, 87–106, and passim.

65. Lyotard, *The Differend*, 135. A fuller discussion of the role of romanticism in Lyotard would need to qualify that his is dark romanticism, the romanticism, e.g., of Wordsworth on the Terror during the French Revolution. We might thus juxtapose Lyotard's recurrent scene of "litigation" and the "supreme tribunal" with the following scene in the *Prelude* (Wordsworth, *The Prelude: 1799, 1805, 1850*, 378 [10.370–77 (1805)]):

> Through months, through years, long after the last beat
> Of those atrocities (I speak bare truth,
> As if to thee alone in private talk)
> I scarcely had one night of quiet sleep,
> Such ghastly visions had I of despair,
> And tyranny, and implements of death,
> And long orations which in dreams I pleaded
> Before unjust tribunals.

Lyotard himself meditates on the French Revolution (*The Differend*, 145ff.). (See also the discussion below of the romantic sublime that Lyotard invokes as the perfect complement to the anxious, painful, or [in Edmund Burke's idiom] "terrible" feeling of the differend.) Of course, my claim is not that Lyotard *is* romantic but only that romanticism is one identifiable contestant in his complex debate of romanticism, modernism, and postmodernism—a triangular face-off of mutually implicated perspectives.

66. See Coleridge, *The Statesman's Manual*, 28–31. We might apply here Paul de Man's comment in "The Rhetoric of Temporality": "The world is then no longer seen as a configuration of entities that designate a plurality of distinct and isolated meanings, but as a configuration of symbols ultimately leading to a total, single, and universal meaning. This appeal to the infinity of a totality constitutes the main attraction of the symbol as opposed to allegory" (188). Two discussions relevant to my mention here of Coleridge on the symbol (especially in light of synecdoche) are de Man, "Rhetoric of Temporality," 191–92; and Knapp, *Personification and the Sublime*, esp. 15.

67. For Rorty's Antipodean myth, see *Philosophy and the Mirror of Nature*, chap. 2. The myth opens on the same sense of defamiliarized culture, of humanity glimpsed across a proscenium of otherness, that readers see staged in the stereotypical New Historicist paradigm or anecdote: "Far away, on the other side of our galaxy, there was a planet on which lived beings like ourselves—featherless bipeds who built houses and bombs, and wrote poems and computer programs. These beings did not know that they had minds" (70). Compare the chapter openings in Greenblatt's *Shakespearean Negotiations* or Mullaney's *The Place of the Stage* (for other examples from Renaissance New Historicism, see n. 1, chapter 1, above).

68. Baudrillard, "The Ecstasy of Communication," 130. As I discussed in the introduction, the bubble universes of postmodern cultural criticism are constitutively mediated; they are forms of media. A fuller exposition at this point of their descent from romantic ordered spaces, spots of time, and so on would need to address the relation between such romantic forms of attention and the ancestral media of ca. 1800 in all their complex superimposition with memory and imagination, i.e., the romantic theory of media (the theory of how the "unmediated vision," to cite the title of Hartman's early book, came to be mediated through the post-Lockean, post–camera obscura mind). For example, to what extent was the "picture of the mind" that Wordsworth makes of Tintern Abbey in one of the great, inaugural poems of tourism already, *avant la lettre*, a "postcard" framed within a mind extended (borrowing McLuhan's notion of media as human "extension") via the pictorial forms and media apparatuses of the time (e.g., engravings, Claude glasses)? More obviously, Blake's ordered space—as Blake criticism has so thoroughly shown in the past few decades—was deeply mediated through such media techniques as relief etching, a firmament-making, -dividing, and -inscribing process of ordering space as incisive as any divine fiat.

As such an allusion to the divine fiat might suggest, the distance between mediation and transcendence is not actually far. I go on next in this chapter to propose a notion of "local transcendence." Linking the idea of media to such transcendence would require only the recognition that media today is a form of transcendence—albeit not a vertical but a lateral transcendence extending in vistas of "more and more" information beyond the horizon. I did not make this connection when I originally wrote this essay in the late 1980s, though there is a premonition in my review of Simpson's *Wordsworth's Historical Imagination*. There I discussed New Historicist "displacement"—the way the method reads literature as displacing or denying history by re-presenting historical traumas "elsewhere"—as the intuition of a "flat apocalypse," "lateral transcendence," or "glide of a refugee from brutal historical experience not to higher worlds (because the New Historicism knows no other worlds) but merely to some other site of historical experience—even if called Self, Mind, or Nature—that is at least not a killing ground" (172).

It was not until I began studying recent information media in the age of "cool" (itself a kind of local transcendence: "I work here, but I'm cool") that I saw how the notion of flat apocalypse or lateral transcendence interfaced with what Steven Johnson calls the "infinity imagined" of today's digital information networks. Johnson writes: "When I think about the gap between raw information and its numinous life on the screen—something I try to avoid doing, because it is a dark and difficult thought, more than a little like contemplating the age of the universe—the whole sensation has a strangely religious feel to it, that sense of the mind trying to reach around a vibrant (and convenient) metaphor to the wider truth that lies beyond. Cathedrals, remember, were 'infinity imagined,' the heavens brought down to earthly scale. The medieval mind couldn't take in the full infinity of godliness, but it could subjugate itself before the majestic spires of Chartres or Saint-Sulpice. The interface offers a comparable sidelong view onto the infosphere, half unveiling and half disappearing act. It makes information sensible to you by keeping most of it from view—for the simple reason that 'most of it' is far too multitudinous to imagine in a single thought" (*Interface Culture*, 238–39). (Johnson uses the phrase "infinity imagined" for the title of his concluding chapter; see also his discussion of cathedrals and infinity imagined [ibid., 42–45]. For my discussion of Johnson, see Liu, *Laws of Cool*, chap. 4 ["Networking"], 158 and passim.) As in *The Matrix* films by the Wachowski brothers, "network" today is one venue for the feeling for transcendence, even if it is complicated by the spirit-emptying rather than -fulfilling "affect of missing affect" that Joshua Clover explores in poetry and criticism on the "feeling for system" or "Weltsystemaffekt" ("Stock Footage").

69. Baudrillard, "The Structural Law of Value and the Order of Simulacra," 66. Compare Adorno on "fragmented transcendence" (*Aesthetic Theory*, 184–85).

70. Keats, *Complete Poems*, 348 ("Ode to a Nightingale," lines 71–72). The original verse refers to "me" instead of "them."

71. Marcus, *Puzzling Shakespeare*, 213, 218.

72. Greenblatt, "Psychoanalysis and Renaissance Culture," 217.

73. Foucault, *Power/Knowledge*, 86.

74. See Liu, *Wordsworth: The Sense of History*, 501 (epilogue).

75. Schor, *Reading in Detail*, esp. 5, 17–41, 141–47. "The detail," Schor writes, "was to become, as Blake had predicted it would, the very 'Foundation of the Sublime'" (22).

76. On Schor's argument about desublimation, see n. 10 above. I take the apt phrase *detail ideal* slightly out of context from Schor's chapter on Freudian detail (see ibid., 70).

77. Lyotard, "Answering the Question: What Is Postmodernism?" 81.

78. Hertz's "The Notion of Blockage in the Literature of the Sublime" is especially relevant to my discussion here. It may be observed, however, that the fact that some of the best work on the sublime in the late twentieth century was psychoanalytically inclined (as in the case of Weiskel and Hertz) or otherwise "self" fixated (an orientation true to the Burkean universe of a single perceiver facing the mountain) indicates that there is an impasse or blockage between such criticism of the sublime and the criticism of culture. The current need to formulate a *cultural sublime*, as it might be called, requires the social parameters of the sublime to be broadened. But it also needs access to the rigor of thought developed by Weiskel, Hertz, and other recent theorists of the aesthetic and subjective sublime. Lyotard's writings on the sublime, e.g., might thus assist us in translating between Longinus, Burke, and Kant (as reexplored by Weiskel, Hertz, and others), on the one hand, and Baudrillard's later, hyperbolical ("astral") sublimities of cultural commentary, on the other. Such a renegotiation of the theory of the sublime would exploit the supplementary interest common to the criticisms both of the sublime and of culture:

textuality and representation. (Jennifer Jones's book in progress, *Virtual Romanticism: Sublime Aesthetics and the Materiality of Experience* [based in part on her dissertation, "Virtual Sublime"], negotiates between the sublime and culture by thinking rigorously about such media phenomena of the romantic era as panorama exhibitions.)

79. Wordsworth, *The Prelude: 1799, 1805, 1850*, 460 (13.52–65 [1805]).

80. Dewey, *The Philosophy of John Dewey*, 173.

81. De Certeau, *The Practice of Everyday Life*, e.g., xxiii–xxiv; Lentricchia, "The Return of William James," 191, 193. I stress that this is just a partial view of the matter. There is also the alternative paradigm in cultural criticism of the subject as innately differential or split.

82. Indeed, it may be predicted that the effort to redefine *locality* or *region* will continue to offer cultural criticism room for innovation—both empirical and theoretical—long after its neoindividualist and often virtually biographical experiments have passed. (By the latter, I mean the obsessional studies in the New Historicism, the New Pragmatism, the new Marxism, or French pragmatism of "More," "Tyndale," "Elizabeth," "Wordsworth," "Marx," "Kant," and so forth.)

83. I do not wish to overlook, however, the dialectical use to which some of these person-concept localisms are put. Klancher, e.g., fashions his notion of a particular readership community ("a reader situated in a particular social space") in an antithetical or other-aware fashion such that individual readership communities define themselves against a sense of competing communities (see *The Making of English Reading Audiences*, 11–12). My critique here is that, however heteroglossic person-concept localisms can be made, they still start on a logic of individual identity. Characteristically: first there is an "I," then a sense of the "other" (from the perspective of the "I" or its plural, "we"), and finally a sense of "community" formed from the antithetical relation between self and other, "us" and "them." The outcome of such logic is that local communities become magnified versions of the "I" in its intersubjective relations. An alternative model, perhaps, could be constructed by thinking through the implications of traditional local history, for which the beginning unit of analysis is characteristically, not identity, but loose, conflicting, overlapping, and multilayered archives of what might be called *distributed identity* (individuals whose identity is registered plurally across a jumble of age, sex, family, village, parish, and other categories). In this model, the distinction between the individual and the collective, and the self and the other, is not a matter of black and white. Rather, there is a whole series of overlapping boundaries involving "I," "we," and "other" in each other.

84. Rorty, *Contingency, Irony, and Solidarity*, 191.

85. For Rorty's thought on the "we" and "we-intentions," see esp. *Contingency, Irony, and Solidarity*, chap. 9 ("Solidarity"). Besides the authorial or generalizing *we/I*, there is also a busload of generalizing *one's*, *he's*, and (especially marked in *Contingency, Irony, and Solidarity*) *she's* in New Pragmatist discourse. The stylistic coordination of all these pronouns (several may occur in the same passage) is at times so complex and intrusive that it signals that "we" are in the presence of an overdetermination (see, e.g., the pronouns in the last paragraph of Fish, *Is There a Text in This Class?* chap. 6 ["Interpreting the Variorum"], p. 173, only part of which I quote below). Put another way, passages especially thick with pronouns in New Pragmatist writing (as in the Rorty and Fish passages I example here) characteristically situate the pronoun on an unstable interface between being an overdetermined feature of style and being an explicit *theme*. It is this doubling of the pronoun that distinguishes the New Pragmatist *we* or *I* from that of other discourses. Most authors engage in acts of consensus building by judicious deployments of *we's*,

our's, and *I*'s (as we have seen in the present essay itself). But the case is different when an author deploys the rhetoric of consensus building to *define* consensus. In this case, *we* or *I* used outside quotation marks to talk about a *we in* quotation marks has the effect less of rhetoric than of foundation. In Barthes's terms in "Myth Today," the pronouns of the New Pragmatism consist of a "second-order semiological system" built on top of a first-order one, and are thus structurally cognate with what Barthes calls ideological "mythology." To follow the lines of Barthes's analysis: the commonsensical speaking voice of the New Pragmatist *we* or *I* is analogous to "nature," and the thematized *we* that defines the local or interpretive community is analogous to connotative ideology, which borrows its felt "reality" from "nature." The thematized *we* of the New Pragmatism, in short, is akin to the patriotism or "French imperiality" signified by the Paris *Match* cover in Barthes's example.

86. Fish, *Is There a Text in This Class?* 173.

87. More fully, my argument is that Fish's careful defense against the charge of interpretive subjectivity suffers a return of the repressed. To ward off the threat of "independent" subjectivity, Fish subordinates subjectivity entirely to the determination of the community, e.g.: "The self is conceived of not as an independent entity but as a social construct whose operations are delimited by the systems of intelligibility that inform it" (*Is There a Text in This Class?* 335). In my view, however, communities are always slightly— but crucially—inadequate or conflicted in their determination of the self in any context, sufficiently so that they force the individual to draw on alternative or past communities to fill in the missing dots. This act of recall or imagination splits the self in a manner that amounts to splitting the perceived interpretive community, and, unless an effort is made to account for such differentiation in the self/community, then the argument that the community determines the self is hollow. More, the argument allows the essence of a foundational, integral self to reappear *as the community itself*, which can too easily seem a singleness because we do not look hard enough at the adequacy of its concept (put pragmatically, we do not test the adequacy of the community as a domain of actions whose consequence is the identity and behavior of member selves). The community becomes subjectivity.

I should add, however, that Fish's later elaboration of the interpretive community, especially in regard to its potential for heterogeneity and change, goes a long way toward thinking the inner differentiation of self or community that I call for (see *Doing What Comes Naturally*, esp. 141–60). A parallel for the interpretive community in this light would be the habitus, which Bourdieu builds, not from identity-as-singleness, but from identity-in-difference: the habitus is a moving horizon of relation between a past context that generates practices and a present context in which those practices are adapted (see Bourdieu, *Outline of a Theory of Practice*, 72–95).

88. Compare Samuel Weber's criticism of Fish: "What has to be investigated and discussed is the process by which [the unity of the interpretive institution] is established, maintained, and disrupted. . . . A tension thus emerges between the given state of the institution, and its tendency to encourage or even demand innovation and transformation. As long as such changes do not call into question the basic premises that endow the institution with its particular identity, they can be rewarded and contained. But when, as today, those changes tend to affect the very founding assumptions of the institution, such containment can no longer be regarded as a given" (*Institution and Interpretation*, 36–37). See also the critique of the concept of the interpretive community in McGann, *Social Values and Poetic Acts*, 188.

89. If this essay had been written after 2001, the reference might have been switched here from Napoleon to the "go-it-alone" *isolatos* understanding of globalism (together

with its dark antitheses, global terror and global warming) that another regime immediately after the events of that year deemed to be manifest destiny.

90. Darnton, *The Great Cat Massacre*, 98.

91. I have written on the subversion/containment problem in chapter 2 above. Carolyn Porter's critique of oppositionality as conceived by the New Historicism is especially apropos to detailism: "By an appeal to richly suggestive 'local episodes' and 'particular historical encounters,' this tautology [that domination dominates] takes on the clothing of historical specificity so that each time it is found, once again, that resistance or opposition serves the interests of the powerful, the conclusion seems to be derived from a densely textured understanding of a particular, historically localized cultural space" ("Are We Being Historical Yet?" 769).

92. For the term *commitment*, cf. Adorno, *Aesthetic Theory*, 349–52 (on "artistic commitment").

93. A full consideration of this topic would need to take up an especially thorny aspect of the pragmatist problem of belief: whether it is possible to view or imagine other people's beliefs qua beliefs. Is it the case that everyone is trapped in a particular belief story whose nature is to make other people's belief stories seem *mere* stories or that no one in the postmodern world is trapped in a belief story because all are to some degree ironists? Such questions about the pragmatics of belief approach a vanishing point when applied to a case like Baudrillard's silent majority. What does this silent majority like "an impenetrable and meaningless surface" believe (Baudrillard, *Selected Writings*, 213)?

Chapter 4

This essay was first presented in preliminary form in 1992 at a session of the Modern Language Association (MLA) convention (one of a pair of sessions entitled "Romanticism and Postmodernism" that I organized for the MLA's Division on the English Romantic Period). My focus in this essay on postmodernism is a symptom of that moment, when it seemed important to make a connection between the romanticism field's recent experimentation with the New Historicism and late-twentieth-century aesthetic and cultural concerns as they appeared in that same decade under the banner of postmodernism. Now, another decade and a half on, I would also want to position such postmodernism as one element in the combined social, economic, political, and cultural now of postindustrialism into which all historical awareness is vanishing. My *Laws of Cool* takes a postmillennial perspective on information culture (and the associated postindustrial ethos of "workplace 2000") as the epitome of the endless, benighted, postindustrial "now." Today's romantics are knowledge workers who imagine they are cool.

The commentaries or vignettes prefacing each section of this essay are based on notes, tape recordings, and photographs of a visit to the Spruce Goose dome in Long Beach, California, on 2 July 1992 (the second of two visits that year). Shortly afterward, the Disney-owned exhibit was shut down and the plane (owned by Aero Club of Southern California/Aero Exhibits, Inc.) was transported north in disassembled sections, beginning in October 1992, to await the building of a new exhibition facility at the Evergreen Aviation Museum in McMinnville, Oregon. The new facility was completed after I wrote this essay. For the recent history of the Spruce Goose, see the Web site of the Evergreen Aviation Museum, esp. the pages entitled "Aircraft and Artifacts: Featured Exhibits—Spruce Goose," "Description," and "Move to Oregon."

1. Baudrillard, *Selected Writings*, 171–72; Jameson, *Postmodernism*, 38–45; Lyotard, *Pacific Wall*; Virilio and Lotringer, *Pure War*, 71–75.

2. Stephanson, "Regarding Postmodernism—a Conversation with Fredric Jameson,"

18. On the topic of postmodernism and history, see also Eagleton, *The Ideology of the Aesthetic*, 377–78.

3. Baudrillard, "The Year 2000 Has Already Happened," 41. The classic paradigm of such historicity is the nostalgia film as studied by Jameson (*Postmodernism*, 19–21).

4. Lyotard, *The Postmodern Condition*; Habermas, *The Theory of Communicative Action*.

5. Benjamin, "The Work of Art in the Age of Mechanical Reproduction," 240. On postmodern distraction, see Jameson, *Postmodernism*, 117. See also Margaret Morse, who, in her study of the postmodern "nonspace" of the freeway, the mall, and television, has said that we know in the agora today only an "ontology of everyday distraction" ("An Ontology of Everyday Distraction").

6. Lyotard, *The Postmodern Condition*, 79–81 (on the "feeling" for the unpresentable, which Lyotard associates with the differend [see also his *The Differend*, 13]); Deleuze and Guattari, *A Thousand Plateaus*, esp. 4; Baudrillard, *The Ecstasy of Communication*; Haraway, "A Cyborg Manifesto," 150; de Certeau, *The Practice of Everyday Life*, xxiv (de Certeau is here quoting Witold Gombrowicz); Jameson, *Postmodernism*, 71, 34, 72. I leave aside here ethics as the third player in the Weberian/Habermasian thesis that meaningful cognition splits apart into specialized realms of instrumental rationality, morality, and aesthetics. As in such works as Lyotard and Thébaud's *Just Gaming*, however, it is clear that, while the postmodern celebration of aesthetics may not require a classical metaphysical foundation (the "truth" or "nature" that once grounded the "beautiful"), it does search for a grounding in ethics (the "good").

7. This is one way to express the main argument of my *Wordsworth: The Sense of History*.

8. Eagleton, *The Ideology of the Aesthetic*.

9. Benjamin, "The Work of Art in the Age of Mechanical Reproduction," 222–23.

10. On the modern obsession with fabricating the "real thing," see Orvell, *The Real Thing*.

11. Relevant here is Deleuze and Guattari's slogan against uniqueness: "Subtract the unique from the multiplicity to be constituted; write at $n - 1$ dimensions" (*A Thousand Plateaus*, 6). Or, as Jameson puts it, postmodernism is the blank parody, the pastiche, of modernist "uniqueness" (*Postmodernism*, 17).

12. Jameson, *Postmodernism*, 38–39, 44, 115–16 (esp. in regard to the "tumbling cube" in the Frank Gehry House in Santa Monica); Morse, "An Ontology of Everyday Distraction," 203.

13. See, e.g., Jan Tschichold's 1928 *The New Typography*. (For further discussion of modernist-era graphic design, see Liu, *Laws of Cool*, 195–205.)

14. Hughes and his engineers designed a cantilevered bra to show off Russell's breasts in the 1943 film *The Outlaw*.

15. On Foucault's laugh, see *The Order of Things*, xv–xvii.

16. Baudrillard, *Selected Writings*, 213.

17. In the "history of distraction" I call for here, the emphasis is on history, as opposed, e.g., to the emphasis on practice in de Certeau's project of recovering the many ways of practical reason.

18. See also chapters 3 above and 5 below.

19. My allusion here is to line 51 of Wordsworth's "Immortality Ode": "But there's a Tree, of many one" (Wordsworth, *William Wordsworth*, 298).

20. Habermas, "The Entry into Postmodernity."

21. Jameson, *Postmodernism*, esp. the sections on architecture; Harvey, *The Condition of Postmodernity*; Soja, *Postmodern Geographies*.

22. Jameson, *Postmodernism*, 3.

23. Habermas, "Modernity—an Incomplete Project," 4.

24. Lyotard, "Answering the Question: What Is Postmodernism?" Habermas, "The Entry into Postmodernity."

25. On delay as a critical concept—i.e., on the difference that delay makes—see n. 45, chapter 3, above. Compare "tmesis" and the spacing apart of beginnings and ends discussed in Hartman, "The Voice of the Shuttle," esp. 344–48. For Hartman, the delay between origins and ends makes a space—an "indeterminate middle between overspecified poles" (348)—capable of sheltering human life and aesthetic figuration from the existential velocity of being, i.e., the condition of pure being without history.

26. Foucault, *The Order of Things*, xv.

27. I borrow the word play on *unfurrowing* and *delirium* from Pynchon, *The Crying of Lot 49*, 104.

28. On "the romantic modernist," see Habermas, "Modernity—an Incomplete Project," 4.

29. Wordsworth, *The Prelude: 1799, 1805, 1850*, 434 (11.341–42 [1805]).

Chapter 5

1. Wordsworth, *William Wordsworth*, ed. Gill, 134 (lines 97–99).

2. Wordsworth, *The Letters of William and Dorothy Wordsworth*, 1:544–45, 546, 548.

3. Weiskel, *The Romantic Sublime*, 6. Kevis Goodman brought this passage to my attention in a private communication.

4. Nancy, "Finite History," 155–56.

5. An allusion to the Borg society in the *Star Trek: The Next Generation* television series.

6. Deleuze and Guattari, *A Thousand Plateaus*, esp. chap. 10 ("1730: Becoming-Intense, Becoming-Animal, Becoming-Imperceptible . . .").

7. I am taking liberties here, of course, with lines 33–39 of Wordsworth's "Elegiac Stanzas Suggested by a Picture of Peele Castle." For the original verses, see Wordsworth, *William Wordsworth*, ed. Gill, 327.

8. The session "Wordsworth's 'Invisible Workmanship' and the Work of New Historicism" was presented at the Modern Language Association convention in Toronto, 29 December 1993. The session, which was organized by Kevis Goodman, featured Goodman, "Making Time for History"; Spargo, "Facing the Other"; and Waldoff, "The Wordsworthian 'I' and the Work of Self-Representation in 'Elegiac Stanzas.'" The present chapter was originally the invited response to this session.

9. See Liu, *Wordsworth: The Sense of History*, chaps. 7 and 1, respectively.

10. I have taken all these terms of negativity from the pages of the New Historicism in the romantics field. Most of the words listed here, e.g., can be found in Levinson, *Wordsworth's Great Period Poems*, chap. 1 ("Insight and Oversight: Reading 'Tintern Abbey'"). My own work in the romantics field often used such vocabulary, especially *denial*. For a discussion of the relations—and differences—between some of these terms, see my review of Simpson's *Wordsworth's Historical Imagination*, 173.

11. On *white mythology*, see Derrida, "White Mythology."

12. Levinson, *Wordsworth's Great Period Poems*, 102.

13. The very notion that "Elegiac Stanzas" "turns around and *registers*" loss, we

recognize, mediates between the poet's and the critic's theaters of action. Registration is an eminently academic—and, more generally, modern—act.

14. Levinson, *Wordsworth's Great Period Poems*, 128.

15. Liu, *Wordsworth: The Sense of History*, 39.

16. By contrast with more activist styles of cultural materialism, of course, even the subversion topos in Renaissance New Historicism is exorbitantly elegiac—as in the tone of the More chapter or the epilogue in Greenblatt's *Renaissance Self-Fashioning*.

17. Nancy, "Finite History," 157.

18. Freud, "Mourning and Melancholia," 244.

19. Lyotard, "Answering the Question: What Is Postmodernism?" 80.

20. Lyotard, "Answering the Question: What Is Postmodernism?" 80. For bringing to my attention the importance of this passage in Lyotard, I am indebted to Ellison, "Someday Bridges Will Have Feelings, Too."

Chapter 6

This essay was originally written in 1989–90. I have for the most part not attempted in the review of the literature to update citations beyond that point, choosing instead to let the review stand for what I term the *zenith* of a certain epoch associated with the New Cultural History and the New Historicism as it intersected with the onset of the theory of interdisciplinarity.

1. Ozouf, *Festivals and the French Revolution*, 39. (The book was originally published in French in 1976.)

2. Furet, *Interpreting the French Revolution*, 46, 48, 78. (*Interpreting the French Revolution* was originally published as *Penser la Révolution Française* in 1978.) I have taken the liberty of gathering together several passages in Furet to demonstrate the overall impact of his emphasis on language.

3. Hunt, *Politics, Culture, and Class in the French Revolution*, 24–25.

4. Baker, "Memory and Practice," 134.

5. Huet, *Rehearsing the Revolution*, 10, 13.

6. Jacobus, "'That Great Stage Where Senators Perform,'" 361–62.

7. Parker, "Reading Wordsworth's Power," 322.

8. Carlson, "An Active Imagination," 23.

9. Kelley, *Wordsworth's Revisionary Aesthetics*, 5.

10. Blakemore, *Burke and the Fall of Language*, 1–2.

11. Liu, *Wordsworth: The Sense of History*, 138.

12. Hunt, "Introduction: History, Culture, and Text." Also informing my discussion here are Furet, "Beyond the *Annales*"; Hunt, "French History in the Last Twenty Years," and review of *Penser la Révolution Français* (translated as *Interpreting the French Revolution*); Darnton, "The Symbolic Element in History"; and Chartier, *Cultural History*, chaps. 1 ("Intellectual History and the History of *Mentalités*: A Dual Re-Evaluation") and 4 ("Text, Symbols and Frenchness: Historical Uses of Symbolic Anthropology").

13. Furet, *Interpreting the French Revolution*, 12.

14. Hunt, ed., *The New Cultural History*; Wilentz, ed., *Rites of Power*.

15. Braudel, *The Mediterranean and the Mediterranean World in the Age of Philip II*, 1:21.

16. Hunt, *Politics, Culture, and Class in the French Revolution*, 13.

17. Chartier, *Cultural History*, 44.

18. Greenblatt, *Renaissance Self-Fashioning*, 4.

19. Bloom, *The Anxiety of Influence*, 139–55.

20. Jameson, *Postmodernism*, 188–90.

21. Eliot, *The Waste Land and Other Poems*, 30 (line 22).

22. Montrose, "Renaissance Literary Studies," 8–9.

23. Thomas, "The New Historicism and Other Old-Fashioned Topics," e.g., 183–84, 193–94; Greenblatt, *Renaissance Self-Fashioning*, 5.

24. See, e.g., CERI, *Interdisciplinarity: Problems of Teaching and Research in Universities*; *Interdisciplinarity: Papers Presented at the SHRE European Symposium on Interdisciplinary Courses in European Education*; Mayville, *Interdisciplinarity*; Kockelmans, ed., *Interdisciplinarity and Higher Education*; and Jurkovich and Paelinck, eds., *Problems in Interdisciplinary Studies*.

25. Fish, "Being Interdisciplinary Is So Very Hard to Do," 21; Palmade, *Interdisciplinarité et idéologies*, esp. 15–44, 56–62, 163–275 (for the term *imperialist*, see 60). The trope of imperialism in referring to disciplinary matrices is ubiquitous: see also, e.g., LaCapra, *Rethinking Intellectual History*, 19 (on "the specter of 'textual imperialism' or 'pantextualism'") and 59 ("No discipline has the imperial right to dominion over a Freud, Marx, Nietzsche, or Joyce").

26. Palmade, *Interdisciplinarité et idéologies*, 21; Kavaloski, "Interdisciplinary Education and Humanistic Aspiration," esp. 225–28; Fish, "Being Interdisciplinary Is So Very Hard to Do," 19.

27. Fish, "Being Interdisciplinary Is So Very Hard to Do," 15–19.

28. Ibid., 18.

29. We can recognize in Fish's criticism of interdisciplinary study's *"revolution tout court"* (ibid., 17) the trace of an older critique of revolution. Fish against the possibility of interdiscipline and for the inevitability of closed minds is Edmund Burke arguing the long war against French revolutionary "theory" and for "prejudice." French Revolution studies, in other words, is not just a convenient but an especially prescriptive context in which to take up the interdisciplinary problem. If the French Revolution is over, as Furet asseverates against presentist Marxist historiography, it is not truly over until current interdisciplinary discourse addresses critically the revolutionary ideologies of "free" thinking that live on within itself. The French Revolution, after all, set a precedent for interdisciplinary thought in the contest between Napoleon's imperial ambition and the metadisciplinary project of the Ideologues. (On ideology in the context of the Ideologues and Napoleon, see Chandler, *Wordsworth's Second Nature*, 217–23; McGann, *The Romantic Ideology*, 7–8, 10; and Kelley, *Historians and the Law in Postrevolutionary France*, 14, 17.)

30. Fish, "Being Interdisciplinary Is So Very Hard to Do," 21.

31. It is well worth comparing Fish's and Kavaloski's critiques. Kavaloski argues that interdisciplinary studies retains an older model of "objectivist epistemology" that allows teachers, "having privileged access to the 'bodies' of knowledge," to "deliver it in measured units to their all-consuming [students]" ("Interdisciplinary Education and Humanistic Aspiration," 227). In essence, this criticism is complementary to Fish's discrimination of the transcendental vantage point implicit in interdisciplinary studies.

32. Geertz, *Local Knowledge*, 20.

33. Macksey, "Introduction: 'A New Text of the World,'" 312 (on the "violation of previously secure boundaries," see also 314); Barthes, "De l'ouevre au texte," quoted in Macksey, "Introduction: 'A New Text of the World,'" 309; Fish, "Being Interdisciplinary Is So Very Hard to Do," 18; Partner, "Making Up Lost Time," 95, quoted in Hunt, "Introduction: History, Culture, and Text," 21.

34. Klein, *Interdisciplinarity*, 78.

35. On the mode of literary defense, see Ferguson, *Trials of Desire*.

36. In essence, I am arguing here for a pragmatist position that goes beyond the "against theory" New Pragmatist view that no theory (interdisciplinary or otherwise) can ever get us out of our present minds into other frames of mind, from our own beliefs into other beliefs. (Thus, to be in our mind is simply to *be* in our mind; other minds as such are unknowable.) My argument is that such a view is tautologically true but only artificially interesting because the in/out dichotomy (as well as the categorical conception of mind or belief it rests on) is inadequate to the complexity of the problem. The tools of discussion are too blunt, so we should find better ones with more gauge settings than true or not true, in or out.

37. Liu, *Laws of Cool*, esp. chap. 1 ("The Idea of Knowledge Work"). This paragraph and the next in the present discussion were added sometime after the original writing of this essay, when research for *Laws of Cool* showed me that a cross-institutional context was needed to understand both the limitations and the possibilities of interdisciplinarity within the academy.

38. An extranet extends the internal network of an organization to other organizations so that, e.g., a business's suppliers can have up-to-the-minute information about planning or manufacturing that can be used to adjust their own businesses symbiotically. Web services are software systems and protocols designed to mediate between different information platforms and applications—so that, e.g., data stored in one proprietary database can be automatically transported into or acted on by another over the Internet. Content-management systems, which generate personal blogs as well as large-scale collaborative sites, allow users to create, edit, and organize content through predesigned, fully integrated systems of Web forms (for data entry), databases (for back-end data management), and stylesheet-managed templates (for output with a well-designed look). One system popular with both personal bloggers and managers of collaborative sites, e.g., is WordPress. *Wikis* is the generic term for a class of applications that allow broad communities of users to create and edit online resources collectively on an anyone-can-edit-anyone-else principle (e.g., Wikipedia). Social networking is exemplified by sites such as MySpace.com or Facebook.com on which users create personal pages interlinked with those of a network of friends. Folksonomic tagging allows users to attach sharable tags or descriptors to online resources via such "social bookmarking" sites as del.icio.us. The notion of Web 2.0 came into currency in the middle of the first decade of the twenty-first century to describe the convergence of these and other developments that encouraged user-created content. Tim O'Reilly wrote the early, influential definition of *Web 2.0* (see O'Reilly, "What Is Web 2.0").

39. Da Vinci: Renaissance man. Von Neumann: mathematician, physicist, computer scientist, economist. Berners-Lee: physicist, inventor of the World Wide Web. In regard to collaborative, grant-driven projects in the humanities, I should acknowledge that some of these are ones I have started (e.g., the Transcriptions and Transliteracies projects) to explore the possibility of hybridizing the humanities research paradigm with the paradigms of other institutions and disciplines. To borrow a concept from Davidson's "Big Humanities and Collaboration," might big business and big science be matched by "big-humanities" projects that adopt other institutional paradigms yet still harvest the rich difference of the humanities? Might a hybrid model of interdisciplinarity be possible?

40. For a more detailed discussion of the contemporary idealization of the corporation as a knowledge or learning organization, see Liu, *Laws of Cool*, esp. 14–22, 43–45. An influential instance of such idealization is Senge's *The Fifth Discipline*.

41. Fish, "Being Interdisciplinary Is So Very Hard to Do," 21.

42. I draw the term *pantextualism* in particular from LaCapra (*Rethinking Intellectual History*, 19) and Macksey ("Introduction: 'A New Text of the World,'" 307).

43. Hunt, *Politics, Culture, and Class in the French Revolution*, esp. 87–119; Paulson, *Representations of Revolution*; Kelley, *Wordsworth's Revisionary Aesthetics*, 170–92, and "J. M. W. Turner, Napoleonic Caricature, and Romantic Allegory"; Jacobus, "'Incorruptible Milk'"; Liu, *Wordsworth: The Sense of History*, esp. 61–137.

44. I refer to the discussion of Velázquez's *Las Meninas* in Foucault, *The Order of Things*, 3–16, and of Hans Holbein's *The Ambassadors* in Greenblatt, *Renaissance Self-Fashioning*, esp. 17–27.

45. To borrow a topos of recent analyses of French revolutionary political discourse, textualism wishes to be "transparent." On transparency in the Revolution, see Hunt, *Politics, Culture, and Class in the French Revolution*, 44–46, 72–74. On the concept of transparency in the work of François Furet, Jean Starobinski, and Marc Richir, see ibid., 44n.

46. Fish, "Being Interdisciplinary Is So Very Hard to Do," 18–19.

47. The fact that my model of interdisciplinary study is binary (restricted primarily to just *two* disciplines at a time) is based on an empirical observation. In a variant of Edgar Allan Poe's critique (in "The Poetic Principle") of the "long poem," we may say that the attention span of the academic mind—limited at any time to, say, a chapter of a book or an hour-and-fifteen-minute seminar—is closed to the extent of being able to grapple seriously with only two simultaneous disciplines. This is especially true if intermedia apparatus (e.g., slide projectors, computer multimedia) are involved because the use of such apparatus itself consumes a great deal of attention. In my experience, trying to deal with more than two disciplines in a single class leads to superficial "anthology" or "survey" thinking.

48. For a more recent, and more thorough, exploration of the concept of intermediation in a new media context, see Hayles, *My Mother Was a Computer*.

49. Feyerabend, *Against Method*; Lévi-Strauss, *The Savage Mind*, 1–33; Paulson, *Literary Landscape*; Appleton, *The Experience of Landscape*; Tuan, *Segmented Worlds and Self*; Deleuze and Guattari, *A Thousand Plateaus*.

50. For introductions to the *new media* field—the term under which digital art, writing, and theory have recently converged—see, e.g., Wardrip-Fruin and Montfort, eds., *The New Media Reader*; Manovich, *The Language of New Media*; and Paul, *Digital Art*.

51. The original passage is as follows: "The postmodern would be that which, in the modern, puts forward the unpresentable in presentation itself; that which denies itself the solace of good forms, the consensus of a taste which would make it possible to share collectively the nostalgia for the unattainable; that which searches for new presentations, not in order to enjoy them but in order to impart a stronger sense of the unpresentable" (Lyotard, "Answering the Question: What Is Postmodernism?" 81).

52. For the relation between mourning and jubilation in Anglo-American and French postmodern theory, respectively, see the discussion of "regret and assay" that concludes chapter 5 above. Of course, as I speculate immediately below, the great work that makes visible the relation between these two theoretical regions and their tonal registers is Julia Kristeva's *Powers of Horror*.

53. Klein, *Interdisciplinarity*, 77–78. See also Bender: "The word [*interdisciplinarity*] itself implies the preservation of traditional disciplinary boundaries and provokes one to think of the critic either as a fugitive living dangerously in limbo between nations or

operating as a kind of extraordinary ambassador moving without portfolio from one sovereignty to another" ("Eighteenth-Century Studies," 87).

54. Deleuze and Guattari, *A Thousand Plateaus*, 422.

Chapter 7

1. For example, Marcuse, "Some Social Implications of Modern Technology," 153; Ellul, *The Technological Society*, xxv. I develop this argument about the slippage between technologies and techniques more fully in my *Laws of Cool*, esp. chaps. 9–10.

2. Watkins, *Throwaways*.

3. Jonathan Arac wrote in the mid-1980s: "A major impetus to the boom in American theory was the hope for a 'new literary history' (the journal of that name was founded by Ralph Cohen in 1969). Yet no accomplished projects have been widely recognized as fulfilling that hope" (*Critical Genealogies*, 1). We can now modify Arac's observation in the wake of the 1990s. The new literary history awaited only a form in which to be recognized: display genres able to bring to market a new notion of the survey or anthology that had, in fact, already circulated throughout the anecdotal openings, collage-like juxtapositions of context and text, kaleidoscopic splinterings of the canon, and other such destabilizations of unified literature in the criticism and theory of the 1980s. Concentrating just on avowedly comprehensive or broad-coverage Anglo-American surveys (about or by American, English, Canadian, or Australian authors) published between 1985 and 1994, we can construct a checklist for our discussion as follows:

Literary Histories

Columbia Literary History of the United States (1988)
A New History of French Literature (1989)
The Columbia History of the American Novel (1991)
The Columbia History of American Poetry (1993)
The Cambridge History of American Literature, vol. 1, *1590–1820* (1994)
The Columbia History of British Poetry (1994)

Anthologies

Joseph's Coat: An Anthology of Multicultural Writing (1985)
The Norton Anthology of Literature by Women: The Tradition in English (1985)
Longman Anthology of World Literature by Women, 1875–1975 (1989)
The Heath Anthology of American Literature (1990)

Readers

American Mosaic: Multicultural Readings in Context (1991)
Decker's Patterns of Exposition (Instructor's Edition) (1992)
Kaleidoscope: Stories of the American Experience (1993)

Literary Guides and Companions

The Cambridge Guide to Literature in English (1988)
The Feminist Companion to Literature in English: Women Writers from the Middle Ages to the Present (1990)
Prentice-Hall Guide to English Literature (1990)

4. Sidney, *An Apology for Poetry*, 155.

5. Ferguson, *Trials of Desire*, 137–62.

6. Sidney, *An Apology for Poetry*, 153.

7. In the following discussion, I develop freely from Greimas, *Structural Semantics*. For the work of Shannon and Weaver, see their *The Mathematical Theory of Communication*.

8. Greimas, *Structural Semantics*, 208. The tabular form I use to apply Greimas's scheme to Sidney and the *Norton Anthology* imitates Greimas's tables for philosophy and Marxism.

9. Sidney, *An Apology for Poetry*, 148, 154.

10. *Norton Anthology of English Literature*, 1:458–59.

11. Compare Perkins: "Literary history is and perhaps must be written in metaphors of origins, emergence from obscurity, neglect and recognition, conflict, hegemony, succession, displacement, decline, and so forth. Thus it activates archetypal emotions. . . . The possible plots of narrative literary history can be reduced to three: rise, decline, and rise and decline" ("Discursive Form versus the Past in Literary History," 369). On death in this context, see Kernan, *The Death of Literature*. On myth in Lévi-Strauss, see *Structural Anthropology*, chap. 11 ("The Structural Study of Myth").

12. In my recent research and teaching focused on bringing the act of literary interpretation into contact (or collision) with other dominant paradigms of knowledge in the academy, including the acts of modeling, mapping, surveying, simulating, gaming, etc., I have been much influenced by Moretti's *Graphs, Maps, Trees* (2005). I have not revised this section of my argument, which, when originally written, alluded to decision trees in such fields as programming or (as I was just beginning to learn) rational-choice theory. But, if it had been available, Moretti's chapter "Trees" (as well as the general tenor of his brilliant little book) would certainly have helped me enrich the idea of logical trees.

13. I borrow very loosely from Ronell's *The Telephone Book*. A trunk line is the long-distance channel between two communications exchanges, each of which is linked in a hub-and-spoke pattern to many phones or terminals. In my conceptual model here, the hero is located at an exchange; calls to or from the sender/helper then switch the relays at the exchange in order to transmit the hero over long-distance lines to another exchange, at which point further relays then pass the hero on through the hub and spoke to the receiver. (On trunk lines and relays, see Clayton, *McGraw-Hill Illustrated Telecom Dictionary*.)

14. Barthes, *S/Z*, 22–23.

15. Jauss, *Toward an Aesthetic of Reception*.

16. Liu, *Wordsworth: The Sense of History*, 3–31. This connection between Wordsworth and Napoleon, however, has not gone uncontested.

17. Auerbach, *Mimesis*, 3–23.

18. Shelley, *A Defense of Poetry*, 517.

19. Eliot, "Tradition and the Individual Talent," 762.

20. Sidney, *An Apology for Poetry*, 143, 144, 145, 147, 154.

21. More fully, the response to a teacher's call can also be a paper or a classroom comment, both of which include (but are not necessarily restricted to) a testing component. For Althusser's example of being "hailed" by a policeman, see "Ideology and Ideological State Apparatuses," 163.

22. Guillory, *Cultural Capital*.

23. Shelley, *A Defense of Poetry*, 517; Gray, "The Progress of Poesy," 169 (lines 54–55).

24. Shklovsky, "Art as Technique," 12.

25. Sidney, *An Apology for Poetry*, 156.

26. Gray, "The Progress of Poesy," 172 (lines 81–82).

27. Taine, *History of English Literature*, 1:10.

28. Eliot, "Tradition and the Individual Talent," 762.

29. Chandler, *The Visible Hand*; Beniger, *The Control Revolution*.

30. I make this argument more fully in Liu, *Laws of Cool*, esp. 4–5, 35. See also the argument about the relation between postmodernism and contemporary business organizations in Dirlik, "The Postmodernization of Production and Its Organization."

31. See, e.g., *American Mosaic* or *Decker's Patterns of Exposition*.

Chapter 8

Suiting style to theme, I have used an incomplete, minimal set of XML tags to mark out the sections of this essay.

1. I use *discourse* in this essay to refer elastically to digitally born, transmitted, and/or received information that is mediated through the combination of the database- and XML-based technologies described below. While, in its narrower sense, *discourse* refers to language-based communication, the term is still apt in the age of multimedia. While a contemporary data stream may consist of digital image, video, or sound, e.g., it is still discursive to the extent that its production, transmission, aggregation, and coordination—in a word, management—are increasingly controlled (in the database and XML system I outline) through such text-based standards as SVG and SMIL (XML-based standards applicable to multimedia).

2. Some academic presses are moving full bore into text encoding—e.g., Cambridge University Press, which now encodes its books in XML to facilitate production (e.g., in the indexing process). My thanks to Kevis Goodman for this information. At the time of this writing, Goodman's book from Cambridge, *Georgic Modernity and British Romanticism*, was being indexed.

3. Examples of proprietary and open-source office suites that committed to XML for their native file formats in the early years of the twenty-first century are, respectively, Microsoft Office and OpenOffice.

4. Kittler, *Discourse Networks*. See also Kittler. *Gramophone, Film, Typewriter*. In the afterword to the second printing of *Discourse Networks*, Kittler writes: "The term *discourse network* . . . can also designate the network of technologies and institutions that allow a given culture to select, store, and process relevant data. Technologies like that of book printing and the institutions coupled to it, such as literature and the university, thus constituted a historically very powerful formation. . . . Archeologies of the present must also take into account data storage, transmission, and calculation in technological media" (369). I discuss Kittler's work further at the end of this essay.

In regard to knowledge work in institutional settings, my *Laws of Cool* studies the concept and its bearing on the contemporary humanities and arts. See esp. the preface to pt. 1 ("'Unnice Work': Knowledge Work and the Academy"), chap. 1 ("The Idea of Knowledge Work"), and app. A ("Taxonomy of Knowledge Work").

5. In 2005, after the publication of the original version of this essay, I started the Transliteracies Project (Research in the Technological, Social, and Cultural Practices of Online Reading) as a Multi-Campus Research Group funded by the University of California system. The project brings together scholars from the humanities, the social sciences, computer science, and other disciplines to study the past and future of reading. The goal

is to understand what it might mean to improve the technologies, interfaces, forms, communities, and practices of online (digital, networked) reading. (For research results and plans to date, see Transliteracies Project Web site.)

However, Transliteracies had not yet been conceived when I first completed the present argument during a half year on a Beckman visiting professorship at the University of California, Berkeley, in 2003. My thanks to Kent Puckett of the Berkeley English Department for helping me start thinking about the new digital reading practices, which, at the time, we were discussing (on the model of "browsing") as "low-cognitive" activities with unexpectedly rich, hidden intelligences.

6. Well-known examples of the digital text or image archives I refer to include the Brown University Women Writers Project, the *Rossetti Archive*, the *William Blake Archive*, and the *Walt Whitman Archive*.

7. The Digital Cultures Project and DARnet were University of California Multi-Campus Research Groups that ran from 2000 to 2005. In such projects as the current version of my *Voice of the Shuttle* or Sharon Daniel and Mark Bartlett's "collaborative systems" for public activism (e.g., *Subtract the Sky*), content is entered in database tables and fields (rather than in markup tags), and it is the database that then drives the display of content on the Web as well as advanced search and query functions. Gill et al., eds., "Database Aesthetics" (which includes contributions from several DARnet members), is helpful in its introduction of the database approach to humanities and arts computing.

8. In the present essay, my critique is external rather than internal to the cultural-history approach (whose inner fault lines I explore in other essays in this volume). That is, I seek to bring postmodern cultural historicism to bear on a problem external to academic method, to make it "useful." The use of academic postmodern historicism, I suggest, is to understand with critical difference the broader contemporary developments with which it overlaps but across which, at an angle, it also cuts. Academic postmodern historicism angles—sometimes acutely—toward a different horizon: not the instantaneous satisfactions and market returns of the New Economy information age, for which there is no history longer than a financial quarter or year, but the critical juxtaposition of instants of satisfaction (and dissatisfaction) in the past *and* present. The goal is to make possible the recognition of both the beauty and the horror that arise from collisions between old and new economies of organized human desire (and its repression). To adapt the exempla that I use in this essay (below): our contemporary postmodern / postindustrial age is also a sick rose. We should not be surprised to find at the heart of its desire for efficient and flexible postindustrial discourse the remnants of an industrial-age rifle factory.

9. This poem by William Blake is the first example in one of the best-known explanations of XML for an academic audience, Sperberg-McQueen and Burnard's "A Gentle Introduction to XML" (published on the Web site of the Text Encoding Initiative [TEI]). While I borrow the example, I have improvised my own, even gentler explanation of XML for this essay, whose audience will, in most cases, be less involved in technology or the digitization of texts than the TEI community.

10. For an introduction to RSS, see Nottingham, "RSS Tutorial for Content Publishers and Webmasters"; and RSS-DEV Working Group, "RDF Site Summary (RSS) 1.0." *RSS* has been understood variously to stand for "Rich Site Summary," "RDF [Resource Description Framework] Summary," or "Really Simple Syndication"—a case study in the semiotic creep of acronyms in information culture (by which acronyms acquire an iconic or pseudoimage status increasingly detached from verbalization).

11. Of course, there are some occasions when it is desirable to use a procedural

approach—e.g., to make a page match up as closely as possible on the sending and receiving ends of an Internet transmission.

12. For my fuller discussion of relational databases, see chapter 9 below. For a helpful explanation and history of relational databases intended for a general audience, see National Research Council, *Funding a Revolution*, chap. 6 ("The Rise of Relational Databases").

13. For the official documentation and specifications of XML (as well as related specifications), see the W3C site, esp. the pages "Extensible Markup Language (XML)" and "XML Core Working Group Public Page" (with links to specifications for XML 1.0 and 2.0). In my own, amateur experimentation with creating XML documents, schemas, and the stylesheets needed to display XML on the Web, I was initially assisted by two books that include sections for a general audience explaining the nature of XML: Young, *XML Step by Step*; and Watt, *SAMS Teach Yourself XML in 10 Minutes*. Also helpful for general explanations of such affiliated XML specifications or concepts as DTDs, schemas, validity, etc. is the O'Reilly XML.com Web site.

One historical difference between the text-encoding and database approaches is that the former followed open standards from the first while the latter has often relied on proprietary database programs. (More recently, developers have begun to use the open-source database MySQL, frequently with PHP scripting to move content back and forth to the Web.) But another difference tended to compensate for the above disadvantage: databases were designed from the first to be reversible in data flow. By contrast with most text-encoded digital archives in the past, therefore, a database-to-Web system could also easily be configured as a Web-to-database system, accommodating two-way interaction with the user (e.g., users could enter or revise content in a database through a Web form).

Despite these past differences, however, the trend is now clearly toward convergence between text encoding and databases. Just as SGML text encoding succeeded to XML (the encoding standard designed to make some of the logical rigor and power of SGML available in a fully distributed, networked, and display-oriented environment), so databases have moved in the direction of communicating (exporting/importing) in XML. (Reciprocally, XML is developing native XML databases and an XML Query language allowing it to act in a manner akin to relational databases.) XML is the glue or splice between the text-encoding and the database worlds.

14. Again, I am borrowing this example from Sperberg-McQueen and Burnard, "A Gentle Introduction to XML."

15. To facilitate the match between the discourse as it is structured on the originating machine and the processing or display formats on the receiving machine, moreover, XML documents are often also attended by an XSLT (Extensible Stylesheet Language Transformations) stylesheet designed to transform XML markup intelligently from one format into another. For display purposes, e.g., a stylesheet can transform XML into XHTML (XML-compliant HTML for Web browsers). For reference guides to these and other technical terms related to XML, see n. 13 above.

16. For Kittler's definition of discourse networks as including both "technologies and institutions," see n. 4 above.

17. Toffler, *The Third Wave*, 185, 273–75.

18. "The Semantic Web . . . is an extension of the current [Web] in which information is given well-defined meaning, better enabling computers and people to work in cooperation" (Berners-Lee, Hendler, and Lassila, "The Semantic Web," 37). The W3C overview page on the Semantic Web quotes this sentence. As the W3C also defines it: "The Semantic Web is the representation of data on the World Wide Web. It is a collaborative effort

led by W3C with participation from a large number of researchers and industrial partners. It is based on the Resource Description Framework (RDF), which integrates a variety of applications using XML for syntax and URIs for naming" (Miller et al., "Semantic Web").

19. *Web services* refers to the concatenation of software and specifications that allow businesses (and other institutions) to create automated, end-to-end or round-trip flows of information across varying hardware and software platforms. The goal is to allow databases or other applications, in effect, to serve each other without intervention so as to better serve end users. For example, the act of purchasing a product online could trigger a whole set of cross-business and cross-system transaction events (one database checking another for product availability, shipping schedules, customer credit information, and so on). To neutralize differences in software at each local end of a transmission, Web services usually require databases to send information to others in the standardized form of XML. A database thus needs to know only how to read XML content into its own processing methods and export again into XML; it does not need to know how to talk directly to another database. For a gentle introduction to Web services, see Lipschutz, "Brave New Apps."

20. The TEI quote is from Sperberg-McQueen and Burnard, "A Gentle Introduction to XML," par. 2.1.

21. The phenomenology of writing I indicate is subtly different from that of writing for most print publications, where it is only apparently true that authors need not know anything about how the content they create will be formatted or set. Relevant here is Johanna Drucker's discussion (in *The Visible Word*, 94–95) of "unmarked" typography (gray, graphically neutral blocks of text), which she identifies with traditional, high literature (most canonically, the Bible). In such typography, neutrality of presentation is really a testament of assumed uniformity of belief, seriousness, reading habits, and so on in the consuming audience—matched to appropriate conventions of genre and presentation in the production of books. Authors in effect know they are writing for an authoritative look. In contrast, the publication medium at the other end of an Internet transmission is far less standardized. It has fewer established generic or other constraints (unless it is a venue designed specifically to mimic some print genre, as in the case of many newspaper sites or, more extreme, sites serving their content in the Adobe pdf format so that a rendered online page looks exactly like a print page).

22. For an explanation of *data island*, see Woychowsky, "XML Data Islands Offer a Useful Mechanism to Display Web Form Data." *Data island* usually refers only to XML code embedded in a Web page that can be "bound" to HTML objects on that page. I coin the phrase *data pour* to generalize the phenomenon. In my usage, a data pour is code embedded in a Web page that is bound to (transfers information to or from) any data repository located *elsewhere*—whether XML data elsewhere on the Web page itself, XML data in separate documents and on separate servers, or database content. In the source code of a Web page, data islands or pours commonly appear as a congested, opaque concentration of non-HTML code or scripting (or non-HTML grafted onto/interwoven with HTML). Functionally, however, the opacity of the code is really transparency (like looking through an aperture or window) to content located elsewhere.

23. *Data island* is commonly used to describe the practice of "embedding" XML-coded data "inside HTML pages," as Microsoft's *MSDN Library* (s.v. "XML Data Islands") for programmers puts it. However, I will prefer the neologism *data pour* because I think it is more descriptive of the function of such embedded code, which is, not to be isolated, but, instead, to flood the foreground reading space with volumes of dynamic content originating in background automated sources seeming to the end user—and often also to the Web author—inexhaustible, unpredictable, and not fully controllable.

24. This is a database in Microsoft's Access program that I created initially in 2001 to house the image gallery for a graduate seminar I often teach, "Landscape and the Social Imaginary: Romantic Landscape and Cyberspace." Though my own database work began with proprietary programs (and also with the ASP scripting language used to create the middleware layer that transfers content to and from the Web), examples could also be drawn from open-source databases and scripting of the sort that my more recent database-to-Web sites draw on (e.g., using the WordPress blog or content-management system). Such sites are open-source "LAMP" applications—an acronym standing for the combination of Linux operating system, Apache Web server program, MySQL database program, and PHP scripting language.

25. This is code from a simple application of XML called *Tracker* (Hypertext Fiction Tracker) that I created in 2002 to illustrate how XML might facilitate teaching and research in the field of electronic literature. (See Liu, "Hypertext Fiction Tracker.") In particular, Tracker was intended to illustrate how XML could help a teacher navigate works of lexia-based hypertext fiction in the classroom (where such works can be difficult to navigate or point to in real time without interrupting the flow of class for an extended hunt and explore). The concept has since been superseded by the ideas articulated in the Electronic Literature Organization's PAD (Preservation / Archiving / Dissemination) initiative, for which I served as the head of the Technology / Software Committee (see Electronic Literature Organization, "PAD [Preservation, Archiving, Dissemination Initiative].") PAD proposes a road map for developing protocols and technologies that facilitate the preservation and scholarly manipulation of hypertextual, interactive, multimedia, and algorithmically generated new media literature.

Edward Falco's *Self-Portrait as Child with Father* is a Web-based hypertext fiction.

26. When I originally wrote this essay in 2002–3, what is now called *Web 2.0* was already being implemented and popularized through blogs, wikis, social-networking sites, etc., though the explicit formulation of the concept lagged by a few years. (See esp. O'Reilly's influential "What Is Web 2.0.") My observations here about data pours apply with even more force to Web 2.0, where user-produced content flows both in and out of back-end databases through "template" Web pages that are often elegant, minimalist designs built around an all-powerful, blind aperture of parameterized code—like a reverse black hole—that sucks all content in and throws it back out again. For example, on the template pages for the WordPress blog engine—one of the more popular (and increasingly general-purpose) content-management systems in the Web 2.0 universe—data pours through a section of the page dominated by non-HTML middleware code called *the loop*, which itself has no content but voraciously calls for content from a database via a structured repeat statement (essentially, "get me something like this, and then do it again and again, until you have exhausted the whole database"). Such loops are a contemporary form—a fetish—of desire. Beyond all need, they are hungry.

27. Manovich, "From Cultural Interfaces to Info-Aesthetics." See also Manovich, "Avant-Garde as Software." In developing this line of argument about the phenomenality of transcendental data sources, I am indebted to Jennifer Jones for an incisive question in a personal communication at an early point in my writing: How do end users, as opposed to the originating designers or programmers who work with the underlying source code, perceive such transcendence as differentiated from any other content that is rendered on a Web page? The presence of a data island, after all, is not explicit unless one looks at the source code, and, in the case of database-driven Web pages, even the source or underlying HTML code that a user might see by using the "view source" command in a browser is screened from view. (The apparent HTML code that produces the Web page a user sees is

generated on the fly by the real code in the background, which includes scripting or other algorithmic processes designed to write content into HTML.)

28. More complex interface designs are possible for data-pour pages, but they are uncommon because they are difficult to create. Complicated graphic design also tends to constrain the kind or quantity of information pulled out of the underlying content source (database or XML repository). My thanks for this qualification to an anonymous reader of this essay when it was originally submitted to *Critical Inquiry* as a preprint to be presented at the 2004 conference "Arts of Transmission" at the University of Chicago.

29. For an example of Web pages created by an RSS news-aggregator program, see the pages generated on the fly on a user's local machine by a free, downloadable aggregator program like AmphetaDesk.

30. For reasons indicated below, I do not develop the relation of religion to computing as more than an analogy. However, such an approach is possible. Stephen Johnson, e.g., discusses the computer interface as contemporary "infinity made imaginable" and compares such interfaces to Gothic cathedrals (*Interface Culture*, 42). See also Mitchum, "Computers."

31. My generic use of the term *protestant* refers to both the main lineages in the genealogy of computer hackers: the older (and still prevalent) tribe of programmers who legitimately jigger systems to create novel, ingenious, or work-around solutions and the newer tribe of transgressive hackers. In my secularized usage, *protestant* alludes to the complex blend of belief in direct data access (rather than priestly mediation) and maverick action that both tribes share. For a fuller discussion of the dual, but uncannily overlapping, heritage of hackers, see Liu, *Laws of Cool*, app. C ("'Ethical Hacking' and Art").

32. A fuller genealogy of the belief structures underlying discourse network 2000 would also need to add alongside the postdivine paradigm of the transcendental sublime the romantic sense of immanental nature (and, as Kittler argues in his discussion of discourse network 1800, of the "mother")—all sources of an original, ulterior, or transcendental source of meaning. For Kittler on the "mother's mouth," see *Discourse Networks*, 25–69.

33. The latter statement is actually XSLT, a specification for stylesheets that "transform" XML documents into some other form (see n. 15 above).

34. Liu, *Laws of Cool*, is a fuller meditation on the condition of postindustrialism.

35. Drucker, *Managing in Turbulent Times*, 226. I also cite this Drucker dictum in Liu, *Laws of Cool*, where I discuss postindustrial business theory at length (see both the preface to pt. 1 and chap. 1).

36. Piez is now working in the private sector as a consultant and developer of electronic text systems. My thanks to Piez for extensive, generous correspondence on Hall and XML following our meeting at the 2001 ACH-ALLC (Association for Computers and the Humanities–Association for Literary and Linguistic Computing) conference at New York University, where I gave a keynote address from *Laws of Cool* in which I speculated in an early, sketchy way on the connection between Taylor and text encoding. In the following discussion, I draw on correspondence with Piez, supplemented by further research into Hall's manufacturing process.

37. Smith, *Harpers Ferry Armory and the New Technology*, 79.

38. Ibid., 79–82.

39. Ibid., 108.

40. On Hall's appointment, see ibid., 155–56.

41. Wendell Piez, e-mail to the author, 20 June 2001. Subsequent citations of Piez reference this letter.

42. Smith, *Harpers Ferry Armory and the New Technology*, 225–26.

43. *Validation* refers to the process of checking the encoded content of a document marked up according to XML against the DTD or schema for that document.

44. On Hall's use of bearing points, see Smith, *Harpers Ferry Armory and the New Technology*, 227.

45. Smith sums up Hall's contribution to industrial manufacture in a way that chimes with my emphasis here on the systemic nature of Hall's innovation as embodied in machine tools and gauges: "What was so startlingly new about the Harpers Ferry experiment was the extent to which Hall had mechanized his operations and the impressive results he had actually achieved. . . . Much of the excitement generated [among observers at the time] can be traced directly to Hall's success in combining men, machines, and precision-measurement methods into a *practical* system of production" (ibid., 249).

46. Taylor, *The Principles of Scientific Management*, 40–48, 65–71, 86–97.

47. Ibid., 77, 79.

48. "In the type of management advocated by the writer, this complete standardization of all details and methods is not only desirable but absolutely indispensable as a preliminary to specifying the time in which each operation shall be done, and then insisting that it shall be done within the time allowed" (Taylor, *Shop Management*, 123). The insistence on standardization despite objections based on the apparent uniqueness of tasks or workers was also explicit in William Henry Leffingwell's early-twentieth-century books applying scientific management to office work (see, e.g., Leffingwell and Robinson, *Textbook of Office Management*, 392–95).

49. Taylor, *Shop Management*, 102–3.

50. Yates, *Control through Communication*. Yates is careful to situate Taylor as only part of a more general phenomenon of "systematic management" (see ibid., 9–11). I am grateful to John Guillory for sending me a manuscript version of his essay "The Memo and Modernity," which first pointed me to Yates's book. Guillory subsequently presented his essay at the same University of Chicago "Arts of Transmission" conference in 2004 (leading to the *Critical Inquiry* issue on that topic) at which I presented the preprint version of this essay.

51. Taylor, *Shop Management*, 102–4.

52. For a discussion of work from industrialism to postindustrialism that focuses in part on the connection between Taylor's "friendly" management and today's "user-friendly" computing interfaces, see Liu, *Laws of Cool*, chaps. 2–4.

53. On the new class, see, e.g., Ehrenreich and Ehrenreich, "The Professional-Managerial Class." For a fuller discussion of the theory of the new class, see Liu, *Laws of Cool*, chap. 1.

54. See Dyck, "Clash of the Titans."

55. Especially interesting are the innovations in office equipment or practices recommended by Leffingwell that eerily anticipate what I have called *discourse network 2000*. Modular unit bins, modular desks, and colored-ink systems for facilitating document-based work, e.g., might be approximated to later hardware and software invented to sort documents in modular and flexible ways (see Leffingwell, *Scientific Office Management*, 22, 25, 20). The most striking premonition is to be found in Leffingwell's codification of improvements in letter writing—i.e., document-content creation (e.g., writing, typewriting), document transmission (e.g., through mechanical conveyance systems in the office), and managed document consumption (e.g., ways of sorting, filing, and copying letters from the public). His approach to office correspondence produced lists of standard paragraphs (or variants of standard paragraphs) that could be prewritten,

classified in a hierarchical classification of paragraph types and topics (not unlike an XML DTD or schema), and then assembled into actual letters to the public or other businesses by selecting, shuffling, and concatenating indexical paragraph numbers. "I have seen a system consisting of over 600 paragraphs easily handled by high-school girls who glibly discussed the relative merits of a letter consisting of paragraphs 'A2, B14, J26' as compared with 'A12, B22, J26,'" he says (ibid., 94). For a typical hierarchy of standard correspondence paragraphs, see ibid., 93. (On the use of standard letter greetings and headings in internal office communications or memos, see Yates, *Control through Communication*, 70–71. Yates's work is especially useful in its analysis of internal office communication as a separate field of discourse.) Such correspondence systems in Leffingwell even came complete with what amounts to XSLT stylesheets, as in the case of the style guide he reproduces at one point that begins: "As we desire uniformity of style in the arrangement of all letters leaving our office, you will please use this letter as a model for future correspondence. . . . Begin the letter addressing the customer one space beneath the dot on the upper left hand side" (Leffingwell, *Scientific Office Management*, 137).

56. Leffingwell and Robinson, *Textbook of Office Management*, 19. A recent ad for IBM's open-standards approach to business information services makes an interestingly similar comparison to the era of manufacturing—specifically, to manufacturing in the wake of Hall's interchangeable parts philosophy. The ad copy begins: "In 1864, a bolt or screw made in one machine shop wouldn't fit a nut made in another machine shop. . . . Until William Sellers proposed a standard, uniform screw. So one part could be made down the street, and another made across town, and assembly could happen anywhere. Everything worked together. Apply the same logic to IT and you arrive at open standards like Linux" (*Business Week*, 22 September 2003, 101).

57. Yates, *Control through Communication*, 81, 80. The phrase "general logical rule for all forms" is from the language of one office systematizer whom Yates quotes.

58. Leffingwell quoted in Yates, *Control through Communication*, 94.

59. Yates, *Control through Communication*, esp. 6–8.

60. For a discussion of synopticism and the trope of vision in Zuboff's interviews with information workers, see Liu, *Laws of Cool*, chap. 3.

61. Not only does almost all the prolific business literature about workplace 2000, workforce 2000, the virtual corporation, and so on emphasize such a break, but so too does much scholarly theory of postindustrialism or postmodernism. The focus has been on the difference between industrialism (with its assembly lines, vertically integrated companies, hierarchical management, and so forth) and postindustrial chaos management, flat or networked companies, team management, and knowledge-work industries. For a critical survey of contemporary business literature in its best-seller mode, see Micklethwait and Wooldridge, *The Witch Doctors*. See also the discussion of such works in Liu, *Laws of Cool*, preface to pt. 1 and chap. 1.

62. Of course, Marx on the alienation of work (especially in those sketchy, early writings published as Marx and Engels, *Economic and Philosophic Manuscripts of 1844*) cannot be taken as our final word. There is also the entire contemporary infrastructure and superstructure of networking to consider, according to which decentralized processes of data circulation morph the concept of alienation (and the early-industrial context of commodification that Marx addressed) into what Manuel Castells calls "network society" and Michael Hardt and Antonio Negri simply "empire," where distributed, incommensurable, and sometimes contradictory modes of data production and consumption extend the theory of work into uncharted territory (see Castells, *The Information Age*; and Hardt and Negri, *Empire*). To survey this territory would require the assistance, not only of

established class theory, but also of more recent new class theory in combination with even newer frameworks of analysis (such as global studies).

63. See Hayles, *How We Became Posthuman*, 17. See also Gessler, "Skeuomorphs and Cultural Algorithms."

64. Taylor and Leffingwell were most successful at standardizing and managing the managerial art of time-motion study, the lower-order function of scientific management. Both, e.g., give elaborate instructions in their works on how to use a stopwatch to study work and chart or analyze the results.

65. My thanks to Rita Raley for the manuscript in progress of *Reading Code*, which includes materials related to her previously published articles on "codework" (e.g., "Interferences").

66. Stallabrass, "The Aesthetics of Net Art." Stallabrass's phrase is "the sublime of data." My thanks to Stallabrass for correspondence and conversation on digital art.

67. Gibson, *Neuromancer*, 180–81.

68. The following passage in Pynchon's *The Crying of Lot 49* speaks eloquently of a transcendental data pour whose revelation is never immediately available to consciousness lived on the interface: "She [Oedipa Maas] could, at this stage of things, recognize signals like that, as the epileptic is said to—an odor, color, pure piercing grace note announcing his seizure. Afterward it is only this signal, really dross, this secular announcement, and never what is revealed during the attack, that he remembers. Oedipa wondered whether, at the end of this (if it were supposed to end), she too might not be left with only compiled memories of clues, announcements, intimations, but never the central truth itself, which must somehow each time be too bright for her memory to hold; which must always blaze out, destroying its own message irreversibly, leaving an overexposed blank when the ordinary world came back" (76).

69. For an introduction to Novak's transarchitecture, see his "Liquid~, Trans~, Invisible~." Novak discussed his notion of allogenesis at a talk on transvergence and allogenesis at the University of California, Santa Barbara.

70. Jevbratt, "Interface: *Every*."

71. Jevbratt explains the color scheme for the *"Every"* interface as follows: "The color of a pixel in the 'every: IP' interface is generated by using the second octet (200.*93*.167.214) for its red value, the third for its green (200.93.*167*.214), and the fourth for its blue value (200.93.167.*214*)" (ibid.). The term *postphotographic* occurs in Ekenberg's prologue to Jevbratt's *1:1*.

72. Jevbratt, "Interface: *Migration*." My discussion of Jevbratt's background as a painter and her interfaces for *1:1* benefits from Jevbratt's own comments about her work in informal talks she has given at the University of California, Santa Barbara, including her talks on 14 January and 17 April 2002.

73. Lyotard, "Answering the Question: What Is Postmodernism?" 81.

74. For a fuller description of cool as a style on the Web, see Liu, *Laws of Cool*, chap. 6. CGI, or Common Gateway Interface, allows programs running on a Web server to be activated by, or transfer information to, Web pages through relatively simple go-between programs (often written in the Perl scripting language). Though still common, CGI scripts are no longer dominant, ceding their role (for efficiency and other reasons) to such more modern scripting languages as ASP and PHP, which are increasingly prevalent for mediating between the Web and programs running on a server. *Push* refers to a method by which a Web server can send fresh content to a user's browser without the user needing to refresh the page.

75. See Liu, *Laws of Cool*, esp. chap. 2. See also Dinerstein, *Swinging the Machine.*

76. See Tschichold, *The New Typography.* On grid design, see Kung, "The Grid System."

77. Kittler, *Discourse Networks*, esp. the chapter titled "The Great Lalulā."

Chapter 9

1. I created the panels here referred to during a leave year spent in Madison, Wisconsin, while I was at work on my *Wordsworth: The Sense of History.* Somewhere in repeated travels back and forth between Madison and New Haven in the succeeding years, the wall charts (carefully folded and packed away for oblivion) were lost.

2. See chapter 3 above. My gratitude to Steven Goldsmith, who, in his introduction to my Beckman lecture, "Transcendental Data," pointed out the relation between the "matrix of detail" in my essay "Local Transcendence" (chapter 3 above) and my later work in information technology and new media.

3. See *Romantic Chronology*, ed. Mandell and Liu, originally created in 1995–96 in the form of static Web pages and then in 1999 migrated to a database-to-Web system. Rita Raley and Carl Stahmer assisted in the original creation of the site.

4. See *Voice of the Shuttle*, ed. Liu, which was originally created in 1994 and then migrated in 2001 into a SQL Server–to–Web database system designed by Robert Adlington and Jeremy Douglass.

5. *OED.*

6. I use *end of history* here in a manner that emphasizes its postmodern and post-industrial connotation as a release from history. However, Francis Fukuyama's now-paradigmatic, neo-Hegelian thesis of the end of history also incorporates the sense of a historical *determination* to be free (motivated by the dual drives of rational economic process and the "struggle for recognition"). See Fukuyama, *The End of History and the Last Man* (whose third part is titled "The Struggle for Recognition"). One of the goals of my present essay is to develop an alternative informational framework for understanding the paradox of "determination to be free"—one that might unchain the understanding of conditional freedom (externally programmed *and* self-programmed freedom) from the neoliberal globalism that today has captured the original Hegelian dialectic and enslaved it to rational economic process.

7. My base text for *The Ninth Bridgewater Treatise* is the second edition as reproduced in vol. 9 of *The Works of Charles Babbage.* (Unless otherwise indicated, all citations are to this version, cited as *The Ninth Bridgewater Treatise* [1989].) However, I have also consulted the first edition (1837).

8. The most noted of the official Bridgewater Treatises—William Whewell's *Astronomy and General Physics Considered with Reference to Natural Theology* (1833)—had dismissed "deductive" mathematics as irrelevant to natural theology. "We have no reason whatever," Whewell said about mathematicians, "to expect from their speculations any help, when we ascend to the first cause and supreme ruler of the universe" (quoted by Babbage on the title page of his treatise). (For facsimile reproductions of Babbage's title pages of 1837 and 1838, both of which bear the quote from Whewell, see *The Ninth Bridgewater Treatise* [1989], iv, iii. For background on the Bridgewater Treatises and Babbage's entry into the lists, see ibid., 5–7; and Hyman, *Charles Babbage*, 136–42.)

In retrospect, Babbage's effort in this treatise to prevent a further widening of the gap between theoretical mathematics and the empirical sciences may be seen to be part of what his modern biographer, Hyman, calls the great, lost "battle for applied science" that he fought throughout his life (*Charles Babbage*, 1). As a compound problem in the metaphysical *and* physical engineering of the universe, we deduce, natural theology must have been a conundrum as irresistible to Babbage as his calculating machines, which also split the difference between pure mathematics and mechanical design.

9. The best-known precedent is William Paley's *Natural Theology* (originally published in 1802), which contains on its first page the famous thought experiment, "Suppose I had found a *watch* upon the ground. . . . "

10. In his appended "Note B," Babbage writes concerning the Analytical Engine: "About October, 1834, I commenced the design of another, and far more powerful engine. . . . As the remaining illustrations [in this treatise] are all drawn from the powers of this new engine, it may be right to state, that . . . at any period previously fixed upon, or contingent on certain events, it will cease to tabulate [an] algebraic function, and commence the calculation of a different one, and that these changes may be repeated to any extent" (*The Ninth Bridgewater Treatise* [1989], 68).

11. This explanation is a simplification in particular of Babbage's second chapter, titled "Argument in Favour of Design from the Changing of Laws in Natural Events" (ibid., 4–11). As Hyman puts it in his biography: "Babbage saw God as a being of science and programmer who defined the entire future of the universe at the time of the Creation as a sort of infinite set of programs" (*Charles Babbage*, 137).

12. Immediately after putting his question, Babbage concludes: "[We] cannot for a moment hesitate in pronouncing that that for which, after its original adjustment, no superintendance is required, displays far greater ingenuity than that which demands, at every change in its law, the direct intervention of its contriver" (*The Ninth Bridgewater Treatise* [1989], 8). He continues: "To have *foreseen*, at the creation of matter and of mind, that a period would arrive when matter, assuming its prearranged combinations, would become susceptible of the support of vegetable forms; that these should in due time themselves supply the pabulum of animal existence; that successive races of giant forms or of microscopic beings should at appointed periods necessarily rise into existence, and as inevitably yield to decay; and that decay and death—the lot of each individual existence—should also act with equal power on the races which they constitute; that the extinction of every race should be as certain as the death of each individual, and the advent of new genera be as inevitable as the destruction of their predecessors; to have foreseen all these changes, and to have provided, by one comprehensive law, for all that should ever occur, either to the races themselves, to the individuals of which they are composed, or to the globe which they inhabit, manifests a degree of power and of knowledge of a far higher order" (10).

13. Babbage's *Ninth Bridgewater Treatise* was published as a fragmentary work and is, in fact, too full of digressions and loose ends to be conceived of strictly as a hierarchy (or nesting) of arguments. My notion of nested here is just a figure for those modules in Babbage's argument that seem clearly subordinate even if we cannot always identify the exact relation of subordination between the various chapters and the overall argument (as would be required for an actual computer program).

14. Babbage includes the relevant excerpt from Laplace in a note appended to his ninth chapter (see *The Ninth Bridgewater Treatise* [1989], "Note C," pp. 70–71).

15. Ibid., 36–37.

16. Ibid., 38. Babbage resumes his meditations on crime and punishment at greater length in chap. 14 of the 1838 edition ("Thoughts on the Nature of Future Punishments"). The break between this paragraph, where the 1837 version of the chapter ended, and subsequent material added in 1838 (discussed below) is indicated by the editor. While I

have quoted only the 1838 text, I have also consulted the first edition, where the paragraph differs only in minor points of punctuation (*The Ninth Bridgewater Treatise* [1837], 116–17).

17. Ibid., 38–39. The biblical allusion at the end of this passage to the "prophet's denunciation" is supplied by Babbage in a footnote: "And Nathan said unto David—*Thou art the man*" (ibid., 39n).

18. Ibid., 38–39n. In transcribing from the *Quarterly Review*, Babbage introduces only minor variations and some punctuation changes. (Compare the original report by Captain Hayes in the *Parliamentary Papers* as quoted in the *Quarterly Review* [55 (December 1835 and February 1836): 253–54].) Except for the two emphases I have added, the emphases that Babbage includes were in the *Quarterly Review* (with slight variations).

After this extract from the *Quarterly Review*, Babbage's note continues: "When the ink was scarcely dry on the paper on which the remarks in the text, suggested by a former description of the atrocities of the slave trade, was written, the following paragraph caught my attention: 'Slave trade.—His Majesty's ship *Thalia*, 31, Captain R. Wauchope, has captured on the coast of Africa, two slave vessels—one the *Félicité*, 611 slaves; the other, the *Adalia*, with 409 slaves. It appears the latter vessel had been chased by the boats of one of our cruizers, and to avoid being come up with she threw overboard upwards of 150 of the poor wretches who were on board, besides almost all her heavy stores.'— *Western Luminary*, May, 1837" (ibid., 39n).

19. Burke, *Reflections on the Revolution in France*, 194–95, 193.

20. I refer to the point in the "Review of Soame Jenyns, *A Free Enquiry into the Nature and Origin of Evil*" when Johnson, coming to Jenyns's argument that those destined to be poor should not be vexed by an education inappropriate to them, asks piercingly (where the italicized phrases are Jenyns's): "Though it should be granted, that those who are *born to poverty and drudgery*, should not be *deprived* by an *improper education* of the *opiate* of *ignorance*, even this concession will not be of much use to direct our practice, unless it be determined who are those that are *born to poverty*. To entail irreversible poverty upon generation after generation only because the ancestor happened to be poor is in itself, cruel, if not unjust" (Johnson, *Samuel Johnson*, ed. Greene, 529).

21. "Anaphora: repetition of same word at beginning of successive clauses or verses" (Lanham, *A Handlist of Rhetorical Terms*, 130).

22. From Wordsworth's "Lines Written a Few Miles above Tintern Abbey" (Wordsworth, *William Wordsworth*, ed. Gill, 134 [lines 94–103]):

> And I have felt
> A presence that disturbs me with the joy
> Of elevated thoughts; a sense sublime
> Of something far more deeply interfused,
> Whose dwelling is the light of setting suns,
> And the round ocean, and the living air,
> And the blue sky, and in the mind of man,
> A motion and a spirit, that impels
> All thinking things, all objects of all thought,
> And rolls through all things.

The *and*'s in this vision of the One Life characteristic of Wordsworth's and Coleridge's work ca. 1798 chime hauntingly against those in Babbage's note quoting the witness of the slave ship. We might say that nature was the universal slave ship for the romantics— somehow at once inevitable ("rolled round in earth's diurnal course," Wordsworth says about Lucy in "A Slumber Did My Spirit Seal" (ibid., 147 [line 7]); propelled by unseen spirits, Coleridge imagines in "The Rime of the Ancient Mariner") *and* free to be piloted by the romantic subject. "Therefore am I still / A lover of the meadows and the woods, / And mountains; and of all that we behold" (ibid., 134 ["Tintern Abbey," lines 103–5]), Wordsworth continues after the "rolls through all things" above—as if he had a choice (akin to Shelley's expansive ethos of "love") in the matter.

23. See also chapter 8 above, where, in the conclusion, I suggest that Turner's *Light and Colour: The Morning after the Deluge* (1843) may be analogized to a transcendental database pouring forth what seems to be a first record: an image of Moses writing the Pentateuch.

24. Bush, "As We May Think"; Nelson, *Literary Machines*. On Nelson's notion of "historical backtrack," see ibid., sec. 3, pp. 12–13 (each section of the work is paginated independently).

25. Raymond Boyce and Donald Chamberlin developed the SQL language at IBM (see Bostrup, "Introduction to Relational Databases").

The discussion of database theory that follows is informed primarily by the following works: Codd, *The Relational Model for Database Management, Version 2*; Date, *An Introduction to Database Systems*; Rob and Coronel, *Database Systems*; and Stanczyk, et al., *Theory and Practice of Relational Databases*. I am indebted to my friend and colleague Amr El Abbadi, a database scholar in the Computer Science Department at the University of California, Santa Barbara, for excellent discussion over the years relating to database theory and research.

26. For a textbook review of hierarchical and network databases, see Rob and Coronel, *Database Systems*, 24–33. Network databases were similar to hierarchical databases in having something like a tree structure, but with the variation that each branch in the data tree could have more than a single parent trunk (or root), thus allowing for more flexible modelings of data.

27. I take the expedient step here of inventing my own example. The example is of the sort well established in database textbooks, whose illustrative instances of tables often premise a typical business use.

28. As William Kent puts it succinctly in "A Simple Guide to Five Normal Forms in Relational Database Theory," an ideal database table—more precisely, a table in "third normal form" and "Boyce Codd Normal Form"—is one in which "each attribute must represent a fact about the key, the whole key, and nothing but the key" (to quote the "slightly paraphrased" version adapted and cited in Date, *An Introduction to Database Systems*, 379). (Kent's original sentence reads: "Under second and third normal forms, a non-key field must provide a fact about the key, us[e] the whole key, and nothing but the key.")

29. On why it is often optimal to stop at the third normal form, see Rob and Coronel, *Database Systems*, 176. On the limitations of SQL, see Codd, *Relational Model for Database Management, Version 2*, 371–89. On SQL's "sins of omission and commission," see Date, *An Introduction to Database Systems*, 98.

30. Nulls were eventually written into relational database theory by Codd, but with deep misgivings about the fact that database programs typically process nulls unsystematically (see, e.g., Codd, *Relational Model for Database Management, Version 2*, 197–98). Nulls have remained controversial. On the incommensurability between three-value logic or nulls and relational theory, see esp. Date, *Introduction to Database Systems*, chap. 18 ("Missing Information"). As Date colorfully puts it, nulls "undermine the entire foundation of the relational model" and "wreck the relational model" (594, 600). There

is even a hint of essentialism in Date's stance. "There is no such thing as a null in the real world," he says (600n). And, of course, from the point of view of the novice or even middling database programmer (as I can personally attest), nulls are the source of fundamental errors. It would be interesting to compare the notion of the null with such philosophical or aesthetic notions now familiar to modern and postmodern humanists as *antithesis* (Hegel), *either/or* (Kierkegaard), *paradox* or *ambiguity* (the New Critics), *mana* and *trickster* (anthropology), *différance* (Derrida), *wasp/orchid* (Deleuze and Guattari), *hybridity* (postcolonial theory), *queer* (gender theory), etc. My own concept of the *ethos of the unknown* is apropos (see *Laws of Cool*, esp., 9, 72, 179, 304–6, 382–83, 385–86). The operational demand that *null* adds to such concepts—one not well accommodated in the humanities—is calculability.

31. Date comments: "Any scalar comparison in which one of the comparands is null evaluates to the *unknown* truth value, instead of to *true* or *false*" (*An Introduction to Database Systems*, 584). For a working out in detail of the implication of nulls for various relational operations, see ibid., 584–612 (chap. 18, "Missing Information").

32. See Rob and Coronel, *Database Systems*, 611–64; and Date, *Introduction to Database Systems*, 694–729.

33. The following summary of MyLifeBits derives primarily from the most detailed of the group's papers that I was able to find at the time of this writing: Gemmell et al., "Living with a Lifetime Store" (esp. the section "Data Model") and "MyLifeBits: Fulfilling the Memex Vision." However, I also cite other papers by the MyLifeBits group where useful.

The influence on the MyLifeBits project of Vannevar Bush and Ted Nelson is self-advertised. For example, the title "MyLifeBits: Fulfilling the Memex Vision" alludes to Bush, while "Living with a Lifetime Store" credits both Bush and Nelson. Even the eye-camera used by Gordon Bell (see below) follows up on Bush's idea for head-mounted, "walnut"-sized cameras recording anything and everything. (Compare other eye-camera recording technology created at Hewlett-Packard and MIT [see Port, "Innovations"; and Emory, "Memory Glasses for Total Recall"].)

34. On Total Recall, see "IBM's Budding Innovators." On LifeLog, see Gage, LifeLog homepage. On Memories for Life, see Fitzgibbon and Reiter, "'Memories for Life.'" On Time-Machine Computing, see Rekimoto, Time-Machine Computing homepage. On Shoebox, see Mills et al., "Shoebox."

35. According to the calculations of the MyLifeBits group, e.g., it would "take you five years to fill up your current 80 GB hard drive" with e-mail, cached or stored Web pages, scanned documents, books in digital form, or digital photos and music, and, "once you upgrade to a terabyte disk [1,024 gigabytes], it will take more than 60 additional years to fill." The group adds that even video "shot 24 hours a day, seven days a week," fits in a terabyte if the video bit rate is kept low or moderate (Gemmell et al., "Living with a Lifetime Store," 2).

36. MyLifeBits Project homepage; Gemmell et al., "MyLifeBits: Fulfilling the Memex Vision," 1.

37. Festa, "Total Recall." The quotations regarding Gordon Bell's hat-mounted camera are from Gemmell et al., "The MyLifeBits Lifetime Store," 1.

38. The MyLifeBits group identifies its core problem in this way: "Once we see the feasibility of collecting and storing vast amounts of information, the challenge becomes making use of it. There is no point in constructing a 'Write Once Read Never' memory" (Gemmell et al., "Living with a Lifetime Store," 2). In succeeding paragraphs, the group

invokes sequentially the approaches of Bush's Memex, Nelson's hypertext, and the database (ibid., 2–3).

39. The MyLifeBits group uses the term *blob* in Gemmell et al., "MyLifeBits: Fulfilling the Memex Vision," 4. For a definition of *blob*, see, e.g., *Hyperdictionary*, s.v. *binary large object*.

40. There have also been efforts to allow computers to analyze blobs automatically. See, e.g., the discussion by the Shoebox project group of its attempts at image index-ing and image-content analysis based on various grid segmentations of an image (Mills et al., "Shoebox," 3–4). However, machine recognition of image files has so far been notably disappointing. The Shoebox group, e.g., concludes: "For the management of personal photograph collections, retrieval both by date and annotations out-performed visual-based retrieval. We conclude that visual-based retrieval tools may not be especially valuable" (ibid., 7).

41. Gemmell et al., "MyLifeBits: Fulfilling the Memex Vision," 3.

42. Ibid., 3–4.

43. See esp. Gemmell et al., "Living with a Lifetime Store," 4–6. There is overlap between the notion of semantically aware "strong typing" in the MyLifeBits schema and Tim Berners-Lee's notion of the Semantic Web based on metadata standards rather than database schemas (see Berners-Lee et al., "The Semantic Web").

44. Gemmell et al., "Living with a Lifetime Store," 7, and "The MyLifeBits Lifetime Store," 3.

45. Programming here is my allegory for historical experience, just as psychoanalysis served the same purpose in "The History of the Anecdote," Joel Fineman's well-known essay on the New Historicism. The escape character that I fetishize is the code for what Fineman, in a passage I touched on in the introduction to this volume, calls "the hole and rim" of the anecdote (61). (The full passage is quoted in n. 45, introduction, above.)

46. Gallagher and Greenblatt, *Practicing New Historicism*, 22, 28. On the relation between Renaissance New Historicism and Tillyard's *Elizabethan World Picture*, see n. 2, chapter 1, above.

47. Gallagher and Greenblatt, *Practicing New Historicism*, 28, 51, 53.

48. On anamorphosis, see Greenblatt, *Renaissance Self-Fashioning*, 17–26 (also discussed in chapter 1 above).

49. In citing the "wreathes of smoke" at Tintern Abbey in Wordsworth's poem as a testament to history-as-displacement, I allude to Marjorie Levinson's strong, subtle read-ing of the poem (see *Wordsworth's Great Period Poems*, chap. 1, esp. 42–43), one of the most definitive and influential of the early New Historicist readings of romanticism.

50. Liu, *Wordsworth: The Sense of History*, esp. 31–51. The tension I indicate here between the levitas and the gravitas of the New Historicist anecdote is comparable to that which Ross foregrounds between the conditional and the categorical in his treatment of the anecdote in "Contingent Predilections" (see n. 25, introduction, above).

51. Gallagher and Greenblatt, *Practicing New Historicism*, 31.

52. Ibid., 51.

53. Compare Ross on the derivation of *contingency* ("Contingent Predilections," 491 [quoted in n. 25, introduction, above). Also apropos to my argument here is Ross on how accidents "enable us to act in ways that go against our conditioning" (ibid., 491 [quoted in n. 46, introduction, above]).

54. Esposito, "The Arts of Contingency," 9, 24.

55. I am grateful for Elena Esposito's fine conversation at dinner on 22 May 2004,

during the University of Chicago Franke Institute's conference "Arts of Transmission" (where she presented "The Arts of Contingency" as a paper).

56. See Elster, *Ulysses Unbound*, 200. See also Elster, *Explaining Technical Change*.

57. For my own discussion of contemporary creativity theory caught in the divergence between rational-choice theory and emergence (or complexity) theory, see Liu, "'A Forming Hand.'"

Works Cited /

To find Web sites that have moved to a different URL since the citations in this book were finalized, readers are advised first to try a search engine. To find sites that are now defunct, or to view past versions of continuing sites, readers can use the Internet Archive's Wayback Machine: http://web.archive .org/. Searching for a URL in this archive returns multiple versions of old Web sites, going back to ca. fall 1996. Web sites that have vanished and cannot be accessed through the Wayback Machine or by other means (e.g., because their content was dynamically generated from databases or because their owners blocked access to automated search engine and indexing "crawlers") are flagged below as "now extinct."

Aarseth, Espen J. *Cybertext: Perspectives on Ergodic Literature*. Baltimore: Johns Hopkins University Press, 1997.

Abrams, M. H. "On Reading Wordsworth's *Lyrical Ballads*." Paper presented at the conference "Wordsworth and the Borders of Romanticism," Yale University, 14 November 1987.

Adorno, Theodor. *Aesthetic Theory*. Edited by Gretel Adorno and Rolf Tiedemann. Translated by C. Lenhardt. London: Routledge & Kegan Paul, 1984.

Aers, David, et al. *Literature, Language and Society in England, 1580–1680*. Dublin: Gill & Macmillan, 1981.

Alien. Directed by Ridley Scott. Twentieth Century–Fox, 1979.

Althusser, Louis. "Ideology and Ideological State Apparatuses (Notes towards an Investigation)." In *Lenin and Philosophy and Other Essays*. Translated by Ben Brewster. London: New Left, 1971.

———. *Lenin and Philosophy and Other Essays*. Translated by Ben Brewster. London: New Left, 1971.

Althusser, Louis, and Étienne Balibar. *Reading Capital*. Translated by Ben Brewster. London: New Left, 1970.

American Mosaic: Multicultural Readings in Context. Edited by Barbara Roche Rico and Sandra Mano. Boston: Houghton Mifflin, 1991.

AmphetaDesk. Homepage. http://www.disobey.com/amphetadesk/ (retrieved 17 October 2003).

Annual Register; or, A View of the History, Politics, and Literature for the Year. . . . London: J. Dodsley, various years after 1758.

Appleton, Jay. *The Experience of Landscape*. Rev. ed. Chichester: John Wiley, 1996.

Arac, Jonathan. *Critical Genealogies: Historical Situations for Postmodern Literary Studies*. New York: Columbia University Press, 1987.

Attridge, Derek, et al. *Post-Structuralism and the Question of History*. Cambridge: Cambridge University Press, 1987.

Auerbach, Erich. *Mimesis: The Representation of Reality in Western Literature*. Translated by Willard R. Trask. Princeton, NJ: Princeton University Press, 1953.

Austin, J. L. *Philosophical Papers*. Oxford: Clarendon, 1961.

Babbage, Charles. *The Ninth Bridgewater Treatise: A Fragment*. 1st ed. London: J. Murray, 1837.

———. *The Ninth Bridgewater Treatise: A Fragment*. Vol. 9 of *The Works of Charles Babbage*, ed. Martin Campbell-Kelly. London: William Pickering, 1989. [This edition is based on the 1838 2nd ed.]

Baker, Keith Michael. "Memory and Practice: Politics and the Representation of the Past in Eighteenth-Century France." *Representations* 11 (Summer 1985): 134–64.

Bakhtin, M. M. [Mikhail]. *The Dialogic Imagination: Four Essays*. Edited by Michael Holquist. Translated by Caryl Emerson and Michael Holquist. Austin: University of Texas Press, 1981.

———. *Rabelais and His World*. Translated by Hélène Iswolsky. Bloomington: Indiana University Press, 1984.

Barlow, John Perry. "A Declaration of the Independence of Cyberspace." Electronic Frontier Foundation, 8 February 1996. http://www.eff.org/~barlow/Declaration-Final.html (retrieved 12 September 2001).

Barthes, Roland. "De l'ouevre au texte." *Revue d'Esthetique*, no. 3 (1971): 225–32. Translated by Josué V. Harari as "From Work to Text" in *Textual Strategies: Perspectives in Post-Structuralist Criticism*, ed. Josué V. Harari (Ithaca, NY: Cornell University Press, 1979).

———. *Elements of Semiology*. Translated by Annette Lavers and Colin Smith. New York: Hill & Wang, 1968.

———. "Myth Today." In *Mythologies*. Translated by Annette Lavers. New York: Hill & Wang, 1972.

———. "The Reality Effect." In *French Literary Theory Today: A Reader*, ed. Tzvetan Todorov, trans. R. Carter. New York: Cambridge University Press, 1982.

———. *S/Z*. Translated by Richard Miller. New York: Hill & Wang, 1974.

The Battleship Potemkin. Directed by Sergei Eisenstein. 1925.

Baudrillard, Jean. "The Ecstasy of Communication." In *The Anti-Aesthetic: Essays on Postmodern Culture*, ed. Hal Foster. Port Townsend, WA: Bay, 1983.

———. *The Ecstasy of Communication*. Translated by Bernard Schutze and Caroline Schutze. Edited by Sylvère Lotringer. New York: Semiotext(e), 1988.

———. "Fatal Strategies." Translated by Jacques Mourrain. In *Jean Baudrillard: Selected Writings*, ed. Mark Poster. Stanford, CA: Stanford University Press, 1988. [Excerpts from *Les Stratégies fatales* (1983).]

———. *Selected Writings*. Edited by Mark Poster. Stanford, CA: Stanford University Press, 1988.

———. "The Structural Law of Value and the Order of Simulacra." Translated by Charles Levin. In *The Structural Allegory: Reconstructive Encounters with the New French Thought* (Theory and History of Literature, vol. 11), ed. John Fekete. Minneapolis: University of Minnesota Press, 1984. [Excerpts from *L'Échange symbolique et la mort* (1976).]

———. "The Year 2000 Has Already Happened." In *Body Invaders: Panic Sex in America*, ed. Arthur and Marilouise Kroker. New York: St. Martin's, 1987.

Belsey, Catherine. *The Subject of Tragedy: Identity and Difference in Renaissance Drama*. London: Methuen, 1985.

Bender, John. "Eighteenth-Century Studies." In *Redrawing the Boundaries: The Transformation of English and American Literary Studies*, ed. Stephen Greenblatt and Giles Gunn. New York: Modern Language Association, 1992.

———. *Imagining the Penitentiary: Fiction and the Architecture of Mind in Eighteenth-Century England*. Chicago: University of Chicago Press, 1987.

Beniger, James R. *The Control Revolution: Technological and Economic Origins of the Information Society*. Cambridge, MA: Harvard University Press, 1986.

Benjamin, Walter. *The Arcades Project*. Translated by Howard Eiland and Kevin McLaughlin. Cambridge, MA: Harvard University Press, 1999. [Prepared on the basis of the German volume (of *Passagen-Werk*) edited by Rolf Tiedemann.]

———. "Theses on the Philosophy of History." In *Illuminations*, ed. Hannah Arendt, trans. Harry Zohn. New York: Schocken, 1969.

———. "The Work of Art in the Age of Mechanical Reproduction." In *Illuminations*, ed. Hannah Arendt, trans. Harry Zohn. New York: Schocken, 1969.

Berners-Lee, Tim, James Hendler, and Ora Lassila. "The Semantic Web." *Scientific American* 284, no. 5 (May 2001): 34–43. Also available at http://www.sciam.com/article.cfm?id=the-semantic-web (retrieved 7 December 2007).

Blade Runner. Directed by Ridley Scott. Warner Bros., 1982.

Blake, William. *Complete Writings*. Edited by Geoffrey Keynes. London: Oxford University Press, 1972.

Blake Archive. See *The William Blake Archive*.

Blakemore, Steven. *Burke and the Fall of Language: The French Revolution as Linguistic Event*. Hanover, NH: Brown University Press/University Press of New England, 1988.

Bloom, Harold. *The Anxiety of Influence: A Theory of Poetry*. New York: Oxford University Press, 1973.

Boas, George. *The History of Ideas: An Introduction*. New York: Scribner's, 1969.

Bostrup, Tore. "Introduction to Relational Databases: Pt. 1. Theoretical Foundation." *15 Seconds* (Jupitermedia Corp.), 22 May 2002. http://www.15seconds.com/Issue/020522.htm (retrieved 26 April 2004).

Bourdieu, Pierre. *Outline of a Theory of Practice*. Translated by Richard Nice. London: Cambridge University Press, 1977.

Braudel, Fernand. *The Mediterranean and the Mediterranean World in the Age of Philip II*. Translated by Siân Reynolds. 2nd rev. ed. 2 vols. New York: Harper & Row, 1976.

————. *On History*. Translated by Sarah Matthews. Chicago: University of Chicago Press, 1980.

Breitenberg, Mark, "'. . . the hole matter opened': Iconic Representation and Interpretation in 'The Quenes Majesties Passage.'" *Criticism* 28 (1986): 1–26.

Bristol, Michael D. *Carnival and Theater: Plebeian Culture and the Structure of Authority in Renaissance England*. New York: Methuen, 1985.

Brodersen, Momme. *Walter Benjamin: A Biography*. Translated by Malcolm R. Green and Ingrida Ligers. Edited by Martina Derviş. London: Verso, 1996.

Brooks, Cleanth. "Irony as a Principle of Structure." In *Literary Opinion in America: Essays Illustrating the Status, Methods, and Problems of Criticism in the United States in the Twentieth Century* (rev. ed.), ed. Morton Dauwen Zobel. New York: Harper, 1951.

————. *The Well Wrought Urn: Studies in the Structure of Poetry*. 1947. Reprint, San Diego: Harcourt Brace Jovanovich, 1975.

Brooks, Cleanth, and Robert Penn Warren, eds. *Understanding Poetry: An Anthology for College Students*. New York: Henry Holt, 1938.

Brown, Paul. "'This thing of darkness I acknowledge mine': *The Tempest* and the Discourse of Colonialism." In *Political Shakespeare: New Essays in Cultural Materialism*, ed. Jonathan Dollimore and Alan Sinfield. Ithaca, NY: Cornell University Press, 1985.

Brown University Women Writers Project. Directed by Julia Flanders. Homepage. http://www.wwp.brown.edu/ (retrieved 20 January 2003).

Buck-Morss, Susan. "Aesthetics and Anesthetics: Walter Benjamin's Artwork Essay Reconsidered." *October* 62 (Fall 1992): 3–41.

Burke, Edmund Burke. *Reflections on the Revolution in France*. Edited by Conor Cruise O'Brien. Harmondsworth: Penguin, 1969.

Burke, Kenneth. *Attitudes toward History*. 3rd ed. Berkeley and Los Angeles: University of California Press, 1984.

Bush, Vannevar. "As We May Think." In *The New Media Reader*, ed. Noah Wardrip-Fruin and Nick Montfort. Cambridge, MA: MIT Press, 2003. [Originally published in the July 1945 *Atlantic Monthly*.]

The Cambridge Guide to Literature in English. Edited by Ian Ousby. Cambridge: Cambridge University Press/Hamlyn, 1988.

The Cambridge History of American Literature. Vol. 1, *1590–1820*. Edited by Sacvan Bercovitch. Cambridge: Cambridge University Press, 1994.

Carlson, Julie. "An Active Imagination: Coleridge and the Politics of Dramatic Reform." *Modern Philology* 86, no. 1 (August 1988): 22–33.

Carnap, Rudolf. "The Elimination of Metaphysics through Logical Analysis of Language." Translated by Arthur Pap. In *Logical Positivism*, ed. A. J. Ayer. New York: Free Press, 1959.

————. "Psychology in Physical Language." Translated by George Schick. In *Logical Positivism*, ed. A. J. Ayer. New York: Free Press, 1959.

Cartelli, Thomas. "Ideology and Subversion in the Shakespearean Set Speech." *ELH* 53 (1986): 1–25.

————. "Prospero in Africa: *The Tempest* as Colonialist Text and Pretext." In *Shakespeare Reproduced: The Text in History and Ideology*, ed. Jean E. Howard and Marion F. O'Connor. New York: Methuen, 1987.

Casanova, Pablo González. "Internal Colonialism and National Development." *Studies in Comparative International Development* 1, no. 4 (1965): 27–37.

Castells, Manuel. *The Information Age: Economy, Society and Culture*. 3 vols. Malden, MA: Blackwell, 1996–98.

Castle, Terry. *Masquerade and Civilization: The Carnivalesque in Eighteenth-Century English Culture and Fiction.* Stanford, CA: Stanford University Press, 1986.

Celoria, Francis. "Chatterton, Wordsworth and Stonehenge." *Notes and Queries,* n.s., 23 (1976): 103–4.

Centre for Educational Research and Innovation (CERI). *Interdisciplinarity: Problems of Teaching and Research in Universities.* Paris: Organization for Economic Co-Operation and Development, 1972.

Chandler, Alfred D., Jr. *The Visible Hand: The Managerial Revolution in American Business.* Cambridge, MA: Belknap, 1977.

Chandler, James K. *Wordsworth's Second Nature: A Study of the Poetry and Politics.* Chicago: University of Chicago Press, 1984.

Charlesworth, Andrew, ed. *An Atlas of Rural Protest in Britain, 1548–1900.* Philadelphia: University of Pennsylvania Press, 1983.

Chartier, Roger. *Cultural History: Between Practices and Representations.* Translated by Lydia G. Cochrane. Ithaca, NY: Cornell University Press, 1988.

Chatterton, Thomas. *The Complete Works of Thomas Chatterton: A Bicentenary Edition.* Edited by Donald S. Taylor with Benjamin B. Hoover. 2 vols. Oxford: Oxford University Press, 1971.

———. *Poems, Supposed to Have Been Written at Bristol, by Thomas Rowley.* 1777. Facsimile reprint, Menston: Scolar, 1969.

Churchill, Sir Winston. Speech to House of Commons. The Churchill Centre, 20 August 1940. http://www.winstonchurchill.org/i4a/pages/index.cfm?pageid=420 (retrieved 10 November 2007).

Civilization. See Sid Meier's Civilization IV.

Clayton, Jade. *McGraw-Hill Illustrated Telecom Dictionary.* New York: McGraw-Hill, 1998.

Clayton, Jay. *Charles Dickens in Cyberspace: The Afterlife of the Nineteenth Century in Postmodern Culture.* Oxford: Oxford University Press, 2003.

Clover, Joshua. "Stock Footage; or, The Representability of World Systems." Paper presented at the conference "The Extreme Contemporary," Stanford University, Center for the Study of the Novel, 12 January 2007.

———. *Their Ambiguity.* Ann Arbor, MI: Quemadura, 2003. [Chapbook and CD.]

Lord Cockburn. *An Examination of the Trials for Sedition Which Have Hitherto Occurred in Scotland.* 1888. 2 vols. in 1. Reprint, New York: Augustus M. Kelley, 1970.

Codd, E. F. "A Relational Model of Data for Large Shared Data Banks." *Communications of the ACM* 13, no. 6 (June 1970): 377–87.

———. *The Relational Model for Database Management, Version 2.* Reading, MA: Addison-Wesley, 1990.

Cohen, Abner. *Two-Dimensional Man: An Essay on the Anthropology of Power and Symbolism in Complex Societies.* 1974. Reprint, Berkeley and Los Angeles: University of California Press, 1976.

Cohen, Ralph. "Innovation and Variation: Literary Change and Georgic Poetry." In *Literature and History: Papers Read at a Clark Library Seminar, March 3, 1973,* by Ralph Cohen and Murray Krieger. Los Angeles: William Andrews Clark Memorial Library, University of California, 1974.

Cohen, Walter. "Political Criticism of Shakespeare." In *Shakespeare Reproduced: The Text in History and Ideology,* ed. Jean E. Howard and Marion F. O'Connor. New York: Methuen, 1987.

Colebrook, Claire. *New Literary Histories: New Historicism and Contemporary Criticism.* Manchester: Manchester University Press, 1997.

Coleridge, Samuel Taylor. *Biographia Literaria; or, Biographical Sketches of My Literary Life and Opinions*. Edited by James Engell and W. Jackson Bate. Vol. 7 of *The Collected Works of Samuel Taylor Coleridge*. 2 vols. in 1. Princeton, NJ: Princeton University Press, 1983.

———. *Essays on His Times in "The Morning Post" and "The Courier."* Edited by David V. Erdman. 3 vols. Vol. 3 of *The Collected Works of Samuel Taylor Coleridge*. Princeton, NJ: Princeton University Press, 1978.

———. *The Notebooks of Samuel Taylor Coleridge*. Edited by Kathleen Coburn. Vol. 1, *1794–1804* (pt. 1, *Text*; pt. 2, *Notes*). New York: Pantheon, 1957.

———. *The Statesman's Manual*. In *Lay Sermons* (vol. 6 of *The Collected Works of Samuel Taylor Coleridge*), ed. R. J. White. Princeton, NJ: Princeton University Press, 1972.

Collingwood, R. G. *The Idea of History*. 1946. Reprint, Oxford: Oxford University Press, 1977.

The Columbia History of American Poetry. Edited by Jay Parini and Brett C. Miller. New York: Columbia University Press, 1993.

The Columbia History of British Poetry. Edited by Carl Woodring and James Shapiro. New York: Columbia University Press, 1994.

The Columbia History of the American Novel. Edited by Emory Elliott et al. New York: Columbia University Press, 1991.

Columbia Literary History of the United States. Edited by Emory Elliott et al. New York: Columbia University Press, 1988.

Daniel, Sharon, Mark Bartlett, and Puragra Guhathakurta, developers. Subtract the Sky. *See* Subtract the Sky.

DARnet. *See* under Digital Arts Research Network.

Darnton, Robert. *The Great Cat Massacre and Other Episodes in French Cultural History*. New York: Vintage, 1985.

———. "The Symbolic Element in History." *Journal of Modern History* 58 (1986): 218–34.

Date, C. J. *An Introduction to Database Systems*. 7th ed. Reading, MA: Addison-Wesley, 2000.

Davidson, Cathy N. "Big Humanities and Collaboration." Paper presented at "SECT III: TechnoSpheres/FutureS of Thinking," University of California, Irvine, 23 August 2006.

Davies, R. R. "Colonial Wales." *Past and Present* 65 (1974): 3–23.

——— [Rees Davies]. "Race Relations in Post-Conquest Wales: Confrontation and Compromise." *Transactions of the Honourable Society of Cymmrodorion*, 1974–75, 32–56.

Davis, David Brion, ed. *The Fear of Conspiracy: Images of Un-American Subversion from the Revolution to the Present*. Ithaca, NY: Cornell University Press, 1971.

Davis, Natalie Zemon. *The Return of Martin Guerre*. Cambridge, MA: Harvard University Press, 1983.

———. *Society and Culture in Early Modern France: Eight Essays*. Stanford, CA: Stanford University Press, 1975.

de Certeau, Michel. *The Practice of Everyday Life*. Translated by Steven Rendall. Berkeley and Los Angeles: University of California Press, 1984.

Decker's Patterns of Exposition (Instructor's Edition). 13th ed. New York: HarperCollins, 1992.

De Landa, Manuel. *A Thousand Years of Nonlinear History*. New York: Zone, 1997.

Deleuze, Gilles, and Félix Guattari. *A Thousand Plateaus: Capitalism and Schizophrenia*. Translated by Brian Massumi. Minneapolis: University of Minnesota Press, 1987.

del.icio.us. Homepage. http://del.icio.us/ (retrieved 7 March 2007).

de Man, Paul. "The Resistance to Theory." In *The Resistance to Theory*. Minneapolis: University of Minnesota Press, 1986.

———. "The Rhetoric of Temporality." In *Blindness and Insight: Essays in the Rhetoric of Contemporary Criticism*. 2d ed., rev. Minneapolis: University of Minnesota Press, 1983.

———. "Shelley Disfigured." In *Deconstruction and Criticism*, by Harold Bloom et al. New York: Seabury, 1979.

Derrida, Jacques. "Structure, Sign and Play in the Discourse of the Human Sciences." In *Writing and Difference*, trans. Alan Bass. Chicago: University of Chicago Press, 1978.

———. "White Mythology: Metaphor in the Text of Philosophy." Translated by F. C. T. Moore. *New Literary History* 6 (1974): 5–74.

Descartes, René. *Discourse on Method and Meditations*. Translated by Laurence J. Lafleur. Indianapolis: Bobbs-Merrill, 1960.

Dewey, John. *Experience and Nature*. In *John Dewey: The Later Works, 1925–1953*, vol. 1, *1925*, ed. Jo Ann Boydston with Patricia Baysinger and Barbara Levine. Carbondale: Southern Illinois University Press, 1981.

———. *The Philosophy of John Dewey*. Edited by John J. McDermott. 2 vols. in 1. 1973. Reprint, Chicago: University of Chicago Press, 1981.

Diacritics 15, no. 4 (Winter 1985). Special issue. *See* "Marx after Derrida."

Digital Arts Research Network (DARnet). Collectively directed University of California Multi-Campus Research Group. Homepage. http://ucdarnet.org/ (retrieved 17 January 2003). [Initiated in 2000.]

Digital Cultures Project. Principal investigator, William Warner. University of California Multi-Campus Research Group. Homepage. http://dc-mrg/english.ucsb.edu/ (retrieved 17 January 2003). [Initiated in 2000.]

Dillon, George L. *Rhetoric as Social Imagination: Explorations in the Interpersonal Function of Language*. Bloomington: Indiana University Press, 1986.

Dilthey, Wilhelm. *Pattern and Meaning in History: Thoughts on History and Society*. Translated and edited by H. P. Rickman. 1961. Reprint, New York: Harper & Row, 1962.

Dinerstein, Joel. *Swinging the Machine: Modernity, Technology, and African American Culture between the World Wars*. Amherst: University of Massachusetts Press, 2003.

Dirlik, Arif. "The Postmodernization of Production and Its Organization: Flexible Production, Work and Culture." In *The Postcolonial Aura: Third World Criticism in the Age of Global Capitalism*. Boulder, CO: Westview, 1997.

Dollimore, Jonathan. "Introduction: Shakespeare, Cultural Materialism and the New Historicism." In *Political Shakespeare: New Essays in Cultural Materialism*, ed. Jonathan Dollimore and Alan Sinfield. Ithaca, NY: Cornell University Press, 1985.

———. *Radical Tragedy: Religion, Ideology and Power in the Drama of Shakespeare and His Contemporaries*. Chicago: University of Chicago Press, 1984.

———. "'Transgression and Surveillance in *Measure for Measure*." In *Political Shakespeare: New Essays in Cultural Materialism*, ed. Jonathan Dollimore and Alan Sinfield. Ithaca, NY: Cornell University Press, 1985.

Dollimore, Jonathan, and Alan Sinfield, eds. *Political Shakespeare: New Essays in Cultural Materialism*. Ithaca, NY: Cornell University Press, 1985.

Douglas, Mary. *Purity and Danger: An Analysis of Concepts of Pollution and Taboo*. London: Routledge & Kegan Paul, 1966.

Drucker, Johanna. *The Visible Word: Experimental Typography and Modern Art, 1909–1923*. Chicago: University of Chicago Press, 1994.

Drucker, Peter F. *Managing in Turbulent Times*. New York: Harper & Row, 1980.

Dyck, Timothy. "Clash of the Titans: SQL Databases." *PC Magazine*, 26 March 2002, 122–38.

Eagleston, A. J. "Wordsworth, Coleridge, and the Spy." In *Coleridge Studies by Several Hands*, ed. Edmund Blunden and Earl Leslie Griggs. London: Constable, 1934.

Eagleton, Terry. *The Ideology of the Aesthetic*. Cambridge: Blackwell, 1990.

Ehrenreich, Barbara, and John Ehrenreich. "The Professional-Managerial Class." In *Between Labor and Capital*, ed. Pat Walker. Boston: South End, 1979.

Eichenbaum, Boris. "The Theory of the 'Formal Method.'" In *Russian Formalist Criticism: Four Essays*, trans. Lee T. Lemon and Marion J. Reis. Lincoln: University of Nebraska Press, 1965.

8½. Dir. Federico Fellini. Embassy Pictures, 1963.

Eilenberg, Susan. "'Michael,' 'Christabel,' and the Poetry of Possession." *Criticism* 30 (1988): 205–24.

———. "Wordsworth's 'Michael': The Poetry of Property." *Essays in Literature* 15 (1988): 13–25.

Eisenstein, Sergei. *Film Form: Essays in Film Theory*. Edited and translated by Jay Leyda. New York: Harcourt, Brace, 1949.

Ekenberg, Jan. Prologue to Lisa Jevbratt's *1:1*. http://128.111.69.4/~jevbratt/1_to_1/jan.html (retrieved 14 October 2003).

Electronic Frontier Foundation. Homepage. http://www.eff.org/ (retrieved 20 January 2007).

Electronic Literature Organization (ELO). *Electronic Literature Collection*: Volume 1. Edited by N. Katherine Hayles, Nick Montfort, Scott Rettberg, Stephanie Strickland. Electronic Literature Organization, 2006. CD-ROM for Macintosh and Windows. Also available online at http://collection.eliterature.org/1/ (retrieved 2 April 2007).

———. "PAD (Preservation, Archiving, Dissemination Initiative)." http://www.eliterature.org/pad/ (retrieved 31 July 2003).

Eliot, T. S. "Tradition and the Individual Talent." In *Critical Theory since Plato* (rev. ed.), ed. Hazard Adams. Fort Worth, TX: Harcourt Brace Jovanovich, 1992.

———. *The Waste Land and Other Poems*. 1922. New York: Harcourt Brace Jovanovich, 1962.

Ellison, Julie. "Someday Bridges Will Have Feelings, Too." Paper presented at the session "Romanticism and Postmodernism" at the Modern Language Association convention, New York, 28 December 1992. [Originally titled "Between Regret and Assay."]

Ellul, Jacques. *The Technological Society*. Translated by John Wilkinson. New York: Knopf, 1967.

Elster, Jon. *Explaining Technical Change: A Case Study in the Philosophy of Science*. Cambridge: Cambridge University Press, 1983.

———. *Ulysses Unbound: Studies in Rationality, Precommitment, and Constraints*. Cambridge: Cambridge University Press, 2000.

Emory, Theo. "Memory Glasses for Total Recall." Associated Press, CBS News online, 2 December 2003, http://www.cbsnews.com/stories/2003/12/01/tech/main586191.shtml (retrieved 4 December 2003).

Empson, William. *Seven Types of Ambiguity*. New York: New Directions, 1947.

Emsley, Clive. *British Society and the French Wars, 1793–1815*. Totowa, NJ: Rowman & Littlefield, 1979.

Erdman, David V. Introduction to Samuel Taylor Coleridge, *Essays on His Times in "The Morning Post" and "The Courier"* (vol. 3 of *The Collected Works of Samuel Taylor Coleridge*), ed. David V. Erdman, vol. 1. Princeton, NJ: Princeton University Press, 1978.

———. "Wordsworth as Heartsworth; or, Was Regicide the Prophetic Ground of Those 'Moral Questions'?" In *The Evidence of the Imagination: Studies of Interactions between Life and Art in English Romantic Literature*, ed. Donald H. Reiman et al. New York: New York University Press, 1978.

Erlich, Victor. *Russian Formalism: History—Doctrine.* 3rd ed. New Haven, CT: Yale University Press, 1981.

Esposito, Elena. "The Arts of Contingency." *Critical Inquiry* 31 (2004): 7–25.

Evans, E. D. *A History of Wales, 1660–1815.* Cardiff: University of Wales Press, 1976.

Everest, Kelvin. *Coleridge's Secret Ministry: The Context of the Conversation Poems, 1795–1798.* Hassocks: Harvester, 1979.

Evergreen Aviation Museum (and Captain Michael King Smith Educational Institute). Home page. http://www.sprucegoose.org/ (retrieved 3 March 2007).

    Secondary pages cited:

        "Aircraft and Artifacts: Featured Exhibits—Spruce Goose." 2004. http://www.sprucegoose.org/aircraft_artifacts/exhibits.html (retrieved 3 March 2007).

        "Description." 2004. http://www.sprucegoose.org/aircraft_artifacts/exhibits_cont1.html (retrieved 3 March 2007).

        "Move to Oregon." 2004. http://www.sprucegoose.org/aircraft_artifacts/exhibits_cont.html (retrieved 3 March 2007).

Facebook. Homepage. http://www.facebook.com/ (retrieved 7 March 2007).

Falco, Edward. *Self-Portrait as Child with Father. Iowa Review Web,* 26 March 1999, http://www.uiowa.edu/~iareview/tirweb/hypermedia/edward_falco/webpages/selfportrait.html (retrieved 17 October 2003).

The Feminist Companion to Literature in English: Women Writers from the Middle Ages to the Present. Edited by Virginia Blain, Patricia Clements, and Isobel Grundy. New Haven, CT: Yale University Press, 1990.

Ferguson, Margaret W. *Trials of Desire: Renaissance Defenses of Poetry.* New Haven, CT: Yale University Press, 1983.

Fernandez, James W. *Persuasions and Performances: The Play of Tropes in Culture.* Bloomington: Indiana University Press, 1986.

Ferry, Luc, and Alain Renaut. *French Philosophy of the Sixties: An Essay on Antihumanism.* Translated by Mary H. S. Cattani. Amherst: University of Massachusetts Press, 1990.

Festa, Paul. "Total Recall." *Computer Shopper,* March 2003, 174. [Interview with Gordon Bell.]

Feyerabend, Paul. *Against Method: Outline of an Anarchistic Theory of Knowledge.* London: Verso, 1978.

Fineman, Joel. "The History of the Anecdote: Fiction and Fiction." In *The New Historicism,* ed. H. Aram Veeser. New York: Routledge, 1989.

Fischer, Michael. Review of *Social Values and Poetic Acts: The Historical Judgment of Literary Work,* by Jerome J. McGann. *Blake: An Illustrated Quarterly* 23 (1989): 32–39.

Fish, Stanley. "Being Interdisciplinary Is So Very Hard to Do." *Profession* (1989): 15–22.

———. "Consequences." In *Against Theory: Literary Studies and the New Pragmatism,* ed. W. J. T. Mitchell. Chicago: University of Chicago Press, 1985.

———. *Doing What Comes Naturally: Change, Rhetoric, and the Practice of Theory in Literary and Legal Studies.* Durham, NC: Duke University Press, 1989.

———. *Is There a Text in This Class? The Authority of Interpretive Communities.* Cambridge, MA: Harvard University Press, 1980.

Fitzgibbon, Andrew, and Ehud Reiter. "'Memories for Life': Managing Information over a Human Lifetime." Grand Challenges in Computing Workshop, United Kingdom Computing Research Committee, 22 May 2003. http://www.nesc.ac.uk/esi/events/Grand_Challenges/proposals/Memories.pdf (retrieved 4 April 2004).

Foucault, Michel. *Discipline and Punish: The Birth of the Prison.* Translated by Alan Sheridan. New York: Vintage, 1979.

————. *The History of Sexuality.* Vol. 1, *An Introduction.* Translated by Robert Hurley. New York: Vintage, 1980.

————. *The Order of Things: An Archaeology of the Human Sciences.* New York: Vintage, 1973.

————. *Power/Knowledge: Selected Interviews and Other Writings, 1972–1977.* Edited by Colin Gordon. Translated by Colin Gordon et al. New York: Pantheon, 1980.

Fowler, Roger. *Literature as Social Discourse: The Practice of Linguistic Criticism.* Bloomington: Indiana University Press, 1981.

Fowler, Roger, et al. *Language and Control.* London: Routledge & Kegan Paul, 1979.

François, Anne-Lise. *Open Secrets: The Literature of Uncounted Experience.* Stanford: Stanford University Press, 2008.

Frank, André Gunder. *Capitalism and Underdevelopment in Latin America: Historical Studies of Chile and Brazil.* New York: Monthly Review Press, 1969.

Freud, Sigmund. "Mourning and Melancholia." In *Standard Edition of the Complete Psychological Works of Sigmund Freud,* trans. James Strachey, vol. 14. London: Hogarth, 1957.

Frow, John. *Marxism and Literary History.* Cambridge, MA: Harvard University Press, 1986.

Fukuyama, Francis. "The End of History?" *National Interest,* no. 16 (Summer 1989): 3–18.

————. *The End of History and the Last Man.* New York: Free Press, 1992.

Fumerton, Patricia. *Cultural Aesthetics: Renaissance Literature and the Practice of Social Ornament.* Chicago: University of Chicago Press, 1991.

————. "Exchanging Gifts: The Elizabethan Currency of Children and Poetry." *ELH* 53 (1986): 241–78.

————. "'Secret' Arts: Elizabethan Miniatures and Sonnets." *Representations* 15 (Summer 1986): 57–97.

Furet, François. "Beyond the *Annales.*" *Journal of Modern History* 55 (1983): 389–410.

————. *Interpreting the French Revolution.* Translated by Elborg Forster. Cambridge: Cambridge University Press, 1981.

Gage, Doug. LifeLog. DARPA (U.S. Defense Advanced Research Projects Agency) Information Processing Technology Office. Homepage. http://www.darpa.mil/ipto/programs/lifelog/index.htm (retrieved 4 April 2004).

Gallagher, Catherine, and Stephen Greenblatt. *Practicing New Historicism.* Chicago: University of Chicago Press, 2000.

Gaudibert, Pierre. *Action culturelle: Intégration et/ou subversion.* 3rd ed. Tournai: Casterman, 1977.

Geertz, Clifford. "Deep Play: Notes on the Balinese Cockfight." In *The Interpretation of Cultures: Selected Essays.* New York: Basic, 1973.

————. *The Interpretation of Cultures: Selected Essays.* New York: Basic, 1973.

————. *Local Knowledge: Further Essays in Interpretive Anthropology.* New York: Basic, 1983.

Gemmell, Jim, et al. "Living with a Lifetime Store." ATR Workshop on Ubiquitous Experience Media, 9–10 September 2003, Keihanna Science City, Kyoto, Japan. http://research.microsoft.com/~jgemmell/pubs/UEM2003.pdf (retrieved 5 April 2004).

————. "MyLifeBits: Fulfilling the Memex Vision." *ACM Multimedia '02,* 1–6 December 2002, Juan-les-Pins, France. http://research.microsoft.com/~jgemmell/pubs/MyLifeBitsMM02.pdf (retrieved 5 April 2004).

————. "The MyLifeBits Lifetime Store." ACM SIGMM 2003 Workshop on Experiential Telepresence (ETP 2003), 7 November 2003, Berkeley, CA. http://research.microsoft.com/~jgemmell/pubs/ETP2003.pdf (retrieved 12 July 2004).

Geoffrey of Monmouth. *The History of the Kings of Britain.* Translated by Lewis Thorpe. Harmondsworth: Penguin, 1966.

Gessler, Nicholas. "Skeuomorphs and Cultural Algorithms." In *HTM Evolutionary Program-*

ming VII: *Proceedings of the Seventh International Conference on Evolutionary Programming*, 229–38. Berlin: Springer, 1998. Also available at http://www.sscnet.ucla.edu/geog/gessler/cv-pubs/98skeuo.htm (retrieved 16 October 2003).

Gibbon, Edward. *The Decline and Fall of the Roman Empire*. Abridged ed. Edited by Hans-Friedrich Mueller. New York: Modern Library, 2003.

Gibson, William. *Burning Chrome*. 1986. Reprint, New York: Ace, 1987.

———. *Count Zero*. 1986. Reprint, New York: Ace, 1987.

———. *Mona Lisa Overdrive*. New York: Bantam, 1988.

———. *Neuromancer*. New York: Ace, 1984.

Gill, Karamjit S., et al., eds. "Database Aesthetics: Issues of Organization and Category in Online Art." Special issue, *AI and Society* 14, no. 1 (2000). Available online at http://time.arts.ucla.edu/AI_Society/ (retrieved 17 January 2003).

Ginzburg, Carlo. *The Cheese and the Worms: The Cosmos of a Sixteenth-Century Miller*. Translated by John Tedeschi and Anne Tedeschi. New York: Penguin, 1982.

Gitelman, Lisa. *Always Already New: Media, History, and the Data of Culture*. Cambridge, MA: MIT Press, 2006.

Goldberg, Jonathan. *James I and the Politics of Literature: Jonson, Shakespeare, Donne, and Their Contemporaries*. Baltimore: Johns Hopkins University Press, 1983.

———. "The Politics of Renaissance Literature: A Review Essay." *ELH* 49 (1982): 514–42.

Gombrich, E. H. *Norm and Form: Studies in the Art of the Renaissance*. London: Phaidon, 1966.

González-Casanova, Pablo. "Internal Colonialism and National Development." *Studies in Comparative International Development* 1, no. 4 (1965): 27–37.

Goodman, Kevis. *Georgic Modernity and British Romanticism: Poetry and the Mediation of History*. Cambridge: Cambridge University Press, 2004.

———. "Making Time for History: Wordsworth, the New Historicism, and the Apocalyptic Fallacy." Paper presented at the session "Wordsworth's 'Invisible Workmanship' and the Work of New Historicism," Modern Language Association convention, Toronto, 29 December 1993. Subsequently published in *Studies in Romanticism* 35 (1996): 563–77.

Graff, Gerald. *Professing Literature: An Institutional History*. Chicago: University of Chicago Press, 1987.

Gray, Thomas. "The Progress of Poesy: A Pindaric Ode." In *The Poems of Thomas Gray, William Collins, Oliver Goldsmith*, ed. Roger Lonsdale. New York: Longmans, 1969.

Greenblatt, Stephen, ed. "The Forms of Power and the Power of Forms in the Renaissance." Special issue, *Genre* 15, nos. 1–2 (1982).

———. Introduction to "The Forms of Power and the Power of Forms in the Renaissance." Special issue, *Genre* 15, nos. 1–2 (1982): 3–6.

———. "Invisible Bullets: Renaissance Authority and Its Subversion." *Glyph* 8 (1981): 40–61.

———. "Invisible Bullets." In *Shakespearean Negotiations: The Circulation of Social Energy in Renaissance England*. Berkeley and Los Angeles: University of California Press, 1988.

———. "*King Lear* and Harsnett's 'Devil-Fiction.'" In "The Forms of Power and the Power of Forms in the Renaissance," ed. Stephen Greenblatt. Special issue, *Genre* 15, nos. 1–2 (1982): 239–42.

———. "Murdering Peasants: Status, Genre, and the Representation of Rebellion." *Representations* 1 (February 1983): 1–29.

———. "Psychoanalysis and Renaissance Culture." In *Literary Theory/Renaissance Texts*, ed. Patricia Parker and David Quint. Baltimore: Johns Hopkins University Press, 1986.

———. *Renaissance Self-Fashioning: From More to Shakespeare*. Chicago: University of Chicago Press, 1980.

———. *Shakespearean Negotiations: The Circulation of Social Energy in Renaissance England.* Berkeley and Los Angeles: University of California Press, 1988.

———. "Towards a Poetics of Culture." In *The New Historicism*, ed. H. Aram Veeser. New York: Routledge, 1989.

Greimas, A.-J. *Structural Semantics: An Attempt at a Method.* Translated by Daniele McDowell et al. Lincoln: University of Nebraska Press, 1983.

Guillory, John. *Cultural Capital: The Problem of Literary Canon Formation.* Chicago: University of Chicago Press, 1993.

———. "The Memo and Modernity." *Critical Inquiry* 31 (2004): 108–32.

Habermas, Jürgen. "Modernity—an Incomplete Project." Translated by Seyla Ben-Habib. In *The Anti-Aesthetic: Essays on Postmodern Culture*, ed. Hal Foster. 1983. Reprint, Port Townsend, WA: New Press, 1998.

———. "The Entry into Postmodernity: Nietzsche as a Turning Point." In *The Philosophical Discourse of Modernity: Twelve Lectures.* Translated by Frederick G. Lawrence. Cambridge, MA: MIT Press, 1990.

———. *The Theory of Communicative Action.* Translated by Thomas McCarthy. 2 vols. Boston: Beacon, 1984–87.

Haraway, Donna J. "A Cyborg Manifesto: Science, Technology, and Socialist-Feminism in the Late Twentieth Century." In *Simians, Cyborgs, and Women: The Reinvention of Nature.* New York: Routledge, 1991.

Hardt, Michael, and Antonio Negri. *Empire.* Cambridge, MA: Harvard University Press, 2000.

Harrison, Gary. "Wordsworth and the Itinerant Poor: The Discourse on Poverty." Ph.D. diss., Stanford University, 1987.

———. *Wordsworth's Vagrant Muse: Poetry, Poverty, and Power.* Detroit: Wayne State University Press, 1994.

Hartman, Geoffrey H. *The Unmediated Vision: An Interpretation of Wordsworth, Hopkins, Rilke, and Valéry.* New Haven, CT: Yale University Press, 1954.

———. "The Voice of the Shuttle: Language from the Point of View of Literature." In *Beyond Formalism: Literary Essays, 1958–1970.* New Haven, CT: Yale University Press, 1970.

———. *Wordsworth's Poetry, 1787–1814.* New Haven, CT: Yale University Press, 1971.

Harvey, David. *The Condition of Postmodernity: An Enquiry into the Origins of Cultural Change.* Oxford: Blackwell, 1989.

Hayden, Donald E. *Wordsworth's Travels in Wales and Ireland.* Tulsa, OK: University of Tulsa, 1985.

Hayles, N. Katherine. *How We Became Posthuman: Virtual Bodies in Cybernetics, Literature, and Informatics.* Chicago: University of Chicago Press, 1999.

———. *My Mother Was a Computer: Digital Subjects and Literary Texts.* Chicago: University of Chicago Press, 2005.

Haynes, Jonathan. "Festivity and the Dramatic Economy of Jonson's *Bartholomew Fair.*" *ELH* 51 (1984): 645–68.

The Heath Anthology of American Literature. Edited by Paul Lauter et al. 2 vols. Lexington, MA: Heath, 1990.

Hechter, Michael. *Internal Colonialism: The Celtic Fringe in British National Development, 1536–1966.* Berkeley: University of California Press, 1975.

Heinzelman, Kurt. *The Economics of the Imagination.* Amherst: University of Massachusetts Press, 1980.

Helgerson, Richard. "Inventing Noplace; or, The Power of Negative Thinking." *Genre* 15 (1982): 101–21.

————. "The Land Speaks: Cartography, Chorography, and Subversion in Renaissance England." *Representations* 16 (Fall 1986): 50–85.

————. Review of *Language as Ideology*, by Gunther Kress and Robert Hodge, *Language and Control*, by Roger Fowler et al., and *Literature, Language and Society in England, 1580–1680*, by David Aers et al. *Comparative Literature* 35 (1983): 362–73.

————. *Self-Crowned Laureates: Spenser, Jonson, Milton and the Literary System*. Berkeley and Los Angeles: University of California Press, 1983.

————. *A Sonnet from Carthage: Garcilaso de la Vega and the New Poetry of Sixteenth-Century Europe*. Philadelphia: University of Pennsylvania Press, 2007.

Hell's Angels. Directed by Howard Hughes. United Artists, 1930.

Hertz, Neil. "The Notion of Blockage in the Literature of the Sublime." In *The End of the Line: Essays on Psychoanalysis and the Sublime*. New York: Columbia University Press, 1985.

Himmelfarb, Gertrude. "The Haunted House of Jeremy Bentham." In *Ideas in History: Essays Presented to Louis Gottschalk by His Former Students*, ed. Richard Herr and Harold T. Parker. Durham, NC: Duke University Press, 1965.

Hirsch, E. D., Jr. *Validity in Interpretation*. New Haven, CT: Yale University Press, 1976.

Hobsbawm, Eric. *Primitive Rebels*. Manchester: Manchester University Press, 1959.

Hobsbawm, Eric, and Terence Ranger, eds. *The Invention of Tradition*. Cambridge: Cambridge University Press, 1983.

Howard, Jean E. "The New Historicism in Renaissance Studies." *English Literary Renaissance* 16 (1986): 13–43.

Howard, Jean E., and Marion F. O'Connor, eds. *Shakespeare Reproduced: The Text in History and Ideology*. New York: Methuen, 1987.

Howell, T. B., and Thomas Jones Howell. *A Complete Collection of State Trials and Proceedings for High Treason and Other Crimes and Misdemeanors from the Earliest Period to the Year 1783, with Notes and Other Illustrations*. 33 vols. London, T. C. Hansard, for Longman, Hurst, Rees, Orme, & Brown, 1809–26.

Huet, Marie-Hélène. *Rehearsing the Revolution: The Staging of Marat's Death, 1793–1797*. Translated by Robert Hurley. Berkeley and Los Angeles: University of California Press, 1982.

Hunt, Lynn. "French History in the Last Twenty Years: The Rise and Fall of the *Annales* Paradigm." *Journal of Contemporary History* 21 (1986): 209–24.

————. "Introduction: History, Culture, and Text." In *The New Cultural History*, ed. Lynn Hunt. Berkeley and Los Angeles: University of California Press, 1989.

————, ed. *The New Cultural History*. Berkeley and Los Angeles: University of California Press, 1989.

————. *Politics, Culture, and Class in the French Revolution*. Berkeley and Los Angeles: University of California Press, 1984.

————. Review of *Penser la Révolution Français [Interpreting the French Revolution]*, by François Furet. *History and Theory* 20 (1981): 313–23.

Hutchinson, William. *The History of the County of Cumberland*. 1794–97. 2 vols. Reprint, East Ardsley, 1974.

Hyman, Anthony. *Charles Babbage: Pioneer of the Computer*. Princeton, NJ: Princeton University Press, 1982.

Hyperdictionary. WEBNOX Corp. http://www.hyperdictionary.com/ (retrieved 12 July 2004).

"IBM's Budding Innovators: Grooming the Next Generation." *PC Magazine*, 1 October 2003, 19.

Iggers, Georg G. "Historicism." In *The Dictionary of the History of Ideas: Studies of Selected*

Pivotal Ideas, ed. Philip P. Wiener. New York: Scribner's, 1973–74. Available online at http://etext.virginia.edu/DicHist/dict.html (retrieved 21 January 2007).

I'll Take My Stand: The South and the Agrarian Tradition, by Twelve Southerners. 1930. Reprint, with an introduction by Louis D. Rubin Jr. and biographical essays by Virginia Rock, Baton Rouge: Louisiana State University Press, 1977.

Interdisciplinarity: Papers Presented at the SHRE European Symposium on Interdisciplinary Courses in European Education, 13 September 1975. Guildford: Society for Research into Higher Education Ltd. at the University of Surrey, 1977.

J. Lloyd Eaton Collection Newsletter (Special Collections Department, Tomas Rivera Library, University of California, Riverside) 1, no. 2 (Fall 1989).

Jacobus, Mary. "'Incorruptible Milk': Breast-Feeding and the French Revolution." Paper presented at the conference "Revolution '89," University of California, Santa Barbara, 12 May 1989. Subsequently published in *Rebel Daughters: Women and the French Revolution*, ed. Sara E. Melzer and Leslie W. Rabine (Oxford: Oxford University Press, 1992).

———. "The Law of/and Gender: Genre Theory and *The Prelude*." *Diacritics* 14 (Winter 1984): 47–57.

———. "'That Great Stage Where Senators Perform': *Macbeth* and the Politics of Romantic Theater." *Studies in Romanticism* 22 (1983): 353–87.

Jakobson, Roman. "The Dominant." Translated by Herbert Eagle. In *Readings in Russian Poetics: Formalist and Structuralist Views*, ed. Ladislav Matejka and Krystyna Pomorska. Cambridge, MA: MIT Press, 1971.

James, William. *Essays in Pragmatism*. Edited by Alburey Castell. New York: Hafner, 1948.

Jameson, Fredric. *The Political Unconscious: Narrative as a Socially Symbolic Act*. Ithaca, NY: Cornell University Press, 1981.

———. *Postmodernism; or, The Cultural Logic of Late Capitalism*. Durham, NC: Duke University Press, 1991.

———. "Postmodernism and Consumer Society." In *The Anti-Aesthetic: Essays on Postmodern Culture*, ed. Hal Foster. 1983. Reprint, Port Townsend, WA: New Press, 1998.

Jarman, Paul. "Madoc, 1795: Robert Southey's Misdated Manuscript." *Review of English Studies*, n.s., 55 (2004): 355–73.

Jauss, Hans Robert. *Toward an Aesthetic of Reception*. Translated by Timothy Bahti. Minneapolis: University of Minnesota Press, 1982.

Jenkins, Geraint H. *The Foundations of Modern Wales, 1642–1780*. Oxford: Oxford University Press, 1987.

Jevbratt, Lisa. *1:1*. Version 2. 2001–2002. http://128.111.69.4/~jevbratt/1_to_1/index_ng .html (retrieved 3 April 2007).

    Secondary pages cited:

    "Interface: *Every*." http://128.111.69.4/~jevbratt/1_to_1/interface_ii/index.html (retrieved 3 April 2007).

    "Interface: *Migration*." http://128.111.69.4/~jevbratt/1_to_1/interface_a/index_s .html (retrieved 3 April 2007).

———. Untitled talks. University of California, Santa Barbara. 14 January, 17 April 2002.

Jewett, William. "'Action' in *The Borderers*." Paper presented at the conference "Wordsworth and the Borders of Romanticism," Yale University, 14 November 1987.

Johnson, Samuel. *Samuel Johnson*. Edited by Donald Greene. Oxford: Oxford University Press, 1984. [Oxford Authors series collection of Johnson's works.]

Johnson, Steven. *Interface Culture: How New Technology Transforms the Way We Create and Communicate*. San Francisco: HarperEdge, 1997.

Johnston, Kenneth R. "Philanthropy or Treason? Wordsworth as 'Active Partisan.'" *Studies in Romanticism* 25 (1986): 371–409.

Jones, Jennifer. "Virtual Sublime: Romantic Transcendence and the Transport of the Real." Ph.D. diss., University of California, Santa Barbara, 2002.

Joseph's Coat: An Anthology of Multicultural Writing. Edited by Peter Skrzynecki. Sydney: Hale & Iremonger, 1985.

Jurkovich, Ray, and J. H. P. Paelinck, eds. *Problems in Interdisciplinary Studies.* Issues in Interdisciplinary Studies 2. Brookfield, VT: Gower / Steering Committee in Interdisciplinary Studies, Erasmus University, 1984.

Kaleidoscope: Stories of the American Experience. Edited by Barbara Perkins and George Perkins. New York: Oxford University Press, 1993.

Kamuf, Peggy. *Signature Pieces: On the Institution of Authorship.* Ithaca, NY: Cornell University Press, 1988.

Kavaloski, Vincent C. "Interdisciplinary Education and Humanistic Aspiration: A Critical Reflection." In *Interdisciplinarity and Higher Education,* ed. Joseph J. Kockelmans. University Park: Pennsylvania State University Press, 1979.

Keats, John. *The Complete Poems.* Edited by John Barnard. 2d ed. Harmondsworth: Penguin, 1976.

Kelley, Donald R. *Historians and the Law in Postrevolutionary France.* Princeton, NJ: Princeton University Press, 1984.

Kelley, Theresa M. "J. M. W. Turner, Napoleonic Caricature, and Romantic Allegory." *ELH* 58 (1991): 351–82.

———. *Wordsworth's Revisionary Aesthetics.* Cambridge: Cambridge University Press, 1988.

Kelly, George Armstrong. *Mortal Politics in Eighteenth-Century France.* Waterloo, ON: University of Waterloo Press, 1986.

Kendrick, Thomas Downing. *The Druids: A Study in Keltic Prehistory.* 1927. Reprint, New York: Barnes & Noble, 1966.

Kent, William. "A Simple Guide to Five Normal Forms in Relational Database Theory." *Communications of the Association for Computing Machinery* 26, no. 2 (February 1983): 120–25. Available online at http:/ / www.bkent.net / Doc / simple5.htm (accessed 3 October 2007).

Kernan, Alvin. *The Death of Literature.* New Haven, CT: Yale University Press, 1990.

Khleif, Bud B. *Language, Ethnicity, and Education in Wales.* The Hague: Mouton, 1980.

Kirschenbaum, Matthew G. *Mechanisms: New Media and the Forensic Imagination.* Cambridge, MA: MIT Press, 2008.

Kittler, Friedrich A. *Discourse Networks, 1800/1900.* Translated by Michael Metteer with Chris Cullens. Stanford, CA: Stanford University Press, 1990.

———. *Gramophone, Film, Typewriter.* Translated by Geoffrey Winthrop-Young and Michael Wutz. Stanford, CA: Stanford University Press, 1999.

Klancher, Jon P. *The Making of English Reading Audiences, 1790–1832.* Madison: University of Wisconsin Press, 1987.

Klein, Julie Thompson. *Interdisciplinarity: History, Theory, and Practice.* Detroit: Wayne State University Press, 1990.

Knapp, Steven. *Personification and the Sublime: Milton to Coleridge.* Cambridge, MA: Harvard University Press, 1985.

Knapp, Steven, and Walter Benn Michaels. "Against Theory." In *Against Theory: Literary Studies and the New Pragmatism,* ed. W. J. T. Mitchell. Chicago: University of Chicago Press, 1985.

Kockelmans, Joseph J., ed. *Interdisciplinarity and Higher Education.* University Park: Pennsylvania State University Press, 1979.

Krapp, Peter. *Déjà Vu: Aberrations of Cultural Memory.* Minneapolis: University of Minnesota Press, 2004.

Kress, Gunther, and Robert Hodge. *Language as Ideology*. London: Routledge & Kegan Paul, 1979.

Kristeva, Julia. *Powers of Horror: An Essay on Abjection*. Translated by Leon S. Roudiez. New York: Columbia University Press, 1982.

Kung, Hans. "The Grid System." In *Graphic Arts Manual*, ed. Janet M. Field et al. New York: Arno, 1980.

LaCapra, Dominick. *Rethinking Intellectual History: Texts, Contexts, Language*. Ithaca, NY: Cornell University Press, 1983.

Lanham, Richard A. *A Handlist of Rhetorical Terms: A Guide for Students of English Literature*. Berkeley: University of California Press, 1968.

Laplace, Pierre Simon, Marquis de. *Philosophical Essay on Probabilities*. Translated by Andrew I. Dale. New York: Springer, 1995. [Translated from the fifth French edition of 1825.]

Leffingwell, William Henry. *Scientific Office Management*. Chicago: A. W. Shaw, 1917.

Leffingwell, William Henry, and Edwin Marshall Robinson. *Textbook of Office Management*. 2nd ed. New York: McGraw-Hill, 1943.

Leiris, Michel. *L'âge d'homme: Précédeé de De la Littérature considérée comme une tauromachie*. Paris: Gallimard, 1972.

Lentricchia, Frank. *Criticism and Social Change*. Chicago: University of Chicago Press, 1983.

————. "The Return of William James." In *The Current in Criticism: Essays on the Present and Future of Literary Theory*, ed. Clayton Koelb and Virgil Lokke. West Lafayette, IN: Purdue University Press, 1987.

Le Roy Ladurie, Emmanuel. *Love, Death and Money in the Pays d'Oc*. Translated by Alan Sheridan. Harmondsworth: Penguin, 1984.

Levinson, Marjorie. "Back to the Future: Wordsworth's New Historicism." *South Atlantic Quarterly* 88 (1989): 633–59.

————. *The Romantic Fragment Poem: A Critique of a Form*. Chapel Hill, NC: University of North Carolina Press, 1986.

————. *Wordsworth's Great Period Poems: Four Essays*. Cambridge: Cambridge University Press, 1986.

Lévi-Strauss, Claude. *The Savage Mind*. Chicago: University of Chicago Press, 1966.

————. *Structural Anthropology*. Translated by Claire Jacobson and Brooke Grundfest Schoepf. New York: Basic, 1963.

————. *Structural Anthropology, Volume 2*. Translated by Monique Layton. Chicago: University of Chicago Press, 1976.

Lewis, Thomas E. "Reference and Dissemination: Althusser after Derrida." *Diacritics* 15, no. 4 (Winter 1985): 37–56.

Lipschutz, Robert P. "Brave New Apps: The Web Services Tools." *PC Magazine*, 1 October 2003, 116–25.

Litvak, Joseph. "Back to the Future: A Review-Article on the New Historicism, Deconstruction, and Nineteenth-Century Fiction." *Texas Studies in Literature and Language* 30 (1988): 120–49.

Liu, Alan. "'A Forming Hand': Creativity and Destruction from Romanticism to Emergence Theory." Paper circulated for the workshop "Development, Creativity, and Agency: New Approaches (A Conversation between Thomas Pfau and Alan Liu)." Conference of the North American Society for the Study of Romanticism, Montreal, 16 August 2005.

————. "Hypertext Fiction Tracker: Conceptual Demo of XML Application." University of California, Santa Barbara, 4 April 2002. http://www.english.ucsb.edu/faculty/ayliu/test/xml/tracker.html (retrieved 20 January 2003).

———. *The Laws of Cool: Knowledge Work and the Culture of Information.* Chicago: University of Chicago Press, 2004.

———. Review of *Wordsworth's Historical Imagination: The Poetry of Displacement,* by David Simpson. *Wordsworth Circle* 19 (1988): 172–81.

———. "Toward a Theory of the Prerequisite: Curing the Canon at Yale." Paper presented at the California Institute of Technology, 12 May 1988.

———. "Transcendental Data: Toward a Cultural History and Aesthetics of the New Encoded Discourse." Beckman Lecture, University of California, Berkeley, 15 October 2003.

———, ed. *Voice of the Shuttle.* See *Voice of the Shuttle.*

———. *Wordsworth: The Sense of History.* Stanford: Stanford University Press, 1989.

Longman Anthology of World Literature by Women, 1875–1975. Edited by Marian Arkin and Barbara Shollar. New York: Longman, 1989.

Lovejoy, Arthur O. *Essays in the History of Ideas.* Baltimore: Johns Hopkins University Press, 1948.

Lovink, Geert. *Dark Fiber: Tracking Critical Internet Culture.* Cambridge, MA: MIT Press, 2002.

Lyotard, Jean-François. "Answering the Question: What Is Postmodernism?" Translated by Régis Durand. In *The Postmodern Condition: A Report on Knowledge,* trans. Geoff Bennington and Brian Massumi. Minneapolis: University of Minnesota Press, 1984.

———. *The Differend: Phrases in Dispute.* Translated by Georges Van Den Abbeele. Minneapolis: University of Minnesota Press, 1988.

———. *Pacific Wall.* Translated by Bruce Boone. Venice, CA: Lapis, 1990.

———. *The Postmodern Condition: A Report on Knowledge.* Translated by Geoff Bennington and Brian Massumi. Minneapolis: University of Minnesota Press, 1984.

———. "A Postmodern Fable." Translated by Elizabeth Constable and Thomas Cochran. *Yale Journal of Criticism* 6, no. 1 (Spring 1993): 237–47.

Lyotard, Jean-François, and Jean-Loup Thébaud. *Just Gaming.* Translated by Wlad Godzich. Minneapolis: University of Minnesota Press, 1985.

Macherey, Pierre. *A Theory of Literary Production.* Translated by Geoffrey Wall. London: Routledge & Kegan Paul, 1978.

Mack, Anne, and J. J. Rome [Jerome J. McGann]. "Marxism, Romanticism, and Postmodernism: An American Case History." *South Atlantic Quarterly* 88 (1989): 605–32.

Macksey, Richard, "Introduction: 'A New Text of the World.'" *Genre* 16 (1983): 307–16.

MacLeish, Archibald. *Collected Poems, 1917–1982.* Boston: Houghton Mifflin, 1985.

Mandell, Laura, and Alan Liu, eds. *Romantic Chronology.* See *Romantic Chronology.*

Manovich, Lev. "Avant-Garde as Software." In *Ostranenie,* ed. Stephen Kovats. Frankfurt: Campus, 1999. Also available at http://www.manovich.net/docs/avantgarde_as_software.doc (retrieved 21 January 2002).

———. "From Cultural Interfaces to Info-Aesthetics (or: From Myst to OS X)." Paper presented at the conference "Interfacing Knowledges," Digital Cultures Project and Microcosms Project, University of California, Santa Barbara, 10 March 2002.

———. *The Language of New Media.* Cambridge, MA: MIT Press, 2001.

Marcus, Leah S. *The Politics of Mirth: Jonson, Herrick, Milton, Marvell, and the Defense of Old Holiday Pastimes.* Chicago: University of Chicago Press, 1986.

———. *Puzzling Shakespeare: Local Reading and Its Discontents.* Berkeley and Los Angeles: University of California Press, 1988.

Marcuse, Herbert. "Some Social Implications of Modern Technology." In *The Essential Frankfurt School Reader,* ed. Andrew Arato and Eike Gebhardt. New York: Continuum, 1988.

Marotti, Arthur F. "'Love Is Not Love': Elizabethan Sonnet Sequences and the Social Order." *ELH* 49 (1982): 396–428.

"Marx after Derrida." Special issue, *Diacritics* 15, no. 4 (Winter 1985).

Marx, Karl, and Frederick Engels. *Economic and Philosophic Manuscripts of 1844.* In *Collected Works,* vol. 3. New York: International, 1975.

Massey, Irving, ed. "Particularism." Special issue, *Criticism* 32, no. 3 (summer 1990).

The Matrix. Directed by Andy Wachowski and Larry Wachowski. Warner Bros., 1999.

Mayville, William V. *Interdisciplinarity: The Mutable Paradigm.* AAHE-ERIC / Higher Education Research Report no. 9. Washington, DC: American Association for Higher Education, 1978.

McCanles, Michael. *Dialectical Criticism and Renaissance Literature.* Berkeley: University of California Press, 1975.

McCarty, Willard. *Humanities Computing.* Basingstoke: Palgrave Macmillan, 2005.

McGann, Jerome J. "Marxism, Romanticism, and Postmodernism." *See* Mack and Rome.

———. *Radiant Textuality: Literature after the World Wide Web.* New York: Palgrave, 2001.

———. *The Romantic Ideology: A Critical Investigation.* Chicago: University of Chicago Press, 1983.

———. *Social Values and Poetic Acts: The Historical Judgment of Literary Work.* Cambridge, MA: Harvard University Press, 1988.

Michaels, Walter Benn. *The Gold Standard and the Logic of Naturalism: American Literature at the Turn of the Century.* Berkeley and Los Angeles: University of California Press, 1987.

Micklethwait, John, and Adrian Wooldridge. *The Witch Doctors: Making Sense of the Management Gurus.* New York: Times / Random House, 1996.

Microsoft Corp. *MSDN Library.* 2007. http:// msdn.microsoft.com/ library/ (retrieved 14 March 2007).

Miller, Eric, et al. "Semantic Web." Version 1.168. W3C, 11 October 2003. http:// www.w3 .org/ 2001/ sw/ (retrieved 13 October 2003).

Miller, J. Hillis. *The Linguistic Moment: From Wordsworth to Stevens.* Princeton, NJ: Princeton University Press, 1985.

———. "The Obligation to Write." President's Column. *MLA Newsletter* 18 (Fall 1986): 4–5.

———. "Responsibility and the Joy of Reading." President's Column. *MLA Newsletter* 18 (Spring 1986): 2.

———. "Responsibility and the Joy (?) of Teaching." President's Column. *MLA Newsletter* 18 (Summer 1986): 2.

———. "Stevens' Rock and Criticism as Cure (Part I)." *Georgia Review* 30 (1976): 5–31.

Mills, Timothy J., et al. "Shoebox: A Digital Photo Management System." Cambridge: AT&T Laboratories, 2000. http:// citeseer.ist.psu.edu/ cache/ papers/ cs/ 17914/ ftp:zSzzSzftp.uk.research.att.comzSzpubzSzdocszSzattzSztr.2000.10.pdf/ mills00shoe box.pdf (retrieved 13 April 2007).

Mink, Louis O. "Change and Causality in the History of Ideas." *Eighteenth-Century Studies* 2 (1968): 7–25.

Mitchum, Carl. "Computers: From Ethos and Ethics to Mythos and Religion: Notes on the New Frontier between Computers and Philosophy." *Technology in Society* 8 (1986): 171–201.

Moisan, Thomas. "'Which is the merchant here? and which the Jew?': Subversion and Recuperation in *The Merchant of Venice.*" In *Shakespeare Reproduced: The Text in History and Ideology,* ed. Jean E. Howard and Marion F. O'Connor. New York: Methuen, 1987.

Montrose, Louis Adrian. "'Eliza, Queene of shepheardes,' and the Pastoral of Power." *English Literary Renaissance* 10 (1980): 153–82.

———. "The Elizabethan Subject and the Spenserian Text." In *Literary Theory/Renaissance*

Texts, ed. Patricia Parker and David Quint. Baltimore: Johns Hopkins University Press, 1986.

———. "Gifts and Reasons: The Contexts of Peele's *Araygnement of Paris*." *ELH* 47 (1980): 433–61.

———. "The Purpose of Playing: Reflections on a Shakespearean Anthropology." *Helios*, n.s., 7, no. 2 (Spring 1980): 51–74.

———. "Renaissance Literary Studies and the Subject of History." *English Literary Renaissance* 16 (1986): 5–12.

———. "'Shaping Fantasies': Figurations of Gender and Power in Elizabethan Culture." *Representations* 2 (Spring 1983): 61–94.

Moorman, Mary. *The Early Years, 1770–1803*. Vol. 1 of *William Wordsworth: A Biography*. Oxford: Oxford University Press, 1957.

Moretti, Franco. *Graphs, Maps, Trees: Abstract Models for a Literary History*. London: Verso, 2005.

———. "'A Huge Eclipse': Tragic Form and the Deconsecration of Sovereignty." *Genre* 15 (1982): 7–40.

Morgan, Prys. "From a Death to a View: The Hunt for the Welsh Past in the Romantic Period." In *The Invention of Tradition*, ed. Eric Hobsbawm and Terence Ranger. Cambridge: Cambridge University Press, 1983.

———. "From Long Knives to Blue Books." In *Welsh Society and Nationhood: Historical Essays Presented to Glanmor Williams*, ed. R. R. Davies et al. Cardiff: University of Wales Press, 1984.

Morgan, Prys, and David Thomas. *Wales: The Shaping of a Nation*. Newton Abbot: David & Charles, 1984.

Morris, Meaghan. "Banality in Cultural Studies." *Discourse* 10, no. 2 (Spring–Summer 1988): 3–29.

Morris, Wesley. *Toward a New Historicism*. Princeton, NJ: Princeton University Press, 1972.

Morse, Margaret. "An Ontology of Everyday Distraction: The Freeway, the Mall, and Television." In *Logics of Television: Essays in Cultural Criticism*, ed. Patricia Mellencamp. Bloomington: Indiana University Press, 1990.

Mullaney, Steven. *The Place of the Stage: License, Play, and Power in Renaissance England*. Chicago: University of Chicago Press, 1988.

MusicMatch. Yahoo! Inc. Homepage. http://www.musicmatch.com/home.htm (retrieved 15 March 2007).

MyLifeBits Project. Microsoft Bay Area Research Center Media Presence Group, Microsoft, Inc. Homepage. http://research.microsoft.com/barc/mediapresence/MyLifeBits.aspx (retrieved 4 April 2004).

MySpace.com. Homepage. http://www.myspace.com/ (retrieved 7 March 2007).

Nancy, Jean-Luc. "Finite History." In *The Birth to Presence*, trans. Brian Holmes et al. Stanford, CA: Stanford University Press, 1993.

National Research Council. *Funding a Revolution: Government Support for Computing Research*. Washington, DC: National Academy Press, 1999. Also available at http://www.nap.edu/readingroom/books/far/ (retrieved 16 October 2003).

Nelson, Theodor Holm. *Literary Machines: The Report on, and of, Project Xanadu concerning Word Processing, Electronic Publishing, Hypertext, Thinkertoys, Tomorrow's Intellectual Revolution, and Certain Other Topics Including Knowledge, Education and Freedom*. Rev. ed. Sausalito, CA: Mindful, 1990. [The cover gives the release number "90.1" by analogy with software releases.]

A New History of French Literature. Edited by Denis Hollier et al. Cambridge, MA: Harvard University Press, 1989.

Newmeyer, Frederick J. *The Politics of Linguistics*. Chicago: University of Chicago Press, 1986.

Nicolis, Grégoire, and Ilya Prigogine. *Exploring Complexity: An Introduction*. New York: W. H. Freeman, 1989.

Nietzsche, Friedrich. *The Use and Abuse of History*. Translated by Adrian Collins. Indianapolis: Bobbs-Merrill, 1949.

The Norton Anthology of English Literature. Edited by M. H. Abrams et al. 6th ed. 2 vols. New York: Norton, 1993.

The Norton Anthology of Literature by Women: The Tradition in English. Edited by Sandra M. Gilbert and Susan Gubar. New York: Norton, 1985.

Nottingham, Mark. "RSS Tutorial for Content Publishers and Webmasters." 12 June 2003. http://www.mnot.net/rss/tutorial/ (retrieved 15 October 2003).

Novak, Marcos. "Liquid~, Trans~, Invisible~: The Ascent and Speciation of the Digital in Architecture: A Story." 2001. Digital/real exhibition. http://www.a-matter.de/digital-real/eng/mainframe.asp?sel=17 (retrieved 20 January 2003).

———. Talk on transvergence and allogenesis. Digital Media Arts Lecture Series, University of California, Santa Barbara, 4 March 2002.

Open Group Base Specifications Issue 6, IEEE Std 1003.1, 2004 Edition. IEEE and the Open Group. Homepage. http://www.opengroup.org/onlinepubs/009695399/ (retrieved 13 June 2004).

    Secondary page cited:

    "Shell Command Language" (chap. 2 of "Shell & Utilities" section). http://www.opengroup.org/onlinepubs/009695399/utilities/xcu_chap02.html#tag_02_02_01 (retrieved 13 June 2004).

O'Reilly, Tim. "What Is Web 2.0: Design Patterns and Business Models for the Next Generation of Software." O'Reilly Media, Inc., 30 September 2005. http://www.oreilly.com/pub/a/oreilly/tim/news/2005/09/30/what-is-web-20.html (retrieved 25 September 2007).

O'Reilly XML.com. O'Reilly & Associates. Homepage. http://www.xml.com/ (retrieved 17 October 2003).

Orgel, Stephen. *The Illusion of Power: Political Theater in the English Renaissance*. Berkeley: University of California Press, 1975.

———. "Making Greatness Familiar." *Genre* 15 (1982): 41–48.

———. "Prospero's Wife." *Representations* 8 (Fall 1984): 1–13.

———. "The Royal Theatre and the Role of King." In *Patronage in the Renaissance*, ed. Guy Fitch Lytle and Stephen Orgel. Princeton, NJ: Princeton University Press, 1981.

Orvell, Miles. *The Real Thing: Imitation and Authenticity in American Culture, 1880–1940*. Chapel Hill: University of North Carolina Press, 1989.

The Outlaw. Directed by Howard Hughes. Howard Hughes Productions, 1943.

Owen, A. L. *The Famous Druids: A Survey of Three Centuries of English Literature on the Druids*. Oxford: Oxford University Press, 1962.

Owen, D. Huw. "The Englishry of Denbigh: An English Colony in Medieval Wales." *Transactions of the Honourable Society of Cymmrodorion*, 1974–75, 57–76.

Ozouf, Mona. *Festivals and the French Revolution*. Translated by Alan Sheridan. Cambridge, MA: Harvard University Press, 1988.

Paley, William. *Natural Theology; or, Evidences of the Existence and Attributes of the Deity from the Appearances of Nature*. 12th ed. London: J. Faulder, 1809. Accessed from the 1998 online version of the University of Michigan Humanities Text Initiative at http://www.hti.umich.edu/p/pd-modeng/ (now extinct; retrieved 13 July 2004).

Palmade, Guy. *Interdisciplinarité et idéologies*. Paris: Anthropos, 1977.

Parker, Andrew. "Futures for Marxism: An Appreciation of Althusser." *Diacritics* 15, no. 4 (Winter 1985): 57–92.

Parker, Reeve. "'In some sort seeing with my proper eyes': Wordsworth and the Spectacles of Paris." *Studies in Romanticism* 27 (1988): 369–90.

———. "Reading Wordsworth's Power: Narrative and Usurpation in *The Borderers*." *ELH* 54 (1987): 299–331.

Parry, Milman. *The Making of Homeric Verse: The Collected Papers of Milman Parry*. Edited by Adam Parry. Oxford: Clarendon, 1971.

Partner, Nancy F. "Making Up Lost Time: Writing on the Writing of History." *Speculum* 61 (1986): 90–117.

Paul, Christiane. *Digital Art*. London: Thames & Hudson, 2003.

Paulson, Ronald. *Literary Landscape: Turner and Constable*. New Haven, CT: Yale University Press, 1982.

———. *Representations of Revolution, 1789–1820*. New Haven, CT: Yale University Press, 1983.

Pechter, Edward. "The New Historicism and Its Discontents: Politicizing Renaissance Drama." *PMLA* 102 (1987): 292–303.

Peek, Katherine Mary. *Wordsworth in England: Studies in the History of His Fame*. 1943. Reprint, New York: Octagon, 1969.

Perkins, David. "Discursive Form versus the Past in Literary History." *New Literary History* 22 (1991): 359–76.

Piggott, Stuart. *The Druids*. London: Thames & Hudson, 1968.

Poe, Edgar Allan. "The Poetic Principle." In *American Poetic Theory*, ed. George Perkins. New York: Holt, Rinehart & Winston, 1972.

Port, Otis. "Innovations." *Business Week*, 6 October 2003, 82.

Porter, Carolyn. "Are We Being Historical Yet?" *South Atlantic Quarterly* 87 (1988): 743–86.

Prentice-Hall Guide to English Literature. Edited by Marion Wynne-Davies. New York: Prentice-Hall, 1990.

Prigogine, Ilya. *See* Grégoire Nicolis and Ilya Prigogine.

Prince, Gerald. *A Dictionary of Narratology*. Lincoln: University of Nebraska Press, 1987.

Propp, Vladímir. *Morphology of the Folktale*. Translated by Laurence Scott. 2d ed. Revised and edited by Louis A. Wagner. Austin: University of Texas Press, 1968.

Pynchon, Thomas. *The Crying of Lot 49*. New York: Perennial/HarperCollins, 1999.

Raley, Rita. "Interferences: [Net.Writing] and the Practice of Codework." *Electronic Book Review*, 8 September 2002. http://www.electronicbookreview.com/thread/electro poetics/net.writing (retrieved 17 March 2007).

———. *Reading Code*. Manuscript in progress.

———. *Tactical Media*. Electronic Mediations Series. Minneapolis: University of Minnesota Press, 2008.

Ranke, Leopold von. *History of the Latin and Teutonic Nations, 1494 to 1514*. Revised translation by G. R. Dennis. London: G. Bell, 1909. Reprint, New York: AMS, 1976. [Translation of *Geschichten der romanischen und germanischen Völker von 1494–1514* (1824).]

Ransom, John Crowe. *The New Criticism*. Norfolk, CT: New Directions, 1941.

———. "Reconstructed but Unregenerate." In *I'll Take My Stand: The South and the Agrarian Tradition, by Twelve Southerners*. 1930. Reprint, with an introduction by Louis D. Rubin Jr. and biographical essays by Virginia Rock. Baton Rouge: Louisiana State University Press, 1977.

Reed, Mark L. *Wordsworth: The Chronology of the Early Years, 1770–1799*. Cambridge, MA: Harvard University Press, 1967.

————. *Wordsworth: The Chronology of the Middle Years, 1800–1815*. Cambridge, MA: Harvard University Press, 1975.

Rees, William. *An Historical Atlas of Wales: From Early to Modern Times*. London: Faber & Faber, 1972.

Reiss, Timothy J. "Montaigne and the Subject of Polity." In *Literary Theory/Renaissance Texts*, ed. Patricia Parker and David Quint. Baltimore: Johns Hopkins University Press, 1986.

Rekimoto, Jun. *Time-Machine Computing*. Sony Computer Science Laboratories, Inc. Homepage. http://www.csl.sony.co.jp/person/rekimoto/tmc/ (retrieved 4 April 2004).

Rhapsody (Rhapsody.Online). Listen.com (RealNetworks, Inc.). Homepage. http://www.rhapsody.com/ (retrieved 15 March 2007).

Rimbaud, Arthur. *Rimbaud: Complete Works, Selected Letters*. Translated and edited by Wallace Fowlie. Chicago: University of Chicago Press, 1966.

Road Warrior. Directed by George Miller. Warner Bros., 1982. [Also known as *Mad Max 2*.]

Rob, Peter, and Carlos Coronel. *Database Systems: Design, Implementation, and Management*. 5th ed. Boston: Course Technology/Thomson Learning, 2002.

Roe, Nicholas. "Citizen Wordsworth." *Wordsworth Circle* 14 (1983): 21–30.

————. "Who Was Spy Nozy?" *Wordsworth Circle* 15 (1984): 46–50.

Romantic Chronology. Edited by Laura Mandell and Alan Liu. Miami University, Ohio/University of California, Santa Barbara, created 1995–96. http://english.ucsb.edu:591/rchrono/ (retrieved 14 November 2000).

Ronell, Avital. *The Telephone Book: Technology, Schizophrenia, Electric Speech*. Lincoln: University of Nebraska Press, 1989.

Roosevelt, Theodore. *The Foes of Our Own Household*. New York: George H. Doran, 1917.

Rorty, Richard. *Consequences of Pragmatism (Essays: 1972–1980)*. Minneapolis: University of Minnesota Press, 1982.

————. *Contingency, Irony, and Solidarity*. Cambridge: Cambridge University Press, 1989.

————. *Philosophy and the Mirror of Nature*. Princeton, NJ: Princeton University Press, 1979.

Rose, Mark. "The Author as Proprietor: *Donaldson v. Becket* and the Genealogy of Modern Authorship." *Representations* 23 (Summer 1988): 51–85.

Rosen, Philip. "Taming the Detail: Film and Historical Spectacle." Paper delivered at the conference "Revolution '89: Interdisciplinary Perspectives on the French Revolution," University of California, Santa Barbara, 13 May 1989. Manuscript courtesy of the author.

Ross, Marlon B. "Contingent Predilections: The Newest Historicisms and the Question of Method." *Centennial Review* 34 (1990): 485–538.

The Rossetti Archive (The Complete Writings and Pictures of Dante Gabriel Rossetti: A Hypermedia Research Archive). Edited by Jerome J. McGann. Institute for Advanced Technology in the Humanities, University of Virginia. Homepage. http://www.iath.virginia.edu/rossetti/ (retrieved 20 January 2003).

RSS-DEV Working Group. "RDF Site Summary (RSS) 1.0." http://web.resource.org/rss/1.0 (retrieved 8 November 2007).

Ryan, Michael. *Marxism and Deconstruction: A Critical Articulation*. Baltimore: Johns Hopkins University Press, 1982.

————. "Postmodern Politics." *Theory, Culture and Society* 5 (1988): 559–76.

Schoenfield, Mark. *The Professional Wordsworth: Law, Labor, and the Poet's Contract*. Athens: University of Georgia Press, 1996.

————. "Wordsworth, Law, and Economics: A Poet's Languages." Ph.D. diss., University of Southern California, 1990.

Schor, Naomi. *Reading in Detail: Aesthetics and the Feminine*. New York: Methuen, 1987.

———. "Rereading in Detail; or, Aesthetics, the Feminine, and Idealism." *Criticism* 32 (1990): 309–23.

Schumpeter, Joseph A. *Capitalism, Socialism and Democracy.* New York: Harper & Row, 1975.

Searle, John R. *Intentionality: An Essay in the Philosophy of Mind.* Cambridge: Cambridge University Press, 1983.

Senge, Peter M. *The Fifth Discipline: The Art and Practice of the Learning Organization.* New York: Doubleday, 1990.

Shakespeare, William. *The Tragedy of King Richard the Second.* Edited by Kenneth Muir. Rev. ed. New York: Signet, 1963.

Shannon, Claude E., and Warren Weaver. *The Mathematical Theory of Communication.* Urbana: University of Illinois Press, 1949.

Shelley, Percy Bysshe. *A Defense of Poetry.* In *Critical Theory since Plato* (rev. ed.), ed. Hazard Adams. Fort Worth, TX: Harcourt Brace Jovanovich, 1992.

———. *Shelley's Poetry and Prose.* Edited by Donald H. Reiman and Sharon B. Powers. Norton Critical Edition. New York: Norton, 1977.

Shirley, John. *Eclipse Corona.* New York: Warner, Popular Library, 1990.

Shklovsky, Victor. "Art as Technique." In *Russian Formalist Criticism: Four Essays*, trans. Lee T. Lemon and Marion J. Reis. Lincoln: University of Nebraska Press, 1965.

———. "Sterne's *Tristram Shandy*: Stylistic Commentary." In *Russian Formalist Criticism: Four Essays*, trans. Lee T. Lemon and Marion J. Reis. Lincoln: University of Nebraska Press, 1965.

SHOUTcast (Nullsoft SHOUTcast). Nullsoft, Inc. Homepage. http://www.shoutcast.com/ (retrieved 15 March 2007).

Sid Meier's Civilization IV. CD-ROM. Hunt Valley, MD: Firaxis Games, 2005. [Computer game.]

Sidney, Sir Philip. *An Apology for Poetry.* In *Critical Theory since Plato* (rev. ed.), ed. Hazard Adams. Fort Worth, TX: Harcourt Brace Jovanovich, 1992.

Simpson, David. "Is Literary History the History of Everything? The Case for 'Antiquarian' History." *SubStance*, no. 88 (1999): 5–16. Available online at http://www.rc.umd.edu/praxis/contemporary/simpson/simpson.html (retrieved 23 January 2007).

———. *The Politics of American English, 1776–1850.* New York: Oxford University Press, 1986.

———. *Wordsworth's Historical Imagination: The Poetry of Displacement.* New York: Methuen, 1987.

Smith, Merritt Roe. *Harpers Ferry Armory and the New Technology: The Challenge of Change.* Ithaca, NY: Cornell University Press, 1977.

Smith, Nigel. "Critical Opinion: The Rest Is Silence." *Essays in Criticism* 37 (1987): 269–80.

Soja, Edward W. *Postmodern Geographies: The Reassertion of Space in Critical Social Theory.* London: Verso, 1989.

Sources of English Constitutional History: A Selection of Documents from A.D. 600 to the Present. Edited and translated by Carl Stephenson and Frederick George Marcham. New York: Harper & Row, 1937.

Spargo, R. Clifton. "Facing the Other: Wordsworth's Critique of Subjectivity in 'Elegiac Stanzas.'" Paper presented at the session "Wordsworth's 'Invisible Workmanship' and the Work of New Historicism," Modern Language Association convention, Toronto, 29 December 1993.

Sperberg-McQueen, C. M., and Lou Burnard. "A Gentle Introduction to XML." Text Encoding Initiative Consortium (TEI), 2003. http://www.tei-c.org/P4X/SG.html (retrieved 17 October 2003).

Spivak, Gayatri Chakravorty. "Scattered Speculations on the Question of Value." *Diacritics* 15, no. 4 (Winter 1985): 73–93.

Works Cited

Stallabrass, Julian. "The Aesthetics of Net.Art." Paper presented at the University of California, Berkeley, 30 September 2003. Subsequently published in *Qui Parle* 14, no. 1 (Fall/Winter 2003–4): 49–72. Also available at http://www.courtauld.ac.uk/people/stallabrass_julian/essays/aesthetics_net_art-print.pdf (retrieved 17 March 2007).

Stallybrass, Peter, and Allon White. *The Politics and Poetics of Transgression.* Ithaca, NY: Cornell University Press, 1986.

Stanczyk, Stefan, et al. *Theory and Practice of Relational Databases.* 2nd ed. London: Taylor & Francis, 2001.

State Trials for High Treason, Embellished with Portraits, Part the First, Containing the Trial of Thomas Hardy, Reported by a Student in the Temple. . . . London: B. Crosby, 1794.

Stavenhagen, Rodolfo. "Classes, Colonialism, and Acculturation: Essay on a System of Inter-Ethnic Relations in Mesoamerica." *Studies in Comparative International Development* 1, no. 6 (1965): 53–77.

Stephanson, Anders. "Regarding Postmodernism—a Conversation with Fredric Jameson." In *Universal Abandon: The Politics of Postmodernism,* ed. Andrew Ross. Minneapolis: University of Minnesota Press, 1988.

Stephen, James Fitzjames. *A History of the Criminal Law of England.* 3 vols. London: Macmillan, 1883.

Sterling, Bruce, ed. *Mirrorshades: The Cyberpunk Anthology.* 1986. Reprint, New York: Ace, 1988.

Stewart, John Hall. *A Documentary Survey of the French Revolution.* New York: Macmillan, 1951.

Stewart, John L. *The Burden of Time: The Fugitives and Agrarians—the Nashville Groups of the 1920s and 1930s, and the Writing of John Crowe Ransom, Allen Tate, and Robert Penn Warren.* Princeton, NJ: Princeton University Press, 1965.

Subtract the Sky. Developed by Sharon Daniel, Mark Bartlett, and Puragra Guhathakurta. University of California, Santa Cruz. Homepage. http://arts.ucsc.edu/sdaniel/new/subtract.html (retrieved 20 January 2003). Documentation and screenshots now archived at http://subtractthesky.net.

Taine, H[ippolyte] A. *History of English Literature.* 2 vols. in 1. Translated by H. Van Laun. New York: Henry Holt, 1879.

Taylor, Frederick Winslow. *The Principles of Scientific Management.* In *Scientific Management, Comprising "Shop Management," "The Principles of Scientific Management," "Testimony before the Special House Committee."* 1947. Reprint, Westport, CT: Greenwood, 1972.

———. *Shop Management.* In *Scientific Management, Comprising "Shop Management," "The Principles of Scientific Management," "Testimony before the Special House Committee."* 1947. Reprint, Westport, CT: Greenwood, 1972.

Tennenhouse, Leonard. *Power on Display: The Politics of Shakespeare's Genres.* New York: Methuen, 1986.

———. "Strategies of State and Political Plays: *A Midsummer Night's Dream, Henry IV, Henry V, Henry VIII.*" In *Political Shakespeare: New Essays in Cultural Materialism,* ed. Jonathan Dollimore and Alan Sinfield. Ithaca, NY: Cornell University Press, 1985.

Terdiman, Richard. "Deconstructing Memory: On Representing the Past and Theorizing Culture in France since the Revolution." *Diacritics* 15, no. 4 (Winter 1985): 13–36.

Text Encoding Initiative (TEI). Home page. http://www.tei-c.org/index.xml (retrieved 7 November 2007).
  Secondary page cited:
    "Guidelines." http://www.tei-c.org/Guidelines/index.xml (retrieved 7 November 2007).

Thirsk, Joan. "The Field Systems in England." In *The Agrarian History of England and*

Wales, ed. H. P. R. Finberg, vol. 4, *1500–1640*, ed. Joan Thirsk. Cambridge: Cambridge University Press, 1967.

Thomas, Brook. "The New Historicism and Other Old-Fashioned Topics." In *The New Historicism*, ed. H. Aram Veeser. New York: Routledge, 1989.

———. *The New Historicism and Other Old-Fashioned Topics*. Princeton, NJ: Princeton University Press, 1991.

Thomas, D. Aneurin, ed. *The Welsh Elizabethan Catholic Martyrs: The Trial Documents of Saint Richard Gwyn and of the Venerable William Davies*. Cardiff: University of Wales Press, 1971.

Tillyard, E. M. W. *The Elizabethan World Picture*. 1943. Reprint, New York: Vintage, n.d.

Toffler, Alvin. *The Third Wave*. New York: Bantam, 1981.

Tomashevsky, Boris. "Thematics." In *Russian Formalist Criticism: Four Essays*, trans. Lee T. Lemon and Marion J. Reis. Lincoln: University of Nebraska Press, 1965.

Transcriptions Project (Transcriptions: Literature and the Culture of Information). Principal investigator, Alan Liu. Department of English, University of California, Santa Barbara. Homepage. http://transcriptions.english.ucsb.edu (retrieved 7 March 2007). [Initiated 1998.]

Transliteracies Project (Transliteracies: Research in the Technological, Social, and Cultural Practices of Online Reading). Principal investigator, Alan Liu. University of California Multi-Campus Research Group. Homepage. http://transliteracies.english.ucsb.edu (retrieved 11 March 2007). [Initiated 2000.]

Tschichold, Jan. *The New Typography: A Handbook for Modern Designers*. Translated by Ruari McLean. Berkeley and Los Angeles: University of California Press, 1995.

Tuan, Yi-Fu. *Segmented Worlds and Self: Group Life and Individual Consciousness*. Minneapolis: University of Minnesota Press, 1982.

Tynjanov, Jurij. "On Literary Evolution." Translated by C. A. Luplow. In *Readings in Russian Poetics: Formalist and Structuralist Views*, ed. Ladislav Matejka and Krystyna Pomorska. Cambridge, MA: MIT Press, 1971.

U.S. Patent and Trademark Office. "Appendix L: Patent Laws." In *Manual of Patent Examining Procedure (MPEP)*. 8th ed. August 2001; latest revision August 2006. http://www.uspto.gov/web/offices/pac/mpep/documents/appxl.htm (retrieved 19 January 2007).

Virilio, Paul, and Sylvère Lotringer. *Pure War*. Translated by Mark Polizzotti. New York: Semiotext(e), 1983.

Voice of the Shuttle: Web Site for Humanities Research. Edited by Alan Liu. University of California, Santa Barbara. Homepage. http://vos.ucsb.edu (retrieved 12 March 2007). [Initiated 1994.]

Waismann, Friedrich. *The Principles of Linguistic Philosophy*. Edited by R. Harré. New York: St. Martin's, 1965.

Waldoff, Leon. "The Wordsworthian 'I' and the Work of Self-Representation in 'Elegiac Stanzas.'" Paper presented at the session "Wordsworth's 'Invisible Workmanship' and the Work of New Historicism," Modern Language Association convention, Toronto, 29 December 1993.

Wallerstein, Immanuel. *The Modern World-System II: Mercantilism and the Consolidation of the European World-Economy, 1600–1750*. New York: Academic, 1980.

The Walt Whitman Archive. Edited by Ed Folsom and Kenneth M. Price. Homepage. http://www.whitmanarchive.org/ (retrieved 11 March 2007). [Initiated 1995.]

Wardrip-Fruin, Noah, and Nick Montfort, eds. *The New Media Reader*. Cambridge, MA: MIT Press, 2003.

Warren, Robert Penn. "A Conversation with Cleanth Brooks." In *The Possibilities of Order:*

Cleanth Brooks and His Work, ed. Lewis P. Simpson. Baton Rouge: Louisiana State University Press, 1976.

Watkins, Evan. *Throwaways: Work Culture and Consumer Education*. Stanford, CA: Stanford University Press, 1993.

Watt, Andrew H. *SAMS Teach Yourself XML in 10 Minutes*. Indianapolis: SAMS, 2003.

Wayne, Don E. *Penshurst: The Semiotics of Place and the Poetics of History*. Madison: University of Wisconsin Press, 1984.

————. "Power, Politics, and the Shakespearean Text: Recent Criticism in England and the United States." In *Shakespeare Reproduced: The Text in History and Ideology*, ed. Jean E. Howard and Marion F. O'Connor. New York: Methuen, 1987.

Weber, Samuel. *Institution and Interpretation*. Minneapolis: University of Minnesota Press, 1987.

————. "The Intersection: Marxism and the Philosophy of Language." *Diacritics* 15, no. 4 (Winter 1985): 94–112.

Weimann, Robert. "History and the Issue of Authority in Representation: The Elizabethan Theater and the Reformation." *New Literary History* 17 (1986): 449–76.

Weiskel, Thomas. *The Romantic Sublime: Studies in the Structure and Psychology of Transcendence*. Baltimore: Johns Hopkins University Press, 1976.

Weisstein, Eric W. "Menger Sponge." MathWorld—a Wolfram Web Resource, 5 March 2005. http://mathworld.wolfram.com/MengerSponge.html (retrieved 23 January 2007).

Wells, Susan. *The Dialectics of Representation*. Baltimore: Johns Hopkins University Press, 1985.

Whewell, William. *Astronomy and General Physics Considered with Reference to Natural Theology*. Bridgewater Treatises on the Power, Wisdom and Goodness of God as Manifested in the Creation, Treatise 3. London: W. Pickering, 1833.

White, Hayden. *The Content of the Form: Narrative Discourse and Historical Representation*. Baltimore: Johns Hopkins University Press, 1987.

Whitman Archive. See *The Walt Whitman Archive*.

Wikipedia. Wikipedia Foundation, Inc. Homepage. http://www.wikipedia.org/ (retrieved 7 March 2007).

Wilentz, Sean, ed. *Rites of Power: Symbolism, Ritual and Politics since the Middle Ages*. Philadelphia: University of Pennsylvania Press, 1985.

The William Blake Archive. Edited by Morris Eaves, Robert Essick, and Joseph Viscomi. Homepage. http://www.blakearchive.org/ (retrieved 20 January 2003).

Williams, Gwyn A. *The Welsh in Their History*. London: Croom Helm, 1982.

————. *When Was Wales? A History of the Welsh*. London: Black Raven, 1985.

Williams, Raymond. *Marxism and Literature*. New York: Oxford University Press, 1977.

Williams, Richard. "Montgomeryshire Worthies." *Collections Historical and Archaeological Relating to Montgomeryshire, and Its Borders* 12 (1879): 184–85.

Wilson, Robert R. "Play, Transgression and Carnival: Bakhtin and Derrida on *Scriptor Ludens*." *Mosaic* 19 (1986): 73–89.

Wilson, Stephen. *Information Arts: Intersections of Art, Science, and Technology*. Cambridge, MA: MIT Press, 2002.

Wölfflin, Heinrich. *Kunstgeschichtliche Grundbegriffe: Das Problem der Stilentwicklung in der neueren Kunst*. 1915. 5th ed. Munich: Hugo Bruckmann, 1921.

————. *Principles of Art History: The Problem of the Development of Style in Later Art*. Translated by M. D. Hottinger. 1932. Reprint, New York: Dover, 1950.

Woodring, Carl. *Politics in English Romantic Poetry*. Cambridge, MA: Harvard University Press, 1970.

WordPress. Homepage. http://wordpress.org/ (retrieved 7 March 2007).

Wordsworth, William. *The Borderers*. Edited by Robert Osborn. The Cornell Wordsworth. Ithaca, NY: Cornell University Press, 1982.

———. *An Evening Walk*. Edited by James Averill. The Cornell Wordsworth. Ithaca, NY: Cornell University Press, 1984.

———. *The Letters of William and Dorothy Wordsworth*. Edited by Ernest de Selincourt. 2nd, rev. ed. 8 vols. Oxford: Clarendon, 1967–93. [Revised by various hands.]

———. *The Poetical Works of William Wordsworth*. Edited by Ernest de Selincourt (and Helen Darbishire). 5 vols. Oxford: Clarendon, 1940–49.

———. *"The Prelude": 1799, 1805, 1850: Authoritative Texts, Context and Reception, Recent Critical Essays*. Edited by Jonathan Wordsworth, M. H. Abrams, and Stephen Gill. Norton Critical Edition. New York: Norton, 1979.

———. *The Prose Works of William Wordsworth*. Edited by W. J. B. Owen and Jane Worthington Smyser. 3 vols. Oxford: Oxford University Press, 1974.

———. *The Salisbury Plain Poems of William Wordsworth: "Salisbury Plain," or "A Night on Salisbury Plain," "Adventures on Salisbury Plain" (including "The Female Vagrant"), "Guilt and Sorrow; or, Incidents upon Salisbury Plain."* Edited by Stephen Gill. The Cornell Wordsworth. Ithaca, NY: Cornell University Press, 1975.

———. *William Wordsworth*. Edited by Stephen Gill. New York: Oxford University Press, 1984. [Oxford Authors series collection of his poems.]

The World Wide Web Consortium (W3C). Home page. http://www.w3.org/ (retrieved 17 October 2003).

    Secondary pages cited:

    "Extensible Markup Language (XML)." http://www.w3.org/XML/ (retrieved 17 October 2003).

    Miller, Eric et al. "Semantic Web." *See* Eric Miller et al.

    "XML Core Working Group Public Page." http://www.w3.org/XML/Core/ (retrieved 17 October 2003).

Woychowsky, Edmond. "XML Data Islands Offer a Useful Mechanism to Display Web Form Data." Builder.com. 25 February 2003. CNET Networks, Inc. http://builder.com.com/5100-6371-1058668.html (retrieved 17 October 2003).

W3C. *See* World Wide Web Consortium.

Yates, JoAnne. *Control through Communication: The Rise of System in American Management*. Baltimore: Johns Hopkins University Press, 1989.

Young, Michael J. *XML Step by Step*. 2nd ed. Redmond, WA: Microsoft Press, 2002.

Zuboff, Shoshana. *In the Age of the Smart Machine: The Future of Work and Power*. New York: Basic, 1988.

Index

and history of thought, 119, 123, 297n25, 297n26; and list forms, 121; and matrix or array forms, 113, 120–21, 137, 295n14; and media or mediation (*see under* media analysis); and poststructuralism (*see under* poststructuralism); rhetoric of (*see under* rhetoric); and romanticism, 123–28, 130, 135, 137; and the subject (*see under* subject and subjectivity); and subversion (*see under* subversion); and symbolic representations (*see under* representations and symbols); and system, 10; mentioned, xi, 7–11 passim, 16–19 passim, 258

cultural materialism, 18, 58, 83, 112, 280n94, 283n5, 293n7, 310n16

cultural poetics, 32, 55, 68

cultural studies. *See* cultural criticism

culture, 5, 33, 81, 100, 116, 123, 130, 135–37 passim; and New Cultural History, 171

custom, 151, 245

cyberpunk science fiction, 110–11, 229–31, 293n1, 294n14

cyberspace, 111

Cybertext (Aarseth), 228

Cymmrodorion, 93, 98, 101

da Vinci, Leonardo, 179

Daniel, Sharon, *Subtract the Sky*, 317n7

DARnet (Digital Arts Research Network), 210, 317n7

Darnton, Robert, 113, 117, 121, 171, 268n46, 310n12; *The Great Cat Massacre*, 134–35, 298n32

data island, 216–17, 221, 234, 319nn22–23, 320n27

data pour, 216–17, 220–21, 319n23, 321n28; artistic or literary analogs of, 229–33, 324n68, 328n23; and Web 2.0, 320n26. *See also* data island

data sublime. *See under* sublime, the

data warehouses, 254

Database Aesthetics (Gill et al.), 317n7

database software, 213, 328n30; management consoles for, 225. *See also* Access; MySQL; Oracle; SQL Server

databases: and anecdotes (*see under* anecdotes and anecdotalism); compared to industrial-age technologies and management, 222–27; compared to XML, 210,

318n13, 319n19; and content management systems, 312n38; in corporations (*see under* corporations and corporatism); and cultural criticisms (*see under* cultural criticism); in cyberpunk science fiction, 111; and discourse network 2000, 209, 210, 214–27 passim, 235–36, 316n1; examples from, 217, 218f, 221; and freedom, 11, 254, 258 (*see also* independence, logical [in databases]); hierarchical model of, 249–50, 328n26; in the humanities and arts, 211, 232, 240, 259, 317n7; and knowledge bases or data warehouses, 254; network model of, 249–50, 328n26; and New Historicism (*see under* New Historicism); object-oriented model of, 250; relational model of (*see* databases, relational); and the Web, 215, 240, 318n13, 320n24, 320n27, 325nn3–4; and Web 2.0, 178, 320n26. *See also* database software; databases, relational

databases, relational, 6, 213, 318n12, 328n25; Codd's theory of, 249–54 passim, 328n30; examples of, 250–52, 253f; and MyLifeBits project, 256–58, 330n38; normalization of, 252–54, 328nn28–29; nulls in, 240, 254, 328n30, 329n31; redundancy and duplicate records in, 252, 254

Date, C. J., 328n25, 328nn28–30, 329n31

David, Jacques Louis, 94

Davidson, Cathy N., 312n39

Davies, Rees, 88, 290n63

Davis, David Brion, 286n24

Davis, Natalie Zemon, 113–14, 268n46

de Certeau, Michel, 112, 115, 117, 136, 142, 162, 308n17; *The Practice of Everyday Life*, 131

De Landa, Manuel, *A Thousand Years of Nonlinear History*, 18

de Man, Paul, 67, 117, 182, 280n95, 287n34, 296n21; "Shelley Disfigured," 183, 297n21; "The Resistance to Theory," 177, 181, 280n94; "The Rhetoric of Temporality," 303n66

de Tracy, Destutt, 175

death of literature. *See under* literature and literariness

decentralization in information technology, 265n15, 323n62

decision trees, 194–95, 197, 315n12